INVISIBLE HISTORY

Afghanistan's Untold Story

by Paul Fitzgerald and Elizabeth Gould

City Lights Books
San Francisco

Text design: Gambrinus

Cover Photograph of the Karta-i-Sakhi neighborhood in Western Kabul by Anja Håvedal

Library of Congress Cataloging-in-Publication Data

Fitzgerald, Paul.
Invisible history : Afghanistan's untold story / by Paul Fitzgerald and Elizabeth Gould.
p. cm.
ISBN-13: 978-0-87286-494-8
ISBN-10: 0-87286-494-4
1. Afghanistan—History. 2. Afghanistan—Politics and government. I. Gould, Elizabeth. II. Title.

DS357.5.F58 2009
958.1—dc22

2008020486

City Lights Books are published at the City Lights Bookstore,
261 Columbus Avenue, San Francisco, CA 94133.
Visit our Web site: www.citylights.com

Praise for *Invisible History: Afghanistan's Untold Story*

"Seasoned journalists Fitzgerald and Gould—co-producers of the 1981 PBS documentary *Afghanistan Between Three Worlds*—deliver a probing history of the country and a critical evaluation of American involvement in recent decades. The authors had just finished a documentary in late 1979 on SALT II (*Arms Race and the Economy*) when Russia invaded the seemingly insignificant country of Afghanistan. In this densely researched work, they study the ancient ethnic makeup of the country, its fledgling attempts at democracy and the catastrophic rise of the Taliban, introduced by Pakistan refugee groups and funded by the Saudis. As the 'meeting place of four cultural zones,' Afghanistan has constantly been overrun by invaders eager to get somewhere else, including Alexander the Great, early Arab armies that converted the country to Islam, Genghis Khan, and the mid-19th century invasion by the British, which sowed the seeds of destabilizing colonial politics that would wreak havoc until the present day. The country lived in perpetual fear of Russian invasion of its northern territories, and it became a natural base for Cold War confrontation. Internally, a conservative, traditional society in which Islam played a pious rather than political role was being radically transformed by the 1970s, 'under the influence of outside religious and intellectual forces.' Most chilling to read is the American government's hot-cold manipulation of the region for its own purposes. As the situation devolved into 'a sea of drugs, covert operations, Islamic revolutionaries, and Maoist cadres,' and U.S. ambassador Adolph Dubs was murdered in February 1979, an aggressive anti-Soviet stance was set in play from Brzezinski to Reagan, and the entrenchment of Islamic extremism was assured. The authors ably demystify Afghan efforts in the wake of 9/11, delineating its destroyed culture and offering a cogent plan for the next American president. A fresh perspective on a little-understood nation."

—*Kirkus Reviews*

"Journalists Fitzgerald and Gould do yeoman's labor in clearing the fog and laying bare American failures in Afghanistan in this deeply researched, cogently argued and enormously important book. The authors demonstrate how closely American actions are tied to past miscalculations—and how U.S. policy has placed Afghans and Americans in grave danger. Long at cultural crossroads, Afghanistan's location poised the country to serve as 'a fragile buffer' between rival empires. Great Britain's 1947 creation of an arbitrary and indefensible border between Afghanistan and the newly minted Pakistan 'from the Afghan point of view . . . has always been the problem,' but particularly after 9/11 American policymakers have paid scant attention to the concerns of Afghans, preferring to shoehorn an imagined Afghanistan into U.S. power paradigms . . ."

—*Publishers Weekly* (starred review)

"From the dawn of the Cold War onward, generations of conservative strategists have eyed Afghanistan as a launching pad first for the subversion of the Soviet Union and then to checkmate Russia in central Asia. To that end, as Gould and Fitzgerald show, since the 1950s the CIA has played games with both reactionary, feudal landlords and wild-eyed Muslim fundamentalists. In their exhaustively documented book, Gould and Fitzgerald reveal how that sort of gamesmanship played havoc with a battered nation of twenty-five million souls—helping to spawn, in the process, the virulent strain of violent Islamism that reaches far beyond the remote and landlocked territory of that war-torn country."

—Robert Dreyfuss, author of *Devil's Game: How the United States Helped Unleash Fundamentalist Islam*

"In this penetrating inquiry, based on careful study of an intricate web of political, cultural, and historical factors that lie in the immediate background, and enriched by unique direct observation at crucial moments, Fitzgerald and Gould tell 'the real story of how they came to be there and what we can expect next.' With skill and care, they unravel the roots of Afghanistan's terrible travail, and lay bare its awesome significance for the world at large. Invocation of Armageddon is no mere literary device. The threat is all too real as the political leadership of a superpower with few external constraints charges forward on a course that is fraught with peril. *Invisible History: Afghanistan's Untold Story* is a critically important contribution to our understanding of some of the most dramatic and significant developments of current history."

—Noam Chomsky

"*Invisible History: Afghanistan's Untold Story* is a much-needed corrective to five decades of biased journalistic and academic writing about Afghanistan that has covered up the destructive and self-defeating U.S. role there. Backed by prodigious research, it shows that successive U.S. administrations deserve much of the blame for the rise of Al Qaeda and the Taliban, and that the increasingly unpopular American military presence in Afghanistan today is likely to prove unsustainable."

—Selig S. Harrison, former South Asia Bureau Chief, *Washington Post*, and author of *Out of Afghanistan*

"*Invisible History: Afghanistan's Untold Story* is a defining work of great wisdom and depth in which the authors get to the bottom of the cauldron that is Afghanistan. We cannot fully understand today's Afghanistan without reading this insightful book. Afghanistan was the first war in the US war on terror. Understanding Afghanistan is the key to the current war. You could not start at a better place than this book. To understand why eight years later it is still being fought, *Invisible History: Afghanistan's Untold Story* is a must read."

—Ahmed Rashid author of *Taliban*, *Jihad*, and *Descent into Chaos*

This book is dedicated to Sima Wali and to her dream of a new Afghanistan becoming a reality.

ACKNOWLEDGMENTS

Afghanistan has been with us so long, it would take a separate book to list all the people who helped along the way. We owe a debt of gratitude to City Lights Books and especially to our editor Greg Ruggiero, who shared our vision and whose thoughtful guidance shepherded this project through its myriad stages. And to Noam Chomsky, whose wisdom and encouragement over many years kept our effort alive. We would also like to express our thanks to the one man, without whose help this book and our thirty-year journey would never have begun.

When the entire western press corps was expelled from Afghanistan following the Soviet invasion, we saw the chance to tell a story hidden from the eyes of the world. Not the Cold War story that force-fit the conflict into the Manichean terms of superpower confrontation as directed from Moscow and Washington, but the story of Afghanistan as seen from Afghan eyes.

In the fall of 1980 we approached Mohammed Farid Zarif, *charge d'affairs* of the Afghan mission at the United Nations for the much-coveted "first" visas to enter Afghanistan. Zarif accepted our explanation that the news blackout made for wild speculation and that Afghanistan needed its own story told. Zarif understood that we would bring the story to the very networks his government had expelled. But even with that precondition, he accepted our word that we would go with an open mind and with no preconceived notions about the crisis his country was in.

Zarif presented our case to the authorities in Kabul and six months later we got the call that the visas were on their way.

In the end, a story about our experience wound up on the CBS Evening News with Dan Rather, but the real story that we discovered about Afghanistan had to wait. For nearly thirty years we have gathered as many of the stories and diverse views as we could find and put them together into one volume. But that original Afghanistan that was opened to us by this one man, who wanted the story of his country told, remains the foundation of an experience that changed our lives forever.

—Paul Fitzgerald and Elizabeth Gould

Contents

PART III. AFGHANISTAN FROM 2001 TO 2008

Introduction

by Sima Wali

Invisible History: Afghanistan's Untold Story is a phenomenal compendium of history, research and critical analysis of the complex dynamics that has led to the death of my home country Afghanistan—a nation as old as history itself. For Afghanistan, the aftermath of the Cold War resulted in large-scale genocide of more than two million civilians and five million war victims, as well as a million handicapped and scores of internally displaced Afghan people.

Before I met Paul and Liz I had spent two decades seeking an explanation for why Afghanistan was sacrificed in the war against the Soviet Union. *Invisible History* unravels this great mystery as it bears testimony for all humanity about one of the great invisible injustices of our time.

I fled Afghanistan for the United States in 1978 after the first Marxist coup overthrew the last member of a dynasty that had ruled my country for nearly 250 years. During that time my family was put under house arrest simply because, as allies to the West, we were on the wrong side of Afghan politics. In my youth my family was very close to the Americans. We admired them. We all believed they shared with us a vision of a greater Afghanistan, where men and women could share in a bright future through education, cultural exchange and economic development. Despite the many obstacles inherent in moving an underdeveloped country like Afghanistan into the twentieth century, it was a time of hope, enthusiasm and promise. Kabul was a peaceful international city then with ancient ties to the East and the West. Tourists flocked from all over the world, especially from the Middle East, to enjoy a cosmopolitan Islamic culture, free from the strictures of extremism.

When I was forced to flee Afghanistan, I left behind that era and a culture that was striving on the path of democracy. It had been a golden era, where the voices of empowered women were heard and recognized by their male counterparts as legitimate and necessary to the development of our country. Back then I was accustomed to the visibility and contributions of women in the Afghan democracy. I was exposed to empowered women in my own immediate family and the larger society who held cabinet posts and worked alongside men in the government. I promised to remain a voice for these people, and I dedicated myself to their memory. I still grieve for the Afghanistan I left behind and the lost opportunities for the democratic-minded Afghan people.

In 1981 I established Refugee Women in Development (RefWID), an international nonprofit tax exempt organization dedicated to helping the world's displaced women and victims of war and genocide make a new way of life for themselves. For twenty-five years my colleagues and I worked to empower women who were affected by major socio-political transformations such as war, civil strife and human rights abuses. From our offices in Washington, D.C. we supported war-affected women and their male counterparts by building their leadership capacities in the nongovernmental sector (NGOs). We conducted our work by providing training, networking and advocacy support to enable local NGOs to provide better services in their communities. Although we worked primarily with women, we also included men in our programs. Our aim was to build the capacities of women to organize their communities and to fully participate in the rebuilding process. By empowering these women and men to reestablish their own shattered lives, Refugee Women in Development helped set the stage for a reconstructed, functioning civil society.

For the twenty years preceding the downfall of the Taliban, Refugee Women in Development was unable to conduct its program inside Afghanistan. Most of our programs were centered in Pakistan. There, I listened to the voices of hundreds of increasingly desperate men and women. I anguished over how to explain what I learned—that despite the growing awareness of the total destruction of the war, the Afghan people were mostly absent from campaigns waged on their behalf in the United States.

I realized then that this callous treatment of my people, who had served the United States in the war against the Soviet Union, would leave them vulnerable to a far more pervasive and determined enemy. That enemy emerged as the Taliban.

During my visits to Pakistan prior to 9/11, the women of Afghanistan and their male escorts braved minefields and dangerous mountain passes to secretly meet with me. I listened to the voices of the Afghan women who ran schools, provided health services and conducted human rights activities while providing social services to Afghans inside Afghanistan and Pakistan. Traumatized and desperate, they constantly spoke of severe poverty, suicide and the growing hopelessness that saw their dreams for a free Afghanistan swallowed by an army of Islamist mercenaries from all over the world armed and supplied by Pakistan. How did the world community allow such heinous crimes to be committed against a nation of twenty-six million people with a large majority of women?

I still hear their cries. During this entire time I carried with me their pleading voices and ultimately their screams, while the world looked away. Now, as we conclude still another decade of war, their screams rise again within me as I witness a Taliban resurgence. The draconian Taliban rule stripped women of their basic human rights. Their edicts against women in Afghanistan led to an introduction of a new form of violence termed "gender apartheid." Strict limitations on women's public space and education led to the galvanization of American women on behalf of Afghan women. This worldwide solidarity with the most oppressed women in the world itself was novel. From that day on, the women's alliance across the globe and their influence on foreign policy was seen as a new and powerful factor in the resolution of the worldwide refugee problem. I can safely state that Afghan women were the canaries in the mineshaft, bearing witness to the inhumanity of a regime against its own citizens.

Still, in the United States today there remains a profound lack of understanding about the Taliban, what political forces they represent and what their objectives are. The void of accurate historical information on their origins has resulted in a succession of dangerous, counterproductive policy initiatives from Washington. The consequences of these initiatives have negated any chance for a successful restoration of an Afghan republic, opened Afghanistan to cross-border raids from Pakistan while at the same time providing a platform for the resurgence of the Taliban.

When the Americans washed their hands of Afghanistan once the Soviets were defeated, many desperate Afghans living in Pakistan became indoctrinated into the Taliban's fundamentalist mentality. Due to the dismal economic conditions following the war, many young Afghan men were either forcibly recruited or voluntarily joined the Taliban out of desperation. Over the years as I witnessed the continuing breakdown of civil society due to the long term effects of war on the Afghan people, I also witnessed the growth of the madrassa system of fundamentalist education in Pakistan. While I was in Pakistan, Afghan refugee familes—with few options to care for their children—confirmed to me that the only way for their boys to receive education was through the madrassas. During that time, the Taliban's influence grew over the Afghan refugees in Peshawar as well as across the border into Afghanistan as the war continued to drain all resources required to maintain civil society. Encouraged by Pakistan but apparently "overlooked" by the Americans, these Pakistani madrassas continued to provide the major source of indoctrination and recruitment for the Taliban and grew stronger by the day.

To set the record straight, the term "Taliban" and the movement itself were unheard of in Afghanistan until 1996. Prior to the Soviet invasion, the Taliban mentality and the madrassa structure did not exist. As an invention of Pakistan's military intelligence with outside help, the Taliban were not recruited from inside Afghanistan but from Pakistani madrassas. This process was funded, not by Afghans, but by the Saudis and other Arab countries who continue to seek the longterm goal of a political and religious transformation of South Asia combined with the dissolution of Afghanistan as a nation state. As Zalmay Khalizad said in his April 1, 2004 remarks at the Center for Strategic and International Studies (CSIS), historically the version of Islam practiced by Afghans was moderate. The Taliban version of Deobandi Islam practiced in Pakistan and the Wahhabism practiced in Saudi Arabia were both alien to Afghan practice. Suicide bombings did not exist in Afghanistan during the Soviet occupation nor even when the Taliban arrived in 1996. The Afghan people never willingly embraced extremist Islam. These ideas were forced upon them under circumstances beyond their control.

Regardless of these understandings, during the debates establishing the post-Taliban government for Afghanistan in 2001, Islamist principles that had never been considered Afghan and were never a part of previous Afghan constitutions were infused into the new constitution. Even the chief justice and the ministry of justice are composed of former Taliban madrassa students. Many in leadership positions in the current government of Afghanistan also subscribe to extremist ideologies of the Islamic kind that were never a part of Afghan politics. And so, where in the past, extremism held little sway within the political process, the conflict between moderates and extremists has now become the norm.

Years after being driven from power by the American military intervention of 2001, today the Taliban enemy is once again reemerging as a tenacious and relentless insurgent force. But even with a military occupation that has lasted more than seven years, the United States and the West in general, do not perceive that their failure in Afghanistan remains a direct result of the long-standing inability of western institutions to adjust to the realities of what needs to be done. It is also a result of the failure to listen to the voices of the vast majority of willing Afghans who are capable of ushering in democratic change. This is a bias that permeated American thinking before September 11, 2001. Unfortunately, despite a wealth of new and empirical evidence, misconceptions about Afghanistan remains in place today.

Following the fall of the Taliban, our central effort was to build a democratic civil society in Afghanistan. Our basic philosophy at Refugee Women in Development has been that the grassroots leadership found in local NGOs play a vital role in promoting a balanced, tolerant, and open society. We developed training programs and networking opportunities for local Afghan organizations by strengthening their institutional and leadership capacities through training programs.

At first we were confident that with a combination of American aid and security, the civil society that I had known in Afghanistan could be restored and expanded throughout the country. This was not to be.

Today, Afghanistan is again depicted in the worst possible light—as a haven for extremists who have hijacked Afghan cultural and religious traditions. The media often promote this misconception, and fail to recognize that the Afghan people have themselves been held hostage to external invading forces. These forces have a vested interest in keeping Afghanistan destabilized and weak. They also have a vested interest in maintaining misconceptions about Afghanistan that prevent the country from getting enough western commitment to realistically establish democratic institutions. The international system of law and diplomacy broke down once over Afghanistan. It must not be allowed to break down again.

Following 9/11 we temporarily had the semblance of a new society, but the Afghan people are yet again seeing the glimmer of hope rapidly dissipate. Although 9/11 was a wake-up call, the realization that events in Afghanistan are directly tied to security in the United States is clouded by a profound misunderstanding.

I no longer fear that Afghanistan will again be abandoned. My fear today is that despite all the initial good intentions, America's overreliance on military methods, targeted missile strikes, chemical spraying, and imprisoning and torturing suspected militants has turned popular opinion in the wrong direction. Combined with an inability to improve the lives of the average Afghan by even a small measure, America is now viewed as an occupier, instead of the friend and ally we want her to be.

While many strides have been made to bring women along in reconstruction schemes, today these advances are tempered by rampant poverty, violence, and lack of water, electricity, and employment among other things. Under current circumstances women are abducted, even jailed, for refusing to accept forced marriages. Honor killings continue and sexual and physical violence have not been adequately addressed especially in the provinces where warlords rule.

Today, the common Afghan man and woman have fear in their hearts and uncertainty about their future.

Although we now have a new constitution in place that guarantees the rights of both men and women, the advances are tempered by rising repression of women's social and political prominence. We, as women, are at peril of anti-modernist forces that are committed to rolling back the newfound gains of Afghan women by hijacking our language and by resorting to the so-called "Islamic" argument. The protection of women as equal citizens does not figure prominently under the new constitution. After having suffered flagrant abuses for more than two decades we cannot and will not stand for unequal protection under the highest law of our nation.

The world community must not be acquiescent with rhetoric, tokenism, or symbolic assurances. What Afghanistan and its people desperately need at this critical juncture is not misplaced charity but long-term strategies for sustainable democracy. This can only be done if the international community makes a permanent commitment to: 1) staying the course of nation building; 2) committing enough finances to sustain long-term development; 3) heeding the voices of the Afghan people especially the moderate Afghans; and 4) involving ever-increasing numbers of women. Afghan women constitute 67 percent of the Afghan population. Building a ravaged nation with only 33 percent of its human resources is simply not sound economics.

As we approach the second decade of the twenty-first century, the world community and especially the United States realize that Afghanistan is a country of very special interest. But despite the West's commitment to Afghanistan it still remains a country whose history and struggle for democracy is largely obscured by myth and propaganda.

In the pages ahead Paul Fitzgerald and Elizabeth Gould clarify and correct the record, and build a foundation upon which the whole story of Afghanistan's past can be appreciated.

It takes courageous hearts, minds and souls to travel the path that Paul and Liz have pursued—particularly for Afghans who have endured and continue to endure unspeakable trauma. Witnessing the massacre of members of my extended family has altered my life and has been the driving force in my quest to inform the world of the insanity in the current war. To this day, I am exposed to the impact this war has on women, men and children, and bear witness to their families' lifelong trauma. It has led me to question why anyone or any institution can claim the right to sacrifice innocent victims while pursuing their own political agendas and economic interests.

Invisible History is filled with ground-breaking analysis, not only for those interested in the more recent politics of Afghanistan, but also for those wanting the larger historical context necessary to grasp the immensity of this tragedy. It will stand as a twenty-first century guide not only to what was lost in the destruction of Afghanistan but to what can still be done to reconstruct a future where all Afghan women and men can live with the peace and plenty they deserve. I commend Paul and Liz for their dedication, courage and professionalism in treading in areas where no soul has dared venture before and in unraveling the complex dynamics of the story of Afghanistan.

PROLOGUE

A Clockwork Afghanistan

It's a battle for the air and the airwaves. As well as dropping bombs and food ration packs into Afghanistan, military strategists in Washington have a new secret weapon in their war on terrorism—the wind-up radio.

—"Clockwork Warfare," *BBC News*, October 10, 2001

I

Round and round like a clockwork Afghanistan: the symbolism didn't really hit home until we returned from our latest trip to that desperate country in the late fall of 2002. Over the course of our stay at a small hotel catering to an international cadre of journalists, aid workers, and UN staffers, we encountered a local artist in the act of painting American icons on the whitewashed wall of the narrow stairwell. During the first few days we witnessed the detailed completion of the New York City Police Department logo overlooking the small first-floor dining room, while in ongoing days the New York City Fire Department logo came to dominate the second-floor stairwell. It was an understandable expression of appreciation from the Afghans, we thought. Throughout our trip we had encountered nothing but thanks from our Afghan hosts who wished America well for liberating them from the oppressive Taliban regime while breaking the cycle of violence that had taken two million lives since 1978.

But when the artist chose to decorate the third-floor stairwell with an artistic rendering of the poster from Stanley Kubrick's classic *A Clockwork Orange* (1971), we came up short. Why mix the real image of sacrifice and public service represented by New York's heroes of 9/11 with the most indelible symbol of Anglo-Saxon cultural savagery ever invented?

In the thirty years since we'd seen the movie, we'd forgotten the sedated, Orwellian future ruled over by criminal thugs that Anthony Burgess's antique British expression had warned of. At the time, it was the tentacles of communism we were persuaded would turn us into the clockwork oranges of Burgess's 1962 book—mind-controlled Sovietized automatons with all "the appearance of an organism lovely with colour and juice but in fact only a clockwork toy to be wound up by God or the Devil or (since this is increasingly replacing both) the Almighty State."[1] But the idea that our own "state" would seek such controls over us freethinking Americans seemed an improbable, if not impossible, prospect.

Since then an endless series of wars in Vietnam, Grenada, Nicaragua, Panama, Somalia, Kosovo, Iraq, and Afghanistan have inched the United States further and further from the principles and practices of a just society while the media's endless fascination with tabloid and video-game warfare has reduced America's collective moral conscience to a vague numbness. But not until 9/11 and the subsequent unilateral engagements in Afghanistan and Iraq did the inevitable outcome of this step-by-step process become apparent.

And so here, thirty years later, we were reminded by an Afghan artist of what we had been warned about by a book and film decades ago, and the meaning of the metaphor was suddenly "[c]lear as an azure sky of deepest summer,"[2] to quote Burgess's protagonist. We in the United States had become the "clockwork oranges," of Burgess's book—the unsuspecting beneficiaries of Britain's violent nineteenth-century imperial obsession with conquering Afghanistan and controlling the gateway to Eurasia. But a story about windup radios didn't shed a clue about how Afghanistan had been stage-managed to turn the clock back on America's disillusioned hearts and minds after Vietnam and Watergate nor how Afghanistan had been used as a pretext for undermining the power and the promise of American democracy.

II

Our involvement in this story began in the summer of 1979 when we began production of a documentary we called *Arms Race and the Economy: A Delicate Balance*. The big international news story of the day was the second round of the Strategic Arms Limitation Talks (SALT II), which had been completed that June. Begun under President Richard M. Nixon in November 1972, it was hoped that the agreement signed by President Jimmy Carter and General Secretary of the Communist Party of the Soviet Union Leonid Brezhnev would further the era of détente and end, once and for all, the Cold War between the United States and Soviet Union.

We had no idea at the time of the key role that Afghanistan would shortly come to play in keeping the Cold War very much alive. As the host of a weekly public affairs program (*Watchworks*) on Pat Robertson's Christian Broadcasting Network affiliate in Boston, I found that the issue had taken on a personal relevance. I had been hired in an effort to balance the ultraconservative Apocalypse-is-coming programming of Pat Robertson, Jerry Falwell, Jimmy Swaggart, and others, that streamed out of the network's headquarters in Virginia Beach. For someone who had worked on the political campaigns of liberals Barney Frank in 1972 for the Massachusetts House of Representatives and Ed Markey in 1976 for the U.S. House of Representatives, this was not difficult to do. But it was Robertson's decision to repeatedly air an anti-SALT documentary titled *The Salt Syndrome*, produced by the American Security Council as "public service," that enabled us to engage the topic of the nuclear arms race. So, on a shoestring budget, we began interviewing individuals who would begin explaining the mechanism of the twentieth century's arms race; its growth and mutation into the domestic economy following World War II, and the mythology that had been created to maintain it.

During the next months Ted Kennedy, Henry Cabot Lodge, John Kenneth Galbraith, George B. Kistiakowsky, Paul Warnke, and numerous others lent their experience to our understanding of SLCMs and GLCMs, Cruise and MX missiles, throw weights, and the all-important canon of the nuclear age—Mutual Assured Destruction (MAD). But the picture that was emerging was anything but clear. It appeared that strategic thought wasn't only a matter of numbers and throw weights, but a dark world of business, science, and politics ruled over by a self-described "priesthood" of experts.[3] A visit to the Arms Control and Disarmament Agency in Washington, D.C., that fall revealed a bureaucracy under attack from not only the Left but also the Right, which accused it of betraying the security of the United States by appeasing an enemy who was bent on America's destruction. But not even after the Soviets crossed their border into Afghanistan that December 27 did anyone realize the full measure of what was occurring. Suddenly and without warning a supposedly insignificant little country called Afghanistan had managed to roll the clock back thirty years on U.S.-Soviet relations and usher in a new and dangerous era of U.S.-Soviet competition and pave the way for a "conservative revolution" in American politics.

By the time our program aired on February 17, 1980, the delicate balance of the arms race and the economy—that is, whether our government should call a halt to the nuclear arms race or commit new trillions to strategic weapons—was no longer at issue. Another set of assumptions had taken hold of the nation, with the media echoing a return to Cold War rhetoric, and the debate refocused on how much was to be spent to counter this "historic moment" of Soviet aggression. Viewed by the emerging right-wing neoconservative establishment as a vindication of their long-standing belief in Soviet iniquity, Afghanistan had reset the clock back to the darkest days of the Cold War and the creation of the national security state in 1947. But in July 1980 an odd new aspect of that war began to emerge.

III

Colin S. Gray and Keith Payne's *Foreign Policy* article "Victory is Possible" (Summer 1980) went unnoticed by the political pundits of the day. Even after three years of attempting to provide a balance to Pat Robertson's apocalyptic philosophy, the stridency of the rhetoric came as a surprise. "Nuclear war is possible," they wrote that summer. "But unlike Armageddon, the apocalyptic war prophesied to end history, nuclear war can have a wide range of possible outcomes."

No longer was biblical prophecy confined to the broadcasts of the Christian Broadcasting Network. Because of the Soviet invasion of Afghanistan the domain of strategic thinking was now being challenged. It seemed that Afghanistan was more than just a "historic moment" in East-West relations as declared by Harvard historian Richard Pipes. Afghanistan had somehow enabled a philosophical shift away from a policy of "realist" diplomacy to a policy of nuclear-war fighting and the New Right was rushing to graft it to an archaic spiritual agenda.

Combining the high-tech weaponry of America's nuclear arsenal with the medieval Catholic doctrine of Just War, Gray and Payne proposed to break the stalemate over the use of nuclear weapons and create a new rationale that would free America from nuclear restraint. Added to Robert Scheer's January 1980 *Los Angeles Times* article in which presidential candidate George Herbert Walker Bush was reported as suggesting that a nuclear war was winnable, it seemed that Afghanistan had become the most important story of a strange and dangerous new era.

Our decision in the fall of 1980 to request exclusive permission from the Afghan government to enter Afghanistan and see for ourselves what the Soviets were up to grew from this realization, and our journey there in the spring of 1981 under contract to CBS News would forever immunize us from the haze of propaganda and chest beating surrounding U.S.-Soviet competition.

Afghanistan was a complex problem—far from the simplistic portrait of black and white, good against evil, portrayed by the American media and the U.S. administration. Ethnic feuding, modernization, chronic poverty, women's rights issues, a 50 percent infant mortality rate, and massive narcotics trafficking were all factors in the country's political instability. Added to that were two hundred years of colonial pressure from Russia and Britain that saw Britain's armies occupy broad swaths of Afghan territory during three separate wars of conquest. But even our personal look at the Soviet occupation couldn't explain why the Kremlin had risked international condemnation in overthrowing the nominally Marxist government of Hafizullah Amin. Nor did it explain the disproportionate American response to the Afghan crisis. Something other than the presence of 75,000

Soviet troops appeared to be driving Afghanistan as the major East-West conflict of the late twentieth century, and we were determined to find out what it was.

Against this backdrop, a return trip in 1983 accompanied by Harvard Negotiation Project director Roger Fisher for ABC's *Nightline* revealed a major clue. Far from being a preparatory step toward the Persian Gulf, the Soviet Union was anxious to extricate itself as quickly as possible from the Afghan quagmire. Talks with Soviet officials in Kabul that spring indicated a Soviet willingness to admit that a "mistake" had been made, to withdraw its forces, and to cool international tensions. Yet this discovery, made by one of the world's foremost experts on crisis negotiation was ignored by the powers that be in both the press and the government of the United States.

A deeper long-range plan seemed to be unfolding in Afghanistan, a plan that even after the events of 9/11 would never make it to the evening news. But that was a deeper story that went far beyond Osama bin Laden and the veneer of American foreign policy. It was a mystical story—apocalyptic in nature, one that bound America's destiny to the ancient mechanism of good versus evil culminating in a great battle at the end of time in a place where civilization began.

Following the attack on the World Trade Center towers on September 11, 2001, we were given the opportunity to speak about our experience to the national media and to provide insight into whom and what the United States might expect from this sudden and shocking turn of events. During this time it came as a great surprise to find that after two decades of direct American involvement in the internal affairs of Afghanistan and a previous bombing of the Twin Towers by Afghan-related fighters, Americans knew virtually nothing about how such a thing had come about. The acquiescence of the major American media in maintaining a silence on the largest covert operation in American history following the invasion of a "limited contingent" of Soviet troops in 1979 had left the greatest democracy on earth without a clue as to who had really just attacked it or what was to be done about it.

In the end, of course, Afghanistan was bombed by American planes and again invaded—this time by a "limited contingent' of American forces. But even after years of direct American involvement in the internal affairs of Afghanistan little was known and less understood about how it brought about the events of 9/11 or the importance of this ancient crossroads to the future of the United States. Even less was known about the evolution of Afghan history, its people, and the centuries of interaction with outside forces that caused Afghanistan to become the staging ground for the end of an old world and the beginning of another. The impact Afghanistan has made on political life in the West and especially in the life of American politics is significant. Manipulated into a mechanism for change by a handful of insightful geopoliticians and defense intellectuals, it has worked like clockwork to produce a series of historic and unstoppable events that have brought our civilization to the edge of a great transformation. The chances that this land, the very place where western civilization began, will soon play a final and decisive role in our future are all but certain. But for most, Afghanistan remains behind the veil—a country whose true purpose and beauty remain hidden from sight, but whose future we ignore at our own peril.

PART I

AFGHANISTAN FROM ANTIQUITY TO THE 1960S

A great deal of what is traditionally denoted in historical studies as Persian, Iranian, and even Indian history involves the cities and principalities of what is now Afghanistan. Composed of tribes that were even at the time recognized as ethnically and culturally distinct, such ancient cities as Kandahar, Bamiyan, Mazar, Herat, Kabul, Bagram, and Balkh played a leading role in the evolving history of the region and the civilized world. Over the millennia, rulers from these cities swept far outside their territories to conquer and for long intervals rule over kingdoms stretching from China to the Caspian Sea. At times Afghan dynasties controlled the fate of Indian and Persian empires, while no less a figure than Zoroaster (Zarathustra) is said to have gained renown as a priest-scholar in the northern Bactrian city of Balkh, now located in Afghanistan, not far from Mazar-e Sharif.

But the ancient apocalyptic religious teachings accredited to Zoroaster take on even more meaning when placed against a backdrop of today's holy war. For what may seem to our modern secular society a hopelessly anachronistic throwback to the past is in fact seen by its mystical holy warrior participants in Washington and elsewhere as the final act in an ancient historical drama.

I.

Problems with the Historical Record

For more than ten thousand years, what is today Afghanistan has been the meeting place of four cultural zones, Southwestern Asia (including North Africa), Central Asia, South Asia and East Asia. Little distinction has been bestowed upon Afghanistan or the history of its people by western historians. In fact, to the West, the larger part of Afghanistan has often seemed invisible, a vacant lot loosely settled by nomads and periodically overrun by great conquerors on their way to somewhere else.

More recently, Afghanistan has suffered at the hands of invaders who in addition to destroying precious historical artifacts and traditions, have seemed intent to remove the country and its history from view. But the study of Afghanistan in both antiquity and the recent past yields many surprises that, depending on the source, can reveal completely disparate images of this ever-evolving, uniquely complex cultural landscape.

Generally dismissed by western academia and U.S. government policy makers, Afghanistan and its people have languished in the shadows, an independent nation whose politics and culture are no better understood today than prior to the Soviet invasion of 1979.

But whether this practice results from an individual or a cultural bias, it is important to recognize that far from being a disadvantage to our understanding, Afghanistan's seeming cultural invisibility has enabled it time and time again to emerge as a stage upon which we have had the privilege of watching some of history's greatest dramas unfold.

A cursory glance at Afghanistan's history reveals a story dating back to the origin of civilization.

The region has been inhabited for at least a hundred thousand years;

Paleolithic peoples are known to have roamed there, while Neanderthal remains dating back thirty thousand years have been found in the Badakhsh n region. Caves have yielded evidence of early Neolithic culture (around 9000–6000 BCE) based on the presence of domesticated animals.[1]

Archaeological research has unearthed Bronze Age sites dating back to both before and after the Indus Valley (Harrapan) civilization of the third to second millennium BCE. Extensive evidence of trade with Bronze Age Mesopotamia and Egypt exists.[2] "Between 3000 and 2000 BCE, as urban civilizations rose in the Nile Valley, the Tigris-Euphrates valleys, and the Indus Valley, peasant agricultural villages served as the backbone of the economy," it is written.[3] The dark-blue lapis lazuli inlaid in Egyptian burial masks can only be identified with Afghan mines, again in Badakhshan. "Lapis Lazuli has been mined in the Badakhshan province of Afghanistan for 6,500 years, and trade in the stone is ancient enough for lapis jewelry to have been found at Predynastic Egyptian sites," according to Bowersox and Chamberlin in *Gemstones of Afghanistan*.[4] In short, Afghanistan and its people have played a central role in the cultural development of southwestern Asia and North Africa since ancient times as a crossroads for trade, conquest, and culture.

Originally known as Aryana, for the mother goddess of the Indo-Aryans,[5] some western historians suggest that variations on the name "Afghan" may go back as early as the third century CE. There are Sasanian references to "Abgan," as a noun referring to Afghans.[6] Ethnic Afghan historian Maulavi Khairuddin maintains however in his *Asrarul Afaghinah* (Secrets of the Afghans) that the name descends from the grandson of King Saul of Israel. "The Afghans, according to their own traditions, are the posterity of *Melic Talut*, (king *Saul*) who, in the opinion of some, was a descendant of *Judah*, the son of *Jacob*; and, according to others, of *Benjamin*, the brother of *Joseph*."[7] Pashtun history maintains the name descends from "Afghana," the commander of King Solomon's army. "Afghans are all Mahomedans of the Suni sect, and according to the Afghan historians they are descended from the Israelites. They take their name of Afghans from the word 'Afghana'; some of them being descended from the Afghana (Commander and Chief) of King Solomon, and others from Jeremiah the son of Saul."[8]

Strategically located at the crossroads to the ancient world's great civilizations, Afghanistan was crisscrossed by the famed Silk Road, a network of routes that linked China to Rome, with wool, gold, and silver carried east while silk and spices were transported west. Nestorian Christianity and Buddhism (from India) both arrived in China via Afghanistan, and for nine centuries the country provided a home for both Buddhist and Hindu faiths.

The Persian Achaemenian Cyrus II the Great established authority over the region in the sixth century BCE. Darius I the Great (ruling from 522–486 BCE) consolidated Achaemenian rule through the satrapies of Aria (north of Herat), Bactria (Balkh), Sattagydia (Ghazn to the Indus River), Kandahar, and Seistan.[9] Alexander the Great conquered the Achaemenians at the battle of Gaugamela in 331 BCE and burned down the cultural and political center of Persepolis during a drunken orgy.[10]

Following the battle the defeated Achaemenian leader, Darius III, was slain by three of his satraps (subordinates), provoking Alexander to pursue them into Afghanistan. "He entered the Afghan area in 330 BCE and met fierce resistance while on the trail of Darius's murderers," writes the noted Afghan specialist Louis Dupree.[11] Dupree observed a fatal flaw in Alexander's Afghan campaign that continues this day to plague military planners with grand dreams of empire over the Hindu Kush. "From the beginning of his Central Asian adventure, however, Alexander failed to realize that he was fighting a nationalist war, not simply destroying an empire. The tribal kingdoms, no longer allies of the defunct Achaemenids, fought to protect their own form of mountain independence and were an important factor which eventually forced Alexander to retreat to Babylon as his troops grew ever more tired and finally rebellious."[12] Alexander would spend two frustrating years in Afghanistan before crossing back over the Hindu Kush, aiming his forces at India. "He had spent more of his life—and lost more of his men—fighting in Bactria and Sogdiana than in any other part of the Persian world," writes Frank L. Holt in *Into the Land of Bones*.[13] Setting out for India in 327 BCE, Alexander left his mark on Afghanistan. Remains of a Greek city founded in 325 BCE have been found at Ay Khanom. Excavations have revealed inscriptions and transcriptions of Delphic precepts describing the stages of a man's life, written in Greek cursive script.[14] In less than a year of Alexander's Afghan campaign, the region was again seething with revolt, but he would not return. Holt writes, "For the remainder of his short life, the king skirted the country in a destructive march down through [what is today] Pakistan and back along the coast to Babylon in Iraq. Every miserable step of the way, the effects of the Bactrian war harassed Alexander and his exhausted army."[15]

As it would for all future would-be conquerors, Afghanistan marked a turning point in Alexander's campaign that hung like a dark cloud over his future. Dupree summed it up dryly: "From that time until he departed the Central Asia steppes, Alexander knew no peace. . . . More fights, more wounds, more deserts, more thirst, more mountains, then Babylon and death."[16]

Following his death in 323, the conquered territories passed to his cavalry commander Seleucus, whose Seleucid dynasty continued to rule from Babylon. The Seleucid satrapy of Bactria (Balkh) established its own kingdom and created its own unique culture by merging both Greek and Indian cultures. Bilingual rock inscriptions in Greek and Aramaic (the official language of the Achaemenians and the Semitic language of the Old Testament books of Daniel and Ezra and of the New Testament) found at Kandahar in eastern Afghanistan date from the reign of King Ashoka 265–238 BCE. But though Greek influence in the region was to last for centuries through the dynasties of Greco-Bactria in northern Afghanistan, Greek control of Afghanistan succumbed to the same internecine strife that destroyed the rest of Greek civilization to the west, ending around 170 BCE.[17]

THE GRECO-BUDDHIST ERA

For nearly two hundred years following the death of Alexander in 323 BCE, Greco-Bactria consisted of a network of city-states ruled by a patchwork of Greek royal dynasties. Adding to the political confusion, nomadic Parthians entered from the west in roughly 248 BCE, penetrating Sogdiana in the north and replacing the Seleucids in Iran. Their rule of the region lasted roughly from 129 BCE to 226 CE.[18]

During this period of political confusion about 135 BCE, remnants of the

Bactrian Greeks ceded control of Bactria to a loose confederation of nomadic Indo-European tribes known as the Kushans. These tribes conquered the region, flourishing from north-central India to the frontiers of China and beyond Bactria. "The zenith of Kushan power was reached in the 2nd century AD under King Kanishka (c. AD 78–144)."[19]

Kushan leadership proved highly cultured, supportive of both the arts and religion. Bactria (Balkh) in northern Afghanistan operated as a major transshipment center on the Silk Road for goods and ideas, and Greco-Buddhist (Gandhara) art flourished there until the coming of Islam. Under Kushan rule, the world's tallest Buddhist statues were carved into a cliff at Bamiyan in the central mountains of Afghanistan during the third and fourth centuries CE. Destroyed by the Taliban in 2001 prior to the U.S. invasion, their absence stands as a mute testament to Afghanistan's vanishing link to the broad-based culture of its past as well as a stark example of modern religious intolerance in action. At the Kushan summer capital, Bagram (just north of Kabul), painted glass from Alexandria, bronzes and alabasters from Rome, lacquers from China, and carved ivories from India have been found, while a major hoard of gold artistry has been excavated at Sheberghan, west of Balkh.[20]

In 241 CE, the Sasanians, a name used to describe the fourth Iranian dynasty and the second Persian Empire, established control over vast parts of Central Asia, including Afghanistan. The large territory of Eranshahr (literally, the realm of the Iranians or Aryans), as the empire was known to the Arabs, extended from the Oxus River to the Euphrates.[21] Eranshahr essentially consisted of modern-day Iran, Iraq, Armenia, Georgia, Azerbaijan, Turkmenistan, Afghanistan, Uzbekistan, Tajikistan, United Arab Emirates, Oman, Qatar, Bahrain, and Kuwait, as well as parts of Turkey, Saudi Arabia, Syria, Pakistan, and China.[22]

This period of Kushano-Sasanian control of Afghanistan ended about the mid fifth century CE with the arrival of the Hephtalites (or Ephtalites).[23] In 244 CE an army of Goths and Germans under Roman emperor Gordian III engaged Sasanian King Shapur I's forces at Massice (Misikhe) on the Euphrates and was defeated.[24] Several years later the Romans suffered another defeat in Syria, losing thirty-seven cities, including the capital,

Antioch.[25] But as each empire wore down the other, as they vied for control of trade routes across the Persian Gulf, Arabian Sea, and Indian Ocean, the gradual Hephtalite encroachment, which had begun around 400 CE, began to supercede Sasanian control.

"The small, disunited Kushano-Sasanian states in Afghanistan could not meet the sudden threat to Bactria in the latter half of the fifth century AD as the Hephtalite Huns rode out of Central Asia."[26] According to Dupree, "The Hephtalite Empire in Afghanistan and northwest India lasted about a century (ca. AD 450–565), extending from Chinese Sinkiang to Sasanian Iran, from Sogdiana to the Punjab."[27] Though their control was finally broken by the combined forces of Sasanians and the western Turks, Central Asian authority Beatrice F. Manz maintains that the 565 CE date "was not the end of Hephtalite power in the region."[28]

The fifth through the seventh century saw Afghanistan's religious centers at Hadda, Ghazni, Kunduz, Bamian, Shotorak, and Bagram host Chinese Buddhist pilgrims. Reportedly motivated by a dream to travel to India, the Buddhist pilgrim Xuanzang recorded his visits to these and other sites in an important account,[29] documenting the widespread but declining influence of Buddhism in Afghanistan.[30] Hindu influence entered Afghanistan from the south and was adopted by both the Hephthalite Huns and the Sasanians. During an especially turbulent period from the eighth to the tenth centuries CE, the Hindu Shahi kings ruled parts of Afghanistan concentrated mostly in and around Kabul and Ghazni. "The Hindu–Shahi Dynasty established itself in Kabul and controlled much of eastern Afghanistan until the ninth and tenth centuries AD," Dupree writes.[31] Excavations north of Kabul and in Ghazni reveal both Buddhist and Hindu relics, suggesting either a mingling or overlapping of the two religions.[32]

651 CE, THE MUSLIMS

The forced introduction of Islam by Arab armies brought an end to the remnants of Graeco-Buddhist society, with 651 considered the end of the Sasanian Empire by most scholars.[33] Islamic historians argue that conversion brought a measure of peace to Afghanistan while over time providing a unifying force in Afghan culture, but the battle for control of Afghanistan had only begun.

Conquered cities rose in revolt and returned to their old religious practices once the invaders had left. Dupree writes, "The first big Arab raid through Qandahar and central Afghanistan took place in 80–81/699–700, when the Arab governor of Sistan was sent to chastise the Hindu-Shahi king of Kabul, who had refused to pay tribute. Even though defeated, the Hindu-Shahi (possibly former Kushans) continued to rule Kabul as vassals of the Umayyid Caliphs (41–132/661–750)."[34] For the next three hundred years Afghanistan became contested ground while giving rise to numerous local Islamic dynasties. Not until the rule of the Saffarids in about 870, did Islam become firmly entrenched, though still not free from conquest. "The Saffarid (253–ca. 900/867–1495), capital at Nimroz, broke the power of the Hindu-Shahi in Kabul, the Buddhist Kushans in Zamindawar, Bost, Ghor, and Qandahar, and even survived as vassals in Sistan under later dynasties," Dupree writes.[35]

A Turkish slave named Alptegin, commander of the Khurasan (capital at Nishapur, Iran) garrison of the Samanids, seized Ghazni with a few loyal Turkish followers around 961 after a failed coup attempt, setting the stage for the rule of the Ghaznavids. "The real founder of the Ghaznavid Empire, Nasir ad-Dawla Subuktigin (366–87/977–97), was son-in-law and one time 'slave' of Alptigin," Dupree writes.[36] Subuktigin and his son Mahmud secured Kabul and the Indus Valley, then conquered the Punjab and Multan, carrying their conquests into the heartland of India. Under their rule, Ghazni became an important city until 1150 when the conquest by Ala-ud-Din Husayn of Ghur drove the last of the Ghaznavids into India. Ala-ud-Din's nephew, Mu'izzud-Din Mohammad, extended the Ghurids' control into India in 1175.[37] With the death of Mu'izzud-Din in 1206 the Ghurid Empire fell to Sultan Ala ad-Din Mohammad, the Khorezmshah, whose dynasty, according to Manz, now extended from the borders of Iraq in the west to the eastern Jaxartes region in today's Kazakhstan.

THE ATOM BOMB OF HIS DAY

Ala-ad-Din Mohammad's empire was short-lived. Dupree writes, "The invincible Khwarazm Shah Turks loosely ruled an empire stretching from India to Turkey but rumors filtered out of Central Asia that a savior was on the way."[38] Medieval Christians assigned the rumor to the legendary "Prester John," a popular European fantasy of the age that had a descendant of one of the Three Magi emerging from a semi-magical, Oriental Christian nation over which he ruled to defeat the pagan and Muslim nations surrounding him. According to Dupree, the Abbasid caliph hoped the "savior" was a Muslim who would reestablish the power and glory of a central caliphate. In 1219 hard reality struck both the Christian and Muslim worlds as Genghis (Chinggis) Khan, a Mongol warlord on a white horse, attacked from the east, driving Ala-ad-Din into retreat on an island in the Caspian Sea. He died there in 1220. Determined to reclaim his father's empire, Ala ad-Din's son Jalal counterattacked and won a surprising victory over the Mongols near Kabul.

Intent on avenging his defeat, Genghis Khan rode on Bamian and laid siege. After his grandson Mutugen was killed in the following battle, the Khan ordered that the city and all its inhabitants be laid to waste.[39] Genghis Khan then defeated Jalal ad-Din at Ghazni. Jalal ad-Din fell back to the Indus River, where he made a final, futile stand.[40] His defeat left western Asia open to a systemic cultural leveling that remains to this day the standard by which all modern catastrophes can be judged.

Although considered "the atom bomb of his day" by Dupree,[41] Genghis Khan failed to dislodge Islam from Central Asia and by the end of the thirteenth century his descendants were themselves Muslim.[42] The dissolution of Genghis Khan's empire following his death in 1227 resulted in the rise of mostly independent principalities throughout Afghanistan which remained divided and factionalized but under Mongol rule (khanates) until the late fourteenth century and the rise of Timur (Tamerlane).[43] The first of the Turkish/Mongol rulers to emerge, Timur united large parts of the country while his successors who ruled from 1405–1507 turned their capital, Herat, into a formidable center for arts and religion. A grandson of Timur built an observatory in Samarqand Uzbekistan and this period is considered a golden age for Afghanistan. But the early sixteenth century signaled the rise of the Turkic Uzbeks in Central Asia whose leader, Mohammad Shaybani, brought this period to an end when they conquered Herat in 1507.[44]

The sixteenth century also saw the rise of a powerful group that would later come to captivate nineteenth-century European orientalists, who saw them as a secret society of assassins that revolved around a Sufi cult operating in the mountains of Afghanistan—the Roshaniya ("illuminated ones").[45] The Roshaniya were inspired by Bayezid Ansari, a philosopher, writer, teacher and Pashtun nationalist known as "Pir Roshan" ("the enlightened one"), named for Roshan ("Shining") Mountain. Ansari's revolutionary-progressive influence on Pashtun culture still reverberates in Afghanistan nearly five hundred years after his birth. "On the occasion a written message from President Hamid Karzai was read out. The president stressed the need for carrying out comprehensive research on the hidden aspects of Pir Rokhan."[46]

According to legends familiar in the west, Ansari's family claimed descent from the "Helpers"—the Ansar—who assisted Mohammad after his escape from Mecca. As a reward his ancestors were initiated into the mysteries of the Ishmaelite religion.[47] Tradition holds that this secret, inner training dates from the time of Abraham's rebuilding of the black stone temple of Kaaba in Mecca, whose name means literally "Cube." Squared upon a mysterious black cornerstone that may be a meteorite, the "Cube" of Mecca carries with it various Cabalistic, Masonic and alchemical allusions to such things as the war of light against dark and the perfection of the material world. In the eyes of Afghan professor Dr. Raj Wali Shah Khattak, "He transformed altogether the lives of many of his disciples through the force of his spriritual knowledge, for he was a practicing Sufi. Pir Roshan was the only person who amalgamated both mystical and political ideology and also proved to be the harbinger of his own vision."[48] A wildly controversial figure in his time, Bayezid Ansari set up a madrassa in Peshawar where he carefully coached those who had been initiated by him in the eight degrees of knowledge leading to perfection. According to some sources he claimed to have received illumination from the supreme being, who desired a class of perfect men—and women—to carry out the organization and direction of the world.[49] Viewed from today's more practical prespective, Pir Roshan is viewed as a Pashtun nationalist (one of the first) dedicated to rebellion against the feudalism of his own Pashtun nobles and the oppression of the Mughal Empire. He is also viewed as a radical social reformer who "advocated the community of ownership or social communism."[50] He would be neither the first nor last Afghan to invoke mystical powers to lead his followers. It has been claimed that the eighteenth-century Bavarian Illuminati society of Adam Weishaupt descended from this cult.[51]

Driven from his father's satrapy in Ferghana in 1504, Babur, a Mughal emperor from Central Asia who had descended from both Genghis Khan and Timur, made Kabul the capital of an independent city-state. In 1522 he captured Kandahar, then Delhi in 1526. "Babur loved Kabul and only moved into India when frustrated in his attempts to regain Ferghana."[52] Defeating Ibrahim, the last of the Afghan kings of India, Babur established the Indian-centered Mughal empire, which lasted for three hundred years and included all of eastern Afghanistan south of the Hindu Kush. According to Dupree, Babur pined for Kabul, writing "The climate [of Kabul] is extremely delightful, and there is no such place in the known world."[53] Considered one of Afghanistan's greatest kings, his body was taken for burial in Kabul nine years after his death in 1530. Today, his shattered and bullet-pocked tomb on the outskirts of the city rules over a desolate landscape.

Afghanistan lay divided between the Mughals of India and the Safavids of Persia for the next two hundred years. Not until the early eighteenth century was there further effort to rid Afghanistan of foreign rule. Beginning in 1709 Mir Wais Khan, prominent figure in the Hotaki Ghilzai tribe, led a successful uprising against the Persians at Kandahar.[54]

Beginning in the mid seventeenth century, these Ghilzai and Durrani Pashtun tribes in the mountainous regions between Afghanistan and what is now Pakistan began to emerge as uniting forces in Afghan history, while their ensuing rivalries and campaigns against outside invaders eventually came to shape world history. Dupree writes, "At Qandahar and Herat major rivalries developed between the Abdali (later Durrani) and the Ghilzai Pushtun, a rivalry still not completely eradicated. Herat remained in Safavid Persian hands until the rise of the Abdali, who had been driven from power in the Qandahar region by the Ghilzai in 1129/1716."[55]

Following the Ghilzai Hotakis example in 1716, the Abdalis of Herat rose up against the Persians and succeeded in freeing their province of Persian rule. Not content with holding Kandahar, in 1721 Mir Wais's son Mahmud led 20,000 men against Esfahan, whose Persian Safavid government surrendered in January 1722 after a six-month siege.[56]

The eighteenth century brought a new era of invaders to the Afghan theater and a new era of social cohesion. Following Mahmud's death in 1725, his successor Ashraf had to contend with an expansive Ottoman Turkish Empire from the west and the Russians from the north. Halting both advances, Ashraf moved to conquer Persia, but was defeated by a rebellious chieftain named Nader Qoli Beg (Tahmasp Quli Khan, "Slave of Tahmasp").

Emboldened by victory, "the outlaw king with a large personal army,"[57] Nader Qoli Beg conquered Herat in 1732 and was elected shah of Persia in 1736. As shah, Nader's 80,000 men seized Kandahar in 1738, then occupied the Mughal capital at Delhi in 1739, gaining the famed Koh-i-Noor diamond and the Peacock Throne as trophies. But although victorious in battle, Nader Beg was assassinated at Khabushan in 1747, bringing his empire to an end while introducing the last and perhaps greatest Afghan empire, the Durrani.[58]

Ahmad Khan Abdali, an Abdali Afghan chieftain and commander of the assassinated shah's 4,000-man bodyguard, was chosen to succeed Nader Beg by a tribal *jirgah* (meeting of tribal leaders). Crowned Badash, Durr-i-Dauran (Shah, Pearl of the Ages), Ahmad Shah changed the title, because of a dream, to Ahmad Shah, Durr-i-Durran (Pearl of Pearls), or Ahmad Shah Durrani. "Since 1160/1747, therefore, the Abdali have been called the Durrani (Ghubar, 1943)."[59] The first Afghan ruler with support from most of the tribal leaders, including their traditional enemies the Ghilzai, Ahmad Shah Durrani united the nation of Afghanistan for the first time in modern history while proceeding to extend Afghan control from Mashhad in northeastern Iran to Kashmir and Delhi in India, from the Amu Darya River bordering Tajikistan, Uzbekistan and Turkmenistan, to the Arabian Sea.[60]

Clearly the first great Afghan ruler of the modern era, over the next quarter century Durrani consolidated his control, making his empire the second most important Muslim kingdom next to the Ottoman Turks. Dupree writes, "But what of the Ghilzai, traditional enemies of the Abdali, and the greatest potential threat to the new Shah? . . . The Ghilzai, once masters of this part of the world, chose to bide their time and work with a winner, but they never again reached their previous pinnacle of power. The Durrani still rule."[61]

Through brilliant leadership, Durrani unified the divergent tribes of Afghanistan and established himself as an example of Afghan identity that would form the foundation for future Afghan kings. Yet upon his death in 1772, the empire began to crumble and with it came the advent of pressure from a new player in the great game for control of Afghanistan.[62]

2.

The British Are Coming

Besieged from the north by Russia and from the west by Iran, with the Ottoman Turks looming in the distance, Durrani's successors now had to contend with an aggressive British empire advancing from the southeast from India and the beginning of a new era of European encroachment fueled by the riches of the opium trade.

A highly lucrative business since the 1700s, when shipments from India often returned profits of more than 400 percent, the Asian opium market's modern era began in 1773, with Britain assuming a monopoly on exports to China.[1] Led by the mercantile interests of the East India Company but guided by a series of British governors, by 1818 Britain's reach had extended into all of western India's opium-growing region. With drug profits fueling the expansion of empire, it was only a matter of time before Russian, British and Afghan tribal ambitions would come face to face over the Hindu Kush. "By 1818, the British completed their conquest of western India, giving them indirect control over the opium districts there," writes Alfred W. McCoy in *The Politics of Heroin*. "The British purchase stimulated poppy production in the west, and the amount of Malwa opium reaching the China coast doubled in just one year."[2]

During this time, control of the Afghan throne at Kabul became a seesaw battle between family members that would rage for most of a century. In addition to the traditional regional antagonists, the entry of Britain and Russia into the struggle would complicate competition for Afghanistan until the end of the twentieth century.

Alarmed by Ahmad Shah Durrani's grandson Zaman Shah's advances into India, the British influenced the Persian king Fath Ali Shah to pressure the Afghan ruler. Fath Ali Shah helped Zaman's half-brother and governor of Herat, Mahmud, seize Kandahar and Kabul, leading to Mahmud's coronation in Kabul in 1800. But the intrigues continued, as Mahmud's ministers plotted with Zaman's full brother, Britain's future puppet Shah Shoja, at Peshawar. Invited to seize Kabul, Shah Shoja arrived and occupied the city, ascending the throne in 1803.[3]

During this time, Napoleon attempted to recruit Czar Alexander I of Russia into attacking the British in India. To complicate matters further, tribal rebellions and external pressures were mounting from the Sikhs in the Punjab to the east and Persians from Iran in the west. Offering to support Shah Shoja against any invasion, the British signed a treaty of friendship in June 1809 at Peshawar. But the weak ruler proved unable to control events and as the British delegation left Peshawar word came that Mahmud had retaken Kabul.[4]

As Dost Mohammad—a member of the Pashtun Barakzay (Mohammadzai) clan—advanced from Kashmir in 1818, he took Ghazni and Jalalabad from Mahmud, establishing the Mohammadzai family dynasty that was to rule on and off for the next 150 years. "Only in Herat did a grandson of Ahmad Shah, Shah Mahmud, retain power (having lost the shah's throne in 1818, he ruled Herat till 1829)."[5] Dost Mohammad took Kabul in 1826. Determined to rejoin his empire with Afghan territory on the other side of the Hindu Kush, he declared a holy war (jihad) and in 1836 marched on Peshawar, determined to retake the city from the Sikhs. But without broad support, Dost Mohammad's attempt failed.[6]

In October 1835, Dost Mohammad dispatched a letter to the Russian czar, Nicholas I, which was delivered by Afghan messengers to Orenburg in May 1836, with the object of establishing friendly relations between Russia and Afghanistan. The governor's aide-de-camp, I. V. Vitkevich, accompanied the messengers to St. Petersburg and was later sent back to Kabul as Russia's representative. On his way, he stopped in Kandahar where he entered into a diplomatic agreement with the Iranians and the Kohandi Khan to form an alliance against the Sadozai ruler of Herat. For British hawks, Vitkevich's actions were a justification for action.[7]

When the shah of Persia, backed by Russian advisers and money, moved on Herat in 1837, the British responded by sending a gifted young political officer—Alexander Burnes—as emissary to Kabul to recruit Dost Mohammad. Needful of British support in retaking Peshawar from the Sikhs, Dost Mohammad welcomed Burnes's mission.[8]

By 1838 Vitkevich's able diplomacy had come to naught when the czar refused to approve the Iran-Afghan treaty and turned his attention from Afghanistan to the Middle East where he sought British help in settling a Turkish-Egyptian conflict. Nevertheless, according to a Soviet historian, "The British continued to use Vitkevich's mission as a pretext for unleasing a war against Afghanistan, alleging that Dost Mohammad's contacts with Iran and Russia threatened the security of British India."[9]

Although adamantly opposed by the British governor-general of India, Lord Auckland, and his political secretary, William Hay Macnaghten, Burnes's plan of returning Peshawar to Dost Mohammad following the death of the aged Sikh leader was the only workable plan. Burnes had argued correctly that only Dost Mohammad could keep the country from disintegrating into tribal feuds, while at the same time protecting British India from Russian and Persian plots. By returning Peshawar to Afghan control, Burnes argued, Britain gained a formidable ally with vast influence over much of Afghanistan. Without him the northwest frontier and much of India could be lost. "A strong Dost Mohammad, Burnes still argued, could keep the country together and resist Russian or Persian encroachment, but a country split into feudal principalities and tribes would invite Russian intrigue aimed at picking them off piecemeal with no great difficulty," John Waller writes in *Beyond the Khyber Pass*.[10]

Macnaghten's arrogant demands for Dost Mohammad to submit to British whim without written terms, combined with British reluctance to cede Peshawar to Kabul, doomed Burnes's efforts from the start. While the ensuing British invasion of 1839 would experience brief success, it would establish a pattern of tragic British blunders that would lay the foundation for a century and a half of conflict.[11]

1839: THE FIRST BRITISH INVASION AND THE BEGINNING OF THE GREAT GAME

Marching into Kandahar in the spring of 1839 with an army of 12,000

British and Indian troops, William Hay Macnaghten's plan for removing Dost Mohammad and forcing Shah Shoja on the Afghan people through military force appeared at first to be an overwhelming success. As the supposedly impregnable fortress at Ghazni fell in July, Dost Mohammad's forces fled, and the army marched on to take Kabul and crown Shah Shoja. But over the next two years, the massive cost of administering the far-flung territory, as well as the constant tribal uprisings Burnes had warned of, turned Macnaghten's plan to disaster.[12] "Many in England intimately connected with India were horrified at the march across the Indus. Lord William Cavendish-Bentinck (first governor-general of India under the Charter Act of 1833) supposedly exclaimed, "What! Lord Auckland and Macnaghten gone to war; the very last men in the world I should have suspected of such folly!"[13]

Plagued by arrogance and incompetence, whittled down by disease, bad weather and better-armed Afghans, by midwinter 1842 the British position grew hopeless and the garrison was forced to flee. Alexander Burnes was killed in the final days of the rioting and his warnings now sounded like prophecy.[14] Within days of leaving Kabul on January 6, 1842, some 17,000 soldiers and camp followers lay slaughtered in the snow between Kabul and Jalalabad. Abandoned by his own regiment of Sikh troops, Macnaghten's darling Shah Shoja was left to his own devices and was assassinated a short time later. An "army of retribution" led by General George Pollock and Brigadier William Nott succeeded in recapturing Kabul that August, but Pollock's indiscriminate revenge harmed friendly Afghans as well as foes, while the architects of the slaughter escaped to the safety of their mountain retreats.[15]

Military defeat was the least important consequence of Britain's first Afghan fiasco and neither Pollock's subsequent rescue of British prisoners nor the burning of Kabul's great bazaar could undo the damage to Britain's Afghan ambition. In addition to providing a lasting military embarrassment, the first Anglo-Afghan war would congeal Afghan sentiment against further British encroachment and drive the Afghans toward an alliance with the Russians. In the end it was decided that the war itself had served little purpose other than to assure Britain's colonial right to unilateral intervention while inflating the Russian threat and ignoring the competence and effectiveness of the Afghan fighters. It was an assessment that would be repeated again and again.[16]

3.

The Great Game

"We'll go there. We'll say to any king we can find, 'Do you want to vanquish your foes?' And we will show him how to drill men; for that we know better than anything else. Then we will subvert that king. We'll seize his throne and establish a dynasty.

"You'll be cut to pieces before you're fifty miles across the border," I said. You have to travel through Afghanistan to get to that country."

—Rudyard Kipling, *The Man Who Would Be King*

To certain nineteenth-century Britons, Afghanistan represented more than just a strategic piece of real estate guarding the doorway to a lucrative Indian empire. Afghanistan represented a living, breathing link to ancient mysteries that had been lost to the modern era. Through the efforts of the late Alexander Burnes and a host of prophecy-driven adventurers, those mysteries would be resurrected and linked with Britain's foreordained destiny.

As the end of the nineteenth century approached, that destiny seemed more and more to favor Britain's ambitions to empire and no one better than Rudyard Kipling would capture the longing for conquest and the spiritual fulfillment of divine right it brought with it. On a practical level, Kipling's rugged adventurers, Peachey Carnahan and Daniel Dravot, represented an advance guard pushing into unexplored territory. On a mystical level their quest to become kings of Kafiristan brought them into realms more in keeping with the spiritual goal of the British empire to weave the light of heaven and the darkness of earth together through an earthly conquest.

As the death and disfigurement of Dravot and Carnahan illustrates, human emissaries into the war of light and darkness often pay a heavy price. But as a century and half of British, Russian and American experience testify, human desires for empire can suffer a similar fate. It's in the colonial politics of mid-nineteenth-century Afghanistan that the root causes of both the Soviet invasion of 1979, as well as over a century's worth of erratic behavior from the West, first take shape. Where these policies were decried by nineteenth-century British historian Sir John Kaye as "a folly and a crime," in his 1874 study of the first Afghan War, Cold War containment analysts a hundred years later would be more generous. Suggesting that the motives of the Indian governor-general, Lord Auckland, were more a desire to avoid war with Russia than an attempt at conquest, modern analysts downplayed British ambitions while mirroring late-twentieth-century American attitudes toward Russian aggression. But according to American University's Richard F. Nyrop and Donald M. Seekins in their 1987 *Afghanistan: A Country Study*, the British invasion was clearly laid out in Lord Auckland's 1838 Simla Manifesto as Britain's imperial right to secure Afghanistan as a buffer state on their western frontier. And it was accepted as such at the time. "The Simla Manifesto stated that the welfare of India required that the British have on their western frontier a trustworthy ally. The British pretense that their troops were merely supporting the tiny force of Shuja in retaking what was once his throne *fooled no one*."[1]

Noting that the manifesto called for withdrawing troops once Shah Shoja was installed, Nyrop and Seekins also observed a theme that would be repeated over the next century and beyond: "Like other interventions in modern times, the British denied that they were invading Afghanistan but claimed they were merely supporting its legitimate government (Shuja) 'against foreign interference and factious opposition.'"[2]

Regardless of how the disastrous war was spun for home audiences in London, in the Afghan mind the war shifted the geopolitical polarity strongly against Britain in favor of Russia. In the decades following the first Anglo-Afghan war, the Russians made steady advances toward Afghanistan, motivated in no small part by British accession of Kashmir in 1846, the Punjab in 1849, and sizeable chunks of Afghan territory between the Indus River and the Hindu Kush, including Sind in 1843, Baluchistan in 1859, and the North-West Frontier in 1895—regions at one time governed by Ahmed Shah Durrani.[3] Nyrop and Seekins write, "The Russians advanced steadily southward toward Afghanistan in the three decades after the First Anglo-Afghan War, and historians of the period generally agree that the Russians were motivated, at least in part, by British intervention in Afghanistan. In 1842 the Russian border was on the other side of the Aral Sea from Afghanistan, but five years later the tsar's outposts moved to the lower reaches of the Syr Darya. By 1865 Tashkent had been formally annexed, as was Samarkand three years later."[4] As a direct result of the previous British occupation, British efforts to establish a legation in Kabul were repeatedly rebuffed, while in London, Britain's policy toward Afghanistan became an increasingly divisive issue.

The first Afghan war haunted British politics for decades, with battle lines drawn between advocates of an aggressive "Forward Policy" of conquest and occupation (Conservatives) and those for maintaining Afghanistan as a neutral buffer state (Liberals). In fact Liberals believed that the natural boundary of India lay at the Indus River (within modern-day Pakistan) and that any attempt to subdue or seize Afghan tribal lands beyond it was futile.[5]

For a time Liberal British governments tended to view Dost Mohammad in a better light. Still seeking to protect their northwest border of the empire from Russian advance, the enlightened 1855 "Treaty of Peshawar" guaranteed Anglo-Afghan cooperation by proclaiming respect for each side's territorial integrity while committing each to be friends of each other's friends. In 1863 Dost Mohammad was allowed to take Herat without British interference. But even thirty years after the first Anglo-Afghan war, Britain's policy toward Afghanistan remained torn between what Afghan expert John C. Griffiths called "half-hearted Imperialists and ill-informed Liberals," and by 1873 was again moving toward an aggressive "Forward Policy." Hedging against Russian moves, Dost Mohammad's son and successor, Sher Ali, approached Britain's viceroy in India, seeking a better relationship between Kabul and London. But if imperial British attitudes wavered between Liberal and Conservative, their common goal of advancing British interests did not. Caught between Russian advances and British ambitions, the pressure on Sher Ali to choose sides increased. Then in 1874 the Conservative government of Prime Minister Benjamin Disraeli dispatched a new viceroy with orders to reimplement[6] the "Forward Policy." Nyrop and Seekins write, "Sher Ali rejected a second British demand for a British mission in Kabul, arguing that if he agreed the Russians might demand the same right. The Afghan ruler had received intimidating letters from the Russians, but the British offered little in return for the concessions they demanded."[7]

Hoping to rebuff British pressure by suggesting to the British viceroy that he could turn to Russia for support, the amir was informed that Britain "could break him as a reed" and was pressed even harder for a permanent British mission.[8]

Fearing a negative public reaction to the return of British soldiers to Kabul, Sher Ali refused. But when the Russians forced their own diplomatic mission on Kabul in July 1878, the game for Afghanistan went into high gear. "Then occurred the event which precipitated the Second Anglo-Afghan War," Dupree writes. "The Russians, without receiving permission from Sher Ali, sent a diplomatic mission under General Stolietov from Samarkand to Kabul in the summer of 1878. Amir Sher Ali Khan tried to stop the mission, but was too late."[9] Insisting on their right to establish a permanent mission to counter Russia's forced intrusion, the British sent a military detachment which was refused entry at Khyber Pass. "Major Louis Cavagnari moved to Ali Masjid, where the Afghan commanding officer, Major Faiz Mohammad Khan, courteously refused permission for the British Mission, led by Sir Neville Chamberlain, to proceed to Kabul."[10] Presenting the incident as a diplomatic insult, the British sent an angry ultimatum to which Sher Ali had no choice but to refuse.[11]

Then, in events which were to be repeated by the Russians almost exactly a hundred years later, the British invaded Afghanistan once again, this time entering the country at three separate locations. Turning north for assistance, Sher Ali was denied support from the Russians and died in February 1879, in failure and desperation. Forced to sign a treaty making his country a British protectorate, and fearful of his people's retribution, Ali's son Yaqub abdicated and a new era in Afghanistan began.[12] "Two factors prevented a repetition of the 1841–42 debacle," Dupree writes, "the generalship of Roberts and the quality of his subordinates, who undertook constant, vigorous sorties beyond the cantonment to keep the besiegers off guard, and the inability (once again) of the tribal khans to maintain a sustained, unified front."[13] Despite these tactical advantages, Britain's worst fears were revived in July 1880 when a British force under Brigadier G. R. S. Burrows suffered a crushing defeat at Maiwand, near Kandahar. According to legend, a Pashtun heroine named Malalai spurred the fighters on to victory by using her veil as a banner, shouting this elegy to remind them of the cost of deafeat: "Young love, if you do not fall in the battle of Maiwand, by God, someone is saving you as a token of shame."[14]

MYSTICAL IMPERIALISM

A minor aside to most western historians but of no small importance to this part of the world were the activities of European secret societies known to be heavily involved in espionage on both British and Russian sides.[15] Reflected in the quasi-Masonic exploits of Kipling's two soldiers in *The Man Who Would Be King*—where the main character, Daniel Dravot, comes to believe himself to be the reincarnation of Alexander the Great—the quest for a spiritual engagement with Afghanistan and Central Asia was an obscure but important factor in the foreign policy of the era. "Some historians have attempted to identify references to the Afghan landscape in the Rig Veda. Others believe that the first identifiable mention of the area now called Afghanistan can be found in the Avesta, the canonical scriptures of the Zoroastrians, plus the teachings of Zarathustra (the Iranian name for Zoroaster, which comes from Greek), its founder."[16] The Avesta establishes for the first time, the duality of good versus evil and the constant struggle between them for control of the universe. As the reputed home of Zoroaster and the Avesta, as well as Gandhara Buddhism, the Roshaniya cult and the founders of the Bektashi, Mevlevi, and Chishti Sufi orders, Afghanistan and its surroundings provided a mystical underpinning to what today is dryly regarded by most observers as mere geopolitics.[17]

With the late-nineteenth-century expansion of empire interwoven with the expectations of Avestic end-time prophecies about to come due, a spiritual movement linking those prophecies to both Russian and British imperial fulfillment began to grow. Drawing on Anglo and Franco-Egyptian Masonic societies for inspiration, this "mystical imperialism" sought to create a syncretistic cultlike foreign policy with the overarching goal of uniting the various religious factions and cultures within the British and Russian empires.

Rudyard Kipling's work was not without its mystical side. Copies of the 1912 Doubleday edition of his 1899 *Plain Tales From the Hills* bear a counterclockwise swastika, a mystical Indo-Aryan sun sign on its cover and frontispiece (shared by Helena Blavatsky's book, *The Secret Doctrine*),[18] long before its adoption and subversion by the Nazi Party.

In their book *Tournament of Shadows,* Karl E. Meyer and Shareen Blair Brysac write that "not just Russia but all Europe was drawn to the esoteric religions and spiritual spices of the Orient. Starting in the Georgian Age, British merchant fleets sailed homeward with mystical creeds and Sanskrit grammars mixed with more earthbound cargoes. The timing was propitious: the light from the East arrived at a moment of moral crisis and revolutionary upheaval in the West."[19]

According to author Robert Dreyfuss in his book *Devil's Game,* during this time, "Many British intellectuals, and not a few imperialists, were seized with a desire to find a sort of holy grail, a unified field theory of religious belief."[20]

Led by the most noted Orientalist of the day, Edward Granville Browne, this passion for a radical pantheism brought the foremost elites of the empire into contact with numerous mystical movements, cults and mystery religions throughout the East, including the progressive Arab Masonic society. According to Meyer and Brysac, despite cries of fraud, "numerous persons of standing in the West" embraced a wide varity of esoteric practices including spiritualism, reincarnation, channeling, the Brotherhood of Masters, Great White Lodges, cosmogenesis, and a host of secret doctrines. "Thus it happened that in Russia and England the Mystical Channel developed into an interesting new medium for imperial intrigues, or in some cases anti-imperial agitation."[21] In fact, Britain's entire program for empire had begun with a heavy dose of occult philosophy inspired by a vision of sacred destiny during the Elizabethan Renaissance. The British East India Company, the primary purveyor of British imperialism in Central Asia, had been given its first royal charter under the reign of Elizabeth I on December 31, 1600, for the purpose of engaging in trade with India. Its cultural and spiritual role, inspired by some of Elizabeth's more cavalier courtiers, like Walter Raleigh, John Dee and Edmund Spenser, had been to transform Britain, through trade and commerce, into a new kind of empire in harmony with the stars and a utopian vision of the universe.[22] In Spenser's work alone, the ancient Zoroastrian metaphors of good versus evil and light versus dark abound, while foreshadowing nineteenth- and early twentieth-century geopolitical concepts of Britain's Halford Mackinder and Germany's Karl Haushofer. "The Faerie Queene is a great magical Renaissance poem, infused with the whitest of white magic, Christian Cabalist and Neoplatonic, haunted by a good magician and scientist, Merlin (a name sometimes used by Dee), and profoundly opposed to bad magic and necromancers and bad religion," Frances Yates wrote in *The Occult Philosophy in the Elizabethan Age*. "The white magic of pure imperial reform is opposed to the bad necromancy of its enemies."[23]

Standing in the distant shadows, with all the potential of becoming the bad necromancer, was imperial Russia. Described as the "World-Island" by nineteenth-century British geographer Mackinder,[24] Russia's geographic position at the center of the Eurasian land mass more than rivaled Britain's as an island fortress. But unlike Britain, Russia's island stood virtually impregnable—overflowing with resources and beyond the reach of Britain's oceangoing armada.

"Mackinder was struck by the ominous implication for an island kingdom whose imperial reach was based on sea power. In theory the new mobility [of railroads] made Russia the master of an invincible interior fortress, which Mackinder called the World-Island," Meyer and Brysac write.[25] Mackinder foresaw Russia, as it emerged into the twentieth century, escaping its history—and with the advancement of railroads—expanding with ferocity toward India. The idea inspired an entire century of religious and geopolitical panic in the West. Between Mackinder, Nazi Germany's geopolitician Karl Haushofer, and American cold warrior James Burnham, Russian dominance of Central Asia implanted an undying nightmare of an apocalyptic horde sweeping from the Russian steppe across Europe and into the Middle East.

Adding their own contribution to the late-nineteenth-century mystical quest were the Russian mystics. Preaching a "secret doctrine" reportedly taught to her by hidden masters in Tibet, Madame Helena Petrovna Blavatsky made her way from Moscow to India to New York and back, weaving herself and her Theosophical Society into British and Russian intrigues. A close friend of Czar Nicholas II and the so-called "mystic Eurasian scholar" Prince Ukhtomsky, she was accused more than once by British authorities of being a Russian spy and conspiring with the Sikhs to overthrow the British occupation of India.[26] Blavatsky's doctrine was in many ways what Robert Dreyfuss described as the "sort of holy grail, a unified field theory of religious belief," that Europe's nineteenth-century imperialists were hoping to achieve. Self-described as the synthesis of science, religion and philosophy, Blavatsky's *The Secret Doctrine* offered the coming twentieth-century world's political and spiritual elite a syncretistic cult-like philosophy that would reorder the planet along racial and spiritual lines and establish a new harmony by fulfilling a universal plan of human evolution.[27]

Henry Wallace, Franklin Roosevelt's vice president, supported an expedition by Blavatsky's successor Nicholas Roerich (also known as Nikolai Konstantinovich Rerikh) in 1934. Intent on establishing a settlement somewhere in the vicinity of the Himalayas, "The Plan," as it was known by Roerich, his wife and their financial supporters, was a continuation of Blavatsky's "Shambhala Project" and was clearly millennial in scope. An acolyte of Blavatsky and Roerich, Wallace expressed his enthusiasm for the project, stating that "the political situation in this part of the world is always rendered especially intriguing by the effect on it of ancient prophecies, traditions and the like"; Wallace anticipated that those prophecies were at last coming due.[28]

A Russian intellectual known to have grappled with late-nineteenth-century mystical imperialism was the Orthodox Christian philosopher Nikolai Fyodorov, who considered the Pamir region of northern Afghanistan (not far from the reputed birthplace of Zoroaster) to be the single most important geographical location on the planet. As George M. Young Jr., an expert on Fyodorov, notes, "Here, according to local legend, was the original site of Eden, and the visible desolation in contrast to biblical and other lush images of the garden emphasizes what we have lost and how great a task of restoration remains."[29] Referred to as the "Moscow Socrates" by his followers, Fyodorov's belief in the resurrection of humanity profoundly influenced Fyodor Dostoevsky and mystic poet Vladimir Soloviev. According to Young, Fyodorov's spiritual geography made the Pamir Range the symbol of all that must be surmounted in the task to make humankind one.

With Russian and British armies encroaching on the borders of Afghanistan, Fyodorov was pleased that the region was finally gaining the attention it deserved in order that the spiritual plan for the human race could proceed and the resurrection of the dead begin.[30] But it would take an additional century to map out the spiritual geography on the path to Shambhala while the collision of the mystical imperialists over Afghanistan would unfold in ways that were both prophetic and apocalyptic.

THE IRON AMIR: 1880–1901

"The British in India, happy at creating a no-man's-land between themselves and tsarist ambitions, faced other problems," Dupree writes. "The Pushtun tribes, almost genetically expert at guerrilla warfare after centuries of resisting all comers and fighting among themselves when no comers were available, plagued attempts to extend Pax Britannica into their mountain homeland."[31] Having narrowly avoided another disastrous defeat comparable to the 1821–42 debacle, Britain's statesmen turned again to the ongoing diplomatic crisis of securing their western frontier following the conclusion of the second Anglo-Afghan war in 1880.[32] Concerned more with Russian expansion than Afghan independence and intent on dismembering Afghanistan by annexing the central and eastern part of the country, Lord Lytton, the Indian viceroy, strategized creating a western Afghan kingdom ruled directly by Britain. This faux kingdom was to oversee what London had determined was the "scientific frontier" of its Indian empire, consisting of the Hindu Kush with the city of Kandahar placed under British suzerainty and the city of Herat annexed to Persia in order to guard its western approaches.[33] But the practical realities of England's first defeat remained a powerful deterrent to Afghan occupation. In addition to being prohibitively expensive to maintain, Afghan tolerance for foreign occupation was notoriously short-lived, while a British presence so close to Russia's recent acquisitions in Central Asia was an open invitation for them to advance to meet them. St. Petersburg resented British intrigues against it through its European allies and saw expansion into Central Asia as a means of countering an encroaching British presence from India. Summed up by Russia's ambassador to London in 1884, Baron de Stael, Afghanistan's importance to the psychology of Russia's strategy was quite clear. "Great historical lessons have taught us that we cannot count on the friendship of England, and that she can strike at us by means of continental alliances while we cannot reach her anywhere. No great nation can accept such a position. In order to escape from it Emperor Alexander II of everlasting memory ordered our expansion into Central Asia, leading us to occupy today in Turkestan and the Turkestan steppes a military position strong enough to keep England in check by the threat of intervention in India."[34]

Although the objective of the "Forward Policy" and the resultant first and second Anglo-Afghan wars had been occupation, London's sudden decision to evacuate Afghanistan and withdraw to the Hindu Kush following their second Afghan invasion reflected Britain's submission to the practical realities of Central Asia and the superior position of Russia's influence in Asia. Viewed by some historians as an effort to appease Russian suspicions and remove any pretexts for Russian advances, the decision by Britain's liberal government to establish Afghanistan as a "buffer state" benefited both empires and would be accepted in principle by both capitals for the better part of the next century. But applied to the fortunes of Afghanistan, that benefit would severely harm the development of the Afghan nation.

Daoud-era Afghan deputy-foreign-minister-turned-historian Abdul Samad Ghaus writes, "as a British protectorate, Afghanistan was kept economically weak and politically isolated. On various occasions the British professed that they wanted Afghanistan to be strong and independent. But a strong and independent Afghanistan meant one thing to them and quite another to the Afghan rulers and people."[35]

According to Ghaus, the British invasions embittered the Afghan people, spawning "xenophobic sentiments that lingered for many years and proved powerful deterrents to Western-style reforms and innovations undertaken by Afghan rulers decades later. The high-handed and aggressive attitude of the British had convinced the population that they would not rest until Afghanistan, the last independent Islamic country in Central Asia, was wiped off the map."[36]

While the Afghans dug in and waited, the Russians continued to probe, playing on Tory-Labor rivalries within the British government. In what would be an near-exact overture to the vicious political struggle over détente and Soviet "intentions" between liberals and conservatives in the Carter administration exactly one hundred years later, Russian and British militarists found common cause, egging each other on by fulfilling the other's prophecies as they battled for control of policy in their respective governments. "Forward Policies, [Prime Minister] Gladstone was convinced, merely provoked or panicked the Russians into acting similarly. He likewise refused to publish details of Kaufman's secret correspondence with Sher Ali, or of the treaty they had signed, lest this rock the boat needlessly at a time when Anglo-Russian relations were momentarily tranquil."[37]

Centered around the Russian acquisition of the ancient city of Merv in what is now Turkmenistan, a new generation of "Forward Policy" advocates heaped scorn on Britain's Liberals, accusing them of naivete, spinelessness and worse in the face of Russian aggression. The peculiar, bilateral, extremist teamwork was not lost on one modern observer of the workings of the Great Game. Peter Hopkirk writes, "The capitulation of Merv [to Russia] was almost as much a triumph for the Russophobes [in Britain] as it was for the Russians, for it was precisely as they had forecast. General Roberts, shortly to become commander-in-chief, India, described the move as 'by far the most important step ever made by Russia on her march towards India.' It would not be long now, warned the hawks, before the Cossacks were watering their horses on the banks of the Indus."[38]

In a preview of twentieth-century Cold War propaganda techniques where East European "dissidents" were employed by the British and U.S. governments to denounce the Soviet Union, Westminster involved an eccentric Hungarian Russophobe named Arminius Vambery, whose jingoistic pro-British lamentations and dire predictions of Russian lust for India earned him the nickname "the Dervish of Windsor Castle." Supported by right wingers in the press who constantly labeled Gladstone's efforts to negotiate with the Russians as appeasement, political opinion began to shift again toward war. Combined with a Russian attack on the Afghan oasis at Panjdeh—a way station on the approach to Herat—the prophecy of a Russian-British confrontation appeared to be fulfilling itself. On the verge of a war neither side wanted but was becoming increasingly unavoidable, the newest leader of Afghanistan would find himself in the middle of history's most difficult balancing act.[39]

A nephew of Sher Ali exiled to Russia during his reign, Abdur Rahman Khan had become the Afghan leader of choice for both British and Russian factions following the close of the second Anglo-Afghan war in 1880. According to Beatrice Manz, he also "came towards Kabul with considerable tribal backing; the English accepted him because they could not help it."[40] It was believed in St. Petersburg that Abdur Rahman, as a Russian protégé, would offset British suzerainty under the 1873 "buffer state" arrangement between the two empires. But as a direct heir to the throne and a capable leader in his own right, he came with his own ambitions for his country.[41]

Hemmed in and pressured from all sides, his power limited to Kabul and a few nearby provinces, Abdur Rahman was first seen by Britain as a momentary solution to their grander scheme of slicing up the country. But as Afghan resistance arose to threaten Britain with additional military debacles, the captive Abdur Rahman was able to establish a fragile independence.[42]

Seizing the two cities critical to the approach to India—Kandahar and Herat—from his cousin Ayub Khan, Abdur Rahman initially discharged his duty as guardian of the buffer between Russia's possessions and British India. But Abdur Rahman received little in return for his service to the crown. Retaining control of Afghan tribal homelands over the Hindu Kush, Britain remained free to renegotiate the fate of the country and its leadership to its own advantage at any time it chose. While relying on Britain for protection against Russia, care had to be taken that too much reliance wouldn't provide a pretext for Russian aggression while too little could encourage it as well. While Britain's acquiescence to the Russian seizure of the northern oasis at Panjdeh in 1885 demonstrated the "limits" of British protection, Afghan requests for weapons to defend themselves were regularly turned down. Ghaus writes, "The amir also felt that his alliance with Britain obligated the latter to assist him with arms and military equipment. The reluctance of the British to respond satisfactorily to his requests for military hardware profoundly embittered him."[43]

With Afghanistan straitjacketed as an official protectorate whose foreign policy and economy (still struggling to recover after two extended wars) was controlled by Britain and under constant pressure for additional concessions, Abdur Rahman began the job of consolidating the first modern Afghan state under a strict policy of isolation.

Brutally suppressing rebellions against him, he tactfully broke the powerful Ghilzai Pashtun chieftains' hold on power by forcibly relocating his enemies to territories he wished to subdue. In Machiavellian fashion, his policies and practices for taming the countryside bore a striking resemblance to tactics practiced by Richelieu and Louis XIV, luring chieftains to Kabul, then destroying their strongholds while they were away. But though dictatorial, the Iron Amir's rule was not despotic. Dupree writes, "Abdur Rahman himself described his task as one of putting 'in order all those hundreds of petty thieves, plunderers, robbers and cut-throats. . . . This necessitated breaking down the feudal and tribal system and substituting one grand community under one law and one rule' (quoted in Wilber, 1962, 19)."[44]

In 1888 Abdur Rahman subdued the powerful Shiite Hazaras, thought to be the descendants of Genghis Khan's Mongol horde, while firmly establishing himself as king.[45] An adventurer with a mystic disposition, he would be guided by prophetic visions and dreams to unite the diverse tribes of Afghanistan under Sunni Islam.

The first Afghan ruler to witness the power of modern technology and organization in the ancient civilizations of Asia, he tentatively began the difficult process of modernization—at times cleverly, at times brutally.

Establishing a system of provincial governors backed by an effective intelligence system, Abdur Rahman managed to collect taxes and suppress dissent while slowly implementing change throughout the country.[46] By enforcing government control through the creation of a national army he reinforced the power of the crown while the creation of a government bureaucracy paved the way for the rise of a small but well-educated and influential middle class. Over his twenty-one-year rule, these changes altered the structure of Afghan tribal organization by replacing the notoriously temperamental tribal authorities with provincial government officials—tribal rules with government rules. But the difficulty of supplanting local tribal authority with a central authority in Kabul, legendary among European observers, was tremendous. Friedrich Engels accurately observed the effect of this irreconcilable dynamic on Afghan politics in a newspaper article written in 1857. "Their indomitable hatred of rule, and their love of individual independence, alone prevents their becoming a powerful nation; but this very irregularity and uncertainty of action makes them dangerous neighbors, liable to be blown about by the wind of caprice, or to be stirred up by political intriguers, who artfully excite their passions."[47]

At the center of a bitter competition for control of Central Asia, the European powers had much to intrigue about, but the boundaries imposed by Russia and especially Britain and the webs of treachery associated with their artful plotting remained the primary irritant—laying the groundwork for destabilization and future disputes that would play a fateful role in Afghanistan and the West's future.

THE DURAND LINE

Within the context of late-nineteenth-century colonial expansion, the creation of the Durand Line demarcating the borders of Afghanistan from Britain's newly conquered territory across the Indus River appeared to be of no extraordinary importance. Yet no border division in the history of colonial conquest could match the ongoing consequences posed by the Durand Line. Created in 1893 by the India's foreign secretary, Sir Mortimer Durand, the 1,519-mile arbitrary border which partitioned "territories and peoples who since time immemorial had been considered part of the Afghan homeland and nation"[48] from British India was received bitterly by Abdur Rahman Khan and remains contested to this day. Seized by British forces and thereafter dubbed the North-West Frontier Provinces of India, these indigenous Afghan territories would always remain lawless, beyond British control and a constant source of friction. A focus of East-West conflict during the Cold War, the territories would become an inspirational source of anti-Soviet pan-Islamic radicalism and subsequently the spawning ground of the radical Islamic human "database" known as Al Qaeda.

Initially agreed to by Abdur Rahman Khan as a means for loosely demarcating areas of political responsibility on either side of the Hindu Kush, in practice the Durand Line would come to mark the western boundaries of the British empire and subsequently the emerging state of Pakistan. Intended by Britain as a step toward pacifying the Pashtun tribal areas and absorbing them, the artificial line that ignored topography, demography and even military strategy did exactly the opposite, laying the foundation for bloodshed even as it was being drawn. While inflaming Afghan nationalism, the cross-border conflict resulting from the arbitrary separation of tribes, families and resources would ignite tensions and rivalries that would give way to a constant state of low-intensity warfare, cross-border infiltration and political instability. Dupree writes, "In his illuminating biography (1900), Abdur Rahman repeatedly states he never considered any Pushtun areas as permanently ceded to the British (also Kakar, 1968, 145). . . . He insisted the 'boundary' delineated zones of responsibility, and did not draw an international boundary. In addition Kakar (1968, 145) presents convincing evidence that the Amir did not actually write the 'I renounce my claims' sentence."[49]

Convinced by his own and numerous others' research that the Durand Line was not, is not and was never intended by either party to be a permanent national boundary, Dupree cites the evidence. "The last paragraph in the final agreement of November 12, 1893, is vague and inconclusive (Caroe, 1965, 463). . . . At what point does coercion cease to be legal? . . . Other British administrators, however, contend the Durand line was never meant to be an international boundary: 'The Durand Agreement was an agreement to define the respective spheres of influence of the British Government and the Amir' (L/P & S/7: Letter from Elgin to Hamilton . . . Vol. 85, Foreign Dept. Letter No. 77, 1896)."[50]

The Iron Amir is still scorned by many Afghans, especially Pashtuns living in the Kandahar border region, and looked upon as a traitor for his acceptance of the boundary.[51] Given the magnitude of the events and the nature of his opponents, others, like former Afghan deputy foreign minister Abdul Samad Ghaus, believe the Iron Amir's compromise may have saved his country from disintegration and succeeded where future leaders would have failed. "Amir Abdur Rahman Khan, by implementing a foreign policy of balance, succeeded in preserving the integrity of Afghanistan. In treading the fine line between firmness and accommodation, he managed to limit British influence in his country and to prevent the spread of Russian influence. He excelled in the art of diplomacy; he knew what was possible and what was not."[52]

Although under constant threat of invasion and partition by Russia and Britain, by the turn of the century Afghanistan's unique position between the world's most powerful empires endowed it with a measure of fragile security. Unable to expand beyond its borders and reclaim lost territory that would have provided a route to the sea, by the year of his death in 1901 Abdur Rahman Khan had unified Afghanistan politically and established a centralized regime. Intent on freeing Afghanistan from feudalism while gaining the country international recognition, through cleverness and ruthlessness he had brought the country partway into the modern world while forging a model that future Afghan royalty would follow.

4.

Twentieth-century Afghanistan

Initiating the new, aggressive "Forward Policy" for the captive tribal regions, British authorities soon found their artificial boundary of little help in gaining control of the wild Afghan territories. Nor was the process of influencing Kabul made easier by the death of Abdur Rahman Khan in 1901. Careful to balance pressure between Russia and Britain, Abdul Rahman's successor, his eldest son Habibullah continued in his father's tradition of playing the interests of one empire against the other and, when appropriate, appealing directly to London over the interests of Calcutta.[1]

Such tactics enabled Habibullah to ward off local pressure for further concessions and controls while gaining him respect in London. But Habibullah's efforts to alter the hated Durand Line were less successful. Further aggravating the relationship was a long-established British practice of renegotiating treaties when each new ruler came to power. Insisting that the agreement with Afghanistan was not between states or even dynasties but purely personal, British viceroy Lord Curzon sought to amend weaknesses in the original 1880 treaty and thus bind Afghanistan closer to Britain by opening the country to trade and a permanent military presence. Dupree writes, "The British demands were rigid (extend British railheads to Kabul and Qandahar; connect the Afghan telecommunications networks with those of India; restrict arms importation though India to Afghanistan)."[2] Demanding among other things a "cessation of incidents on the Indo-Afghan border" and that Afghanistan put a stop to "Afghan intercourse with eastern Pashtun tribes," Habibullah countered with demands for a renegotiated Durand Line. When told by Britain's legal representatives that territorial agreements were permanent while all others were subject to renegotiation he reluctantly accepted the border agreement, but bided time.[3] He would not have long to wait.

The new century would see profound changes in the fortunes of the great power arrangements as the Boer War and Japan's crushing victory over Czarist Russia would temper both British and Russian enthusiasm for conquest and make the two countries allies. The 1907 Anglo-Russian Convention, signed August 31 in St. Petersburg, saw Russia and Britain agreeing on the division of Persia, while codifying the redrawn borders of Tibet and Afghanistan.[4] As the second decade of the century wore on, both British and Russian moves became increasingly defensive. Although they allowed Afghanistan more flexibility in trade and foreign policy, the concerted actions of the two superpowers, without participation or even representation from any of the affected parties, infuriated the amir. Alarmed that weakness and not strength might have provoked the two previously hostile powers to come together to divide up Persia and Tibet, fear spread that the long-sought partitioning of Afghanistan would soon be on the table as well.[5]

As the Great War approached, with Russia and Britain allied against the Central Powers, anti-British sentiment grew inside the Afghan court, fostered by Habibullah's sons Amanullah and Nasrullah. Now a player in the ever-expanding Great Game and with imperial ambitions of its own, an emboldened Germany embraced its own variation of mystical imperialism and with it a plan to upend the existing world order. Against the backdrop of a declining Ottoman Empire, a growing independence movement in India, and a Communist revolutionary underground that would unseat the czar's best-laid plans, Amir Habibullah Khan would soon be faced with the most difficult decision of his reign.

GERMAN HOLY WAR

As Britain and Russia's mystical imperialists quested for a syncretistic religious belief system that could unite the Christian world with the Buddhist, Hindu and Muslim inheritance of Central Asia, a third force was emerging that would tempt those very same Central Asian peoples with one of their own.

Referred to by *The Great Game* author Peter Hopkirk as "a new and more sinister version of the old Great Game,"[6] the secret holy war launched by Germany's Kaiser Wilhelm was the beginning of an aggressive new drive by Central Europe's most powerful nation to break the British-Russian hold over Central Asia. Working through the Ottoman Empire's sultan in Constantinople, German plans called for a Muslim uprising that would encompass Russian Central Asia, Afghanistan, Iran, Burma, and, in the end, India. Intended not only to dispossess Britain of its vast colonial wealth, the plan foresaw the destruction of Britain's entire empire, replacing it with a Teutonic empire run from Berlin via Constantinople. Sweeping in scope, the entire operation required little but promises to Britain's embittered Asian enemies. But if fulfilled, the result would mark a striking new development in modern warfare—marrying the world's most advanced industrial state to the world's second-most-populous religion and resurrecting the medieval concept of holy war. As Hopkirk observes, "Although a plan to launch a Holy War was first and foremost Kaiser Wilhem's, Enver Pasha [Turkey's military attaché to Germany] too had been quick to see its merits as a means of fulfilling his own dreams. It was his suggestion, weeks before Turkey entered the war, that Berlin should send a carefully chosen team of officers to take part in a secret joint Turco-German mission whose objective would be to bring both Persia and Afghanistan into the war."[7]

Though Germany's industrialized jihad played well in the imperial war rooms of Berlin and the salons of Constantinople, the clever Amir Habibullah of Afghanistan found it a dangerous option.

Visited by a delegation of anti-British Indian expatriates and hardened German military intelligence officers in the fall of 1915, Habibullah played the polite host, personally serving his German guests from his pre-tasted plates. Having informed Habibullah that Germany always recognized Afghanistan's independence, Werner Otto von Hentig and Captain Oskar Niedermayer's job was to convince the amir that Afghanistan would be richly rewarded for joining them in holy war. "On reaching Kabul, the mission's task would be to persuade the Emir of Afghanistan to join the sacred cause and order his troops and wild tribesmen through the passes into British India. So hostile were the Afghans towards the infidel British, Enver's spies in Kabul assured him, that the Emir would require little coercion."[8]

But for the next months Habibullah remained uncommitted, unwilling to play his hand until the outcome of Germany's European war was clear. Still, a plan that would return large swaths of India to Afghan control and crown the amir the ruler of it all was a magnetic lure to many in Habibullah's court, while the two Germans—referred to by the British as the "the Angels of Darkness"—were more than a match for Britain's mystical imperialists, à la T. E. Lawrence.[9] A Russian intercept of the German plan indicated broad support among the population, suggesting that the arrival of a 1,000-man force of Turkish and German soldiers would be enough to encourage thousands of disgruntled Pashtun warriors to stream down on India through the narrow mountain passes.[10]

So alarmed was India's British viceroy at the potential for a widespread holy war that he wrote to the amir, warning him of the real possibility of a German-sponsored "coup d'état" should he resist their pressure. London advised him to arrest the Germans and ship them off to India.[11]

Well-accustomed to intrigues both foreign and domestic, the amir knew that a roundup of Germans and their anti-British Afghan supporters would provide exactly the excuse his enemies were waiting for. Playing to both sides, he continued to bargain. As spiritual leader of his people, all that was needed was Amir Habibullah Khan's word to enact a holy war. But though a sacred cause, taking on both Russia and Britain would require more than German promises.[12]

Knowing that it would take months to ratify, in December 1915 the amir agreed with von Hentig to a formal treaty of friendship under which he would receive the latest rifles, artillery and matériel needed to modernize the Afghan army. Unbeknownst to the Indian viceroy and under the strictest secrecy, the amir also promised to send a delegation of diplomats to Persia to further an alliance with Turkey and Germany. In addition, Germany would open a supply route through Persia by which military aid, engineers and advisors could travel.[13]

Although extremely impractical from a tactical military point of view, according to former Afghan deputy foreign minister Ghaus, the Turkish-

German plot was deadly serious and had great potential for success: "The Niedermayer-Hentig expedition was viewed by some as an opéra-comique episode. It was nothing of the sort. The Germans were convinced that the defense of India could be breached through Afghanistan and that it was not impractical to launch an offensive against the subcontinent from Afghan territory. In fact, during the early stages of their talks with the amir, they were quite certain that conditions were favorable for such an undertaking."[14]

By the late winter of 1916 the amir had lost faith in a German victory and turned his back on the idea of an alliance. Following the war's end in 1918, the British turned a blind eye to his having initialed the treaty with von Hentig and all appeared forgotten.[15] But resentment lingered long and hard among the Afghan people. In their eyes, not only had the amir abandoned his Islamic-Turkish ally in favor of the infidel British, he had failed to successfully leverage the German intrigue against British concessions. Expecting to be rewarded with full independence or territorial concessions for his maintenance of a strict neutrality during Britain's most vulnerable moment, the amir was stunned by Britain's return to their colonial, business-as-usual-approach following the war. Ghaus writes, "The only reward the amir had received from the British during the war was a letter from King George V addressing him as 'Your Majesty' instead of 'Your Highness' and praising him for his neutrality."[16]

But the business of Afghanistan was no longer as it had been. World War I had cracked the old world order and even Afghanistan, a remote hinterland as far as most of the world was concerned, would never be the same. In less than a year following the armistice, Habibullah Khan was assassinated, and whether he was killed for his role in the German plot or in retribution for his failure to restore Afghanistan's tribal homelands, it was evident that von Hentig and Niedermayer had tapped into a volatile reservoir.

AMANULLAH

Habibullah's third son, Amanullah, acceded the throne in February 1919. Having urged his father to publicly declare Afghanistan's support for Germany and the Central Powers at the outbreak of World War I,[17] he represented a radical departure for the conservative monarchy. He declared Afghanistan's independence in his first inaugural speech, and he wasted no time in demanding an audience with British officials. Trapped by their own long-standing insistence on negotiating Afghan treaties on a personal basis with the amir, the British were hard-pressed to deny Amanullah the opportunity to present his grievances. Yet Lord Chelmsford, the British viceroy, did just that, citing his bereavement over the amir's death as an excuse for delay.[18]

Knowing Britain's reluctance to negotiate even the slightest territorial concessions, Amanullah and his advisors moved simultaneously on two fronts. Countering with the one thing Britain feared most, a tribal mutiny on the frontier with India was quickly organized, which Amanullah backed with Afghan army troops. Reacting to this series of provocative incidents, the British attacked once again, embarking on the third Anglo-Afghan war in eighty years in June 1919.

"At first, the Afghan troops were victorious against the startled British," Dupree writes. "Many Pashtuns in the paramilitary Frontier Scouts deserted the British to fight with the Afghans, and they were joined by many tribesmen from both sides of the Durand line."[19] The British responded to their early defeats by escalating the conflict, bombing Kabul and Jalalabad by air. But times had changed. Both sides quickly sued for peace.[20]

Acknowledging that "there were profound changes in the political outlook in the Middle East, which were caused by 'general unrest, awakened national aspirations, the pronouncements of President Wilson, and the Bolshevik catchwords,'"[21] Lord Chelmsford acceded to Amanullah's demand. Signed on August 8, 1919, "The Treaty of Peace between the Illustrious British Government and the Independent Afghan Government," otherwise known as the "Treaty of Rawalpindi," guaranteed Afghanistan's independence in its internal and external affairs. But the actual geographical line (the Durand Line) where the treaty's internal affairs became an external threat remained an open wound.[22] Disregarding the uncertainties, in perhaps the boldest diplomatic move ever taken by an Afghan amir, Amanullah immediately opened direct talks with Russia's new Bolshevik regime. "Mohammed Wali Khan, a close advisor to Amanullah, was sent to Moscow, where he was received by Lenin on October 18, 1919," Ghaus writes. "It was the first time since the downfall of Amir Sher Ali Khan that an Afghan ruler had so openly tendered a hand of friendship to the 'barbarian' of the north. Would his destiny be the same as that ill-fated amir's?"[23]

Britain's control over the Pashtun tribal areas, governed on paper by British India, bordered more on wish fulfillment than any strategic reality. Between 1849 and 1890, forty-two military operations were conducted that did little more than reconfirm the stubborn independence of the mountain warriors. According to Alfred W. McCoy in his book *The Politics of Heroin*, an 1897 incursion into the Peshawar district with thirty thousand troops was so ineffective that the British were forced to adopt an even more desperate policy of containment. "Unable to beat the Pashtun (Pathan) warriors, the British adopted a punitive policy known in the officers' mess as *'butcher and bolt'*—that is, march into the offending village, butcher the available civilians, and bolt before the tribe's warriors could retaliate."[24]

Confident that the British would return the southern Afghan tribal provinces of Waziristan and Baluchistan to Afghan control, or at least allow their establishment as independent states, Amanullah was taken aback when the British government did neither. In fact, in one final effort to secure access to the approaches to India, Britain claimed even further territory west of the Khyber Pass in an undemarcated section of the Durand Line.[25]

Off to such a rocky start, it wasn't long before the tribal areas seethed once again with rebellion, but this time the world's largest empire pushed back with even greater ferocity. Long used as a means for pressuring Britain, the volatile tribal areas west of the Indus River embodied the heart and soul of the Afghan nation, the majority of which were ethnically Pashtun. Deeply connected through family, tribal allegiance, and devotion to Islam, Amanullah continued to bargain with Britain, offering a permanent alliance against Moscow in exchange for the return of these Afghan territories or the complete independence of "trans-Durand-Pashtuns."[26] But Britain would have none of it. Resentful of the upstart King Amanullah as well as the loss of Afghanistan itself, Britain now unleashed an aggressive new "modified forward policy"[27] on the tribal areas. Aimed at a total pacification of the unruly tribes and an end to infiltration from across the artificial border, the program was characteristically ruthless and bloody. Referred to as the "police action of 1919–1920," ten thousand Afghans and five thousand Indian troops engaged in a five-day mutual slaughter over a single mountain pass that resulted in two thousand British and Indian dead, and four thousand Afghan dead.[28]

Frustrated by his efforts to engage Britain as a mature nation, and rebuffed continually and completely in his attempts to repatriate Afghan territories under British control, Amanullah reluctantly turned to Moscow, ratifying a Russo-Afghan treaty in August 1921.[29] Viewing full Afghan diplomatic relations with Moscow as a defeat for British diplomacy, Britain's negotiator, Henry Dobbs, finally countered with a watered-down treaty of his own, but the new realities of Afghan independence from their former colonial occupier were cast.[30] Having eschewed the protection of British oversight and control of its foreign policy, Afghanistan was on its own to deal with its friends and enemies as best it could.

AFGHANISTAN IN TRANSITION

Weakened by World War I and faced with a growing list of economic problems, Britain's foreign policy relied increasingly on covert action and subterfuge to undermine the expanding challenges to the empire. During this time numerous alliances would be established with radical pan-Islamic groups, not unlike those cultivated by Germany's von Hentig and Niedermayer. According to *Devil's Game* author Robert Dreyfuss, this policy of intentionally targeting maturing Islamic republics like Afghanistan for destabilization would lead to the birth of an uncontrollable and radical hybrid of Islam. "Juggling factions like balls in the air, the British spent the years between 1918 and 1945 trying to balance the king, the tribal leaders, the emerging middle classes, the army, and the clergy in each of these states, always with an eye toward preserving British power. Sometimes the king would get too strong, and form an alliance with the army; in that case the British would try to break the alliance of king and generals by favoring tribal chieftains instead. Sometimes, if the tribes or ethnic groups got too uppity, the British would deputize the army to crush them. The Islamic right emerged amid this shifting balance. It provided a vital counterweight to England's chief nemesis: the nationalists and the secular left."[31]

Having nurtured the founding father of radical Islam, Jamal al-Din "al-Afghani,"[32] as well as husbanding the growth and influence of the ultra-extremist Wahhabist tribe of Al Saud since the mid–1860s,[33] Britain's employment of antinationalist elements in Afghanistan was a natural by-product of a foreign policy steeped in mystical imperialism. With a growing need to counter the secular left, a revolutionary communist presence, and a surging Afghan nationalism, Afghanistan's most reactionary Islamists and Britain found a perfect marriage.

Championed for his reforms as well as his anti-imperialism, Amanullah came to be viewed in the East as a beacon for moderate Islamic nationalism. Overseeing Afghanistan's escape from a feudal mindset through education, human rights and the construction of a modern civil society, his enlightened leadership would make him an extraordinary figure even today.

Inspired by the father of modern Turkey, Kamal Ataturk, Amanullah attempted drastic changes by reforming the army, instituting the solar calendar and requiring western dress in parts of the country.[34] But it would be the issue of women's rights for which Amanullah would gain the most notoriety, by discouraging the veil and the oppression of women, and abolishing slavery and forced labor, while introducing secular education as well as education for girls and nomads. Instituting Afghanistan's first constitution in 1923, he took the truly revolutionary steps of giving women the right to vote, guaranteeing civil rights to all minorities, and establishing a legislative assembly, courts, and penal, civil, and commercial codes, as well as prohibiting revenge killings and abolishing subsidies for tribal chieftains and the royal family.[35]

But for all the progress toward democratic modernity, Amanullah's program for change encountered stiff opposition. Opposed not so much for his social reforms—which were generally accepted as principled and in keeping with Islamic law—Amanullah faced his greatest challenge by attempting to centralize authority in Kabul at the expense of the mullahs.[36]

Mistrusted as much for these social reforms as his perceived closeness to enemies Germany and communist Russia, Amanullah found himself a natural target for British subterfuge as well.

A violent rebellion in the border town of Khost that was quelled by the Afghan army after intense fighting in 1924 raised suspicions of a British plot. "It was believed by many that the rebellion was a reaction by conservative elements to Amanullah's social reforms, particularly public education for girls and greater freedom for women," Ghaus writes. "The general public never entirely subscribed to such theories. Britain was seen as the culprit in the affair, manipulating the tribes against Amanullah in an attempt to bring about his downfall."[37]

Although hindered by extremist reaction and constant tension on the border with India, Amanullah's reforms had by 1927 gained a wide measure of popularity and support from the growing merchant and middle classes. With financial and technical assistance from the Soviet Union, Turkey, Germany, Italy and France, Amanullah was fulfilling his predecessor's dream of building a modern, independent Afghan state.[38] Received warmly during a tour of Europe, he pressed his case in London for the return of Pashtun territories in what Ghaus describes as "a rather uncomfortable meeting with Sir Austen Chamberlain," and returned to Kabul in the summer of 1928 in triumph.[39]

But in his absence the tone had changed. Buoyed by his European reception and intent on pushing through an even more liberal constitution, guaranteeing the complete liberation of women, the abolishment of the veil, and land reform (that promised a redistribution of wealth), Amanullah was greeted with suspicion. "[W]hen Amanullah returned home in July 1928, the country was not the same as he had left it nine months before. An atmosphere of unrest and apprehension prevailed," Ghaus writes.[40] Easily provoked by outside agents and already threatened with the loss of power and local autonomy, the mullahs' outraged reaction to Queen Soraya's removal of her veil at a public ceremony was all that was needed to ignite the insurrection.[41] Described as charming and dynamic by his admirers, impulsive and tactless by his British critics, Amanullah had by May 1929 been forced by the rebellion to flee, leaving the country in the hands of a murderous and well-armed Tajik bandit named Bacha Saquo (son of a water carrier) who took the name Habibullah Kalakani.[42]

Given the history of the region and Britain's antagonism to his rule, not to mention the absolutely reactionary stance toward any challenges within its empire, not all believe that the unfortunate Amir Amanullah's personality or his progressive policies were solely to blame. "Some British officials saw a modernizing of Afghanistan as a threat to British rule in India since it offered an example of the kind of progress free Asians could achieve," writes Former ambassador Leon B. Poullada in *Reform and Rebellion in Afghanistan, 1919–1929*. "This was especially true among the British military."[43]

Lost to a history that was mostly unknown and certainly of little concern to the American government at the time, it is worthwhile to consider Amanullah as a golden opportunity, overlooked, misunderstood and lost by the United States. Poullada's account of U.S.-Afghan relations going back to 1828 rings with irony as he tells the story of America's first diplomatic foray by an unusual young junior State Department officer from the U.S. embassy in Tehran, Cornelius Van H. Engert. Not officially sanctioned due to a lack of funds and most probably lack of interest, Engert was only the sixth American ever to be issued a visa to travel to Afghanistan.[44]

In 1923 an American tourist, Mrs. Jeanne Vancouver, toured the country and reported her observations back to the State Department, "strongly recommending greater Amercian interest in and recognition of, Afghanistan." She was referred to Allen Dulles who "duly noted and recorded [her views], but no action was taken on them."[45]

This studied lack of action on Afghanistan from the man who would become the first and longest-serving director of U.S. central intelligence was mainly derived from a long tradition of American cooperation with and acquiesence to British interests in the region. It is, of course, wishful thinking, but had the United States been further developed in the uses of its own diplomacy and established an independent relationship with the politically progressive Amanullah free of British oversight, U.S.-Afghan relations today might be far different. Yet nuance and vision were never the strong points of American diplomacy and as the international scene grew more complex, the United States let the Afghan ball fall to other nations who viewed Afghanistan in a very different light.

Within the year, the renegade Bacha Saquo declared himself king, ruled cruelly, and found himself at the end of the noose for his trouble. Easily overthrown by Amanullah's former army commander-in-chief, General Mohammad Nadir Khan, with the help of the British military, Amanullah's ten-year experiment in progressive Afghan politics had ended. But his impact on the Afghan psyche remained. Dismissed by western pundits as an unusually long-lived anomaly, his fate was not lost on that majority of Afghans aware of the nature of the "game" at stake and how it was played out between Moscow, London and Calcutta. Ghaus writes, "Afghans in general remain convinced that the elimination of Amanullah was engineered by the British because, in their view, he had become too friendly with the Russians and an obstacle to the furtherance of Britain's interests. To this day 'eyewitness' accounts abound in and around Kabul of surreptitious contacts that took place between Sacao [Saquo] and members of the British legation, of canned English food found in Sacao's trenches, and of Lawrence of Arabia, the famous British secret agent T. E. Lawrence, roaming the Afghan countryside posing as a holy man and inciting the tribes to rise against Amanullah."[46]

NADIR SHAH

Declared king of Afghanistan on October 17, 1929, Nadir Shah abolished Amanullah's progressive reforms immediately, and then set about reuniting the Afghan nation along the more subdued lines of Abdur Rahman Khan.[47] His renewal of the 1921 treaty with Britain indicated his submission to the status quo regarding Afghanistan's relations to the British empire—including the Durand Line.[48] But the disorder brought about by that enforced relationship made any normalization of relations impossible regardless of Nadir Shah's willingness to bend to British demands. Redoubling their efforts to bring the tribal areas on their side of the Durand Line into line with the perceived security needs of what they called their "scientific frontier," Britain again launched a ferocious military campaign in 1930 that nearly ended in catastrophe. As Britain was about to lose control of Peshawar to the tribal warriors, only the use of massive aerial bombardments on the civilian Afghan population was enough to prevent a total rout.[49] But despite the internationally acknowledged crimes committed on his fellow trans-Durand-Pashtuns, Nadir Shah remained detached. So coldly calculated were these Guernica-like atrocities by Britain's ruling elite, MIT professor Noam Chomsky would point out sixty years later, "Winston Churchill felt that poison gas was just right for use against 'uncivilized tribes' (Kurds and Afghans, particularly). Noting approvingly that British diplomacy had prevented the 1932 disarmament convention from banning bombardment of civilians, the equally respected statesman Lloyd George observed that 'we insisted on reserving the right to bomb niggers,' capturing the basic point succinctly."[50]

Shoehorned into position between two hostile empires, an increasingly unstable tribal region, and a revolutionary Indian independence movement known as the Khudai Khidmatgaran ("Servants of God"), also known as the Red Shirts,[51] Nadir Shah's options were limited. Presenting a new constitution in 1931, it first appeared that he'd incorporated many of the ideals put forward by Amanullah, but in fact he'd created a constitutional monarchy, guaranteeing his family broad powers to rule.[52]

More in the manner of a mid-twentieth-century military dictator supported by foreign interests (in this case British) than a genuine civilian chief executive or even an Afghan amir, in a very short time Nadir Shah had calmed the countryside by emphasizing traditional Islamic values. Receiving the support of the more extremist mullahs as a result, he began to fashion a vastly more conservative Afghanistan than his predecessor, Amanullah. Health care, a banking system, a restoration of industry, and an overall economic plan were Nadir's immediate contributions to restoring the peace. The climate of security he helped to create brought a measure of growth to business and commerce.[53] But Afghanistan's unstable political situation, especially in the unresolved tribal areas, was a drag on the economy that no amount of military intervention could overcome.

Keen on the delicate balance required of Afghan independence, one of Nadir Shah's major foreign policy tasks was to reestablish Afghanistan as a neutral buffer state, while convincing a hostile Soviet Union that he was not a tool of British imperialism. Complicated by his acceptance in 1931 of some ten thousand rifles, five million cartridges and £180,000 from the British political agent in the Kurrum valley, this wasn't easy.[54] Nor did his failure to assist the trans-Duran-Pashtuns in their struggle with anything more than encouraging words aid his popularity. Added to Nadir Shah's net political deficit was Britain's continued use of the brutal and senseless "Forward Policy" in the tribal regions, which after nearly a century of failure, had long since moved from being an actual policy to being a form of psychological dependency for addressing Britain's universal fear of "barbarian hordes" from the north.

Marking him as a British puppet, a hardened corps of Afghan nationalists rejected Nadir Shah's authority and by 1932 the followers of Amanullah were plotting against him.[55] Although Nadir Shah was lionized by western pundits as a peacemaker and nation builder with his new 1931 constitution (in effect until 1964), some Afghans view him in a different light. According to a short biography posted on Afghanistan Online, "After becoming king, Mohammad Nadir fought hard against people who wanted to restore King Amanullah to the throne. He also reversed many of the modernization plans set forth by King Amanullah, and favored up to various religious extremists. Mir Ghulam Mohammad Ghobar, one of Afghanistan's most respected historians, describes Mohammad Nadir's rule as tyrannical. Nadir pinned ethnic groups against one another, (Tajiks and Pashtuns), raped, destroyed, and pillaged the Shamali area to the north of Kabul."[56]

One of Nadir Shah's foreign policy accomplishments in 1932 was to sign a treaty of friendship with Saudi Arabia and Iraq, both countries then under the guidance of Great Britain. But these moves were not enough to placate his increasingly disgruntled Pashtun majority or quell demands from the nationalist-modernists at home.[57]

Nadir's brother Aziz, the Afghan envoy to Germany, was assassinated in 1933 by an Amanullah supporter who declared that Nadir Shah had betrayed his country and the Pashtun tribes under the control of the British. Joined by "disillusioned nationalists and impatient modernists," the rebellion spread. Three months later, on November 8, Nadir himself was assassinated by the adopted son of "a notorious pro-Amanullah sympathizer," writes Ghaus, "whom Nadir Shah had executed a year before on charges of fomenting a tribal rebellion in the southern province for Amanullah's benefit."[58]

Nadir Shah's death brought an era of rapid change and political destabilization to an end. He was replaced by his young son, Zahir Shah, although his brother Mohammad Hashim Khan would rule in Zahir's stead until May 1946.[59] But Afghanistan's opportunity to act as an "example of the kind of progress free Asians could achieve,"[60] in their transit from feudalism to modernity, had passed. The assassination of Nadir Shah did nothing to resolve the state of affairs regarding the trans-Durand-Pashtuns and if anything it isolated them even more. But the issue of a free and united Pashtunistan composed of ethnic Afghans bordering Afghanistan but lorded over by the British would not go away. As the Durand Line solidified into a permanent border between the opposing states, the importance of the Pashtunistan issue and control of the border tribes began to reverberate beyond Central Asia and into the Middle East.

The 1930s saw numerous efforts to incite the tribes to rebellion, secession, or unification with Kabul. As World War II approached, some bore the markings of a covert Axis operation. One of the stranger episodes, known as the "Pir Shami affair," occurred in 1938 when a Syrian holy man named Said al-Jilani (Pir Shami) emerged in Waziristan to declare exiled king Amanullah the legitimate ruler of Afghanistan. Claiming a spiritual lineage to a famous Sufi, Shaikh Abdul Qadir Jilani, he proceeded to raise an army of Wazirs and Mahsuds, then marched on the small border town of Matun with the intention of seizing Kabul.[61] Bribed by the British governor of the North-West Frontier Province, Sir George Cunningham[62] to the tune of £25,000 sterling, Jilani soon quit the rebellion and left India on a British plane. But the expedient manner by which the holy man was dispatched opened a window on the covert workings of the pan-Islamic holy war that was, even then raging between Britain and Germany. Linked by Sir Olaf Caroe, the last British governor of the North-West Frontier Province, to the Nazi collaborator Al-Hajj Amin al-Hussaini, mufti of Jerusalem, he speculated on the possibility of a Nazi plot on the northwest frontier through Jilani's Middle Eastern network of Islamic radicals. What Caroe failed to mention was the debt that Al-Hajj Amin al Hussaini owed to Britain's own mystical policy makers and intelligence agents for his role in the bizarre drama.

Dreyfuss writes, "Meanwhile, in Palestine, Haj Amin, the Nazi-leaning, viciously anti-Semitic firebrand, climbed to power beginning in the 1920s with overt backing from the British overseers of the Palestine Mandate. Together, Banna [Hassan al-Banna—founder of the radical Muslim Brotherhood] and Haj Amin would be responsible for the worldwide spread of political Islam. The two men tied Wahhabi-style ultra-orthodoxy to the pan-Islamic ideals of Jamal al-Din al-Afghani and—with Saudi funding—created the global enterprise that spawned Islam's radical right, including its terrorist wing."[63]

KING ZAHIR SHAH—1933

Following the ascension of Nadir Shah's only son, Zahir, to the Afghan throne on November 8, 1933, the effort to create an independent foreign policy amid the tortured rise of Afghan self-governance began to take hold. Like many educated Afghans, the 19-year-old Zahir Shah had been schooled by the French.[64] Now King Zahir Shah's political education was about to begin at the hands of his powerful uncles Shah Mahmud Khan, Shah Wali Khan, and Mohammad Hashim Khan and his cousin Mohammad Daoud, who would rule the country from behind the scenes. Throughout the reign of Zahir Shah, Mohammad Hashim, Mahmud and Mohammad Daoud successively occupied the post of prime minister.[65]

It was under the direction of these men that Afghanistan began to look away from both the British and the Russians toward the French, Italians, and especially the Germans, for assistance in modernization. Steering away from adjacent powers with obvious colonial interests, since 1921 Afghan leaders had expressed hope that the United States would take a leading role in developing Afghanistan's natural resources.[66] Yet, despite repeated overtures, the U.S. government's response remained distant and often confusing. While Afghanistan signed treaties of friendship with ten European countries, America stayed away, claiming, among other things, "the absence of any important interests." One brief effort that was undertaken began in 1937 when the Inland Exploration Company was granted a seventy-five-year lease on oil exploration. But Inland quickly paid a penalty and withdrew, leaving the disappointed Afghans to speculate whether the move wasn't motivated by Russian or British pressure.[67] Left with few choices, Afghanistan would again look to Germany and find a willing partner. Lacking influence in the region and quite late to the Great Game, their involvement in Afghanistan's development grew quickly throughout the 1930s. Following the rise of the National Socialists (Nazis) to power in 1933, Afghanistan would be courted aggressively as a potential military ally.[68]

By 1938 Germany had become the single most important player in Kabul's modernization scheme and in 1939 extended long-term financial credits for the purchase of machinery and technical skill. Between 1937 and 1939 German-Afghan commerce increased tenfold in addition to providing the one thing both Russia and Britain had consistently denied Afghanistan—a military training and equipment program designed to bring the Afghan army up to western standards.[69]

As Germany prepared for war, Afghanistan's geopolitical position would be seen by Berlin as an ideal base from which to harass Britain or, if necessary, to reenact the von Hentig–Niedermayer scheme of 1915. Perennially at odds with Britain over the trans-Durand tribal areas, Kabul did little to discourage its European allies from acting on its behalf. "In this propitious environment," Ghaus writes, "the Germans and Italians had busied themselves, among other things, with creating difficulties for Britain in the trans-Durand regions. Their agents, sometimes working together, had succeeded in establishing contact with anti-British elements in the tribal areas. Chief among these at the time was Haji Mirza Ali Khan, the famed Fakir of Ipi, who since 1937 had been engaged in leading anti-British uprisings in Waziristan."[70]

To Berlin's geopoliticians, Afghanistan could provide the logistical base for attacking India as well as extending geopolitician Karl Haushofer's Lebensraum into Central Asia. Meyer and Brysac write, "A distinguished procession of Germans had taken special interest in Central Asia, beginning with Alexander von Humboldt, a founder of modern geographic science and author of *Zentralasien* (1843). . . . He was followed by the pioneering geographer Carl Ritter; Hedin's own teacher, Ferdinand von Richthofen; . . . and by Haushofer, the geopolitician, whose belief that Germany's destiny lay to the East became a vital ingredient of Hitlerism. But among Nazis like Himmler this fascination was not just strategic and geographic; it was racial."[71] The belief that the ancient "high civilizations of the East and West" were of a common origin was not unique to the German Nazis. British scholars like Sir William Jones (1746–1794) had stoked the fires of a racial connection between the West and the East for two centuries.[72] German scholar Friedrich Schlegel proclaimed in 1808 that Sanskrit was the linguistic godparent of German, Greek, and Latin, brought to northern Europe by migrating Aryans. "Friedrich Max Muller (1823–1900), a Fellow of All Souls and Boden Professor of Comparative Philology [at Oxford] . . . enthusiastically contended that Anglo-Saxons, Teutons, and Indians all belonged to the same 'Aryan race,' signifying that British rule in India was a 'gathering in,' a kind of family reunion," Meyer and Brysac write.[73] To the National Socialists' more extreme ideologues like Alfred Rosenberg, one of Hitler's chief Aryan ideologists, Afghanistan may have represented an even greater opportunity. "Haushofer is supposed to have proclaimed the necessity of 'a return to the sources' of the human race in Central Asia. He advocated the Nazi colonization of this area, in order that Germany could have access to the hidden centres of power in the East," Oxford historian Nicholas Goodrick-Clarke writes in *The Occult Roots of Nazism*.[74] Although dismissed by Goodrick-Clarke as a "spurious account" of occult doctrines erupting in the policies of the Third Reich, Rosenberg's enthusiasm for a "family reunion" of Aryans via Afghanistan cannot be entirely discounted, having taken a direct hand in the creation and implementation of Germany's Afghan policy. In accordance with the racial and mystical views of Nazi Party founders such as Rosenberg, Afghanistan could also have been viewed as the hub of a Central Asian dream realm, fulfilling the Nazi Party's Aryan destiny. By returning the Germanic peoples to the origins of their creation, the country would have been seen as central to the Nazis' belief in a cosmic cycle of humanity's return to a prehuman godlike state. Very much in the vein of Russian mystic Nikolai Fyodorov's Pamir-centered belief system, Rosenberg's virulent mix of Nazi racial theories with ancient Zoroastrian, paganism and Vedic Hinduism undoubtedly helped to shape Germany's pre–World War II engagement with the region. As director of the Foreign Policy Office (APA) of the Nazi Party, "Germany's outstanding pagan philosopher"[75] at times even overruled Germany's brilliant Nazi foreign minister Joachim von Ribbontrop on the disposition of the country. "Germany, suspecting the Hashim government of being biased in favor of the British," writes Vartan Gregorian, "initially considered replacement of the Afghan regime with ex-king Amanullah or a member of his family. Begun on the basis of an Italian suggestion, the *Amanullah project* was dropped in 1940 because of the opposition of Alfred Rosenberg."[76]

Given Britain's open hostility and Afghanistan's perpetual fear of a Russian invasion of its northern territories, Germany's assistance was considered vital as a hedge against outside interference. But Germany's shocking nonaggression pact with the Soviet Union was of dire concern. Heartfelt gratitude for the financial and advanced technical support provided by the Germans not withstanding, the Soviet Union's involvement in the 1939 nonaggression pact added a new level of jeopardy. Complicating matters further were two incidents that struck at the heart of Afghan fears. First was the disclosure in January 1940 by the commander-in-chief of Germany's land forces that in the coming confrontation with Britain, Germany expected Soviet forces to expand into Afghanistan. Second was von Ribbontrop's assumption, stated in November of that year to the Soviet foreign minister, that the Soviet Union's territorial ambitions "would presumably be centered south of the territory of the Soviet Union in the direction of the Indian Ocean."[77]

Pressuring the Afghan government to ease its policy of neutrality, Germany's support for a restoration of the Durrani Empire—the return of Baluchistan, Sind, Kashmir, the western Punjab and the port of Karachi—most likely allayed any fears of a German betrayal. In fact, documents released after World War II suggest that as late as June 1941 certain Afghan officials spoke forcefully of joining Germany in the war against Britain. Leon Poullada writes, "Abdul Majid Zabuli, the Afghan Minister of

National Economy, with a long experience in Germany, and Faiz Mohammad Zikria, the Foreign Minister, spent considerable time in Berlin bargaining with the Germans and holding out promises of cooperation and even alliance in return for recognition of Afghan claims of territories now part of British India. Faiz Mohammad was received by Hitler and reportedly told him that 'Afghanistan hopes to receive help from Germany whom it considers an elder and more advanced Aryan brother.'"[78]

But any further plans for a combined Afghan-German-Soviet invasion of India were demolished by Germany's surprise invasion of the Soviet Union on June 22, 1941. The consequent Anglo-Soviet alliance and their joint occupation of Iran that September shocked the Afghan leadership even further. Surrounded on all sides by Allied armies, there was little room for diplomatic maneuvering. Afghanistan was to submit to Allied demands or risk occupation. The presentation of formal notes by Britain and the Soviet Union requesting the ouster of German and Italian citizens sealed the deal.[79] There was little recourse for the Afghan government but to return Afghanistan to an enforced neutrality.

THE WAR YEARS—1940s

By guaranteeing a strict neutrality to Britain and the Soviet Union while reluctantly yielding to their demands, Afghanistan managed to escape the fate of neighboring Iran during World War II and avoided occupation.[80] But the involvement of a neophyte United States added a new dimension to Afghanistan's complex struggle to maintain its survival. Speeded personally by Franklin Roosevelt in a memorandum to Acting Secretary of State Sumner Welles in March 1942, the United States opened an American legation in Kabul for the first time on June 6 of that year. Welcomed warmly by King Zahir Shah, the American envoy extraordinary and minister plenipotentiary Cornelius Van H. Engert assured the king "that America was bending every effort to help cure this sick world, first by destroying the forces of evil and second by a scrupulous observance of the principles of law and morality in our relations with other nations."[81]

Although pleased with America's interest, the seasoned Afghan rulers had more on their minds than belated assurances. Meeting later that summer with the power behind the throne, Prime Minister Mohammad Hashim Khan, Engert was warned that the "democracies had made some fearful mistakes and had lost many opportunities [to avoid war] during the past 20 years,"[82] including support for the League of Nations. Hashim Khan also warned Engert that if Germany prevailed in its war in Russia it would have "far-reaching results for Afghanistan whether the Afghans liked it or not."[83] Reflecting on the current military situation in Russia, Hashim Khan stressed that he was not pessimistic by nature, "but as a practical man with heavy responsibilities he had to face realities and he would welcome signs that the democracies would not go on making mistakes indefinitely."[84]

By August, Hashim Khan's concern for the Allies' inability to defeat Germany impressed the American minister enough that Engert requested that a few American bomber squadrons be flown to Northeast Persia as a token show of force to "raise the morale of the Afghan government." Engert's assessment of the overall Afghan position vis-à-vis the allies was grim, given the Afghan leadership's "lack of confidence in British and Allied generalship and strategy and consequently in the ability to win the war decisively or even to hold India."[85] In addition, he cautioned that the northern provinces' reactionary mullahs held no affection for America's "godless" Soviet allies, wisely speculating that since "Russia and Great Britain have as in Iran been looked upon as the two traditional enemies of Afghanistan, it is hardly surprising that the present situation should have brought out much of the latent pro-German sentiment in the vague hope that the Axis Powers, being hostile to both the old enemies, might in some way prove Afghanistan's salvation."[86]

Engert's lengthy analysis revealed that Hashim Khan and his brothers had good reason for concern, fearing the real possibility of deposed ex-king Amanullah "arriving on the Russo-Afghan border supported by Axis arms and money to raise the standard of revolt." He recommended that the United States act to firm up their support of the ruling family while there was still time, warning that as long as there was any doubt about the "United Nations" ability to win the war, "the Afghan government will want to run with hare and not with the hounds."[87]

That December of 1942, U.S. Secretary of State Cordell Hull cabled Engert, informing him that the Office of Lend-Lease Administration desired to send a Mr. Gordon Bowles, an American citizen, for the purpose of exploring alternate supply routes to China should passage through Burma and Iran be blocked by German or Japanese offensives.[88] But the Americans were soon to discover that the impact of a century of British and Russian colonial expansion made even a simple request a matter of diplomatic wizardry.

Addressing a warning by William Phillips, Roosevelt's personal representative in India, that in return for expelling Axis nationals from Afghanistan both British and the Russians agreed to honor Afghan neutrality,[89] Engert was dismissive of Afghanistan's most important concern. Cabling Washington that the "Soviets never gave any assurances re: supply routes and that Britain merely promised not to open such routes without cooperation of Afghans," he assured the State Department that things could be worked out. But Afghanistan's refusal to be drawn into the Allied war plan held firm. "Because of the many overtures by the Afghan government to obtain a resident American mission in Kabul, Engert expected a whole-hearted friendly reception and little difficulty in performing his mission. Instead he found a good deal of hostility toward America's allies (though not toward America itself) and substantial resistance to his overtures, as well as strong residual sympathy for the Axis."[90]

Germany's devastating defeat at Stalingrad in February 1943 alleviated America's immediate concerns about the need for additional supply routes, but the Russian military victory did introduce what would soon become the major postwar concern. Despite an admission that since June 1941 "there has been practically no Bolshevist propaganda in Afghanistan," American minister Engert speculated on the potential complications of a Soviet victory and the effect of that possibility on the Allied war effort. Acknowledging that the "fear and dislike of Russia . . . blinds most of the Afghans to the dangers based on an Axis victory," Engert observed that "the intentions of her Russian neighbor have never been considered above suspicion. . . . There is therefore, no desire to see Russian arms emerge victorious from the war."[91] Added to Kabul's continuing economic emergency exacerbated by British parsimony and the lingering effects of the cutoff in German assistance, Engert viewed a Soviet victory in Central Asia without strong western countermeasures as having the potential for a major political crisis. He urged American economic support wherever possible and took pride in the few small measures made to accommodate Afghan requests.[92]

By the spring of 1943, Engert's warnings foreshadowed Cold War rhetoric as he reflected on the consequences of an Axis defeat, speculating that "Afghanistan's only hope of escaping communism and maintaining her independence lies in close friendship with Great Britain and the US."[93] But as much as Engert grasped the Afghan dilemma, his projection of Afghan "hope" may have been mere wish fulfillment, given the oft-used Afghan tactic of biding time in hope of getting the better deal from more powerful opponents.

When the prospect of an Allied victory improved that fall, Afghanistan's minister to Washington, Abdul Hussain Aziz, made his country's position regarding both Britain and Russia clear. In meetings with Assistant Secretary of State Adolf A. Berle Jr. and Secretary of State Hull, Afghanistan's minister reiterated the primacy of Afghanistan's territorial claims, insisting that "the only issues at present existing between Afghanistan and Russia or between Afghanistan and Great Britain which are not capable of settlement by compromise are those affecting the frontiers."[94] In a harbinger of what was to come, Secretary of State Hull also emphasized in his letter to Engert that in the Afghan minister's personal opinion "any attempt to settle these questions in a manner contrary to Afghan wishes would result in immediate military action by the Afghans," adding that "the Afghan-Indian frontier presented no problem so long as the British remained in India, but that the Government of Afghanistan would never permit that the tribesmen along the present northwest frontier of India should be subject against their will to the control of Indians."[95]

Given that Engert represented a secular American government dealing for the first time with the wholly Muslim nation of Afghanistan, his cautious attention in a letter to the American secretary of state[96] "to the possibility of establishing American missionary activities in Afghanistan," raises surprising questions about American priorities and the unspoken role of religion in American diplomacy. His suggestion for approaching the Afghans after the war "in a perfectly detached manner and as part of the spiritual reconstruction of the world in harmony with the ideals for which we are fighting," appears remarkably idealistic for an American bureaucrat, especially in the light of today's brutal doctrine of targeted assassinations and preemptive war. But his suggestion that a scheme might be made more workable "provided they are *not called* [emphasis his] 'missionary'" and his recommendation that "carefully selected American teachers and doctors would in itself constitute 'missionary' work of the highest order," smacks of the groundwork for a covert intelligence operation in the making.[97]

Despite foot-dragging by the Indian government, Engert helped improve Afghanistan's dire import-export status to such a degree that the country actually generated a large surplus in its balance of payments for the first time in its history by selling much of its agricultural produce to Allied forces. But as the war drew to a close, Afghanistan's difficult relations with its eastern neighbor took on a vastly more dangerous and complex character.

In what appeared a positive start to postwar relations, in 1945 the United States initiated the Helmand River Valley irrigation and hydroelectric project in southern Afghanistan. But the project's impact was anything but helpful. Arranged by the politically well-connected Morrison-Knudsen Company, the project bled Afghanistan's substantial dollar reserves that had been built up feeding Indian troops during World War II. With the company failing to do the necessary engineering surveys prior to construction, the two major dams and extensive canal system flooded the valley floor and ruined crops.[98] A subsequent analysis by a subsidiary company of Knudsen paid for by the United States put all the blame on the Afghans. Not until the king's cousin Mohammad Daoud became prime minister in 1953 were the problems addressed, but only after years of lost revenue from Afghanistan's most productive valley.[99]

Faced with the sudden dissolution of British India, the Durand Line and the future of Afghan tribal homelands bordering the Indus River became the number-one issue of the day. As articulated to the U.S. secretary of state by Afghanistan's minister to Washington in 1943, Afghanistan's claims to territory seized during the period of Russian and British colonial expansion remained unchanged and would, if left unresolved, lead to war. In fact, questions remain to this day whether Britain ever truly honored the terms of the original 1893 agreement imposed on the Afghans. According to Nyrop and Seekins's *Afghanistan: A Country Study*, "Boundary limitations were agreed upon between Durand and Abdur Rahman before the end of 1893, but there is some question about the degree to which Abdur Rahman willingly ceded certain areas. Scholars have found in his papers and autobiography indications that he regarded the Durand Line as a delimitation of areas of political responsibility, not permanent international frontiers, and that he did not explicitly cede control over the areas (such as Kurram and Chitral) that had already come under British control under the Treaty of Gandamak. The amir's reluctant agreement to the Durand Line was only achieved with an increase of his subsidy from the British government and quiet threats by Durand."[100] Tolerated by Afghan rulers only so long as Britain remained in control of India but never accepted as a permanent boundary, the division of British India into Hindu India and Muslim Pakistan posed a final and permanent disillusion with Britain on the part of Afghanistan's leadership. Long awaited as the opportunity for which long-standing grievances would be addressed and longer-standing conflicts resolved, the decision by Britain's last viceroy to India, Lord Louis Mountbatten, to exclude Afghanistan from the official Partition Agreement would raise Afghan ire at the worst possible moment. Disallowing the option for an independent Pashtunistan favored by both Kabul and the Pashtun tribes of the North-West Frontier Province, the British administration offered the tribes the option of joining with either India or Pakistan instead.[101] Still smoldering over the unresolved division of Pashtun homeland, the bloody creation of the state of Pakistan in 1947 set Afghans against Pakistanis from the outset while setting in motion a series of events that would drive Afghanistan toward the Soviet Union. In addition to institutionalizing Afghan grievances over the artificial boundary, Britain's parting act hobbled the Afghan economy, permanently denying Afghanistan its former territory over the Hindu Kush as far as the Indus River—thereby maintaining Afghanistan's landlocked status. Afghan concerns aside, the ill-conceived creation of a Muslim Pakistan was in itself a disaster, placing Pakistan between two hostile neighbors and guaranteeing conflict. Hassan Abbas, a former Pakistani police official now at Tufts Fletcher School of Law and Diplomacy, writes, "The new nation was awkwardly cut from British India in two separate pieces, an East and a West Pakistan that happened to be eight hundred miles apart, with India situated in between. The partition was accomplished by a merciless communal slaughter of Muslims by Hindus and Sikhs and vice versa—17 million people were shunted across frontiers of the two states created by partition to reach their homelands—millions vanished. For the Muslim migrants, the road to Pakistan was covered in blood and ashes."[102]

The blood and ashes would also smother any chance for a normal relationship with Afghanistan, transforming the issue of the trans-Durand-Pashtun tribal areas from a bloody colonial flashpoint to a permanent, deadly, strategic, Cold War hot spot. At the same time, by establishing a militarized prototype Islamic state, alienated from both India and Afghanistan and devoid of economic resources, Britain guaranteed Pakistan's chronic instability.

Not satisfied with the accord, Afghanistan rejected the outcome of the so-called North-West Frontier Province plebiscite and declared it null and void, insisting that self-determination for the Pashtun tribes on both sides of the border was the only solution. According to observers like Ghaus, the British failure to resolve the Pashtun issue grew from an assumption that the umbrella of an "all Muslim Pakistan" would somehow magically resolve all differences. Instead, the British—in their haste to abandon the region—compounded their mistake, overlooking, Ghaus writes, "that the Pashtun people were not geographically part of the subcontinent and had no affinities, ethnic, linguistic, or cultural, with the races of India."[103]

With the British gone, Afghanistan escalated the war of words, denouncing the plebiscite as illegal and ridiculing the newly created state as artificial. In retaliation, Pakistani media outlets returned the insults, attacking all things Afghan, including the royal family.[104] To make matters worse, Pakistani officials took full advantage of their control over access to the sea, denying or delaying Afghan shipments to Pakistani ports while neglecting to protect Afghan goods already inside the country.[105] In response the Afghans retaliated diplomatically, voting in September 1947 to deny Pakistan admission to the United Nations—the only country to do so.[106]

Following the establishment of an independent Pashtunistan movement by the government of Afghanistan, the government of Pakistan hardened its position regarding the territories. In June 1948, Pakistan arrested Pashtun leaders in the North-West Frontier Province while sharply elevating the level of military occupation. The action provoked the Afghan monarchy of King Zahir Shah to renounce the Durand Line and demand the return of its territory. Shaken by Afghanistan's response, Pakistan's leadership called for even closer military ties with the United States. Following the aerial bombing of the village of Mogholgai inside Afghanistan, Kabul convened a Loya Jirga (Afghan tribal assembly) which voted its full support for a separate independence for the tribal areas from Pakistan.[107] According to noted American anthropologist Louis Dupree, the Jirga also authorized the Afghan government to abrogate all of Afghanistan's treaties with Great Britain regarding the trans-Durand-Pashtuns.[108]

A natural base for Cold War confrontation, Afghanistan was quickly returning to its traditional role as a buffer state between empires—only this time as a strangely unique competition for Soviet and American Cold War rivals. By March 1948 that competition saw the American contingent of engineers, technicians and teachers grow to become the largest of any other foreign state, with Afghanistan looking to the United States for assistance in many fields. In a memorandum to President Harry Truman,[109] Secretary of State George Marshall advised raising the level of the diplomatic mission to Afghanistan to full ambassadorial status, insisting that despite "the difficulties implicit in its contiguity to the Soviet Union, [the country] endeavors to align itself with the Western democracies." Yet by that November, Afghanistan's economic minister, Abdul Majid Khan, expressed concern over the American commitment to Afghanistan's development, anxiously questioning American intentions, warning that "time was growing short, and Afghanistan must have an answer soon."[110] Fearing correctly that the United States was giving less than its full attention to his country, Majid hinted to his American hosts that without financial and military assistance the problem of the economically backward tribal areas could soon become an American problem. Recalling Afghanistan's longstanding lack of an adequate self-defense, Majid chided Richard S. Leach of the Division of South Asian Affairs, saying, "As a rusty gun is dangerous to the owner and his neighbors, a 'rusty' economy is likewise full of peril." That December Majid further linked Afghanistan's request for military aid to the nascent Cold War, issuing a fateful prophecy, "indicating his belief that a war between the US and USSR is inevitable, and said that when war came Afghanistan would of course be overrun and occupied. But the Russians would be unable to pacify the country. Afghanistan could and would pursue guerilla tactics for an indefinite period. Abdul Majid said that the early supply of light military equipment for internal defense was closely related to the possibility for a long and determined resistance to some future aggressive action by the USSR."[111]

The end of the British occupation of India did bring a brief period of domestic liberalization to Afghanistan, with the election of numerous progressive members to Parliament. With the war over, a heightened sense of national pride emerged and a nationwide public debate over long-suppressed issues began. Suddenly Kabul University became a locus of intellectual activity with fundamentalists, moderates and communists side by side for the first time in Afghan history. For a time, press censorship was relaxed and opposition political groups were allowed to form. Nur Mohammad Taraki, the leader of one such group—the Wikh-i-Zalmayan (Awakened Youth), would later become president following the 1978 Marxist coup.[112]

None of this was cause for celebration in the U.S. as Cold War-anti-communist fever swept the country. With Congress establishing the Central Intelligence Agency to coordinate and oversee America's military intelligence apparatus, the U.S. policy of containing the spread of Soviet influence would collide with Afghan liberalization.

Modeled closely on British India's Political and Secret Service from the days of the empire (the Raj), the CIA's lineage would be proudly compared in the 1980s by Britain's foremost military historian Sir John Keegan in nineteenth century-Kiplingesque-terms as having "assumed the mantle once worn by Kim's masters, as if it were a seamless garment."[113] In addition to the mantle, the CIA would also receive the mandate of Kim's master, adapting a century-old British political strategy for putting pressure on the Russian empire's southern flank. Applied to Afghanistan, that strategy soon found the U.S. aligning itself with Pakistan's British-trained military establishment, which was by 1948 emulating Britain's aggressive "Forward Policy" of Afghan destabilization in the North-West Frontier Province. Pressed by Afghanistan's Economics Minister Abdul Majid for an equal share of military assistance, the U.S. State Department assured their cooperation.[114] But Pakistan's failure to address the border dispute and that country's ongoing confrontation with India over the province of Kashmir undermined Afghanistan's appeal.

By 1950, American concern for Afghan territorial claims in the North-West Frontier Province were limited strictly to the "strategic importance of the Pakistan-Afghan frontier, the lack of an integrated defense of the Indian subcontinent since the British withdrawal, and the need for Afghan tribal cooperation in providing for the security of this region."[115]

But the State Department's remedy, stated in its official policy report for Pakistan that year, appeared more concerned with the post–World War II reconstruction of Europe as a hedge against communism than the economic progress of either Pakistan or Afghanistan. "We stress our conviction that the recovery of these [Western European] countries from World War II will ultimately make the most effective contribution to Pakistan's security and economic progress."[116] Stated succinctly in the April 3 report, the plan for addressing security concerns relied more on bluff than substance, leaving Pakistan to settle its border disputes, defend its territory and grow its economy, while hoping that the "Commies will do their part in our behalf if we follow up with expanded USIS activities."[117]

Put another way, U.S. policy toward Afghanistan and Pakistan in 1950 relied essentially on doing nothing, hoping in the end that U.S. propaganda and the fear of Russian communism alone would be enough to satisfy American needs: "In the final analysis U.S. government's problem in South Asia is a selling job and for reasons indicated in paragraphs above the relentless publicizing of our side of the story and exposure of Soviet imperialism seems to be a major and most effective implement at our immediate disposal."[118]

Despite America's distraction with rebuilding Europe, Afghanistan continued to look toward the United States for leadership as well as economic and political support, and did receive agricultural and educational assistance through the U.S. International Cooperation Administration. Afghanistan also received generous assistance from the United Nations for both economic and social programs. But the Afghans were surprised and disappointed by the Truman administration's flat refusal to honor Afghanistan's military requests despite positive recommendations by the U.S. embassy in Kabul. Kabul was also frustrated by America's unwillingness to pressure Pakistan into resolving the issue of an independent Pashtunistan, despite numerous halfhearted attempts to mediate the dispute. In fact, instead of affording the Afghans due consideration for their legal right to question the legitimacy of the Durand Line, the United States interpreted Afghanistan's persistent overtures as a threat "to place themselves under Soviet auspices"[119] if the United States refused to back their demands.

Viewed from the perspective of Afghan Deputy Foreign Minister Ghaus, the reluctance to embark on a more equitable post-colonial policy toward Afghanistan resulted partly from American inexperience but even more from the fear of detaching from Britain's colonial apron strings: "The Americans did not know much about Pashtunistan and its ramifications, and the little they did know they learned from the British, who held no great sympathy for the Afghan position. Besides, the Americans were impressed by the English-speaking, British-trained, pro-Western Pakistani officials, who, together with Britain, quickly convinced Washington of the value of Pakistan as a bulwark of Western concepts wedged between neutralist, left-leaning India and backward, unfamiliar Afghanistan, that could easily be taken by Russia 'whenever its broader objectives would be served.'"[120]

Biased by Britain against Afghanistan's stubborn independence from the outset, the negative American response to repeated Afghan pleas for military assistance was further complicated by the growing influence of a new

Cold War mythology. That mythology, Manichean by design, intentionally viewed Third World postcolonial nationalism in much the same light as Soviet communism and acted against it accordingly. Hemmed in, but sheltered by treaties and mutual agreements between Britain and Russia throughout the colonial era, Afghanistan's independence-obsessed leadership viewed America's new exclusive alignment with Pakistan with alarm. This simplistic American policy acted as a self-fulfilling prophecy—alienating many of the newly independent, postcolonial republics like Afghanistan, branding them as enemies, denying them resources, and forcing them toward the Soviet sphere of influence. Summed up by Robert Dreyfuss in his *Devil's Game*, the policy rejuvenated the worst elements of an old-world imperialism at just the moment when a fresh, modern American approach was expected by the developing world: "During the Cold War, from 1945 to 1991, the enemy was merely not the USSR. According to the Manichean rules of that era, the United States demonized leaders who did not wholeheartedly sign on to the American agenda or who might challenge Western and in particular U.S. hegemony. Ideas and ideologies that could inspire such leaders were suspect: nationalism, humanism, secularism, socialism. But subversive ideas such as these were also the ones most feared by the nascent forces of Muslim fundamentalism. Throughout the region, the Islamic right fought pitched battles against the bearers of these notions, not only in the realm of intellectual life but in the streets. During the decades-long struggle against Arab nationalism—along with Persian, Turkish, and Indian nationalism—the United States found it politic to make common cause with the Islamic right."[121]

Located at the geographic center of Persian, Turkish and Indian nationalism, Afghanistan, with its struggle for modernism, independence and recognition, now faced a new and confusing enemy in this strange American policy. Despite the resistance of the radical mullahs, Afghanistan's leadership had for a hundred years slowly advanced the cause of progressive reforms in education, government and women's rights. Despite the opposition of British agencies intent on undermining Kabul's political stability in order to perpetuate Afghanistan's economic dependence, Afghan rulers had successfully courted French, Italian and especially German investment. Now here in the birthplace of the Zoroastrian war of light against darkness, Afghanistan was suddenly confronted by a black-and-white American policy that was at once regressive, dualist, and especially antimodernist in its simplicity and intent.

5.

A Background to Cold War Policy

"Who rules East Europe commands the Heartland; Who rules the heartland commands the World Island; Who rules the world Island commands the world."

—Halford Mackinder

While the institutional narrative on the origins of the Cold War generally tends to cite the cruelty and rapacious qualities of Stalin's Soviet Union or simply the spread of communism as its prime motivation, it does not explain the extreme black-and-white nature of America's new policy or why that policy would include perceived or imagined *noncommunist* threats.

Following World War II, with the Holocaust and the dropping of the first atomic bomb fresh in their minds, American war planners clashed over what course to take against the Soviet Union. Henry Wallace, Roosevelt's vice president and Truman's secretary of commerce, lobbied for peaceful coexistence. A friend and follower of Theosophist Nicholas Roerich and a serious presidential contender, Wallace did not view Soviet communism as a threat. If anything, Wallace shared the Theosophists' assumption that the events in Russia were part of a cosmic plan and that the long-awaited "'revolution of the spirit,' would follow and complete the Bolshevik Revolution," as Bernice Glatzer Rosenthal writes in *The Occult in Russian and Soviet Culture.*[1] This belief was also shared by numerous early Soviet groups, like the workers art movement, the Proletkult. Combining Christian, Masonic, Anthroposophical and Theosophical beliefs—Proletkult writers, playwrights and artists believed themselves to actually be the anticipated spiritual "third revolution." Promising to open the way to the future, their confident rhetoric for materializing the spirit of the masses envisioned a desperate enemy for whom judgment day had come. "For the old, dark capitalist world, it [the third revolution] is more terrifying, more dangerous than any bomb. They know very well that physical revolution is only a quarter of the Bolshevik-Soviet victory. But a spiritual revolution—that is the whole victory."[2] Intended to replace the bourgeois arts with a pure spiritual expression of the working class, Proletkult was vehemently opposed by Lenin's chief theorist and commander of the Red Army Leon Trotsky whose twisted logic argued that a workers' art made no sense since by the time the working class developed its own art form, the working class itself should have ceased to exist. More questionable still was the idea that *anything* spiritual could emerge from the brutal, congealed, "atheist" culture of Stalin's Kremlin—let alone succeed it. Yet at least as recently as the 1940s the esoteric strains of Rudolph Steiner's Anthroposophy and Nicholas Roerich's Theosophy resonated beneath the cold political exterior of Soviet culture and, equally as surprising, in American culture as well.[3] From the perspective of Wallace, whose openly spiritual trek through a dozen of the world's religions from Christianity to Judaism to Zoroastrianism to Islam had been dedicated to creating a new world order, the opportunity to forge a progressive alliance with the Soviets by abolishing poverty, war, and human suffering (spiritual and physical) would have been the fulfillment of the Theosophists' dream agenda, known at the time as the Great Shambhala Project.[4] Seen in the globalist geopolitical terminology of Halford MacKinder or Karl Haushofer, ceding Eastern Europe, Central Asia or any part of the Eurasian land mass to Russia amounted to the fulfillment of an horrendous prophecy.[5]

Despite senior diplomat George Kennan's middle-of-the-road proposal to coerce the Soviets into freeing Eastern Europe through political and economic measures (containment), influential figures in the Democratic Party proffered an aggressive, warlike strategy instead. Renouncing the Democratic Party's pro-Soviet politics of the war years, a group of anti-Stalinist liberals headed by Eleanor Roosevelt, Hubert Humphrey and Arthur Schlesinger Jr. vowed a "two front fight for democracy, both at home and abroad."[6] Backed by organized labor, industry and the growing economic influence of the military-industrial partnership forged during World War II, the intellectuals of the so-called anticommunist Left would, under the cover of the Truman Doctrine, fabricate the rigid, paranoid architecture of the Cold War, incarcerating the Soviets, if not the Russian people themselves, behind a curtain of iron rhetoric, labeling them in the black-and-white terms that are usually the province of Manichean heretics.[7]

Heading this quasi-religious exercise was the State Department's director of policy planning, "Vicar of Foreign Policy" Paul Henry Nitze. Considered by some the creator of the Cold War, Nitze's sanctimonious pronouncements set the tone for a strange new kind of warfare and the newly emerging managerial class needed to prosecute it.[8] Urged on by Secretary of State Dean Acheson to "scare the daylights" out of President Truman, Nitze composed a top-secret paper in April 1950 titled "United States Objectives and Programs for National Security."[9] Also known as National Security Directive 68 (NSC 68), the paper warned of the "Kremlin's design for world domination," and argued forcefully that since Russia was inescapably militant, the Kremlin's goal would be the "ultimate elimination of any effective opposition," predicting that 1954 was the year of ultimate danger. Echoing the primal concerns of Mackinder and Haushofer, the document also warned that "Soviet domination of the potential power of Eurasia, whether achieved by armed aggression or by political and subversive means, would be strategically and politically unacceptable to the United States."[10] Years later in his memoir, Acheson admitted that the document exaggerated the threat but revealed he'd wanted it that way in order "to so bludgeon the mass mind of 'top government' that not only could the President make a decision but that the decision could be carried out."[11]

CREATING THE SELF-FULFILLING PROPHECY

Although encouraged by China, not Russia, and nothing like what NSC 68 anticipated, communist North Korea's advance into the South in June of that year raised Nitze's reputation to the rank of prophet and the document to the level of prophecy. Exploiting memories of British appeasement and humiliation at Munich in 1938, Nitze's NSC 68 magically transformed Acheson's exaggerated threat into the bludgeon he'd hoped for, shielding Truman's Cold War Democrats from any effective criticism or, more importantly, a less ideological analysis of Soviet intentions.

With the imagined threat of an imminent Communist expansion now the official wisdom and an imagined Kremlin plot lurking behind it all, a "new class" of corporate defense manager began the urgent task of imagining their own aggressive "Forward Policy" to counter it.

Generally unknown to the outside world—with little or no connection to either the American people or the mainstream foreign-policy establishment—these men, now termed "defense intellectuals," would be sold to the American public as modern-day high priests, "whose wisdom would be taken for granted, their assumptions worshiped as gospel truth, their insight elevated to an almost mystical level and accepted as dogma," according to Fred Kaplan in *The Wizards of Armageddon*.[12] Politically, what the term "defense intellectual" actually represented was a strange brew of philosophical, anti-modernist, ex-Eastern-European-Communist-turned-anti-Stalinist fringe, miraculously souffléed by Wall Street, Madison Avenue and the Central Intelligence Agency into a new "managerial class." Initially attached to a postwar air force research project called RAND (created by Douglas Aircraft for the purpose of advancing the uses of airpower), the new elite would grow and prosper in a morally and intellectually detached universe. Outside the traditional American diplomatic establishment, RAND's unconventional thinkers would go on to mix Cabalistic mathematical game theories with Marxist-Leninist agitation propaganda while applying their concepts to American politics and foreign policy.[13]

Kaplan writes, "It was, at the outset, a small and exceptionally inbred collection of men—mostly economists and mathematicians, a few political scientists . . . a new elite that would eventually emerge as a power elite, and whose power would come not from wealth or family or brass stripe, but from their having conceived and elaborated a set of ideas."[14]

Licensed by NSC 68 and underwritten by Wall Street to "think the unthinkable," this self-created "new" class would bring the best and worst of Europe's prewar scientific and intellectual dialogue to their new hybridized American reality, mixing techniques of social control pioneered by both Nazis and Bolsheviks with the University of Chicago's Merriam school of thought. "Charles Merriam led the way," Kaplan writes, "with his provocative discourses on American politics, expounding on the now common but then utterly earthshaking thesis that the essence of all politics lay not in structures of organizations or the Bill of Rights or the Electoral College, but in *power*—who uses it, for what ends, in what political context, against whom."[15]

The switch from the traditional law-based foreign policy of the previous century, with its reliance on treaties, councils and international law, was an astonishing course correction for a United States whose founding principles warned of the dangers of monarchies and sinister foreign entanglements. If anything, what America offered the war-ravaged world of 1950 was an example of living by such enlightened policies. Yet here was an aggressive new gang of unknowns given the keys to the kingdom with the mission of rewriting the core directory of the United States along the lines of Niccolò Machiavelli's *The Prince*.

Described by Kaplan as "thermonuclear Jesuits" for their near mystical authority over policy—the Merriamites owed as much to Leon Trotsky as St. Ignatius of Loyola, marrying Trotsky's vision of a Fourth International with its virulent anti-Stalinism to Nitze's anti-Russian crusade. Transformed by former Trotskyist-turned OSS-CIA operative James Burnham from a permanent communist revolution to a permanent managerial one, the agenda for a permanent Cold War had been set.[16] Michael Lind writes in the *Nation*, "The idea that the United States and similar societies are dominated by a decadent post-bourgeois 'new class' was developed by thinkers in the Trotskysist tradition like James Burnham and Max Schachtman, who influenced an older generation of neocons. The concept of the 'global democratic revolution' has its origins in the Trotskyist Fourth International's vision of a permanent revolution. The economic determinist idea . . . is simply Marxism with entrepreneurs substituted for proletarians as the heroic subjects of history."[17]

Housed at think tanks such as RAND and organizations such as Americans for Democratic Action, the Committee on the Present Danger and the CIA-sponsored Congress of Cultural Freedom, ex-Trotskyites like Albert Wohlstetter, Burnham and Irving Kristol supplanted Henry Wallace as the new seneschals of America's emerging national security and foreign policy intelligentsia,[18] remolding and shaping it in the rational terminologies of an apocalyptic new science while infusing it with the racist irrationality of old European grudges. Encouraged further by the Soviet development of the hydrogen bomb, the stage was set for profound changes in America's peacetime status, with the U.S. government embracing a permanent state of war and the institutions necessary to maintain it. Together with the CIA's British mandate and its obsessive focus on Eurasia as "World Island,"[19] Afghanistan would find itself once again in the path of someone's imperial destiny, a destiny now backed by the power of the nuclear bomb and a weird circle of ex–communist revolutionaries intent on finding a way to use it.

THE 1950s

"It seemed Afghanistan had no place under the protective umbrella of the United States, which the Afghans mistakenly believed had acquired responsibility for filling the vacuum left by the departure of the British from India," former Afghan deputy foreign minister Ghaus writes.[20]

Failing to redress the Pashtunistan issue, confrontations on both sides of the border with Pakistan continued to escalate. A 1950 protest march crossed the Durand Line with the intention of planting flags on the banks of the Indus as a reminder of Afghanistan's pre-British border. It resulted in Pakistan embargoing Afghan fuel tankers from crossing the border for three months. Without fuel, Afghanistan again turned to Moscow, resulting in a "barter and trade agreement" providing for aid in construction of petroleum storage facilities, oil and gas exploration, and permission for the free transit of goods to Afghanistan across Soviet territory. Beneficial to Afghanistan, the move predictably fulfilled American fears of growing Soviet involvement.[21]

Opposed to Afghan nationalism and deeply suspicious of Soviet influence, the United States by the spring of 1951 had once again rebuffed

Afghan requests for military assistance. An additional Afghan request that summer saw the United States demanding a $25-million payment in cash, delivery through Pakistan that would require Pakistani approval, and a renunciation of any claim to Pashtunistan as conditions. Clearly intended to prevent Afghanistan from arming itself, but not offering protection in return, the U.S. decision to unilaterally support its new ally Pakistan without addressing Afghanistan's longtime claims and security concerns produced predictable results. Overlooking the fact that Afghanistan's delicate neutrality had relied for over a century on British military power, U.S. policy makers undermined their own stated ambition of maintaining Afghanistan as a "buffer state" against Soviet designs in Central Asia and the Middle East while at the same time encouraging Soviet influence.[22] This pattern of disregarding Afghan concerns worsened as the United States continued to move closer to Pakistan militarily and diplomatically.

More politically isolated than ever, unable to modernize its army, and economically stagnant, Afghanistan's leadership faced a crossroads. In 1952 relations with Pakistan were again inflamed when Pakistan's prime minister was assassinated by an Afghan citizen. Accepting Kabul's denial of involvement, the immediate crisis cooled, but the Pashtunistan issue festered.[23]

Inspired by the rise of strong, independent Muslim nationalists like Mohammad Mossadeq in neighboring Iran and Gamal Abdel Nasser's Egypt, in 1953 King Zahir Shah appointed his cousin and brother-in-law Mohammad Daoud prime minister.[24] A fierce nationalist, the tough, smart, and determined Daoud immediately gained the attention of the United States by making the Pashtunistan issue a priority and turning toward the Soviet Union for financial and military support. Western-educated and authoritarian, Daoud immediately cracked down on dissent and liberalization, rolling back reforms and political openness. One victim of the crackdown was Babrak Karmal, future leader of the Soviet-favored Parcham (Banner) Party who would later go on to align himself closely with Daoud.[25] Another casualty was Nur Mohammad Taraki, godfather to the Khalq Party (the Masses), who was at the time employed as the press attaché to the Afghan embassy in Washington. In what was described as a "bizarre" incident by Afghan historians Nancy and Richard S. Newell, following the induction of Mohammad Daoud as prime minister, Taraki called a press conference to announce his resignation as press attaché and to denounce the Afghan government. Announcing his intention to seek political asylum in Britain, six weeks later he emerged at an Afghan consulate in Pakistan, declaring that he had been misquoted. Out of work and out of favor with Daoud's government for his misstep, Taraki set up an independent translation service that did business with, among others, the U.S. embassy and USAID.[26] "During the late 1950s he began to write radical fiction in which Afghan society was depicted as unjust and degraded. He became the center of a circle of radical writers and intellectuals but never was arrested or jailed, apparently much to his chagrin."[27]

As political unrest simmered under Prince Daoud's crackdown, it exploded next door in Iran that same year with the CIA overthrowing democratically elected Premier Mohammad Mossadeq.[28] Designed to guarantee U.S. control over Iran's oil supply, the coup spawned resentment and a permanent distrust of American intentions in the Muslim world. With Shiite Iran now wedded by force to the U.S. Cold War policy of containment, Daoud faced pressure on both the Pakistani and Iranian fronts. At his urging and with tacit support from the Soviet Union, uprisings increased along the border with Pakistan.[29] Labeled the "Red Prince" in the American press[30] for his growing closeness to the Soviet Union, Daoud tried to offset American concerns by opening the country to western social influence, and the next ten years saw a major strengthening in government agencies, education and public works.[31] Yet the continued tactlessness of American diplomatic efforts kept the Afghans distanced from American goals. Two events embodied Kabul's frustration. The first was a 1953 state visit by Vice President Richard Nixon who unceremoniously informed the Afghans that they had no justifiable claim to Pashtunistan.[32] The second came a year later after a private appeal for armaments by Daoud's brother Mohammad Naim to Secretary of State John Foster Dulles resulted in a thoughtless breach of diplomatic etiquette by the United States.[33]

Complicating relations even further was the U.S. ambassador to Kabul, Angus Ward. Appointed ambassador to Afghanistan by the Truman administration in 1952 following a tumultuous career, Ward was found "guilty of constant breaches of the rigidly conventional behavior that Foreign Service officers demand of one another."[34] Abandoned without protest by the State Department for three months when captured following the Communist Chinese takeover of Mukden in 1948, the Canadian-born Ward's crude and abrasive style clashed with the clever and urbane Daoud. Openly hostile toward Daoud's fierce independence and Soviet drift, Ward quickly turned even the simplest misunderstandings into open warfare, driving Daoud even further from American interests.[35] Described as "the Frontiersman" in an April 2, 1956, *Time* magazine article, the former lumber salesman, army officer, and timber evaluator for the Bureau of Internal Revenue was well suited to Truman's good-versus-evil, Cold War, confrontational approach, an approach that in the case of Afghanistan served little purpose.[36]

Unwilling to be drawn into an active Cold War alliance against the Soviet Union through the Southeast Asia Treaty Organization (SEATO), unable to gain the level of economic development requested from any of the western nations, and facing growing public demands for modernization, Daoud was left with few options. Stepping in where the U.S. Export-Import Bank had already refused to go, by funding grain silos, flour mills and an asphalt factory to pave Kabul's streets, the post-Stalinist Soviet Union rapidly gained a level of influence in Kabul undreamed of under British dominion.[37] In March 1955 the frontier dispute boiled over again, with Pakistan closing the border for five months, refusing transshipments of goods to or from Afghanistan. Afghan appeals to both Iran and the United States for alternate routes to the Persian Gulf or Arabian Sea were denied as "economically impractical." Faced with economic ruin, Afghanistan turned once again to the Soviet Union. Renewing its 1950 transit agreement, that August it signed an even more comprehensive "barter protocol" guaranteeing petroleum, building material, and "rolled ferous metals" in exchange for Afghan goods. With the border situation now tenser than at any time since World War II and guarantees of safe transit through Soviet territory, that August Afghanistan dipped into its limited hard-currency reserves and paid Czechoslovakia three million dollars in cash for new weapons. Capitalizing on the good will, a visit by Nikita

Khrushchev and Soviet Premier Nikolai Bulganin that December of 1955 cemented the deal with the gift of a hundred-bed hospital and fifteen city buses for Kabul's public transit system, with Bulganin openly expressing sympathy for the "question of Pashtunistan."

Although later downplayed by Soviet authorities, Bulganin's report to the Supreme Soviet expressing solidarity with Afghanistan on the rights of Pashtuns to "self-determination as any other people" played to a long-standing and painful theme in Afghan history while winning the Russians closer relations than at any time in history.[38]

In 1967, Sovietologist Marshall Goldman commented on the efficacy of Soviet policy on Afghanistan, writing, "Soviet Foreign Aid has been immensely successful. The Russians have avoided most forms of political interference. . . . Russian aid projects have been well-suited to Afghanistan's needs."[39] With the self-fulfilling logic of the 1950s Cold War, both Russia and the United States viewed the other's efforts at economic assistance with paranoia.

In his memoirs, Nikita Khrushchev recalled, "America was courting Afghanistan. . . . At the time of our visit there, it was clear to us that the Americans were penetrating Afghanistan with the obvious purpose of setting up a military base."[40]

A year later, in 1956, the United States issued the Baghdad Pact Planning Study on Communist Inspired Threat to West Pakistan. Finally recognizing the importance of the Pashtunistan issue to their own efforts at containing the Soviet Union, the study warned of a clear opportunity for the Soviets to align with disgruntled Afghans "in the creation of a Pakhtoonistan ally that borders on the Arabian Sea, [and] places the Soviets in the position . . . of posing a threat to sea lines of communication in the Persian Gulf, the Arabian Sea, and the Indian Ocean."

Warnings that a succession of Afghan leaders had been broadcasting to their American counterparts since at least 1917 had finally been heard. But the American realization came too late. In July 1956, Daoud finally secured the military assistance Afghanistan had been seeking since the time of Amanullah, but not from the Americans as he had hoped. Thoroughly convinced of American intransigence following his previous and final failure to secure military assistance from the United States in 1953, Daoud accepted a $32.4-million dollar loan from the Soviet Union. Supplied with modern weapons and training, Afghanistan began a transformation that within two decades would grow their armed forces from 44,000 haphazardly trained soldiers and police to a modern force of over one hundred thousand, with an air force of an additional ten thousand.[41]

Jolted by the ramifications of their poor judgment, that December the president's National Security Council recommended helping the Afghans to settle their differences with Pakistan over the Pashtunistan issue and encouraging the Afghans to seek military aid from American and other western sources.[42] But the long-standing opportunity to "win" Afghanistan had been lost. From that day forward, the official technical language of the Afghan military would be Russian, with the entire military establishment—air force, army tank corps and paramilitary police—bound exclusively to Soviet trainers, spare parts and technicians.[43] Washington appeared strangely confused at Daoud's decision, offering vague recommendations but with no real idea of the importance of Afghanistan to the future of its own policy. Veteran Afghan observer Henry S. Bradsher remarked incredulously, "There was no detectable sense of irony in the secret [1956] NSC study, no reference to the repeated American spurning of Afghan military aid requests before the Soviet deal, no recognition of the effects of America's arming Pakistan, apparently no institutional memory of what had gone before."[44]

Now unable to gain influence in Afghanistan through its military, the United States resorted to seeking a political advantage through civilian projects. One case, referred to as "curious" by Bradsher, involved road building and the building of an international airport at Kandahar. Once again contracted to the Morrison-Knudsen Company, the airport appeared on the surface to be an additional fifteen million dollars' worth of American incompetence. Sold to the Afghans as a means to reestablish Afghanistan as a necessary stopover for travel to and from the Orient, the airport came online just as long-range jets made such stops unnecessary. Further taking into account its impractical location that required that all fuel be trucked in over bad mountain roads from neighboring Pakistan, the airport was deemed "a monument to poor planning" by the State Department.[45] Below the surface, however, the airport served a very special function which author Bradsher foretold in his 1985 book would be military and strategic in nature, as we were to see in 2001. "A number of sources, both military and civilian Americans who declined to be identified, said Qandahar was a potential United States Air Force base for wartime use. It became in American military planning a 'recovery base' where bombers could land after attacking Soviet targets in Siberia or Central Asia that were too distant from their takeoff points in Western Europe or North Africa for them to have the fuel to get home."[46]

But even with the potential political and strategic benefits of a military staging ground come war with the Soviet Union, to the American foreign policy establishment Afghanistan the nation remained misunderstood and largely ignored. Ambassador Leon B. Poullada, a senior American diplomat who'd served in Afghanistan as an economic advisor, viewed Washington's efforts at peaceful competition with Moscow as hopelessly outclassed, citing American inefficiency, red tape, poor quality administration and above all a "bumbling American diplomacy, which mishandled the military aid and Pashtunistan issues."[47] In his final analysis, Poullada laid the blame for the loss of Afghanistan to the Soviet Union squarely on the back of the U.S. government—citing Stanford's Anthony Arnold: "The history of American military aid (or lack of it) can be summarized by noting that American failure over the years to respond to the genuine security needs of Afghanistan in any serious fashion contributed to the fatal decision of the frustrated Afghan leadership under Daoud to permit Soviet penetration of the Afghan armed forces. The Communist cells established by the Soviets inside the Afghan army and air force were the effective units which staged the bloody coup in April, 1978."[48]

Fumbling diplomatically and outmaneuvered militarily, American activities settled on another "curious" goal of both educating Afghanistan's civilian leaders while at the same time working covertly to recruit and enlist a core of extremist pan-Islamist-Muslim religious leaders to undermine Soviet and secular influence. This policy set in motion a series of events that would also bring the United States in contact with the some of Afghanistan's long-suppressed ethnic minorities such as the Hazaras and Tajiks.

Working through front groups like the Asia Foundation, the CIA began furthering the course set by British intelligence a century before by aiding religious extremists intent on subverting the modernization efforts of the Afghan government.[49] Another obvious target of the covert effort was Soviet influence on future political leaders. According to author Robert Dreyfuss, a special effort was made to influence student groups. "During the 1950s and 1960s, the Asia Foundation provided significant support to Kabul University and had several modest projects that dealt with Afghanistan's organized Muslim community. According to John and Rose Bannigan, longtime Asia Foundation officials who worked for the foundation in both Pakistan and Afghanistan in the 1960s, the organization helped the Islamic Research Institute in Lahore, Pakistan. . . . 'We were also involved with the major universities, through the departments of Islamic theology,' John Bannigan says. . . . 'The students were target number one,' he says."[50]

As important as recruiting foreign students was to the CIA's goals of infiltrating targeted nations, the Asia Foundation played an even more important role at hooking America's intelligentsia into the agency's mythology by crafting the company's propaganda for domestic consumption. According to Victor Marchetti and John D. Marks in *The CIA and the Cult of Intelligence*, "The focus of the Asia Foundation's activities was overseas, but the organization's impact tended to be *greater* in the American academic community than the Far East. Large numbers of American intellectuals participated in foundation programs, and they—usually unwittingly—contributed to popularizing of CIA ideas about the Far East. Designed—and justified at budget time—as an overseas propaganda operation, the Asia Foundation also was regularly guilty of propagandizing the American people with agency views of on Asia."[51]

According to Rose Bannigan, another Afghan "target" of the Asia Foundation's largesse was Afghanistan's most noteworthy clerical family, the Mojadidi. Holding the rank of *pir* (saint) within the Naqshbandiya Sufi order (named for Bahauddin Naqshband who died in 1389),[52] the Mojadidi family was also Afghanistan's largest landlord, leading the revolt against Amanullah's land reforms in 1929.[53] Alleged at the time to have been in the pay of British intelligence, by the 1950s the family, with its financial and political interests, clashed with the fierce nationalism of Mohammed Daoud, who, according to Richard and Nancy Newell, and not surprisingly, "disliked any form of political independence that might threaten his power."[54] Eventually exiled by Daoud, a scion of the family, Sibghatullah Mojadidi, fled to Copenhagen, where he ran a Libyan-financed Muslim center.[55] He would later become a factor in one of the stranger episodes of covert American policy as one of the numerous anti-Soviet mujahideen leaders supported by the United States, albeit one of the least effective.[56]

Beverley Male writes, "[Sibghatullah Mujaddidi] was a close relative of Mohammad Ibrahim Mujaddidi, the Hazrat of Shor Bazaar and Afghanistan's most influential religious figure. . . . The Mujaddidi family derived their religious authority from their claim to descent from the prophet Mohammad. They had consistently placed this authority at the disposal of the most reactionary groups and had been rewarded with lands and honours."[57]

Behind the growing U.S. support for Muslim extremism in Afghanistan lay an odd "fringe" element of the American national security bureaucracy better known for its expertise in self-promotion than its actual effectiveness. Known during the Carter administration as the Nationalities Working Group, the unorthodox program to destabilize Soviet Central Asia by encouraging Muslim extremists of the Naqshbandi order was the brainchild of a Russian exile named Alexandre Bennigsen. The son of a Russian count in St. Petersburg prior to the Bolshevik revolution, Bennigsen dedicated his life to finding ways to negate Soviet power. Migrating through various French universities and a fifteen-year sojourn through Turkey, Iran, Syria, Lebanon, Egypt, Jordan and Afghanistan, the so-called European academic came to passionately invest in the power of secret Sufi brotherhoods (*tariqat*) to transform Central Asia.[58] Citing Soviet sources as to their fanaticism, danger, and effectiveness, Bennigsen saw in the Naqshbandi Sufi extremists the ideal means for accomplishing his lifelong goals and transferred his radical beliefs to a generation of like-minded national security managers at the University of Chicago and RAND. Placing his hopes on a violent strain of Islamic mysticism, Bennigsen came to believe that the long-hoped-for spawn of radical Islam was finally erupting inside the Soviet Union and that the efforts of "mystical Sufi brotherhoods (*tariqa*) fighting to establish the reign of God on earth"[59] had the best chance of unseating Soviet rule throughout the region.

"According to Bennigsen," Dreyfuss writes, "the most significant of the Sufi brotherhoods were a secret society called the Naqshbandiya, a Freemason-style fraternity closely tied to the elite of Turkey, which had long-standing connections in Central Asia. 'The Naqshbandiya adepts have a long tradition of 'Holy War' against the Russians,' wrote Bennigsen. His conclusion was that nationalism in Central Asia was inextricably bound up with radical Islam."[60]

Regarded as controversial, if not absurdly unrealistic in the late 1950s, Bennigsen's views would grow to almost cult-like status as the influence of RAND's anti-Stalinist defense intellectuals grew inside the Washington establishment.[61] But as the 1950s came to a close Afghanistan had more to fear from the growth of foreign-influenced domestic political threats than external ones.

Maintaining low-level training and education programs, the United States aided promising Afghan students by sending them to American universities. One standout was the dynamic Hafizullah Amin. Born in 1929 to a lower-middle-class Pashtun family, Amin's success as a teacher and organizer moved him rapidly into favor with the Daoud government. Handpicked by U.S. administrators to participate in a UNESCO/Columbia University program to address Afghanistan's chronic shortage of teachers, Amin was sent to New York in 1957.[62] He later completed a master's degree at Columbia—coincidentally at a time when future national security director Zbigniew Brzezinski was gaining prominence as a professor there.[63]

According to his biographer Beverley Male, Amin attended summer classes in political science and economics at the University of Wisconsin in 1958 and became radicalized, joining the Socialist Progressive Club. He later claimed to have become a Marxist that summer, but would conceal his emergence as a communist leader until much later.[64]

Male finds Amin's early years as a communist organizer enigmatic.

"Hafizullah Amin's early career gives scarcely a hint of the formidable figure who would later emerge to assume the leadership of the PDPA [People's Democratic Party of Afghanistan]. His political activity was directed towards the radicalization of Afghan teachers and through them, of the rural population."[65]

Amin was again chosen in 1962 by the Americans to attend Columbia, this time as a doctoral candidate. A standout as a student leader, Amin rose quickly to become the president of the Afghan Student Association.[66]

A disclosure in *Ramparts* magazine a decade later would reveal the CIA's sponsorship of that same Afghan Student Association during that period.[67] With no specific mention of Hafizullah Amin, it is known that the CIA targeted Third World foreign students "destined to hold high positions in their home countries in a relatively few years," according to Victor Marchetti in his expose *The CIA and the Cult of Intelligence.*[68] In a few years Hafizullah Amin would fit that profile, leaving Columbia and returning to help Nur Mohammed Taraki in his creation of the leftist, predominantly Ghilzai Pashtun, Khalq (Masses) Party.[69]

Whether Amin was recruited as a CIA double agent at this time to covertly organize opposition to the Red Prince, Daoud, is still a matter of some dispute.[70] But as the 1950s came to a close, Afghanistan entered its most productive and stable period of modern history. Confident that he had finally returned Afghanistan to a "buffer state" status between the two superpowers, Mohammed Daoud bragged to U.S. reporters, "I feel happy when I can light my American cigarette with a Russian match."[71] Assertive and confident in his own rule, successful at remaining officially nonaligned and host to dozens of successful international aid programs, Mohammed Daoud celebrated the fortieth anniversary of Afghan independence by borrowing a chapter from the now legendary King Amanullah. Intentionally provoking religious mullahs, Daoud ordered his ministers' wives unveiled on the reviewing stand, then challenged the religious establishment to show one verse in the Koran that mandated the veil. When the infuriated mullahs protested further, he jailed them.[72] Widely acknowledged for his success at the difficult task of modernization, Daoud's move was deeply resented by the conservative clergy. Although at the peak of his popularity, he faced growing opposition within government and his own royal family to his tyrannical rule.

THE 1960s

The accession of General Mohammad Ayub Khan to lead Pakistan following his 1958 coup d'état was a major development in the fate of Pakistan-Afghanistan relations. An aggressive militarist and Pashtun, Khan's declaration of Pakistan's military might during his first meeting with Afghan Foreign Minister Mohammad Naim (Daoud's brother) enraged Daoud. Ayub Khan's boast that he could, if he wished, "take Kabul within a few hours"[73] reignited the Pashtunistan issue by empowering old tribal rivalries, but this time with far more serious Cold War implications.

On May 1, 1960, Pakistan's cooperation with the United States became the center of a U.S.-Soviet crisis and a major embarrassment to the Eisenhower administration. Since 1956 the United States had operated a huge airfield and secret intelligence facility near Peshawar from where U-2 overflights into the Soviet Union gleaned significant amounts of intelligence data. It was from this base that Francis Gary Powers flew his U-2 and was shot down over the Soviet Union fifteen days before a scheduled summit between the United States and the Soviet Union. The incident proved to be a serious credibility problem for the administration when President Eisenhower first denied—then admitted—complicity.[74] The summit in Paris collapsed when Soviet Premier Nikita Khrushchev walked out following Eisenhower's failure to apologize for the incident.[75] Occurring during an election year, the hoopla proved a boon to the supporters of presidential candidate John F. Kennedy, whose hawkish advisers (including Paul Nitze) sought any opportunity to destabilize U.S.-Soviet relations.[76]

Shortly after the event, Khrushchev informed Pakistan's ambassador at a diplomatic reception that he had drawn a red bullseye around the disputed city of Peshawar, then approached Ayub Khan and his staff and warned, "Don't play with fire, gentlemen."[77]

According to Hassan Abbas, the threat rattled the headstrong Pakistani strongman, but in typical fashion the Pakistanis were quick to shift the blame onto the Soviet KGB and a lowly Afghan "cook" at the base, who somehow "managed to sufficiently tamper with the gadgetry of the ill-fated plane so that when Gary Powers thought that he was flying well outside the Soviet missile range, the delusion was laid to rest with a missile hit."[78]

Discovering how an Afghan cook managed to penetrate a top-secret American spy installation, break into a secure hanger and successfully tamper with what at the time would have been the most sophisticated electronics on the planet without getting caught, would require its own book. But what ruffled the Pakistanis more than the alleged security breach, the shoot-down or even Khrushchev's threat, was the policy of the incoming Kennedy administration.

Convinced that support for Ayub Khan's military machine was a waste of money, Kennedy's advisors changed tack and improved ties to India instead.[79] Taking a page from Afghanistan's book, Pakistan countered by courting Soviet help in oil and gas exploration.[80] To make matters worse, Ayub Khan renewed a policy of aggressive tribal assimilation into the exclusively Pashtun territories of the North-West Frontier Province, a tactic considered by Mohammed Daoud to be a direct attack on Pashtun independence.[81] Afghan-Pakistani relations turned even more sour during this period when Pakistan openly claimed that Afghanistan was subverting its control of Pashtun tribal areas. Closing their consulates in Afghanistan, Pakistan demanded that Afghanistan do the same.

Duly antagonized, between September 1960 and May 1961 Daoud twice sent Afghan troops dressed as tribesmen into Pakistan to assist pro-Pashtunistan groups and twice the Afghans were repelled.[82] In retaliation Khan used American-supplied F-86 jet fighters, and for a time seized Afghan territory. Escalating the conflict on September 6, 1961, Afghanistan closed the border and severed diplomatic relations.[83]

With neither side capable of victory or willing to compromise, tensions grew, with the Soviets reaping a propaganda bonanza. Afghan farm products destined for market enjoyed unlimited support, with the Russians "airlifting almost all the entire fruit crop to the Soviet Union."[84] Unable to cross the border, American equipment and supplies destined for use on U.S. projects rusted at Pakistan's docks, further marginalizing American influence as German, Japanese and UN aid arrived through Europe and Siberia via transit agreement with the Soviet Union.[85]

Tensions increased further with China's 1962 invasion of northern India, highlighting to the world the growing Sino-Soviet split. Facing the growth of Chinese-supported Maoist political parties on their borders and intent on securing their southern border from guerrilla attack, the Soviet leadership had more reason than ever to value Afghan friendship.

Concerned with this sudden growth of Soviet influence and seemingly more aware of Afghan sensibilities, the new Kennedy administration offered the services of Livingston T. Merchant (ambassador to Canada) as special envoy, but neither side found cause to soften their position. Nor did a personal appeal by the shah of Iran in a visit to both capitals in the summer of 1962 move either Daoud or Ayub Khan from their rigid stand.[86]

Despite the extensive Soviet assistance, pressure was mounting on Daoud. His autocratic style and unyielding position on the Durand Line had created mounting political problems while the economic implications were staggering. Instead of forcing Pakistan to change its approach to Pashtunistan, Daoud's policies had only succeeded in further exposing Afghanistan's economy to Pakistan's diplomatic whims while making Afghanistan's demands appear unreasonable. That March of 1963, with the standoff approaching two years, concern over Daoud's foreign policy reached a consensus within Afghanistan's ruling elite.[87] Something had to change.

It did, as King Zahir Shah—content up until then to act as a figurehead—asserted his rule. According to Ghaus, influential Afghans believed that in additional to harming the Afghan economy, the prolonged border closing did nothing to help the Pashtunistan issue, while it did increase Afghan dependence on the Soviet Union and—worst of all—could have been viewed as a forfeiting of existing routes through Pakistan.[88] Added to this was the long-standing discomfort within ruling circles of his autocratic style and unwillingness to advance a multi-party democracy. Without broad support, Daoud bowed to the internal pressure. Asking Daoud to step down as prime minister, Zahir Shah appointed a committee to draft a new constitution while renewing a pledge to make Afghanistan a more democratic society. Made public on March 9, 1963, Daoud's resignation ended an era of unrivaled growth and expansion for Afghanistan in all areas of public administration, including public infrastructure, health care, education and commerce.[89] But most lasting and perhaps troublesome to his Cold War–era detractors in the United States, Iran, and Pakistan was his modernization of the Afghan armed forces through Soviet assistance. By 1978 this program would see 3,725 military personnel sent to the Soviet Union for military training and political indoctrination.[90] This factor alone would eventually play a decisive role in Afghanistan's future, as King Zahir Shah's liberal rule opened the way for long-suppressed Islamic and socialist political parties to force political change—backed respectively by a radicalized Soviet-trained military and Saudi-financed extremists.[91]

Although a major factor in opening Afghanistan to Soviet influence, Daoud's legacy was largely misunderstood in the West, a victim of the simple-minded, Manichean approach to foreign policy forged by America's national security managers. John K . Cooley writes, "Western commentators—few of whom really understood Afghan politics or society then, nor understood their complexities later on, when the West became embroiled in its proxy war with the Russians—wrongly called Daoud 'the Red Prince.' They believed, though the Soviets themselves did not, that the support of [leftist] PDPA (People's Democratic Party of Afghanistan) elements in his successful bid for power made him automatically a tool or a satellite of Moscow."[92]

AFGHANISTAN'S "EXPERIENCE" WITH DEMOCRACY

With "Soviet-leaning" Mohammed Daoud gone and King Zahir Shah implementing a new constitution in 1964, American concerns over Afghanistan's direction lessened. Despite Soviet inroads under Prince Daoud, Washington believed, writes Cooley, that "the combination of government vigilance, the traditional dislike for Russians in Central Asia for what they had done to the Muslim religion north of the Amu Darya, and the upward mobility within the Afghan system were assumed to reduce or even eliminate any Marxist pressures."[93] Despite this, U.S. policy managers were wary of the king's independence from American decision making, quietly determining that he would not be allowed to play the United States against the Soviet Union the way his predecessors had played the British.

Unconvinced of the country's strategic value, Washington relied on the Peace Corps, American University Field Services, and USAID to shoulder American interests, building schools while continuing to target prospective exchange students.[94]

As Afghanistan's population went through changes over the course of the 1960s through mass education, unforeseen tensions within Afghan political life grew out of class, ethnic and religious divisions. On the one extreme was the growing class of foreign-educated elite, running the nation's bureaucracy. On the other were the radical Islamists, increasingly frustrated at the growing modernization of Afghan life. In between were the officer corps, drawn from the wealthier Afghan families and increasingly radicalized by Soviet influence, and the ethnic minorities—Hazara, Tajik, Turkmen and Uzbek, each with its own culture and history, and each with its own political agenda. Finally there were the ethnic Pashtuns themselves, whose familial alliance with their fellow tribespeople in Pakistan's North-West Frontier Province was a constant source of destabilization and whose cultural dominance was a perpetual irritant to the minorities.

Signing the new constitution in 1964, King Zahir Shah reemphasized the role of these ethnic minorities as well as the importance of women's rights to the growth of the Afghan nation.[95] In an effort to display political reform, the new constitution barred members of the royal family from politics, a provision directed specifically at Prince Daoud.[96] But with a near 90 percent illiteracy rate and a narrow political base of support, Zahir Shah's plans for a parliamentary democracy faced impossible odds.

Nevertheless, when Afghanistan's new parliament formed on January 1, 1965, it gave great hope to advocates of democratic change, with women gaining numerous seats.[97] That same year the People's Democratic Party of Afghanistan was formed by seven prominent reform advocates, including Nur Mohammad Taraki, Babrak Karmal, and Taher Badakhshi. Although viewed as bourgeois by the prevailing authority on the matter, the Soviet Union, the loose coalition of forces—some doctrinaire Marxist, some Maoist, some simply pro-monarchy reformist—would be viewed by the Americans with an eye on its most radical elements and regarded as "communist."[98]

But the workings of the PDPA immediately revealed deep divisions between its major factions—Khalq (the Masses), led by Nur Mohammed Taraki and Hafizullah Amin, and Parcham (Banner), led by Babrak Karmal, with Taher Badakhshi leaving within a year to form his own Maoist party, Setam-i Melli (Against National Oppression).[99]

Violently opposed to the Pashtun-nationalist-dominated PDPA, the Maoists—including the larger faction known as Shola-e-Jawid (Eternal Flame)—provided a common political milieu for Afghanistan's minority Shia population and Iran's *majority* Shia population, as well as a pipeline for a shared Chinese-Iranian intelligence connection to the Tajik and Hazara tribal areas of eastern and northern Afghanistan.[100]

Likewise Khalq and Parcham each served as an avenue for Soviet intelligence, though hardly a source of reliable or predictable influence on the political process. As the proponents of a conservative socialist approach more in keeping with Moscow's wishes, Parcham was composed mostly of Soviet-educated army officers, westernized intellectuals, and bureaucrats, while Khalq's leadership reflected the more broad-based and poor, Pashtun peasant class. The dissension and especially personal rivalry between the two would eventually break out into the open, with Karmal breaking from Taraki and forming an alliance with ousted Prince Daoud.[101]

Bradsher writes, "While Parcham took a pragmatic line of seeking temporary alliances on the long road to Communism, Khalq favored class struggle and a hard line. Two other factions appeared. One named for the newspaper *Shu'la-yi-Jawed* ("Eternal Flame"), was openly inspired by the Cultural Revolution then under way in China. The other was *Setem-i-Melli* ("Against National Oppression"). It was led by Badakhshi from the original PDPA central committee, who came to represent regional resentment to Pushtun domination, especially Tajiki opposition to it."[102]

Having been a loyal adherent to Daoud, serving in "prestigious and influential posts,"[103] Hafizullah Amin's student organizing and criticism of the king apparently drew the American government's disapproval. Expelled from the United States in 1965, a year before he was to receive his doctorate, he returned to Afghanistan just in time to join Taraki as a student organizer. According to Beverley Male, the reason for Amin's expulsion remained a curiosity even to him, when he claimed in 1979 that the American authorities said he had been summoned by the government of Afghanistan, but in Kabul the government told him it had been the American authorities who'd ousted him.[104] Either way, someone wanted Hafizullah Amin in Kabul and he arrived just in time for the first elections held under the new constitution in August–September 1965. Attached to Nur Mohammed Taraki—the former would-be defector and U.S. embassy translator—Amin soon proved to be a powerful force in building Khalq's political base among Afghanistan's growing student population.[105]

Singling out the communists and particularly Babrak Karmal's Parchamists for setting back the cause of democracy in Afghanistan, Ghaus follows the traditional bipolar American Cold War line, believing the Soviet Union "pressed for the formation of the PDPA as a Soviet outlet in Afghanistan,"[106] to counter an Afghan rapprochement with Iran and the development of a liberal, western-style parliamentary system. But though Taraki visited Moscow at the invitation of the International Department of the Communist Party of the Soviet Union Central Committee *following* the creation of the PDPA, there is no evidence to suggest that Moscow worked with any factions of the PDPA to subvert a western-style democracy. If anything, Moscow strongly advised Taraki to work within the Afghan system to gain political legitimacy for his party while forbidding local KGB agents from making contact with him unless absolutely necessary. According to Soviet KGB defector Vasiliy Mitrokhin, "Taraki should be told that 'because of the relations between our countries and the existing situation in the country, he should follow a moderate liberal-democratic course and gain the support of leftist activists. In this way a base will be made for the development of the democratic movement which will act as a basis for the practical activities of the PDPA. For this it is necessary to also use legal possibilities, in particular the setting up of student and youth organizations, trade unions and so on.'"[107]

Taraki was also advised, Mitrokhin writes, "to be extremely cautious in his party work until the authorities had given permission for the party to act officially,"[108] although—like all other political parties—some aspects of his activities in setting up the party could not avoid being conducted under illegal conditions.

As disdainful of the Afghan Communists as of his former KGB comrades, Mitrokhin paints a vivid picture of the dissension in the PDPA's ranks, with the competition between Taraki and Babrak Karmal evident in Taraki's very first meeting in Moscow. "Taraki then divulged his suspicions about contacts between his deputy Babrak and Afghan counter-intelligence. He based his ideas on the fact that Babrak was the first political prisoner to be freed by the authorities in 1952. The Residency rejected such allegations and considered that these rumors were aimed at discrediting his [Taraki's] rival and bringing division and distrust into the ranks of the PDPA."[109] Nor (according to Mitrokhin) was Parcham's Babrak Karmal immune from spreading rumors, undermining Taraki's reputation and suggesting that his revolutionary ambitions might not be all they seemed. "Taraki and Babrak were totally unable to do their party work together. Babrak accused Taraki of taking bribes, having contacts with Americans, owning four cars, and having 400,000 Afghani deposited in a Pashtu bank. The Residency defended Taraki as it had done previously with Babrak. It viewed him positively and considered him a true and sincere friend of the USSR who co-operated conscientiously [and] observed the rules of secrecy and carried out an assignment in the American embassy."[110]

Attempting to be evenhanded in their dealings with the Afghan Marxists, Moscow's concerns about Taraki's personality emerge early in the Mitrokhin material—illustrating their reluctance to treat him as a qualified Communist leader. "Taraki was noticeably depressed when he was told in August 1968 about the forthcoming conference of Communist Parties in Moscow and the decision not to invite the PDPA. He bitterly remarked that Moscow did not consider him a Communist whereas in Afghanistan everyone without exception called him a Communist. He felt that the Kremlin had insulted the PDPA. In September 1968 the Center asked the Residency to vet Taraki thoroughly using operational technical means."[111]

Failing to make the grade in Moscow, Taraki fell back on the young and dynamic Hafizullah Amin to bolster the ranks of Khalq and organize the party. But as Mitrokhin reveals, his worsening behavior, his resentment, and his choice of the American-educated Amin may have given Moscow even more reason to be suspicious of his judgment.

"But as a person Taraki was a complex and contradictory character. He was painfully vain, often took jokes made about him in the wrong way and enjoyed being given a lot of attention. This became particularly noticeable after his visit to the Soviet Union."[112]

Mitrokhin paints a vivid picture of the runner-up status that Taraki and his Khalq faction would hold for most of their lifetime as a political party, disqualified by Moscow for being Communist wannabes struggling for recognition and doomed to play second fiddle to Babrak Karmal's skillful leadership and brilliant rhetorical style.[113] Openly sympathetic to Amin, Male views Babrak Karmal's willingness to compromise with Zahir Shah's government (by softening Parcham's rhetoric) as aimed intentionally at weakening Taraki.[114] But according to Mitrokhin's KGB archive, Moscow's dissatisfaction with Taraki's wildly revolutionary agenda and his personality flaws left little room for opposing Marxist parties.

Mitrokhin writes, "In his turn Taraki expressed his dissatisfaction with Moscow's delaying tactics and the way it sent books, publications of the Iranian Tudeh Party, and so on. 'If the Soviet comrades consider that the time is not yet ripe in Afghanistan for a party such as the PDPA to be established and function, then it must be disbanded and I must go abroad to India, Syria or Ceylon and undertake literary work.'"[115] Following the split of Khalq and Parcham in 1967, Khalq nearly disappeared from the public arena, overwhelmed by Karmal's decision to work within the king's constitutional framework. Male writes, "So low was its profile in contrast to that of Babrak Karmal and the Parchamites, that Louis Dupree, a seasoned observer of Afghan politics, seemed unaware that Taraki's group existed and regarded *Parcham* as Khalq's successor: surely the effect Karmal had hoped to achieve."[116]

Rarely mentioned in the annals of Afghan history during this period was China's growing influence on the Afghan political scene represented by the Maoist Setam-i Melli and Shola-e-Jawid, ignored entirely by Mohammed

Daoud's deputy foreign minister Ghaus in his *The Fall of Afghanistan*. Male and Bradsher rightly see the rise of Mao's minions as a major political development in Afghanistan, especially in light of the role they would soon play in the worsening of the Sino-Soviet split and Nixon's decision to open relations with China. Male writes, "Like Settem-i-Melli, [Shola-e-Jawid's] politics were radical left but anti-Pashtun. The logic of international politics was such that both tended to be pro-Chinese—China supported Pakistan which opposed 'Pashtunistan.' The intrusion of the Sino-Soviet dispute into the politics of the Afghan left further complicated an already complex situation."[117]

Even more complex—not to mention relevant to future events—was the relationship between Taraki and Amin's Khalq and the Shola-e-Jawid, who on the surface appeared as enemies but apparently found common cause in their growing antipathy toward Parcham and the Soviet Union. Male writes, "Khalq was much less committed to the idea of Pashtunistan than Karmal's Parchamites which represented a common enemy for both. It only required Khalq disillusionment with the USSR for its leaders to turn to Shu'la-yi-Javid as a natural ally and a channel of communication with China and Pakistan. *It appears that such a development occurred in 1979 and was a significant factor in persuading the USSR to intervene in Afghanistan.*"[118]

Following the Treaty of Tehran in 1963, which ended the diplomatic stalemate over trade and access routes through Pakistan, King Zahir Shah succeeded at improving relations with General Mohammad Ayub Khan. Though not resolved, both sides agreed, Dupree writes, "to approach all mutual problems in accordance with international law, and 'to continue to create an atmosphere of good understanding, friendship and mutual trust'"[119] with the strong implication that Pashtunistan would be on the agenda.

Intent on defusing the long-term crisis once and for all, Afghanistan remained strictly neutral, as Pakistan once again entered into war with India over the territory of Kashmir in 1965. Nor did Afghanistan press the Pashtunistan issue publicly, though the king stated that Afghanistan could not drop the issue or completely normalize relations "until the troublesome question of Pashtu-speaking tribesmen could be settled between the two countries."[120]

During the constitutional period of King Zahir Shah's "Experiment in Democracy," relations also warmed between Kabul and Tehran, with the United States and the Soviet Union looking on more or less passively. But where Daoud's controversial reign had produced rapid economic development, economic progress under Zahir Shah languished. By 1969 strikes and demonstrations plagued the economy, with the government closing down both Karmal's Parcham newspaper and the Maoist *Sho'la-yi Jawed* in an effort to contain unrest.[121] By that year radical Islamists had also reemerged as a political factor, especially in the countryside where the farm economy was worsened by a period of prolonged drought.[122] But the nature of the extremist Islamic opposition to the monarchy arising at Kabul University in the late 1960s was far different from the home-grown variety known to previous Afghan monarchs like Amanullah. As noted by Robert Dreyfuss in his *Devil's Game*, throughout the 1960s the pan-Islamic movement known as political Islam had changed the face of Afghanistan's traditional religion.[123] Having fled Afghanistan for mosques in Egypt and Saudi Arabia during Daoud's reign, Afghanistan's leading clerics returned under the king's well-intentioned but ineffectual rule. Educated and radicalized by the Muslim Brotherhood (al-Ikhwan al-Muslimun), which they established in Afghanistan as the Jamaat-i Islami (Islamic Society), they battled and organized—from 1965 until 1972—against a growing Communist influence at Kabul University.[124] Dreyfuss writes, "Although Afghanistan society had always been a conservative, traditional one in which Islam played a central role, the version of Islam that prevailed in the country, at least until the 1960s, was pious but not political. Islam in Afghanistan was a faith and not a sociopolitical credo. But under the influence of outside religious and intellectual forces—especially Egypt's Muslim Brotherhood, Pakistan's Islamic Group, and the international organization of the Brotherhood based in Geneva and led by Said Ramadan—Afghan Islam underwent a critical transformation."[125]

As an ancient crossroads, Afghan Islam had absorbed numerous traits from other faiths and cultures as well as a tolerance for a personalized mystical religious experience virtually unknown to the arid Wahhabist Islam of the Middle East. As a land where the expression of piety and religious tradition were manifested with a prismatic pluralism, Afghanistan was irresistible to Europe's mystical imperialists—a jumping-off spot from which to not only conquer the gateway to India, but the soul of the "World Island" as well. As told by Steve Coll in his best seller *Ghost Wars*, Afghanistan owed its unique spiritual qualities to a number of factors. "As conquerors riding east from Persia and south from Central Asia's steppes gradually established Islam as the dominant faith, and as they returned from stints of occupation in Hindu India, they brought with them eclectic strains of mysticism and saint worship that blended comfortably with Afghan tribalism and clan politics. The emphasis was on loyalty to the local Big Man. The Sufi strain of Islam became prominent in Afghanistan. Sufism taught personal contact with the divine through mystical devotions. Its leaders established orders of the initiated and were worshiped as saints and chieftains. Their elaborately decorated shrines dotted the country and spoke to a celebratory, personalized, ecstatic strain in traditional Afghan Islam."[126]

The radical Islam of the Muslim Brothers returning to Afghanistan from exile in the late 1960s and early 1970s shared none of the "celebratory, personalized and ecstatic" traits of Afghan Islam—nor did it offer itself as a political or economic reform movement. Instead, what reentered Afghanistan following its exile was a violent, antimodernist hybrid (described by French expert Olivier Roy as more akin to the extremist Catholic sect Opus Dei than anything native to Afghanistan)[127] which at first challenged the weakened boundaries of the old patriarchy, then in triumph broke free from traditional limits on violence and clan rivalries.

Key to the success of this new strain of political Islam was a surprising organizational element that would evolve over time into one of the stranger ingredients of the coming Islamic revolution. In a century of fringe movements, twisting allegiances, double agents and secret agendas, the role of Marxist-Leninist political theory has been a guiding light for leftists' politics, but scarcely thought of as a spiritual guidepost for Afghanistan's religious right. Yet the modern founders of radical Islam and particularly the Muslim Brotherhood could lay claim to such a lineage. Inspired by the same rhetoric and the same cause (the overthrow of the state), both Said Ramadan and the prominent Egyptian Islamic revivalist Said Qutb's plan for a reorganization of Islamic society are linked straight to the revolutionary instruction manuals of Marx and Lenin: "Historians have compared Qtub's pamphlet, 'Milestone' to V. I. Lenin's 'What is to be done?' and deals with tactics and strategies that lead to dismantling the nation-state and regrouping the ummah under the laws of Shariah, prescribed by Allah himself. Qtub was to Osama bin Laden what Karl Marx was to Lenin, or justification for dictatorship of the proletariat."[128]

Radicalized during a two-year educational stay in the United States, as the Afghan Hafizullah Amin would be a decade later, Qutb wrote his manifesto, *Signposts*, while imprisoned in Egypt for the attempted assassination of Egyptian President Gamal Abdul Nasser, and it became the basis for Afghanistan's radical transformation. But added to Qutb's revolutionary oratory was a mystical link that transformed Lenin's political credo into a manifesto for holy war. Dreyfuss writes, "[Burhanuddin] Rabbani translated *Signposts* into Dari, the Afghan language of learning. The returning Afghan professors adapted Qutb's Leninist model of a revolutionary party to the local tradition of Sufi brotherhoods."[129]

Linked to the CIA and Britain's MI6 by Swiss intelligence,[130] Qutb and Ramadan's Muslim Brotherhood would take root in Afghanistan through the efforts of Burhanuddin Rabbani and his followers.[131] By the beginning of the new decade their violent revolutionary tactics would consume Kabul University as young radical Islamists, secretly supported by the United States, rose to oppose leftists and communists, secretly supported by the Soviet Union. The most radical opposition to the king's reforms at this time was centered around a handful of professors at Kabul University, Abdurrab Rasul Sayyaf, Burhanuddin Rabbani, and Gholam Mohammad Niyazi, who, according to Dreyfuss, was "a major beneficiary of CIA support through the Asia Foundation."[132] Intent on overthrowing the monarchy and establishing a Muslim caliphate, Rabbani's recruits were both the most ambitious and the most ruthless. Two of his most outstanding followers, the Panjshiri Ahmed Shah Massoud and the Pashtun Gulbuddin Hekmatyar, would go on to become poster boys in the American media for America's secret war against Moscow, as "fiercely religious freedom fighters." But as students at Kabul University in the late sixties, Hekmatyar and

Massoud earned ugly reputations as dangerous fanatics, punishing women with disfigurement and political opponents with beatings and death. As founding members of the Jamaat-i Islami in Afghanistan (Islamic Society), both Massoud and Hekmatyar's followers were known to be violently misogynist—throwing acid in the faces of women who did not wear the veil. An Afghan woman who now resides in the United States describes one such attack at Kabul University that she personally witnessed:

> Before and after my graduation from Kabul University, I was writing and producing History and Teachers Training programs for Kabul Radio. Kabul Radio provided free transportation for its part-time professionals to the radio station, located in Wazir Akbar Khan/Shashdarak part of Kabul, Afghanistan. In one of the summer days between 1968–1970, the radio driver drove me to the University of Kabul to pick up a professor to host one of my programs. I went inside the Faculty of Letters, waited for the professor in the hallway.
>
> In the lounge area there were six or seven students (boys and girls) standing and chatting. I saw another two young men (eighteen or nineteen years of age) entering the lounge from the main entrance. They were holding hands in a very peculiar way as if they were hiding something, together, in between their hands. The item looked like a cough syrup bottle. . . . I [watched as the] the two men approached a very attractive stylish young student who was wearing mini-skirt (above her knees, not too short). Suddenly the two young men passed her by from both sides. This was very unusual and strange. The two men's hands unclenched and then [they] walked away from the young student very fast, exiting from the right side of the lounge, running toward the Faculty of Engineering.
>
> Meanwhile, at the exact time when the two men passed by the young girl, I heard a harrowing scream of a woman, "Oh! God, I am burning, I am burning." We all rushed toward the woman, saw the young woman pointing to her knees and crying. The scene was horrifying. Her skin was peeling off the flesh. I thought her nylons

were ripped and dangling down, in fact it was her skin. The injuries were above and below her knees. The driver heard the commotion, rushed to the lounge. I told him that a student [was] injured. He grabbed the girl, held her in his arms, dashed toward his jeep. He drove the victim with two other friends to the nearest hospital. . . .

I waited for the driver on the road with other students who were discussing the incident. They were saying that the two men were not from the same campus [but] "some politically motivated people [who] target women and [spray] acid on whoever wore short skirts or indecent clothing." The students also said that the two young attackers probably were from the Hezb-i-Ekhwan-el-Muslimeen (the party of the Muslim Brotherhood). They said that Adela, the young victim, was not a member of any political party, because her father was a high-ranking government official. But she was targeted because of her un-Islamic wardrobe.

Later on, I learned from some of the professors that the assailants were Ahmadshah Panjshiri (from Panjshir provice) and Gulbudin Kunduzi (from Kunduz province). At that time people didn't know about the assailants' last names. Up to date, I do not remember if . . . any criminal investigation took place about the incident.

I had not seen the two assailants before nor [did I see] them after the incident. But I . . . vividly remembered the two pairs of eyes of those assailants after twelve years when they became famous for their fights against the invading army of the USSR. I saw their photos all over the world as mujahideen.[133]

That parliamentary election of 1969, communist Babrak Karmal (Parcham) and Hafizullah Amin (Khalq) gained seats, but most moderate liberals and women lost out. Although their organizing activities were technically illegal, western-style political parties also formed during this period, most notably the Afghan Social Democratic Party and the Progressive Democratic Party of former prime minister Mohammad Hashim Maiwandwal. But instead of ensuring the popularity of the Afghan government by broadening the political base through participation, the proliferation of small political parties only worsened the parliamentary deadlock.[134] In only a few years the parliament had come to represent the same old power structure that had kept Afghanistan mired in its old ways. With conservative clerics, landowners, and businessmen dominating, only the organized leftist parties remained as a force for progressive reform. But even in this PDPA leaders Babrak Karmal and Nur Mohammad Taraki could not agree, maintaining the PDPA split along ethnic and ideological lines in violent feuding.[135]

As the experiment in democracy failed to bring about social reform, the country splintered into extremes of religious conservatives and leftists while leaving moderates behind. Faulted for not backing his own initiatives, the king failed to shake up the old order and generate positive economic activity, which weakened the monarchy. Turning to repression, his control of events soon diminished, trapped between the struggle of two extreme ideologies and the interests of three superpowers.

Against this backdrop, the threat of renewed warfare over Kashmir hovered over India and Pakistan.[136] Adding to the pressure was the ongoing Sino-Soviet diplomatic split which saw the Soviets massing forces on the border of China's Xinjiang province.[137] Stagnating economically and politically, Afghanistan ended a decade that had begun with hope for a broad democratic reform faced with a growing internal unrest, the emerging dangers in a changing South Asia, and a mutating Cold War.

Keen to assess whatever openings were available to the United States amid this growing mass of confusion, that year, after gaining the White House, Richard Nixon's national security advisor Henry Kissinger set out to define America's interests around the world in a series of policy statements. Issued in August 1969, the report on Afghanistan reiterated the conventional wisdom, calling for the preservation of Afghan independence, the creation of a viable political and economic system, the prevention of undue Soviet influence, and the improvement of ties with Pakistan and Iran.[138] But in the eyes of the Nixon White House, Afghanistan continued to offer nothing of value as either a trading partner, a route for U.S. trade, or a source of oil or scarce strategic metals. Nor did Afghanistan provide the United States with any significant defense, intelligence, or scientific facilities.

Still, Nixon's geopolitically conscious national security advisor did not allow Afghanistan to fall far from view. A visit by Vice President Spiro Agnew to Kabul in early January 1970 demonstrated that the Afghans were already aware that a major shift in U.S. policy regarding "our possible altered stance with reference to the Chicoms"[139] was in the works. Carbon copied to Kissinger, the memo offered no hint at what that might mean to the growing destabilization in the area, but the implications were clear. Noting that "there is no love lost," for the Chinese, Agnew cited "the sensitive Afghan relationship with Russia, from whom the Afghans receive a very substantial amount of aid."[140] Together with the knowledge that unmet economic expectations were at the root of the public unrest and U.S. financial commitment was falling, there was little the United States could do but be understanding, according to the Afghans.

Pressing Agnew on the Pashtunistan issue, the Afghan king emphasized that it was Pakistan's stubborn resistance to regional cooperation between Iran, Turkey, India, and Afghanistan that was responsible for the region's insecurity, not Afghanistan. And that were it not for "the absolute refusal of the Pakistanis to enter into any economic, or developmental schemes with the India government,"[141] things might have been different.

Unstated in the Agnew memorandum was any reference to the special relationship Pakistan shared with the United States nor of Nixon's unofficial 1969 visit, where he asked Pakistan's new president Yahya Khan to intervene with the Chinese on his behalf. Recalled in an interview for PBS's *American Experience*, former Pakistani foreign secretary Sultan Mohammad Khan revealed that by August 1969 cold warrior Nixon's desire to exploit the Sino-Soviet split was already in play: "He mentioned to Yahya Khan that [he was] thinking of re-establishing contact with China, [saying that it has] 'been almost two decades [since] we broke relations with them and there has been no official contact and when time is right, I'd like to get in touch with you to help us and act as an intermediary in the establishment of relationship.'"

Intended to offset the perceived U.S. loss of credibility resulting from the Vietnam debacle, in retrospect Nixon's decision to play what historians call the "China card," was an ominous turn of events for Afghanistan.

Bordering two superpowers and precariously balanced between the United States and the Soviet Union politically, Afghanistan had little wiggle room for diplomatic maneuvers. With Nixon's eyes on China, Parchamists, Khalqis, Islamists and Maoists protesting in the streets of Kabul, and Pakistan's oppressive president, Yahya Khan, empowered as emissary to Peking by the United States, time seemed to be running out for King Zahir Shah's "Experiment in Democracy."

Afghanistan had escaped the worst of World War II and the U.S.-Soviet Cold War competition that followed it in the 1950s and 1960s, but the Cold War confrontations of the 1970s would bring shocking new realities to the ancient kingdom. Viewed positively by the U.S. embassy, Zahir Shah's weaknesses were nonetheless glaringly apparent, to the point where embassy political officer Charles Dunbar saw him as something of a victim of his own success. Citing his indecision as "the foremost obstacle to economic modernization and indeed, to the development of the sort of system envisaged by the Constitution,"[142] Dunbar recognized that the failure of the king's program resided in his flawed administration of power, not in the overwhelming desire of the population for modernization. In fact, as political officer, Dunbar realized that it was Afghanistan's overwhelming desire for rapid change that undermined the king, not its backward tendencies:

> In the first place, during the seven years of the experiment, Afghans have become acutely conscious, and indeed jealous, of the personal freedoms guaranteed them under the 1964 Constitution. This consciousness has manifested itself in hitherto undreamed-of criticism of the government by members of parliament, students, and the free press. This criticism has done much to shape the course of events since 1963. Many educated Afghans carry the Constitution in their pockets and quote from it extensively, and it is clear that, however much they may criticize the experiment as a royally-inspired charade, they have developed some faith in the document as a guardian of their rights.[143]

Afghanistan's new religious right also had much criticism for the experiment, mainly for the freedoms the constitution *did allow*, specifically those related to encroaching modernity and the liberation of women. As early as that June of 1970, Dunbar had carefully observed the movements of the conservative religious demonstrators in the streets, noting (without reference) in his first paragraph that it was the Asia Foundation–supported Mojadidi family who had spurred the protests: "1) The original demonstrations in Kabul were inspired by the Mojadedi family, probably with tacit support from some elements of the government and the Royal Family. However as the situation developed, the Mojadedis left the field more to the provincial mullahs *whose aim was to set back the clock socially on a wide front* [our emphasis]."[144]

A cool professional, whom we have encountered on numerous occasions over the last three decades, Dunbar offers, in his "Tentative Assessment," a fascinating American perspective on the resurgence of Afghanistan's religious right at a critical moment as well as speculations as to what it could mean to Afghanistan's future.

At first directed at Babrak Karmal's "pro-communist" Parcham newspaper for using a religious term to praise Lenin on the hundredth anniversary of his birth, the protests quickly devolved into an anti-leftist free-for-all with mullahs bemoaning "the spread of 'atheistic communism,' the RGA's [Royal Government of Afghanistan's] soft attitude toward the threat from the left, and the general decay of the moral fiber of the nation."[145] Tiring of that, the mullahs moved on to a more reactionary agenda as the protests wore on, with the speeches dwelling "more on *the need for shielding women from education and exposure to the world outside the harem* [our emphasis] than to Parcham and Lenin."[146]

Comparing the situation to Amanullah, Dunbar held out the possibility that the insurrection could grow but concluded optimistically that "the 1970 religious demonstrations may ultimately come to be regarded as proof of the mettle of the 'new order' introduced into the country forty years ago with the coming of the Yahya Khel [the families of Nadir and Zahir Shah] and refined with the advent of the experiment in democracy."[147]

Ending his diplomatic tour, Dunbar's optimistic but bureaucratically compartmentalized view omitted the impact of American policy designs that would soon see Henry Kissinger secretly jetting off to Beijing as a prelude to Nixon's historic opening to Communist China. Nor did it anticipate that the stagnant economy and the internal pressures created by the king's indecisive leadership would set the stage for a shakeup at the palace. Lastly and most ironically, Dunbar's final observation—that the mullahs' lack of success at generating widespread support throughout the country "served as proof that unswerving devotion on the part of large segments of the population to reactionary religious causes was no longer a given in Afghanistan"[148]—would by the end of the decade be proved wrong, as the most extreme of Afghanistan's religious community would soon be empowered by Dunbar's *own government* to set back the clock socially on a wide front.

During the next two years the king's program fared no better, with the added bad luck of a persistent drought dragging the economy to an even lower performance than usual. The enduring malaise found the government slow to respond and ineffective when they did. As famine set in, starvation spread. By the spring of 1972 more than eighty thousand Afghans and Afghan nomads were estimated to have died. The World Bank and International Monetary Fund claimed that corruption was to blame.[149] A new prime minister educated in Muslim theology in Cairo and international law at Columbia University—Mohammad Moosa Shafiq Kamawi—was appointed that December.[150] But despite a promising six months, opinion inside and outside the royal family had already coalesced against the king. In the words of a confidential State Department research study published in March 1973, "By the end of 1972, after nearly a decade of trial and error, King Zahir's 'experiment' with parliamentary government had reached a standstill."

Citing the lack of central planning, the absence of seniority among ministers and the general chaos in the cabinet, the report placed the blame squarely on Zahir Shah and his unwillingness to share power. With Zahir Shah jockeying with a carefully selected handful of officials to maintain control, the absence of any effective governing mechanisms prevented the government from responding to even the most basic concerns. One analysis by former Kabul University professor Mohammad Hassan Kakar in his book *Afghanistan: The Soviet Invasion and the Afghan Response* cited the paralysis caused by the king's unwillingness to carry out enacted legislation as reason for the government's collapse: "The king's failure to sign the Political Parties Bill, the Municipalities Bill, and the Provincial Councils Bill, all passed by parliament, prevented national, provincial and municipal governments from taking root. The premiers relied on his good will."[151] But goodwill wasn't enough. King Zahir Shah was ill-prepared for the forces merging to confront him. With the Afghan middle class now expanded from a few thousand to approximately a hundred thousand,[152] the king's process alone could not create the institutional or economic changes necessary to meet its growing expectations. Nor could he manage the delicate process of advancing liberal reforms while at the same time containing the rising tide of foreign-based Islamic radicalism.

That spring an incident occurred regarding an American Protestant missionary group and its medical facility, the Noor Eye Clinic. Reported in a February 1973 cable to be "the only Christian edifice in Afghanistan," the chapel on the grounds of the facility had been torn down on direct order from Prime Minister Shafiq. In fact, not only had the building been torn down, the ground underneath had been bulldozed for fear the staff was using underground tunnels to celebrate secret rituals.[153] Initially chastising Shafiq for such rash behavior and its potential for a negative impact on the U.S. public, a follow-up cable from the embassy to the secretary of state that March revealed with alarm that the clinic's American staff had ignited a diplomatic crisis by engaging in "illegal missionary activity" which was "deeper and more serious than we had been led to believe." Rebounding on the embassy, the prime minister was now under heavy political pressure to end not only "the private, Protestant Missionary–supported medical assistance program," but all medical assistance programs, to "assert his independence from the Americans plus his Islamic orthodoxy on this issue in order [to] counter his opponents."[154]

Caught in the embarrassing disclosure of American complicity in a Christian plot, the ambassador was called upon to give his personal guarantee that there would be "NO PROSELYTIZING." Yet, the saga of the Noor clinic continued.

A few months later, the clinic would find itself again at the center of controversy, but this time as a "fortuitous event which could alter Noor's precarious future."[155] On the morning of June 25, Zahir Shah departed suddenly for London for medical attention for an eye injury incurred in a game of volleyball, following a consultation with the clinic's doctor Herb Friesen. Despite the fact that the king's minister of health, Dr. Majid-Seraj, informed an embassy officer that the "injury is not especially serious and should not require surgery,"[156] the King's decision to leave the country, accompanied by his daughter and son-in-law General Abdul Wali, was taken as a sign by his enemies.[157]

Three weeks later, with King Zahir Shah recuperating at a health spa on the island of Ischia in Italy, former prime minister Royal Highness Sardar Mohammad Daoud retook control of the country after a ten-year absence.[158] Addressing the nation over Radio Kabul at 7:40 a.m. on the morning of July 17, he announced that the progress made during his years as prime minister had been shattered by the king's pseudo-democracy, that progress had been choked by anarchy, and that despite all the distortions propagated by the king's government, "the Afghan people and the outside world knew of the total collapse of economic, social, political, and administrative conditions, brought about by the incompetent regime."[159]

Neither Afghanistan's friends nor enemies would disagree. Declassified American documents acknowledge the king's failings, Daoud's popularity, and the nearly unanimous international recognition of his new regime within hours of the coup. With little official resistance from the king's government, by that afternoon Mohammad Daoud had assumed the title of head of state, raised the issue of Pashtunistan, announced that the 1964 constitution was suspended and that a "Central Committee" had been formed to run the country with the intention of creating a republic.[160] Daoud's surprising return after ten years in political limbo was cause enough for American concern. His invocation of the Pashtun issue and revocation of the Helmand River Treaty, together with his choice of partners in the coup, set off alarms in neighboring Pakistan, Iran and, most of all, the CIA. Aided by Babrak Karmal's Soviet-trained Parchamists in the military, Daoud's return to power was immediately assumed by many to have been motivated, if not planned outright, by the Soviet Union—fitting perfectly (in their view) into the Soviets' Cold War schema for world domination. The Afghans, of course, protested.[161]

In a visit with Daoud's sixty-two-year-old brother, Prince Naim, American ambassador Robert G. Neumann speculated openly that the Soviets at least knew about the coup in advance and might have encouraged the move. But Naim was adamant. "Let me speak completely frankly and as one gentleman to another gentleman that the Russians knew nothing more about this in advance than the King."[162]

Cable after cable from the American embassy in Kabul repeated the same theme: "Soviet embassy counselor went out of his way to deny any advance Soviet knowledge of Daoud's coup. Soviets, he insisted had absolutely nothing to do with the coup and were surprised as anyone else when it occurred."[163] Prince Naim even quoted Soviet ambassador Alexander Puzanov as saying to Daoud, "Even I did not know this was coming."[164] But speculation continued. In conversations with Neumann, Dr. Wahed Karem, director general for political affairs, expressed shock that "the talk from abroad, especially Iran, Pakistan and the UK (BBC) [was] that this was a 'RED COUP' and that Afghanistan was now more subject to Soviet direction." Opinion in Pakistan took an especially conspiratorial tone, where a "majority of observers took for granted that coup was [the] result [of] Soviet manipulation and pressure."[165] Going even further, the detailed "View From Quetta" cable cited Pakistani speculation that Soviet general secretary Leonid Brezhnev had ordered the coup after receiving an impression of U.S. war weariness and preoccupation with domestic affairs following a Washington summit, concluding that it was safe to take a major step to bolster the Soviet position in South Asia and Persian Gulf region without the U.S. responding.[166]

Others saw the coup as a countermove by the Russians to a mysterious, new, anti-Soviet "Chinese-Iranian-Pakistani-Arabian peninsula Axis with U.S. support"[167] rising against it. In the end, none of it was true. The Afghans had been telling the truth. The coup was a product of Afghanistan's complex internal dynamics, not the sinister product of the Kremlin's geostrategic planning. As Ghaus explained, "The leftist complexion of the Central Committee generated speculation that Mohammed

Daoud was only a figurehead used by the Communists in their ascension to power. The reality, however, was quite different. He was, in fact, the one who had masterfully used them to gain control of the country."[168]

But the reality mattered little. By Cold War definition, the coup automatically became a self-fulling prophecy, easily fitting the mantle "Soviet inspired." Daoud had not been the only member of the royal family to realize that the constitutional monarchy could not survive nor was he the only former prime minister plotting to overthrow the king.[169] A situation report from the American ambassador hints strongly that the United States itself may have played a role in the king's removal, with Neumann suggesting that the United States could not stall the recognition of Daoud's government for long, fearing the "*tie to the London meeting will dawn on Afghans* [authors'emphasis] and we shall lose initial momentum we have gained—Daoud is a man who suspects quickly."[170]

As recalled by longtime Afghan expert Selig Harrison, although intended by Daoud to return Afghanistan to economic if not political health, the coup instead opened Afghanistan to the cruel realities of the twentieth century and the vortex of Cold War rivalries then massing in the region: "Once Daoud ousted the King and established his shaky new republic, however, Kabul rapidly became a Cold War political battleground. As factionalism, corruption, and political uncertainty grew, externally backed forces began to jockey for position in preparation for the power struggle expected to follow the elderly Daoud's death."[171]

A CIA report listed the Shah's concerns. "Before the coup, the Shah of Iran was already concerned about Soviet influence in Afghanistan. Daoud's cordial relations with the USSR may jeopardize the ratification of a pending treaty . . . as well as the access to road and port facilities that the Shah has promised to Afghanistan. The Shah is likely to view any threat to Pakistan's unity as a threat to Iran."[172]

Well aware that Pakistan tended to embellish its intelligence on Afghanistan to suit its needs, the reporting American embassy officer in Quetta noted, "[S]ome of my contacts exaggerated their fear of the Soviet hand in [the] Afghan coup for my benefit in order to push [the] case for stronger U.S. support for countries in this region threatened by alleged

Soviet machinations."[173] Even two weeks after the coup, the embassy in Islamabad was still trying to sort fact from fiction.

"Comment: As with other cases in which PAK officials profess to see Soviet machinations directed against them, difficult to tell how completely PAKS believe their own assertions. In this instance, little doubt that most PAKS actually do see Soviet hand in Daoud's coup. At same time, seems equally apparent that they are consciously stressing this point in talks with U.S. officials in hopes of impressing USG with their need for material support."[174]

Regardless of the veracity of the claims or apparent American concerns, the momentary uncertainty enabled the Pakistanis to carry their program forward. Acting under Pakistan's new prime minister, Zulfikar Ali Bhutto, Major General Naseerullah Khan Babar, governor of Pakistan's North-West Frontier Province, used the opportunity to activate Afghanistan's Arab-trained extremist cells already in place. As told by Lutz Kleveman in his 2004 book, *The New Great Game: Blood and Oil in Central Asia*:

> Babar first meddled in Afghan affairs in 1973, after Mohammed Daoud had overthrown his cousin King Zahir Shah in Kabul and established a left-leaning, anti-Islamic regime. With calls for a Great Pashtunistan growing louder once again, the Daoud regime was potentially dangerous to Pakistan. In an effort to destabilize it, Babar, who was then governor of NWFP, brought Afghan Islamist Professor Burhanuddin Rabbani and two of his most outstanding students, Ahmed Shah Massoud and Gulbuddin Hekmatyar, to Peshawar. With the knowledge of only a handful of conspirators, including then-president Zulfiqar Ali Bhutto, Babar set up secret military camps to train young men and several dozen other Afghans as guerrilla fighters. The curriculum for Massoud and Hekmatyar, then still friends, included the use of assault rifles and battle tactics. Babar then sent the talented Massoud to the Panjshir valley for a bloody partisan attack on Afghan government forces. Daoud got the message and became more accommodating.
>
> A triumphant Babar then secretly took his young mujahideen

> to Islamabad and introduced them to the U.S. ambassador, and a successful yet ultimately tragic alliance was born. After the Soviet invasion of Afghanistan in 1979, the Americans knew exactly whom to send into battle against the Red Army.[175]

The decision to support Bhutto's covert action campaign against Daoud was a fateful decision for the United States and Afghanistan, in effect renouncing the "experiment in democracy," while turning the clock back forty years on direct American and western efforts to help modernize the ancient kingdom. Long the hoped-for salvation to Afghanistan's political and social backwardness for generations of Afghan leaders, the U.S.-supported campaign to destabilize Daoud's shaky new regime empowered Afghanistan's most antidemocratic elements at the moment it could least afford it. By doing so it set in motion a series of events that would eventually demolish the country's embryonic infrastructure and political aspirations, while providing the Pakistanis with the opportunity to resuscitate Britain's hoary "Forward Policy" to make it work.

After one hundred years of imperial pressure, begun under the British, to break Kabul's control of the key passageway from India to Eurasia, this had finally been realized under American guidance, hidden under the cover of the Cold War.

Cordovez and Harrison write, "The coup created an unprecedented vacuum in Kabul, where the monarchy had traditionally provided the only focus of legitimate authority for a society divided along tribal, ethnic, and religious lines. Moreover it abruptly upset the uneasy equilibrium between the West and the Soviet Union that had prevailed in Afghanistan throughout the Cold War."[176]

Seizing the opportunity to fill the "unprecedented vacuum"[177] left by Daoud's delegitimizing of the Afghan monarchy, by that fall Babar's plan for destabilization had evolved into a full-fledged conspiracy to overthrow Daoud's republic and replace it with an Islamist, Pakistan-friendly regime. According to Bradsher in his updated 1999 analysis, the Islamists had also recruited members inside the military beginning in 1972 and at the onset of Daoud's action initiated their plan: "Massoud said that two days after

Daoud's coup he and other Muslim Youths began contacting military officers to try to organize their own coup. When their efforts were discovered, five persons were killed in the first publicly acknowledged political executions in Afghanistan in more than forty years."[178] Met by stiff resistance, Massoud, Hekmatyar, and reportedly twenty of their followers fled to Pakistan. Welcomed by Bhutto, trained by Naseerullah Babar, and reportedly supported by the CIA, they were soon joined by up to five thousand recruits, fulfilling the dream of a pan-Islamic jihad long envisioned by both British and German holy warriors of a previous era.[179]

In the face of such pressures Daoud moved quickly and secretly to assemble his government and consolidate power by isolating leftists—immediately assigning the Parchamists to rural posts or distant diplomatic missions.[180] Some observers attributed his sudden anti-leftist moves to Babar's aggression on the NWFP.[181] Others considered it a repetition of Daoud's old tricks.[182] Many saw it as a combination of both.[183] Whatever the reason, within six months of Daoud's coup, Babrak Karmal and Parcham were in rapid decline. Instead of having an influence upon government policy, Parcham's ideology made them immediately suspect within Daoud's inner circle as well as scapegoats for the outside pressure the government was getting.[184] Neither did Khalq waste the opportunity to capitalize on Parcham's ill favor, at one point offering to serve up loyal Khalqis to replace corrupt Parchamists. In an effort to distance himself from any further identification with the left, Daoud proclaimed in a speech in late February 1974 that his government had no connection with any political faction, group or movement.[185] The official report, titled "National Interests above Every Thought, Ideology," made it clear. As he had stressed in the 1950s, Daoud's major concern was for building the Afghan nation. In the bipolar Cold War world of 1953 he had aligned with the USSR to advance Afghanistan's security and independence after making numerous failed overtures to the United States.[186] In the bipolar Cold War world of 1974, he would be perceived as moving in the opposite direction. But within the perception of Afghan reality and the reality itself were a world of subtle differences. His plan came together slowly and in fits and starts, choosing bits and pieces of the radical PDPA program and discarding others. With the coup planned for fall 1973, the King's volleyball accident and his subsequent U.S.-recommended departure for London had caused the small contingent of communist plotters in the military to act spontaneously, guaranteeing surprise, but leaving their small faction without a workable post-coup plan for helping Daoud organize a government.

Politically wedded to the Parchamists, scorned by the Khalqis, and isolated as well from the numerous moderate political parties that had formed over the constitutional period, neither time nor circumstance were on Daoud's side. More importantly, the political climate had changed in the ten years of his exile.

Daoud's predicament was not lost on U.S. Secretary of State William Rogers. Seeing U.S. aid as a bargaining chip, he instructed the Kabul embassy on how to leverage Daoud's tenuous status against Russia, knowing that the United States had a lot of cards to play: "One assumption of these tactical ideas, on which we are asking your comments, is that Daoud will recognize that he needs us more than we need him, that he will therefore ask us to stay on our terms, rather than accept our continuing presence on his terms, a strategy which he used so successfully in the 1950s. We believe that Daoud will wish not to be forced into position of greater reliance on USSR in a period when Afghanistan is faced with increased suspicions from other neighbors."[187]

One neighbor by whom Daoud was held in the utmost suspicion was Iran, the primary beneficiary of the Nixon-Kissinger strategy in South Asia. Arming the shah with the highest-tech military weaponry had become a strange passion, mixing geopolitics, slick salesmanship and old-fashioned Yankee boondoggle. By 1973 Iran had already contracted to buy $2 billion in weapons, the biggest arms deal ever to date, including 175 jet fighters and 500 helicopters, as well as a wide variety of guided missiles.[188] According to Anthony Sampson in his 1977 exposé, *The Arms Bazaar*, the United States was supplying Iran with a virtual orgy of destruction, unparalleled in history and unregulated by any policy, agency or jurisdiction: "It was the first time that any non-industrial country had been allowed to reach the same level as the United States in the 'state of the art.' There had been no major review beforehand and Nixon's decision was passed to the Pentagon with no chance to revise it. It opened the way for the Shah's next massive expansion and thereafter (as one Pentagon official explained to me) the Pentagon had difficulty in maintaining any logical policy towards Iran."[189]

By 1974 the Pentagon was shipping nearly half the total of worldwide U.S. military exports to Iran. Composed of virtually any conventional arms it wanted, the deal was negotiated personally and privately by Nixon, Kissinger and the shah himself, while the U.S. undersecretary for the Middle East, Joseph Sisco, was left waiting in his hotel room alone.[190]

Daoud viewed the shah's excess with the same disdain he reserved for his cousin, King Zahir Shah, anticipating his future more accurately than most American observers were willing to admit at the time: "Daoud and his people are suspicious of Iran and the Shah. . . . Influenced by their recent coup experience they transfer it, only too readily, to an analysis of Iran, preferring to see the shah as an unpopular, power driven ruler (Wahid Abdullah, deputy Foreign Minister who is more passionate than others but may therefore reflect real underlying sentiments, calls the Shah a 'MADMAN') who will soon share the fate of Zahir Shah, if not worse. This may be an extreme view but it is shared by some."[191]

Seeing his own country as the locus of strategic importance and Reza Shah Pahlavi as mad for believing otherwise, Daoud's suspicion did not prevent him from being drawn into Tehran's web of intrigue or its vast oil-fed spending spree. Encouraged by the Americans, Iran extended forty million dollars in low-interest credits in 1974 as part of a promised ten-year two-billion-dollar aid package. A proposed rail and highway link to the Persian Gulf also promised to obviate the need for transit routes through the Soviet Union.[192] But the shah's largesse disguised a hidden agenda. While publicly endorsing a policy of cooperation and friendship with Daoud, Iran was privately engaged in a massive covert operation against him that linked the intelligence agencies of a half dozen countries in a grand scheme to undermine the Muslim underbelly of the Soviet Union. Referred to earlier in U.S. cables as the "Chinese-Iranian-Pakistani-Arabian peninsula Axis: Supported by the United States," the ad-hoc consortium of intelligence agencies of these nations acted on three separate occasions in Daoud's first year to overthrow him, coordinating uprisings and coup attempts through the shah's secret police (SAVAK), Pakistan's Inter-Services Intelligence agency (ISI), and the CIA.[193]

Cordoverz and Harrison write, "Among the less visible, subterranean aspects of the Shah's offensive was expanded activity by his intelligence agency SAVAK, which attempted to challenge the well-established KGB. Covert operatives from Saudi Arabia, Pakistan, India, China, and a variety of Persian Gulf and Middle Eastern countries also filtered into the Afghan capital during the years after 1973."[194]

Viewed "proudly as an example of Iranian-American cooperation," the operation brought SAVAK and the CIA together in a campaign of destabilization and collaboration, with SAVAK funneling American communications gear, money and weapons to the numerous right-wing Afghan extremists.[195] Linked to the Cairo-based Muslim Brotherhood and the Wahhabist Muslim World League, a well-financed Arab invasion soon flooded Kabul, as well, with Saudi Arabia's newly acquired oil money and right-wing Islamic orthodoxy. "As oil profits skyrocketed, emissaries from these newly affluent Arab fundamentalist groups arrived on the Afghan scene with bulging bankrolls. Like SAVAK, they hired informers who attempted to identify Communist sympathizers throughout the Afghan government and armed forces."[196]

Unable to sustain any consistent momentum for change under these influences, Daoud and his government drifted into an Iranian embrace. Now clearly obsessed with the extent of the communist influence in the military, by early 1974 Daoud had set up alternate training programs with India and Egypt, and by July had removed up to two hundred Soviet-trained officers.[197] Later he would agree to a small U.S.–sponsored officer training program, as well.[198] Once expert at maneuvering the intricacies of Afghan tribal and ethnic politics, Daoud's drift to the right revealed a dangerous uncertainty. As he rejected dialogue with his opponents, the numerous plots hatched against him were brutally crushed. An attempted coup by former prime minister Maiwandal resulted in Maiwandal's allegedly accidental death from torture following his arrest.[199] In his late sixties, alienated from the monarchists, progressives, leftists and fundamentalists, pressed for economic reform by the burgeoning middle class, the aging autocrat was no match for the emerging storm he had taken on. Retreating from issues he once championed—Pashtunistan and opposition to the unpopular Helmand River Treaty—he soon lost the support of the nationalists. Returning to the 1950s policy of state ownership and strict government control over business, he alienated the private sector.[200]

Criticized by both left and right, and battered by rising dissent, in 1975 Daoud pledged to bring the country together with the creation of his own political party, the National Revolutionary Party. But his decision that year to break completely from Parcham and his subsequent demand that both Parcham and Khalq disband and join his party, reverberated from Kabul to Moscow. Content to "look the other way," when it came to Daoud's treatment of the fractious Afghan communist parties, Daoud's newfound attraction to Iran and Arab influence worried Moscow. "Daoud's decision to break with the Parchamites, coupled with his pro-Tehran drift, provoked a significant change in Soviet policy toward the Afghan communist movement during 1976. Until then, Moscow had shown little concern over the debilitating Parcham-Khalq split. . . . As the year progressed, however, the Soviet line began to change."[201]

Already weakened by Daoud's purges, Parcham withered under the new arrangement while Khalq grew. In the years following the 1973 coup, Amin's stepped-up recruitment of military officers gave Khalq two to three times the superiority in key positions, while defectors from Parcham swelled the numbers further. Total estimates of both factions vary widely.[202] Having favored the Parcham-Daoud alliance initially, by 1976 the Soviet Union was ready to reconsider. Devastated by the loss of Middle East ally Egypt in 1972, and, according to Bradsher actually on the decline in overall Third World influence,[203] Moscow finally moved to force Khalq and Parcham together. In June of that year, the Iraqi Communist Party newspaper *Tariq Al-Shaab*[204] called for communist unity in Afghanistan, agreeing to recognize Taraki as the leader of the unified movement.

Certainly the least favored of the two communist leaders, Moscow's belated acknowledgment of Taraki owed as much to the rising star of Hafizullah Amin as it did to the failed efforts of Babrak Karmal to develop a working relationship with Daoud.[205] Karmal and his Parchamites had been Moscow's favorite all along, socially upper-class, Persian-influenced and urbane.[206] In fact Parcham shared so much in common with the royal family, including family ties, that the Khalqis referred to them as the "Royal Communist Party."[207]

Ironically, the Khalqis were very much the new kind of Afghan citizen the monarchy had hoped to create with its progressive educational policies and political reform movement: stubborn, independent and nationalistic. According to Harrison, "the Khalqis represented the rising, newly educated, lower-middle-class Pushtuns from small towns and rural areas who not only wanted Pushtun influence to be dominant inside Afghanistan but also favored active efforts to reclaim the lost territories."[208]

Clearly the most dynamic of the leftist parties, the politically volatile Khalq was still feared by Moscow leaders, who viewed them as "too radical, too headstrong and too unpredictable." At the center of Moscow's concern lay Taraki's right-hand man, Hafizullah Amin. One important factor, usually ignored or disregarded in the U.S. effort to package the Afghan conflict in black-and-white terms, was the competition between Soviet intelligence forces and the confused, contradictory, and purely Byzantine results that followed. In Afghanistan, this competition pitted the Soviet military intelligence unit of the Glavnoye Razvedyvatelnoye Upravleniye—Main Intelligence Directorate (GRU)—against the Komitet Gosudarstvennoi Bezopasnosti—Committee for State Security (KGB). Born during the Bolshevik era and tasked with political as well as intelligence responsibilities, the two services had been rivals since their inception. Founded by Felix Dzerzhinsky in 1917, the KGB (originally known as the Cheka) was responsible for internal and external security, making it a kind of combined CIA and FBI.[209] Crushing internal political dissent, the KGB was responsible for maintaining an ideologically pure, single-party system inside the Soviet Union as well as recruiting ideologically sympathetic candidates in the intelligence services of other countries.[210] So effective was the KGB at undermining dissent and protecting the goals of the Bolshevik revolution throughout the 1920s and '30s that Nazi theoreticians Joseph Goebbels, Rudolph Hess and Heinrich Himmler took on the KGB as the model for their own secret state police organization known as Geheime Staatspolizei, the Gestapo.[211]

The GRU was an equally powerful but even more secretive organization in charge of military intelligence. Founded by Lenin himself in 1918 as a check on both the Communist Party and the Cheka, the GRU acted alternately as an overt and covert force, advising allies and spying on the military capacities of foreign governments through human spies (HUMINT) and signals intelligence (SIGINT), while operating a special branch of elite shock troops known as Spetsnaz.[212] So powerful was the GRU that the general secretary of the Communist Party could not enter GRU headquarters without submitting to a security check.[213]

The Moscow-brokered marriage of Khalq and Parcham in 1977 brought both services into direct competition for the Afghan left. Establishing a formal relationship with the leadership of each faction, over the next two and a half years they would play a direct role in the events leading up to the Soviet invasion. Assigned to assist and advise, the two rival intelligence services quickly came to play favorites in the partisan feuding, with the GRU creating its own exclusive spy network in the military and the KGB doing likewise with the PDPA's civilian leadership.[214] Unknown to both, however, were the doings of Hafizullah Amin. Maintaining his own network of agents within the military despite the merger of the Khalq and Parcham, Amin's unsupervised operation proved increasingly problematic from Moscow's perspective. "Amin's freewheeling style, together with the fact that he had gone to the United States twice for postgraduate studies financed by U.S. aid grants, made him suspect in the eyes of the GRU and KGB alike."[215] His New York–based Afghan Student Association, of which he was national president, had been exposed as a CIA front by *Ramparts* magazine as a result of receiving funds from the CIA-supported American Friends of the Middle East—an organization founded by Cornelius Van H. Engert, Franklin Roosevelt's wartime envoy to Kabul.[216] Amin's Teacher Training School operated largely on funds from a Columbia University aid project,[217] which legendary Afghan expert Louis Dupree recalled operated as a front for the CIA. According to a Harrison interview with Dupree, Amin knew the CIA men well: "He took American money for his school and then, behind their backs, recruited the brightest teachers for the Communist Party. But you can imagine how it all looked to the Russians."[218]

Knowing that Taraki did not fit the Soviet mold of approved communist leadership and that Amin maintained strong ties to the U.S. embassy must have made Amin's organizing of communists look very strange indeed. Added to that was the concern of Daoud himself, who, though clearly bending under the strains of leadership, by 1977 took issue with the United States over its connections to the Marxists. Bradsher writes, "As he aged and tired Daoud seemed to become more suspicious, choking effective government by insisting upon personally approving too wide a range of matters. He saw plots everywhere, probably rightly. He asked—virtually ordered—the American embassy to quit keeping contacts with leftists, just as the shah had halted U.S. intelligence contacts with the religious opposition that was to overthrow him."[219]

With Amin operating out of sight of the GRU and KGB, and with American intelligence maintaining such open contact with the so-called communists that Daoud had to demand it be stopped, there was little wonder at Moscow's desire to rein in Kabul's bickering Marxists before they eliminated each other or even Daoud.

Though Moscow was troubled by Daoud's drift toward Tehran, by 1977 the shah's effort to woo Afghanistan into its military camp had clearly run its course. As foreseen by Daoud's people at the outset, the shah's dreams of grandeur had exhausted Tehran's treasury while severely damaging his credibility in the region. By the end of that year, the reality of the shah's failure to meet his obligations was as obvious to Daoud as was the reality of Afghanistan's reliance on the Soviet Union.

Bradsher writes, "Although the question of Iranian political police—SAVAK—operations in Afghanistan would arise later, the fact was that by 1977 any Soviet fears of Iran's cutting Afghanistan away from Soviet influence should have been waning. The Soviet bloc ended up putting far more aid into Afghanistan during the Daoud presidency than the combined total of Iran, other Muslim countries, and the West."[220]

Despite Daoud's interdict on American contact with the Afghan left (to which Bradsher maintains the Americans did not wholly comply), he placed no restrictions on Soviet contacts with Afghanistan's leftists during this period, in a rather clear sign that he trusted the motives of Soviet state security more than his own regarding police plots and coup attempts. But that was soon to end. Behind Daoud's decision may have been concern for the structure of his new constitution that established his National Revolutionary Party as the sole political party in Afghanistan.[221] Intended to address long-standing problems, Daoud's cabinet instead represented the worst of Afghanistan's old system, packed, writes Bradsher, "with his old friends and their sons, with royal hangers-on, people incapable of providing fresh dynamism for a still cumbersome, inefficient administration, people with vested interests that prohibited a meaningful implementation of a promised land reform program."[222]

One old friend who was appointed minister of the interior was Qadir Nuristani. A tough anticommunist hard-liner, Nuristani's crackdown on the left produced predictable results, with the Soviets acting on Daoud's behalf in early 1977 to stop an angry Amin from staging a coup. Amidst this, an official visit by Daoud to Moscow that spring to renew the Soviet Union's commitment to Afghan development produced a heated confrontation with General Secretary Brezhnev. Reprimanded sharply by the increasingly ill and incoherent Brezhnev for allowing a small U.S. team to install seismic and satellite equipment in northern Afghanistan,[223] the increasingly senescent Daoud responded angrily: "[W]e will never allow you to dictate to us how to run our country and whom to employ in Afghanistan. How and where we employ the foreign experts will remain the exclusive prerogative of the Afghan state. Afghanistan shall remain poor, if necessary, but free in its acts and decisions."[224]

According to Ghaus, "Nothing like Brezhnev's words to Daoud had ever been heard in any high-level Russo-Afghan meeting. It was obviously an intentional outburst by which Brezhnev had wanted to demonstrate the Soviet annoyance with the new trends in Daoud's domestic and external policies."[225]

Although viewed by some as *the* pivotal moment that drove the Russians to find a communist alternative to Daoud's increasingly erratic behavior, the truth is far more complex. Intentional or not, the incident had little impact on the immediate relationship between Kabul and Moscow. The very next day representatives of both countries signed an economic agreement that extended Afghan-Russian cooperation for twelve more years while expanding Russian technical assistance into numerous fields. Upon return, Afghanistan's official relations with Moscow continued as they had before, with Daoud expressing bewilderment at Moscow's fears. Yet for all parties, both internal and external, subterranean events were taking on a life of their own. That July saw the formal union of Khalq and Parcham in a move shepherded by the KGB. Also that July, Prime Minister Zulfikar Ali Bhutto of Pakistan was overthrown in a midnight coup by his trusted army chief of staff, General Mohammad Zia-ul-Haq, a man bent on opening Central Asia to the pan-Islamic Muslim Brotherhood and advancing the cause of building an Islamic nuclear weapon.[226]

By the end of 1977, Daoud's deteriorating political position resulted in an increasing number of desperate measures that further undermined his rule. Repulsed by his descent into repression and murder, that November his brother Mohammed Naim and six of his cabinet members briefly resigned in protest.[227] With few allies inside the government, Daoud now found himself trapped in a political bind not uncommon to prior Afghan rulers. But where Amanullah, Nadir Shah and Abdur Rahman Khan had labored in obscurity between Russian and British empires, the Cold War was about to prove a far more daunting enemy than Afghanistan had ever faced.

PART II

AFGHANISTAN FROM THE 1970S TO 2001

6.

Team-B

The Vietnam War had proved an economic, strategic and political watershed for the United States with the unintended consequence of driving American Cold War foreign policy away from aggressive competition and confrontation with the Soviet Union to a policy of détente and arms limitation. By the time of the bicentennial celebration of the United States in 1976, the debate within Washington's national security bureaucracy raged over whether that policy should continue and, if not, where American policy should be directed next. Coming on top of the Watergate scandal and the Arab oil embargo, the American military defeat a year earlier in Vietnam had shaken America's leadership and shattered the morale of the defense establishment to the core. As described by Fred Kaplan in *The Wizards of Armageddon,* "Vietnam brought out the dark side of nearly everyone inside America's national security machine. And it exposed something seamy and disturbing about the very enterprise of the defense intellectual. It revealed that the concept of force underlying all their formulations and scenarios was an abstraction, practically useless as a guide to action."[1]

Proving with 59,000 American fatalities that the use of force in securing victory was nothing more than an illusion, in the final summer of their power the remains of Richard Nixon's secretive brain trust, embodied in men such as Donald Rumsfeld, Dick Cheney, Paul Wolfowitz and Richard Perle, struggled to lay a foundation for rebuilding America's military mythology. In response to a series of articles in the *Wall Street Journal* and *Strategic Review* by University of Chicago professor, RAND theorist, former Trotskyite, and neoconservative icon Albert Wohlstetter, Gerald Ford's CIA director George H. W. Bush opened an outside door to a small, right-wing corps of like-minded defense intellectuals. Well known as a harsh opponent of the strategic principle of Mutual Assured Destruction (MAD) and a perennial advocate of the kind of policy that had failed in Vietnam, Wohlstetter's attack was intended to send a message to Soviet and American policy makers, alike.[2]

Anne Hessing Cahn writes, "Wohlstetter's charges were the opening salvo of a movement determined to destroy détente and to steer U.S. foreign policy back to a more militant stance vis-á-vis the Soviet Union. The critics of détente were certain that the Cold War was far from over and were determined that American hegemony should not disappear."[3]

Known as Team-B, Wohlstetter's hand-picked men brought to work in 1976 revived assumptions that were as old as the Soviet Union itself. It might even be said that the thinking of the group-mind represented by Team-B was so old-world and elitist as to predate the very existence of the Soviet Union. Led by an obscure Harvard professor of Czarist Russian history named Richard Pipes and composed of a unique combination of ex-U.S. military men, retired cold warriors, neoconservatives, and right-wing ideologues, the members of Team-B—Lt. Gen. Daniel Graham, (Ret.) Dr. Thomas Wolfe of RAND, General John Vogt, (Ret.) Ambassador Fay Kohler, Paul Nitze, Ambassador Seymour Weiss, Maj. Gen. Jasper Welch of the USAF, and Paul Wolfowitz of the Arms Control and Disarmament Agency—shared the conviction that détente and Strategic Arms Limitation Talks were nothing more than a Soviet scheme.[4] That scheme was to bargain and talk America into a false sense of security while Soviet agents and proxies subverted American influence both political and military around the globe. Drawn together by their anticommunism and mutual affiliations with a well-established consortium of Wall Street brokerage houses, think tanks, universities and defense contractors (otherwise known as the military-industrial complex), the Team-B members were driven to cast off the hard-won institutional, financial and moral restraints to waging a nuclear war, and their critique of that year's National Intelligence Estimate or NIE left the intelligence establishment reeling.[5]

The Soviets were preparing for a "third world war" and were nakedly expansionist, they claimed in their top secret 1976 report. Given military superiority and the will to use it, they reasoned, at some point in the near future the Russians would make a strategic move that the United States would be militarily unable to stop. "The intensity and scope of the current Soviet military effort in peacetime is without parallel in twentieth century history," they wrote that December, "its only counterpart being Nazi remilitarization of the 1930s."[6]

The assessment at the time was considered radical and, by many, intentionally misleading. Paul Nitze had done this sort of thing originally in NSC 68 and again in the late 1950s with the help of like-minded defense intellectuals at RAND, hounding President Eisenhower to advance the use of nuclear weapons and play "catch-up" with an imagined Soviet threat in the now infamous "missile gap."[7]

The scary assumptions of Soviet strength had been wrong, as the first satellite reconnaissance photos revealed in January 1961. "Even Air Force analysts were embarrassed by the pictures. The images starkly rebutted the estimates of Air Force Intelligence."[8] But the fear they generated had put John Fitzgerald Kennedy into the White House, renewed an arms race that had been slowed to a standstill by Eisenhower, and brought the United States to the brink of nuclear war.

In fact, declassified documents indicate that Kennedy's deputy defense secretary, Roswell Gilpatrick, actually approved an attempt to start a war, with a plan in 1962 to lure or provoke Cuba into an overt hostile reaction against the United States that "would in turn create the justification for the U.S. to not only retaliate but destroy Castro with speed, force and determination."[9]

James Bamford writes, "Codenamed Operation Northwoods, the plan, which had the written approval of the Chairman and every member of the Joint Chiefs of Staff, called for innocent people to be shot on American streets; for boats carrying refugees fleeing Cuba to be sunk on the high seas; for a wave of violent terrorism to be launched in Washington D.C., Miami, and elsewhere. People would be framed for bombings they did not commit; planes would be highjacked."[10]

Again in 1963, Paul Nitze, then assistant secretary of defense, proposed to the White House "a possible scenario whereby an attack on a United

States reconnaissance aircraft could be exploited toward the end of effecting the removal of the Castro regime."[11]

In the end it was concluded by President Kennedy's science advisor Jerome Wiesner that these men were reflecting only a "mirror image" of their own intentions on the Soviets and not the Soviets' intentions themselves.[12] But seventeen years later they were projecting themselves even further into the mirror by suggesting that the CIA completely misunderstood Soviet intentions, that the Soviets believed nuclear war was "inevitable" and were so emboldened by their growing superiority (or the Soviet leaders' perception of it) that "they could be expected to act with greater confidence and less concern for U.S. sensitivities. In fact, there are disturbing signs that the latter is taking place. Recent evidence of a Soviet willingness to take increased risks (for example, by threatening unilateral military intervention in the Middle East in October 1973, and supporting the Angola adventure) may well represent harbingers of what lies ahead."[13]

But it was in their claim that the Russians would first "intimidate smaller powers . . . adjacent to the USSR . . . where pro-Soviet forces have an opportunity to seize power but are unable to do so without military help," that the Team-B assessment attained a level of prophecy.[14]

Though present on the fringes of previous administrations (at least beginning with Truman) and certainly adept at bludgeoning the mass mind of top government, the infusion of the extreme and neoconservative right into a highly irregular oversight role over the mainstream CIA represented a disturbing new addition to the American intelligence process. The former deputy director of intelligence at the CIA, Ray S. Cline, was said to deplore the experiment. "It means, Cline said, that the process of making national security estimates 'has been subverted,' by employing, 'a kangaroo court of outside critics all picked from one point of view.'"[15]

Admittedly ideological, the neoconservative heritage of the group sprang not from a traditional American school of conservatism or even conservative anticommunism, but from the anti-Stalinist communist left. Disciples of the radical communist castoff Leon Trotsky, the neocons were personally motivated by a capitalist evangelism that somewhere between 1938 and 1968 had exchanged the international communist revolution for a global capitalist one.[16] Inspired by the writings of former Trotsky acolyte and OSS operative James Burnham,[17] the neocons' "managerial revolution" had forged a winning alliance of business, defense and radical religion that would come to view western liberal democracy as "suicide"[18] and Stalin's Kremlin descendants as an evil to be eradicated. Gathered together in Team-B, they intended to eliminate both.

Backed by the president's Foreign Intelligence Advisory Board vice chairman, Leo Cherne, and the father of Cold War thinking, Paul Nitze,[19] Team-B produced a report that eviscerated the mainstream CIA along with its methods for gathering intelligence.[20]

At the time, with the United States and Soviet Union still embracing the policy of mutual interest known as détente and long-deterred from planning for nuclear war by the acceptance of Mutual Assured Destruction, the idea that the Soviets were preparing to actually fight a nuclear war was considered ludicrous and by many dangerously irrational.

Vietnam had more than demoralized the American army. Known within the defense establishment to have been an exercise in game theory, Vietnam undercut RAND's much hyped hypothesis for fighting and winning nuclear wars through a doctrine known as *counterforce*.[21] While not only confirming that counterforce was useless against a determined enemy, Vietnam demonstrated that such wars could actually inflict greater harm on the prosecutor than the prosecuted. But Team-B was intent on sidestepping that conclusion while determined to remove any CIA obstacles to the contrary.

A *New York Times* account quoted one source saying that the Team-B confrontation with the CIA had produced "absolutely bloody discussions" during which the outsiders accused the CIA of dealing in faulty assumptions, faulty analysis, faulty use of intelligence and faulty exploitation of available intelligence.[22]

Even outgoing president Gerald Ford distanced himself from the report, telling reporter Hugh Sidey of *Time* magazine that, "The Soviet buildup is not a sudden surge. It has been a long-range problem. I don't necessarily think that the buildup is for adventures around the world. It is my feeling that they are doing it because they feel it is necessary for their own security."[23]

But throughout the next three crucial years, Richard Pipes, Paul Nitze, Richard Perle and a growing network of neoconservative defense intellectuals managed to construct enough of a bipartisan coalition to sway public opinion that the Soviets were preparing to expand beyond their borders.[24] With events in and around Afghanistan heating up, it was only a matter of time before the focus of their attention narrowed.

THE SOUTH ASIA PROGRAM

By early 1978 the entire region of South Asia and Iran had become increasingly militarized and unstable. Flooded with American high-tech weapons by Nixon and Kissinger, Iran's economy and social structure were at the breaking point. The potential for disaster, which the "Nixon doctrine" fostered in Iran, had been neither unpredictable nor unpredicted. An August 1976 U.S. Senate Foreign Relations Committee report stated flatly that the policy was out of control, going so far as to cite the increasing potential for Americans to be taken hostage should the country descend into crisis. More unsettling yet was the disturbing trend observed by journalist Anthony Sampson who wrote in his 1977 book *The Arms Bazaar*, "The idea of the Nixon doctrine, of arms without troops, was turning itself around. The weapons were making their own demands in terms of 'white collar mercenaries,' and were creating their own kind of neo-colonialism, while the Shah was determined to assert his own authority. It was an explosive combination."[25]

Distrustful of the shah's intentions but lured by his wealth and influence, when questioned about his relationship, Daoud admitted to the "new realities" facing him and his country.[26] But the signs of the strain SAVAK was placing on Afghanistan's delicate internal politics were everywhere, with British ambassador and Afghan specialist Roy Crook warning that "if it goes too far and too fast, [Teheran's policy] will surely upset the Russians and produce a reaction."[27]

Daoud's options were now fatally limited. Whatever role the shah's secret police had actually played in ferreting out leftists from Daoud's increasingly paranoid regime, SAVAK's duplicitousness had only further weakened its support, while providing more reason than ever for the PDPA's beleaguered members to accept a Khalq-Parcham unification. The shah's military threat to Afghanistan's independence was real. Combined with Pakistan, it could have spelled the end of Afghanistan's independence almost immediately.

Ruined economically by nearly constant warfare and the relentless pursuit of nuclear technology, by 1978 Pakistan's political-military leadership faced desperate choices. Daoud's position was even worse. In a further blow to his credibility, his decision to back away from confrontation and forge an agreement on the Pashtunistan issue removed the last restraints from both his nationalist supporters and his enemies in Khalq.[28] Fueled by outrage at what appeared to be Daoud's "sellout" to Pakistan and by the conviction that an agreement on the perennial issue of the Durand Line loomed ahead, the coup that Daoud had been madly keeping at bay in the end became a fait accompli.

THE GREAT GAME RESUMES

Daoud's reaction to the new external realities was to move further into the miasma of Middle East politics and cement ties with U.S. Islamic allies Egypt, Saudi Arabia and Pakistan. On a visit to Egypt, Daoud was toasted by an admiring Egyptian president, Anwar Sadat, who, in a clear reference to the Soviet Union, openly goaded the Soviet ambassador by referring to Daoud as a wise nationalist who rejected alignments based on subservience to foreign powers.[29] Having filled his cabinet with repressive hard-liners who often took matters into their own hands, Daoud scheduled a visit from the shah of Iran in June and prepared to visit President Jimmy Carter at the White House in September.[30] With a 20-percent inflation rate and 65 percent of his domestic budget financed by foreign aid, it was a future he no longer had a claim to.[31]

When his hard-line interior minister Abdul Qadir Nuristani bragged that it was time to "finish off" the communists, the political and economic reality that had been brewing for years outside the narrow confines of the palace erupted. Whether ordered by Nuristani or not, the assassination of Babrak

Karmal's strategist Mir Akbar Khyber on April 17, 1978, outside his home, lead to protests by thousands.[32] As the first in a number of key assassinations with profound international ramifications, Khyber's death remains unsolved but bursting with possibilities. "A spokesman for Daoud officially blamed [Gulbuddin Hekmatyar's] Hezbe Islami. Louis Dupree, then living in Kabul, concluded that the murder was directly or indirectly arranged by Interior Minister Nuristani."[33] The PDPA publicly accused Daoud's government as well, citing its well-known campaign of targeting the left.[34] A third and more sanguinary account emerged from Ghaus who believed that it was Hafizullah Amin himself who had ordered his henchman to kill the strategist Khyber as part of a subplot to remove any competition prior to seizing power.[35] In retrospect, Ghaus's reasoning makes sense. The previous August, one of Karmal's next-door neighbors, Inam-ul-Haq Gran, had been shot and killed outside his home. A pilot with Ariana airlines, Gran was said to bear a "striking" resemblance to Karmal. The time between Gran's death and Khyber's also saw the elimination of numerous other Parchamites whose deaths, according to Ghaus, occurred under mysterious circumstances: "Probably old animosities, coupled with the necessity of securing control of the party by Khalqi elements, inclined Amin, who by then had become the active leader of the Khalqi faction and established strong ties to the military, to resort to a more radical and effective method of eliminating the recalcitrant Parchami leadership. No Parchami of stature was to be allowed to challenge Amin's authority in an eventual PDPA government."[36]

Oddly enough, when all Parcham and Khalq leaders spoke at Khyber's funeral, including Taraki and Karmal, only Amin was missing. When on the night of April 25 the hard-line Nuristani arrested the seven leading figures, Amin was not among them.[37] Despite reports that Daoud suspected that a coup was imminent, Nuristani's police overlooked communist sympathizers in the military. Subjected to house arrest, Amin was left free to contact these cells and throughout the night organized Daoud's overthrow.[38]

Details differ from account to account. In what was referred to as "the accidental coup" by Dupree[39] and "the script of a Grade B movie" by Harrison,[40] the next few days witnessed a confused, haphazard enterprise that was more a struggle for control of Afghan communism than a struggle with the nonexistent forces loyal to Daoud.[41]

Unlike previous Afghan coups where the action had occurred between members of the royal family and participants had avoided bloodshed wherever possible, the violence toward Daoud and his family, including small children—was vicious and vindictive.[42] It would become a hallmark of succeeding Afghan regimes as they struggled and failed to control the disintegrating social order brought on by the Cold War. Technically a military coup led by Air Force Chief of Staff Lt. Col. Abdul Qadir and described as such in official documents of the day,[43] by April 30 the government had transformed from being the Revolutionary Military Council to the Revolutionary Council of the Democratic Republic of Afghanistan.[44] Reflecting the influence of the KGB on civilian PDPA decision making, Moscow's director of foreign intelligence, Vladimir Khrychkov, insisted on an equal representation of Khalq and Parcham. According to Harrison, Karmal's local KGB contact, Vilioz Osadchy, wanted the PDPA to refrain from leadership entirely, urging him "to form a coalition headed by non-Communists in which the PDPA would share power. Osadchy warned that an overtly communist regime would provoke concerted conservative opposition and that the PDPA was not strong enough to rule on its own."[45] Hafizullah Amin and the Soviet GRU believed otherwise.[46]

An analysis on May 1, by William G. Bowdler, director of the Bureau of Intelligence and Research at the U.S. Department of State, was more candid about the coup, noting,"Members of the Khalq Party (a pro-Soviet Communist Party) have assumed nearly all the cabinet positions, including the leadership of the ruling National Military Revolutionary Council (NMRC)," stressing that Khalq had spent the last "15 years concentrating on advancing the cause of Pushtun irredentism at Pakistan's expense [while] the Khalq leadership repeatedly accused the Daoud regime of failing to pay attention to the issue."[47]

Sizing up likely Pakistani and Iranian reactions and its impact on the United States, Bowdler cited the fact that "Islamabad and Tehran have long been worried the Khalqists in Afghanistan might take over if Daoud left the scene," and suggested that the two U.S. allies would likely press for more weapons as a result of the takeover.[48]

Bowdler's comments reveal the depth of detailed information available to the State Department regarding Taraki and Amin's Khalq faction, emphasizing that the Soviets would need to become more involved with the regime specifically "in order to restrain it from adventurism that might upset the stability of the region."[49] They also reveal that the shah had far more involvement in Daoud's government than has previously been admitted—having actually prepared an invasion force to intervene should the communists take over in Afghanistan. "The Shah has described the Khalq Party coup as part of Moscow's 'grand design' for encircling Iran. He noted that he had warned Presidents Nixon, Ford and Carter of this threat. *Although his armed forces have been building a capability to intervene militarily in Afghanistan for several years* [authors' emphasis], the process has not been completed. With the apparent collapse of resistance within Afghanistan, we doubt that Iran will intervene."[50]

The shah's influence over Daoud has long been a subject of debate within knowledgeable circles, with Selig Harrison viewing it as pivotal to Daoud's demise and Henry S. Bradsher presenting it as exaggerated. But the shah's motivation for securing Afghanistan against Moscow was of no small concern, either to Washington's defense intellectuals or Tehran's royal family. With the shah inflated first by the Nixon-Kissinger White House to a position of twentieth-century Persian emperor and regional policeman, the accession of the Russophobic Zbigniew Brzezinski in 1977 to the post of national security advisor[51] pushed the twentieth-century Cold War policy of containing the Soviet Union through a time warp back to an obsessed nineteenth-century European historical recipe for confronting Russian imperial expansion. John K. Cooley writes, "Ardeshir Zahedi, his [the Shah's] son-in-law, then Iranian Foreign Minister, was constant in his efforts to impress American listeners with the urgency of the Soviet threat to South Asia; especially Afghanistan. . . . He showed me a map of Baluchistan, a huge tribal area shared by Iran, Pakistan and Afghanistan which purported to show that Moscow planned to realize the old dream of Peter the Great and subsequent czars to push through to the warm-water ports of the Indian Ocean. Under such pretexts of a largely non-existent Soviet agitation among Baluchi tribal separatists, the Pakistani and Iranian armed forces waged a rude war, using jet planes and helicopter gunships, against the Baluchis in the late 1970s."[52]

Given that Tehran had secretly been building a capability to intervene militarily in Afghanistan for years and was already at war in Baluchistan—a tribal area with a legendary historical, ethnic and political alignment to Kabul—it would seem that the shah was more aggressively involved in Afghan politics than many experts have indicated thus far. With the death of Daoud, that involvement would expand exponentially, but in more subtle and pervasive ways than an all-out invasion.

THE STAGE IS SET

In the strange, often inverse world of Afghan politics, where the communist Parcham faction of the PDPA was jokingly referred to as "Royal Communists" for their loyalty to the status quo, the emergence of Khalq at center stage represented a dilemma for the Russians. From early indications, the State Department's position toward Daoud's successor regime appeared cautiously hopeful. Despite the immediate pledge of solidarity with the Soviet Union, the accession of former U.S. employee Taraki was greeted warmly by U.S. ambassador Ted Eliot who signaled Washington that Taraki was intent on maintaining Afghan independence.[53] Eliot also stressed to Taraki that "one other matter of importance to the United States is the stability of this region of the world. I said we have been delighted at the progress that has been made in recent years in developing regional cooperation."[54] Nor was Taraki's reply that Afghanistan needed to include Soviet participation in the region's stability a cause for undo concern by Eliot. The State Department's policy review on Afghanistan dated only two months earlier, February 27, 1978, had made it clear that the Soviets had no interest in shaking up the status quo. If anything, the Soviets were viewed by the United States as a moderating influence whose interest in "a politically stable Afghanistan, could conceivably provide a future occasion to work simultaneously in order to prevent the advent of serious post-Daoud domestic turmoil."[55]

In his meeting, Eliot went on to paint a flattering portrait of the new Afghan leader: "Comment: Taraki is a slim, white haired professional man who looks somewhat older than 61. He has the charm and empathy that one learns to associate with Afghans. He is clearly hardheaded and exhilarated by his success. When he is particularly enthusiastic about a point he is making his eyes assume a fierce, almost fanatical intensity. Our conversation was extremely cordial and was also, I think, a real dialogue."[56]

The response of national security advisor Zbigniew Brzezinski to the April 28 Afghan revolution was not cordial—revealing to knowledgeable sources that the Carter White House did not speak with one voice on the coup or its consequences. From its inauguration in January 1977, the new Carter administration had struggled from within on U.S.-Soviet relations and whether a harder line should be assumed vis-à-vis arms control and perceived Soviet expansion. As recently as January 1977, Ford's outgoing defense secretary, Donald Rumsfeld, had maintained the Nixon-Kissinger line on détente while viewing China as the most serious threat.[57] Convinced that an "arc of crisis" was developing with the Russians, from the Indian subcontinent to the Horn of Africa, by April 1978 Zbigniew Brzezinski had moved that policy 180 degrees into line with Team-B's aggressive anti-Soviet approach. In favor of fast-tracking the so-called China card against the Soviet Union, Brzezinski, who had traveled to China only weeks after the Taraki-Amin takeover, used the Khalq coup in late April as an opportunity for promoting a revolutionary U.S.-China military buildup. Citing nearby Afghanistan specifically as a frightening example of the Soviet grand design for the region, Brzezinski mimicked the dire Team-B predictions, offering to share high-level secrets about Soviet intentions with the astonished Chinese.[58]

Raymond L. Garthoff writes, "Whether President Carter fully realized it, in overriding Secretary of State Vance's objections and sending Brzezinski to Beijing he set in train the development of a rapprochement with China on an anti-Soviet basis. The President did not intend the China card as a counter to Soviet and Cuban activities in Africa, but his action had much broader and deeper consequences . . . it is very unlikely he realized he was giving priority to Chinese relations at a time and in a way that would contribute to American-Soviet estrangement."[59]

A subtlety lost on the president, the view from Moscow of the events in Kabul and Beijing were anything but reassuring. Had the coup been a part of a Soviet "grand design" as alleged by Brzezinski and the shah, it was hard to imagine a less likely candidate than the charming and empathetic Taraki and his ruthless henchman, Amin. Had the Soviets designed the overthrow of Prince Mohammad Daoud it was sure that Parcham's Babrak Karmal would have gotten the call. But the Taraki-Amin duo were nothing but an enigma to the Russians and within months were sending shockwaves reverberating back to Moscow.

The former often employed by the U.S. embassy, the latter equally if not even more entrenched, Nur Mohammad Taraki and Hafizullah Amin had raised Moscow's suspicions of being CIA from the beginning. By masterminding a bloody coup of the Moscow-friendly Afghan royal family and forcing Afghanistan onto the Soviet plate just as Brzezinski moved to embrace a pro-China, anti-Soviet foreign policy, they had some in Moscow convinced.

"Amin was regarded as CIA, not by everyone in the Soviet System, but by certain elements in the KGB," former Carnegie Endowment senior fellow Selig Harrison revealed after speaking with Soviet insiders. "I think if we'd not had the specific circumstances which they regarded as CIA manipulation, they'd have stayed out. But our whole policy, the way we were treating the Soviet Union—definitely created a mindset which was partly responsible for their coming into Afghanistan."[60]

Arriving in Kabul that July of 1978 was the new U.S. ambassador, Adolph Dubs. A World War II Marine Corps veteran and Soviet specialist, Dubs was viewed with added suspicion from Moscow, but also uncertainty from Washington. One of the few American specialists aware of the growing shift in American policy around Afghanistan, he had ordered that a research paper be prepared on a possible Soviet invasion before he left. But no one at the State Department had taken him seriously. Instead Dubs went on to pursue a policy with Taraki-Amin mainly on his own.[61]

Harrison viewed Dubs, who met with Amin fourteen times, as following Secretary Vance's State Department line by working to bring Amin over to the American side: "He came out there with a very sophisticated conception of what he was going to do, which was to try to make Amin into a kind of Tito, a Ceausescu, in other words, detach him." Harrison continued, "I met him out there that summer. He was alone and I had a long evening with [him]. He saw Amin fourteen times when he was Ambassador. . . . and this greatly alarmed the Russians who thought that he might be a CIA agent anyway."[62]

According to Harrison, Dubs's plan also alarmed Brzezinski: "Of course Brzezinski thought this was all nonsense. He saw Afghanistan as a great vindication of their point of view. . . . Brzezinski represented a different approach [to Dubs], which was all part of a self-fulfilling prophecy."[63]

Working closely to gain his confidence, Dubs quickly understood that Amin was a fierce nationalist first and a loyal communist second. According to Harrison, Amin had even bragged to him that the Soviets needed him more than he needed them. But the trick would be to keep a back door open to American influence while not triggering Soviet countermeasures that would shut the operation down. Combined with Brzezinski's rhetoric and covert maneuvering with the Chinese, the task proved difficult.

Cordovez and Harrison write, "Brzezinski and Dubs were working directly at cross-purposes during late 1978 and early 1979. As he boasts in his memoirs, Brzezinski had steadily eroded [Secretary of State] Vance's power, persuading the President to transfer jurisdiction over the CIA from the Inter-Agency Policy Review Committee, headed by the secretary of state, to the National Security Council's Special Coordinating Committee which Brzezinski chaired as National Security Advisor. This control over covert operations enabled Brzezinski to take the first steps toward a more aggressive anti-Soviet Afghan policy without the State Department's knowing much about it."[64]

With the anti-Soviet Team-B agenda being worked covertly from China, Pakistan and Iran, Dubs was playing a risky game. "He knew how subtle an operation it had to be. He had no illusions it could be done quickly or that it could ever necessarily be seen as a Tito. He [Amin] would still be pretty close to the Russians, but he'd have more freedom of action and it would be enough to make it safe from our point of view,"Harrison told us in his interview.[65]

But as Dubs's relationship to Amin developed, political divisions within the Afghan government widened. Accused of a conspiracy to overthrow the PDPA, April coup plotter Defense Minister Abdul Qadir was arrested by Amin in August and executed. In September, Babrak Karmal was packed off to Prague as ambassador.[66] In addition, by the fall of 1978 the Chinese had actively joined the game, secretly training Gulbuddin Hekmatyar's forces in "ultra subversive activities" in secret camps over the border with Pakistan in Xinjiang province.[67] Working in concert with the shah's SAVAK, the Chinese also moved to train Muslim Shiite Hazara and Maoist Tajik factions of the PDPA now alienated by Taraki and Amin's purges.[68]

John Cooley writes, "Qiao Shi, a veteran supporter of Mao, had been especially active in Eastern Europe during the 1970s, when the Sino-Soviet dispute still raged, promoting Chinese influence in countries like Albania (which expelled the Chinese in 1976), Yugoslavia, and Romania. In 1978, on the way home to Beijing from one of his Balkan missions, Qiao Shi stopped over in Tehran to see the Shah of Iran, who was ill with cancer and whose throne and authority were already under fire from a rising tide in popular, Islamists revolution. Qiao Shi proposed to the Shah a new alliance to thwart Soviet expansion especially in neighboring Afghanistan."[69]

Referred to by various names, including the Safari Club, the Cercle, the Enterprise, the Consortium, and the 61, the covert effort aimed at destabilizing Afghanistan could be traced back to the earliest meetings between Henry Kissinger and his Communist Chinese counterparts.[70] Kissinger had used these various groups as proxies during the waning stages of the Vietnam War to accomplish missions that an increasingly beleaguered Nixon administration could not be seen doing on its own. A kind of foreign-policy version of his Watergate plumbers unit, the "others" as Kissinger referred to them, set the stage for what was to become the largest covert effort in American history. Cooley writes, "The 'others' in Kissinger's era of the early 1970s, a time of rehearsal for the approaching adventure in Afghanistan, were a set of unlikely colleagues and allies of circumstance. These allies, in a rough order of their actual value rendered to the U.S. were: France's late Count Alexandre de Marenches, chief of external French intelligence from 1972 to 1982; President Anwar al-Sadat of Egypt from

1970 until his murder in 1981; the Shah of Iran, until his dethronement in 1979 by Khomeini's revolutionaries, and King Hassan II of Morocco, a discreet but valuable friend of the United States since his enthronement in 1960."[71] Together with Saudi intelligence chief Kamal Adham and the young Baathist Iraqi strongman Saddam Hussein, the Safari Club proved a highly effective method of destabilizing Afghanistan.[72]

Using a comparable set of allies, in 1977 Brzezinski took up where the Safari Club left off. But the transfer of power from détente back to Cold War did not go smoothly. Team-B's concerns were considered wild exaggerations by many seasoned intelligence professionals who believed rightly that politicizing intelligence would eventually destroy the entire process. The Vietnam War had begun with politicized intelligence at the Gulf of Tonkin and continued through the Tet offensive, leaving military intelligence and the CIA badly mauled from a self-inflicted wound. Much was known about Soviet State Security's ideologized intelligence units like the KGB, and as much was known of their weaknesses due to their need to fit intelligence into a Marxist-Leninist framework. One American expert who stood at the center of this controversial process was John Arthur Paisley. A product of the merchant marine and the University of Chicago where he studied international relations, Paisley officially joined the CIA in 1953 in the newly created Electronic Intelligence Branch as an economic intelligence officer. Rising over time to the job of deputy director of the Office of Strategic Research, Paisley was central to the CIA's intelligence on both Soviet and American military capabilities. What little has been published about Paisley has him "running" Lee Harvey Oswald into the Soviet Union as a spy at the Minsk radio factory, befriending Soviet defector Yuri Nosenko, and liaising with the White House's so-called plumbers unit to ferret out security leaks. Pressured by Nixon and Kissinger to politicize intelligence on Soviet intentions in order to justify increased defense spending in 1969, Paisley balked. Sent on sabbatical to London to study at the Imperial Defense College, he returned in January 1971 and was tasked with assembling a team to negotiate the first round of Strategic Arms Limitation Talks (SALT I). Deeply immersed in the growing Soviet-American dialogue, he was later tasked with helping to select the members of Team-B while overseeing the classified material available to them.[73]

Paisley's influence can be seen in the opinion of both Henry Kissinger's dismissal of Team-B as "nothing more than an effort to 'sabotage SALT II,'"[74] and Carter's incoming CIA director Stansfield Turner, who came to see the Team-B report as "no big thing." Billed as the "Intelligence Community Experiment in Competitive Analysis," the Team-B's effort at first seemed a stillborn attempt at resurrecting the Cold War.

Anne Hessing Cahn writes, "The immediate reaction of the incoming Carter administration to Team-B was likewise negative. To some on the transition team it looked like blackmail calculated to head off any moves toward more accommodation with the Soviet Union."[75]

But blackmail may have been only a start for the right-wing defense intellectuals of Team-B who flat-out refused to accept the dark implications of Vietnam as a sign of moral and intellectual breakdown. Paisley's liberal credentials and his resistance to slanting intelligence against the Soviets sat poorly with the neoconservatives' tortured campaign to restore America's military ethos. Team-B member Daniel O. Graham was said to describe Paisley as a "weepy liberal who was too soft on the Soviets."[76] Others were not so kind. Turning viciously on their critics, the Team-B braintrust lashed back.

"One member of the A Team, David S. Sullivan, of the CIA's Office of Strategic Research, came to the conclusion that Paisley had been put into place to prevent the B Team from seeing important classified material. As a result, Sullivan began leaking classified documents concerning the SALT I negotiations to [Richard] Pipes and [Daniel] Graham. He also passed these documents to Richard Perle, who was at the time working for Senator Henry Jackson."[77]

As the uproar grew, in August 1978 Sullivan accused both Kissinger and Paisley of being Soviet moles.[78] On September 24, as Hafizullah Amin turned the up the heat in Afghanistan and U.S. ambassador Dubs worked furiously to keep the Soviets from catching fire, Paisley packed up his briefcase with classified documents and set off alone to write an important report in his motorized sailboat, *Brillig*. It was the last time Paisley was seen alive.[79]

A year and a half earlier, just as the divided Carter administration team first set foot in the White House, an influential group of intelligence operatives gathered in London. Drawn together by veteran British intelligence officer Brian Crozier, the object of the meeting was to address the crisis caused by Stansfield Turner's new policies. From Crozier's perspective, Turner's efforts at cleaning house by firing four hundred Soviet experts had left the entire security apparatus of the United States in a state of near collapse.[80] What was needed—and urgently—was a privatized international intelligence operation that would bypass the official intelligence services of the world in order first to provide reliable intelligence in areas which governments were barred from investigating, either through recent legislation (as in the United States) or because political circumstances made such inquiries difficult or potentially embarrassing, and to conduct secret counter-subversion operations in any country in which such actions were deemed feasible.[81]

Called "The 61," Crozier's elite group, which included unnamed American congressional staffers and "the remarkable General Vernon ('Dick') Walters,"[82] would provide a unique venue for directing an unseen and for the most part unknown war of subversion against perceived or imagined Soviet threats around the world—while simultaneously preparing the final chapter in an internal Communist feud that had spanned four decades.

Crozier writes, "Why the '61'? I asked. 'Because the Fourth [Communist] International split,' he replied. The reasoning was abstruse. There had been four Internationals, of which the third was Lenin's Comintern. The Fourth International was the Trotskyist one, and when it split, this meant that, on paper, there were five Internationals. In this numbers game, we would constitute the Sixth International, or '61.' On this tenuous basis, the organization was known among its members, as 'The 61,' and members or conscious contacts were known as 'numerical.'"[83]

From the fall of 1978 on, Brzezinski's anti-Soviet campaign dominated Carter's rhetoric and policy, rolling back détente and sending clear signals to Moscow that the United States was severely hardening its position on a broad series of previously agreed-to issues. Raymond Garthoff writes, "By September 1978 he (Carter) had virtually gutted the [Comprehensive Test

Ban Treaty] negotiations, by reversing the U.S. position so that now the United States would define a 'comprehensive' nuclear test ban to *permit* small nuclear tests ('experiments'). This radical change in the U.S. position was only one in a series in the CTB negotiations, but it was a critical one and left the negotiations foundering."[84]

7.

The 1979 Winter Nightmare

With the fall of the shah of Iran on January 16, 1979,[1] the entire post–World War II structure of U.S. security policy in the Middle East and South Asia dissolved in a swirl of religious fervor. By February 11, the shah's army had disintegrated and the Shiite cleric Ayatollah Khomeini taken control. Pakistan, the home of anti-nationalist Islamist radicals trained in the Middle East, seethed with unrest. Breaking under the strain of internal strife and heightened external pressure from China and Pakistan, Afghanistan was quickly becoming dangerously unstable. Still, Dubs continued his mission, convincing Amin to renew and expand a shuttered U.S. military training program for Afghan army officers. Pressing Washington to actively cease destabilization and keep America's options open, Dubs was working against the tide. Cordovez and Harrison write, "Ironically, while Brzezinski was promoting armed opposition to Amin, Dubs was continuing to nurture his dialogue with the Afghan leader."[2]

A long *Time* magazine article that January hinted at the possibility that Dubs might have been making progress. "The new government in Afghanistan of President Noor Mohammed Taraki is commonly thought to be in Moscow's pocket, especially since it recently signed a friendship treaty with the Soviets. There are signs however, that this too may be an exaggeration. During Taraki's visit to Moscow last month President Brezhnev reportedly chided him for behaving too obsequiously before the Russians, which he felt made the Afghan leader look bad. As soon as they got back to Kabul, Afghan officials began to drop hints that they would welcome more Western aid. Apparently, the Russians are not altogether satisfied with their new client regime in Kabul."[3]

Word of Amin being a CIA agent spread through Kabul and rebounded back to the American embassy. So alarmed was ambassador Dubs by the rumors that he challenged the CIA station chief over their veracity. Steve Coll writes, "He was told emphatically that Amin had never worked for the CIA, according to J. Bruce Amstutz, who was Dubs's deputy at the time. . . . Officers in the Near East Division of the CIA, who would have handled Amin if he were on the agency payroll, also said later that they had no contacts with him when he lived in New York or later."[4]

That same month, Brzezinski's NSC director of South Asian affairs, Thomas P. Thornton, arrived in Kabul. Meeting with Amin, he provided a "negative assessment" of the regime, recommending that any additional aid be cut off, further weakening Dubs's already strained effort.[5]

As the progress in "stability" that U.S. ambassador Ted Eliot had bragged so enthusiastically about only eight months before to Taraki dissolved into a sea of drugs, covert operations, Islamic revolutionaries, and Maoist cadres, all the forces that had been building since Mohammed Daoud's 1973 coup came together.

On February 14, St. Valentine's Day, in a shocking few hours that permanently shattered the prevailing assumptions about the future of U.S.-Soviet relations, U.S. ambassador Adolph Dubs was kidnapped, held hostage, and murdered. Seized by the Maoist PDPA splinter group Setam-i Melli and taken to the exposed second-floor room 117 at the Kabul Hotel, Dubs's subsequent death at the hands of Amin's police force would permanently turn the tide of détente and arms control, and shift the balance of authority toward Brzezinski and Team-B, while making Afghanistan a permanent base for holy war.[6]

With the president and secretary of state out of Washington and temporarily out of the command loop, events quickly slipped out of control. On that the same day, leftists stormed the U.S. embassy in Tehran.[7] Reluctant to reveal the covert game being played against the Russians, the growing alliance with the Chinese, and the internal division over Brzezinski's aggressive application of an anti-Soviet agenda, the Carter administration delivered itself into the hands of the Team-B program. Unable to communicate with Hafizullah Amin directly, U.S. embassy officials stood by in the hallway only footsteps away, unable to stop Amin's police from storming the room. Whether the ambassador was killed by the kidnappers or the rescuers could not be determined. Neither the Soviets nor the Afghans would comply with requests by American investigators for forensic evidence. Nor would the United States explain numerous inconsistencies in its response to the crisis—nor disclose the nature of a conversation between Dubs and a U.S. embassy officer through the hotel-room door regarding the Setam-i Melli's motives.[8]

A cable from Deputy Secretary of State Warren Christopher on February 16, two days after the murder, warned specifically that "future traffic regarding the identity or motives of the terrorists involved in the kidnapping and killing of Ambassador Dubs should be [classified] EXDIS,"[9] meaning exclusive distribution only to officers with an essential need to know.

Seizing on the event as proof of the Soviets' murderous intent, Brzezinski used Dubs's murder as a springboard for action, putting the blame on Soviet advisors, whom the Americans claimed had ordered Afghan marksmen to shoot from a rooftop overlooking the hotel. The U.S. media obliged in the official line, with *Time* magazine referring to the kidnappers as "right-wing Shi'ite Muslims opposed to Afghanistan's pro-Soviet regime"[10] and *Newsweek*, on March 5, calling them "militant Muslims" and "fiercely independent, deeply religious tribes," despite author Ron Moreau's first-hand knowledge of their left-wing, Maoist orientation.[11] Moreau had previously helped establish the CIA's cover for the Muslim rebel support that was about to flow in the February 26 edition, speculating from a Muslim rebel camp in Peshawar that the kidnapping had been a "put-up job by the Kabul regime and the Soviets" in order that "the U.S. would not heed the rebels' pleas for aid." Adding that unnamed "U.S. congressional sources" stated "the Russians had wanted Dubs to die . . . [Dubs] had been trying to wean the Afghans away from Moscow, and his death guaranteed that significant inroads would not be made for months—if ever,"[12] the article left little doubt where the blame was being laid.

But if Moscow had killed Dubs to destroy his mission and take over Afghanistan as the story contended, then Washington's reaction to Dubs's death only advanced that agenda. Declaring in the *Guardian Weekly* on April 29 that "as a result of the incident, the U.S. considers Afghanistan as a communist country past recall," Washington's insiders seemed to be writing off Amin as hopelessly pro-Soviet. Yet only nine months later, after the Soviet invasion, President Carter would be mourning Amin's loss, declaring that Afghanistan's "leaders had been struggling to retain a modicum of independence from their huge neighbor."[13] Which was it?

The two seemingly contradictory American positions unveiled the inner workings of the Team-B transformation inside the White House, with Brzezinski supporting the destabilization of Amin's regime while simultaneously decrying Soviet efforts to remove him. Having long accepted that Afghanistan resided within a Soviet sphere of influence and that the United States had no strategic interest, in order to benefit from the consequences of destabilization Brzezinski's game plan required that Afghanistan be repositioned 180 degrees in the public's mind.

Part of that repositioning occurred within weeks of the Dubs killing when an Afghan army garrison in Herat rose up against their Soviet advisors, killing not only the Russian soldiers, but their wives and children as well.[14] If Dubs's murder had cut off any chance for a U.S. entente with Amin, the Herat uprising gave Zbigniew Brzezinski the validation to actively support a jihad. "The resistance killed a lot of Russians and the Russians were very upset." Harrison said in his interview. "But it gave a shot in the arm to the image of the resistance. That was March of '79. So the coincidence of Dubs's death and the Herat uprising was . . . well, it gave Brzezinski control of the policy from then on."[15]

Ordering an increase in support for Muslim radicals in Pakistan following Herat, Brzezinski directed that U.S. aid be sent to the burgeoning Chinese-supplied, mujahideen training camps in order to "orchestrate and facilitate weapons purchases and related assistance," according to Harrison. In May of that year, in a fateful decision that still haunts the United States, the CIA's station chief in Islamabad, John Joseph Reagan, pledged American military support to a known religious fanatic and heroin trafficker, Gulbuddin Hekmatyar.[16]

Dismissed by the western media, none of these events were lost on the state-controlled Soviet press. An April 10 article in *Pravda* reported the training of rebel forces in Afghanistan's Kunar, Paktia, and Nangarhar provinces, "directed by officers of the Pakistani armed forces, as well as by American, Chinese and, recently, even Egyptian military advisors."[17] The report also cited the role of Afghanistan's Maoist factions, revealing the extent of the international nature of the axis of powers working together against Taraki-Amin's struggling PDPA. "The Chinese special services stepped up their operations among the Afghan Maoist organizations Sholee Javid and Sorha, urging them to cooperate with the extremely reactionary, promonarchist Moslem Brothers. At the request of that organization's leader Gulbeddin Hekmat-Yar, the Chinese authorities agreed to accept up to 200 Moslem Brothers for special courses in saboteur training."[18]

The United States was long aware of the Shola-e-Jawid's Maoist credentials, their radical-left influence on the Shia minority, their destabilizing influence on Afghanistan's political scene and their penchant for violence. "All factions share a pro-Peking radicalism of varying shades, a 'distaste' for parliamentary activity (anything that smells of 'social democratic' revisionism arouses that special wrath reserved for traitors as opposed to class enemies), a willingness to spill blood on appropriate occasions, and great appeal to the increasing numbers of radical youth."[19]

The 1973 assessment of the Afghan Maoists also anticipated that at some point these traits would be put to use. "Sholai as a whole is also the only leftist group in the country which has endorsed terrorism as an acceptable political tactic, and it appears likely that some elements of Sholai will eventually put this theory into practice."[20]

Although Soviet efforts to avoid an invasion would continue throughout the spring and summer, events were signaling that a full-fledged campaign on the Soviets' southern border had begun, a campaign that was, according to Brzezinski, intentionally designed to precipitate a Soviet invasion.

Dreyfuss writes, "In the *Nouvel Observateur* interview, Brzezinski admitted that his intention all along was to provoke a Soviet invasion of Afghanistan—even though, after the Soviet action occurred, U.S. officials expressed shock and surprise. 'We didn't push the Russians to intervene, but we knowingly increased the probability that they would,' said Brzezinski." "'Now,' he told President Carter in 1979, 'we can give the USSR its Vietnam war.'"[21]

It also expanded a process of "off the books" CIA operations that revolutionized the financing and liability of U.S. covert operations. This process would have broad ramifications for the future of terrorism.

By mixing heavy-handed tribal politics with radical land reform and aggressive educational programs, Amin had quickly alienated the Soviets and lost much support in the countryside. By purging his party and the military cadres of non-Pashtuns, he opened the Tajik and Uzbek minorities to Chinese influence.[22] With the Chinese known to be training rebels and aiding the development of Pakistan's nuclear weapons program by exporting opium to the West through Hong Kong, Amin now faced Chinese competition for tribal loyalties.[23] Stimulated by players like France's Alexandre de Marenches, Britain's Brian Crozier, remnants of SAVAK, and Pakistan's Inter-Services Intelligence (ISI), the guns-for-drugs program would finance the privatization of covert operations in South Asia.[24] Once created, the process would act as a corrosive solution to Soviet influence—too powerful to overcome, but, once established, too lucrative to stop.

For twenty years, Brzezinski and the CIA maintained the cover story that the Soviet invasion of Afghanistan was a naked act of aggression while arming the so-called mujahideen rebels was simply an act of self-defense. In the 1998 interview with a French news magazine *Le Nouvelle Observateur*, Brzezinski changed that story, admitting for the first time that the program had begun fully six months before as part of a plan to "draw the Russians into the Afghan trap."[25] Whether Brzezinski's single act of arming the rebels was the deciding factor in pushing the Soviets to invade six months later is irrelevant at this late date. In hindsight it is easy to see how his manipulations triggered the last phase of an elaborate scheme already set in motion by Nixon, Kissinger, and an axis of interests working to lure the Soviets into a confrontation wherever they were certain to lose.

Setting the tone for the horror that was about to begin, on April 4 Pakistan's leader General Zia-ul-Haq executed deposed president Zulfikar Ali Bhutto.[26] That spring President Carter was provoked to cut all aid to Pakistan's military by the revelation of Zia's efforts to develop an atomic bomb.

In Afghanistan, resistance to the Taraki-Amin regime was growing, with Hafizullah Amin viewed more and more by the KGB station and the 4,000

Soviet advisors as the problem.[27] That summer Moscow pressed for ending PDPA rule and establishing a noncommunist government with Daoud's former prime minister, Nur Ahmed Etemadi succeeding Taraki as president. Informing the American embassy in detail of their plan, the Soviets revealed that Amin would be removed by the end of summer in order to form a "national democratic" regime.[28] While officially portraying Soviet efforts to remove Amin as "interference" in Afghanistan, the U.S. embassy viewed the end of the Khalqi regime with relish, speculating that August on the potentially far-reaching benefits of Moscow's dilemma. "The fall of radical leftist and Soviet backed regime could well have positive repercussions for the US throughout the third world by demonstrating that our adversaries' view of the 'inevitable' course of history is not necessarily accurate."[29]

Fully aware of the consequences of turning back the clock, especially for women, the Kabul embassy nonetheless embraced the idea, setting the United States on a course starkly opposed to modernizing and secularizing the Afghan state while transforming the United States into an active sponsor of its destruction. "Conversely, a regime based essentially on the 'fundamentalist' tenets of Islam would probably not place highest priority on social and economic reform (e.g. the 'manifesto' of the 'Islamic party of Afghanistan' calls for the reimposition of 'purdah,' the subjugation of women to a life of exclusion, and probably inevitable widespread [retribution] aimed at Khalqois would have negative human rights implications, no matter how justified retribution against some Khalqois officials might appear to be. On balance, however, our larger interests, given the DRA's extremely close ties to Moscow, would probably be served by the demise of the Taraki and Amin regime."[30]

A shrewd survivor, Amin sidestepped the Soviet effort, rallying support to his side while isolating Taraki further—forbidding him to grant interviews to foreign reporters.[31]

The Carter administration, now firmly in Brzezinski's camp and wanting only "to 'sow shit' in Russia's backyard,"[32] rejected the offer as well. Instead, Brzezinski pushed through the presidential finding that "would bring a military intervention by the Soviets," even though the United States could not appear to "push" them to intervene.

Designed to "draw the Russians into the Afghan trap," Brzezinski's plan worked like magic on the aging Politburo bureaucrats, Brezhnev, Kosygin, Chernenko, and others. Adamantly refusing to commit combat troops, an interim plan was hatched that September to make Babrak Karmal prime minister and send Amin overseas as an ambassador. The plan backfired dangerously when, in a convoluted series of events, a group of Taraki's supporters known as the Gang of Four took matters into their own hands and tried to assassinate Amin in the presence of the Soviet ambassador A. M. Puzanov. Left to the mercy of Amin, both Taraki and Etemadi were soon dead, murdered at the hands of Amin's increasingly ruthless execution squads.[33]

Now aware that the Soviets were conspiring to remove him from power by any means possible, Amin challenged Moscow. Calling a conference of Communist ambassadors in Kabul, including those of China and Yugoslavia, while excluding Soviet Ambassador Puzanov, Amin's foreign minister, Shah Wali, decried Soviet involvement in the affair.[34]

More convinced than ever of Amin's untrustworthiness, the Soviets saw China's hand behind the Afghan disturbances. On September 10 Moscow radio quoted the British *Daily Telegraph*, citing secret sources in Kashmir, that Chinese troops had been put on alert in western China, "that is in the troops on the border with Afghanistan in the region of the minor Pamirs. Chinese troop movements near the border of Afghanistan are yet more evidence the Beijing leaders are out to pressure the government in Kabul."[35] Even the conservative British business magazine the *Economist* backed up Soviet claims in its September 1 edition, stating flatly that "China continues to arm the insurgents."[36] Yet, in the United States, the Chinese hand remained largely invisible, either masked by the mainstream media's sanitized focus on the Islamist resistance or disguised by overtly pro-Chinese propagandists posing as impartial journalists. The growing pro-Beijing and anti-Soviet slant on Afghanistan even found its way into the mainstream American press through activist, pro-Chinese, American journalists like David Kline, in a series of special reports for the influential *Christian Science Monitor*. A freelance journalist, Kline wrote reports on Afghanistan that spanned the key turning points in Soviet decision making from August

1979 until April 1980. Unbeknownst to most American readers was that Kline also wrote for a periodical named the *Call* which was referred to in the American Marxist publication *Guardian* as an "organ of the pro-Beijing Communist Party (Marxist-Leninist)."[37]

Confusing matters further was the startling but less-well-known American assumption that Amin's Khalq Party was itself Maoist. Writing in the *Washington Review of Strategic and International Studies* in July 1978, three months after the Khalq coup, the former U.S. ambassador to Kabul (1966–73) and senior associate at the Center For Strategic and International Studies (CSIS), Robert G. Neumann, revealed that Khalq, "the somewhat larger and more dynamic of the two [parties], was regarded during my service in Afghanistan as 'Maoist,' which did not necessarily mean subservient to China but denoted a category of Marxist radicalism referred to, at different periods, as 'left-wing deviationism.'"[38]

Maoist left-wing deviationism or not, through September, the Soviets persisted in pursuing a strategy of nonintervention and keeping the Americans informed of it. A cable from the U.S. embassy in Kabul summarized Soviet thinking that month. "Point 12. It is also possible that the Soviets do not even feel themselves irrevocably committed to the PDPA, itself. Local Soviet diplomats take pains to make clear that their government's commitment is limited to 'saving the revolution' and to the preservation of its social and economic gains (e.g., the campaign against illiteracy, the elimination of feudal control over women and marriage, the abolishment of usury for agricultural credits, and land reform). As Soviet officials have stated on several occasions: 'The clock cannot be turned back.' This formulation of Soviet views has been taken by some observers to mean that the USSR could live with a non-khalqoi successor regime which would undertake to preserve these 'progressive' gains."[39]

As Amin consolidated power and outside military support for the insurgency increased, Moscow's reluctance for military intervention weakened. In an attempt to assess the effectiveness of invading Afghanistan, in October a unit of thirty KGB special forces, code named the "Zenith group,"[40] arrived in Kabul to secretly survey public opinion across Afghanistan. Reporting back that an invasion would be opposed by the entire country

regardless of political affiliation, they concluded that there was no way to win without exterminating the entire population.

Within weeks the growing popular revolt in Iran made any prior restraint meaningless. On November 4, militant university students again stormed the U.S. embassy in Tehran, this time seizing sixty-three U.S. diplomats and three other U.S. citizens. By November, the already dire situation in Pakistan, which *Time* magazine had described earlier in the year as "nothing if not unstable,"[41] worsened, as rioting extremists in Islamabad burned the U.S. embassy to the ground. Realizing that his efforts to keep free of Soviet control were futile, the ever-resourceful Hafizullah Amin appeared to turn rightward, reaching out in desperation to fellow Ghilzai Pashtun Gulbuddin Hekmatyar and Pakistan's Zia-ul-Haq for help. In what would seem a complete reversal of his radical "Marxist" policies, Amin was said to propose abandoning the revolution and setting up an Islamic state with his fundamentalist rival. In an interview with an Afghan official who had been close to Amin at the time, Amin's gamble was seen as being not as far-fetched or as far right as it seemed. According to this man,[42] Amin had always maintained relations to the radical mullahs on both sides of the Durand Line in Afghanistan and Pakistan throughout his career. Even as a representative of Khalq in parliament, Amin had extended himself to the clerics, assuring them that though they had disagreements he was above all a Muslim and would not violate his faith. Despite reports in the western press that Amin's government was in danger of collapse that fall, it was Amin's strength, his leadership abilities and his unpredictability that troubled the Russians and even the Americans most. Combined with the collapse of U.S. influence in Iran and the overt assistance China and the United States were providing Islamic rebels through Pakistan, Amin clearly understood that he had no other choice but to make a radical break with his northern neighbor. What was not understood was the limited amount of time and the amount of American support he needed to do it. Cordovez and Harrison write, "When the Red Army invaded, the standard American explanation was that Moscow had to intervene to save a toppling Communist regime. However Archer K. Blood, who was Chargé d'Affaires of the American embassy beginning in mid-October, told me in 1981 that 'the regime was not in danger of falling. The whole Embassy agreed on this.'"[43]

In a 1989 interview, Blood admitted that the whole motive for Soviet intervention had been intentionally confused by the Americans from the beginning, first in an effort to make the Russians look bad, but more importantly to make the U.S. support for the mujahideen look more effective than it really was. "'Our idea, of course,' said Blood, 'was to keep Afghanistan alive as a story to embarrass the Russians. Of course, we played up any successes of the resistance and any troubles the government had.'"[44]

Whatever his original status with the Americans, by December 1979 Amin was expendable. Assured that he was "doing a Sadat" on them, the way Egypt's Anwar Sadat had gone over to the Americans in 1972,[45] and convinced that the United States would not stand idly by as their hostages languished and their massive investment in the shah dried up next door in Iran, the Soviets' creaking bureaucracy descended inexorably into panic mode.

DECEMBER 27, 1979

As Zenith forces shot their way through to the Tajbeg Palace on the grounds of the Dar Ul Uman with orders to remove Hafizullah Amin and install Babrak Karmal as the new leader of Afghanistan, Moscow had little idea of the storm of international criticism that would follow its desperate course.[46] "The Soviet invasion was clearly not the first step in the expansionist master plan of a united leadership. Rather, it was the reckless last act of a narrow Stalinist in-group that was starting to lose its grip even in 1979."[47]

More afraid of their own weakness than convinced of their own superiority, the Soviet leadership seemed unable to grasp the complexities of the blunder they had just committed and how it was set to be used against them. At a conference in Oslo in December 1995, titled "Afghanistan and the Collapse of Detente," one of the Kremlin planners—Soviet General Valentin Varennikov—protested vehemently to Brzezinski and his deputy at the time, General William Odom, that their assumptions of Soviet intentions had been wrong. Cooley writes, "Varennikov then described a scenario in the minds of Soviet leaders in 1979. Suppose, he said, that

Afghanistan 'fell' to U.S. and Pakistani aggression. The U.S. could then deploy short-range missiles there, threatening Soviet strategic missile fields including ICBM's in Kazakhstan. If Washington then decided, as the Soviets believed it would, to counter a threat from revolutionary Iran by invading Iran 'to replace Khomeini with the Shah [then in exile but still alive] or someone else you liked,' a Western 'invasion' of Afghanistan would follow. The Kremlin's inner circle also believed by then that Amin was probably an American agent. This, Varennikov reminded the Americans, 'was *our* sphere of influence' and 'our borders, not yours.'"[48]

Carter's CIA director, Stansfield Turner, echoed what would be Brzezinski's later admissions on his knowledge of Soviet plans.[49] But where Brzezinski and Odom still maintained that the Soviet action had been a strategic threat to the United States, in hindsight Turner's perspective sixteen years on proved unusually sympathetic to his old enemy: "The CIA had a pretty good feel for the preparations in the Soviet Union for invading Afghanistan and the probability that they would. But I don't think we had the understanding of the reasons they did that. I don't think we understood the cultural, historic influences that pushed them into that position. It might have helped us ward the whole thing off if we had understood the deeper currents in the situation."[50]

But the situation *was* understood by those in the administration on the other side of the growing Vance-Brzezinski divide as well as written into U.S. policy planning statements as far back as 1941. SALT II negotiator Paul Warnke saw the chances for the congressional ratification of his agreement—which Carter and Brezhnev had signed just the previous June 18[51]—evaporate with the Soviet invasion. But in Warnke's eyes that invasion would never have occurred, had Carter committed to his and Cyrus Vance's moderate policies, instead of those of Brzezinski and the Team-B:

> [If our opinion had prevailed instead of the Team-B] I don't think there would have been any Afghanistan invasion by the Soviet Union. I remember it was about Thanksgiving of 1979 that I was at a party given by some defense contractor and there was a group of people from the Soviet embassy. And one of them came up to me

> and said, 'we have concluded that SALT will not be ratified.' And he said, 'I'm afraid that as a result you will see a bad change in what the Soviet Union does.' And then subsequently I was told that the Politburo had voted on the Afghanistan issue something like six times. And five times those who were against moving into Afghanistan won. But by the sixth time, apparently the hard-liners said, 'look, you're getting nowhere with the United States. You can't even get SALT II ratified, even though we've made all the major concessions. So, as a consequence, why should we hold back? Things aren't going to get any worse if we move into Afghanistan.' And I think that basically was the missed opportunity, that we could in fact have reached an overall agreement with the Soviet Union.[52]

In the end, Warnke believed that the Nitze-Brzezinski view of the Soviet Union was a chimera, a phantom. Until he died, he believed firmly that the Soviet Union was "basically more afraid than they were aggressive,"[53] and would soon have come around regardless of what the United States did. But even as the stolid Politburo members signed the protocols for an invasion that would eventually lead to their own undoing, neither the Soviet premier nor the U.S. president and his secretary of state would comprehend the underlying nature of the old game they had just signed onto.

As a transition president, Jimmy Carter had promised to lift an America humiliated by defeat in Vietnam into a new era, through vision and compassion. Instead, he had played and been played by the right-wing and neoconservative establishment into using Afghanistan as a lure for their own well-known pursuits. That decision would not only weaken the moderate elements within his administration, but would so undermine his credibility as a leader that even his own party would challenge his renomination for president in 1980.[54] With Carter seen as a bewildered neophyte and pawn in the hands of smarter men with a deeper agenda, Afghanistan—coupled to his ongoing inability to resolve the hostage crisis in Iran—would serve two purposes. Internally, by undercutting U.S.-Soviet diplomacy in one broad stroke, the neoconservatives managed to bring on a wholesale revision of U.S. policy and practices dating back to the Roosevelt administration. Externally, the neoconservatives were now in a position to advance a paranoid, apocalyptic international agenda, with the intention of sparking an unrelenting holy war against the Russians, on their own turf.

SOVIET INTERVENTION 1980–1989: THE AFGHAN WAR BEGINS

The impact of the Soviet invasion on the American scene was immediate and permanent. A January 2 *MacNeil/Lehrer Report* featured, among others, Team-B leader and "Soviet expert" Richard Pipes and former American ambassador to Afghanistan Theodore Eliot, who together used the invasion to cement the Team-B exaggerations into place as the new American reality. In the knowing tone of an experienced Russophobic, Eastern European "Sovietologist/Kremlinologist," Pipes described imperial Russia's longing for Afghanistan "for a very long time," and how that longing was directly connected to their expansionist aims, saying that "it is not a rich country, but it is a superb springboard from which to launch offensives both into the Indian subcontinent and into Iran and the Iranian Gulf," while emphasizing that "if they get away with it in Afghanistan, there'll not only be great danger for our whole mideastern position but we will have encouraged them to engage in actions of this sort in other parts of the world, including for example, Southeastern Europe or possibly Western Europe."[55]

Taking the lead from Robin MacNeil, Pipes summed up by taking the opportunity to signal that not only was détente dead, but so was the word "détente" itself, as if—like the old Soviet Symbolists—the very word contained an inherent power that if used magically could make it attain reality.[56] "I think we've dropped the word. I've never believed détente was anything but a public relations concept, because the Russians, even at the height of détente, have not foresworn their ultimate objectives or even the means of attaining them."[57]

This was no circumlocution. This was Kremlin-speak. Pipes's warning verbally announced the dawning of a new era where a secret war conducted by bands of mythical Kiplingesque warriors would magically erase the memory of Vietnam while bringing an evil empire of atheist, Bolshevik heretics to their knees—and President Carter was listening. In a State of the Union speech patterned by Brzezinski along the lines of the 1947 announcement of the Truman Doctrine, Carter announced a host of programs designed to punish the Soviets for their Afghan indiscretion while simultaneously fulfilling the mandate of Team-B for a greatly expanded military.[58]

But even in this Carter misplayed his hand. Garthoff writes, "Not only did the administration go overboard in tossing almost everything movable onto the sacrificial bonfire of sanctions, but it tied the whole to the obviously unattainable maximum aim of getting the Soviets to withdraw from Afghanistan. . . . President Carter and Secretary of State Vance seem not to have learned an important lesson from the recent painful experience in Cuba: it is self-defeating to term not acceptable a situation that cannot be changed and that must, *faute de mieux*, be accepted."[59]

Garthoff's words are a veteran State Department expert's signature statements on the calculated madness that seemed to possess the moment, with a confused Soviet leadership pursuing a war that they knew could not be won, and a flailing U.S. president lashing out with demands that were at once impossible to fulfill and self-defeating if done so. "Much of the administration's foreign policy had already been taken hostage along with the embassy staff in Tehran in November. Now the president chose to make American relations with the Soviet Union and détente hostage to the latter's decision to keep its troops in Afghanistan—even, in a perverse way, to Soviet fortunes in suppressing the Afghan resistance."[60]

Even in Zbigniew Brzezinski's opinion President Carter overplayed the Soviet invasion by repeatedly calling it "the greatest threat to peace since the Second World War,"[61] canceling trade agreements, and boycotting the 1980 Summer Olympics.[62] Demanding that the Soviets withdraw their forces while waging a covert war to draw them in and keep them there, Carter was engaging in a cynical masquerade—demanding something that was not intended to be met. But the invasion did provide Brzezinski and his neoconservative colleagues with a windfall of pretexts for a long-planned expansion of U.S. military power and an excuse for taking an active role in the Middle East. Dismissing Soviet accusations of U.S. duplicity, the UN condemned the invasion while Brzezinski flew off for immediate talks with Zia-ul-Haq in Islamabad to undo congressional restrictions on financial aid.[63] Eventually authorizing $3.2 billion in cash and high-tech weapons under the Reagan administration, the Soviet invasion transformed Pakistan overnight from an international pariah to the United States' third-largest aid recipient.[64] The Durand Line and Pashtunistan issue, which had riled Afghan rulers for over a century, had come full circle, now with the full might of the United States reviving Britain's unmet ambitions for control beyond the Hindu Kush.

Within weeks, seven major mujahideen groups were lined up in Peshawar to receive U.S. aid, with Pakistan's Inter-Services Intelligence Directorate (ISI) assigned the job of steering the money. Over the next ten years billions would flow with little to no CIA oversight. With the well-known Gulbuddin Hekmatyar as the principle recipient, the CIA's purpose was apparently never to establish a democratic or even pluralistic Afghanistan. In fact Brzezinski's view was not concerned with Afghanistan at all. Dreyfuss writes, "As Ayatollah Khomeini was busily creating his Islamic Republic of Iran, Zbigniew Brzezinski and the CIA launched their Islamic-right army in Afghanistan. But it was more than just an Afghanistan strategy. Brzezinski's effort was designed to implement a cataclysmic view of the Bennigsen school, to use the Islamic right as a sword against the USSR itself."[65]

At the center of game planning from its inception, the RAND Corporation dispatched analyst Francis Fukuyama to the North-West Frontier Province (Pashtunistan) from May 25 to June 5, 1980, to assess the Soviet's chances of winning the war. Briefed by the ISI and friendly journalists, Fukuyama interviewed the key players, including Lt. Gen. Fazle Haq, governor of the North-West Frontier Province.[66]

Fukuyama revealed in his "trip report" that the Soviet Union had already reached a stalemate in Afghanistan that, given the history of conflict there, was unlikely to change. Based on his observations as a Sovietologist, the Soviets' "sensitivity to casualties" indicated a reluctance on their part to engage the mujahideen directly and was a sure sign that they were unlikely to escalate the conflict further. He also spelled out the divided nature of the insurgency, writing, "They tend to be more interested in their power position than in contributing to the success of the insurgency as whole."[67] This fact was to plague the U.S.-supported effort for the entire war and destroy what was left of the country afterward.

The "mujahideen freedom fighters," as they were soon to become known, were headquartered in the Pakistani city of Peshawar. Long contested by the Afghans and the British, the city soon became the staging ground for the seven major groups. Jamaat-i Islami was led by Burhanuddin Rabbani and composed primarily of Tajiks from the North. Ahmed Shah Massoud, an acolyte of Rabbani, led Jamaat fighters into battle against the Soviets. Hezb-i-Islami, led by Gulbuddin Hekmatyar, is the most extreme and anti-American of the groups. Closely bound to Pakistan's ISI, Gulbuddin Hekmatyar was to receive the bulk of the U.S. money and support despite criticism that he rarely engaged the enemy. Ittehad-i Islami was led by Abdurrab Rasul Sayyaf, who had been released from prison by Hafizullah Amin. Younas Khalis also headed a group called Hezb-i Islami-(Khalis), which had split from Hekmatyar's group. The three less-extreme factions were led by Pir Sayed Gailaini of the National Islamic Front for Afghanistan, a leader within the Qaderiyyah Sufi order who could trace his lineage back to the prophet Mohammad; Mohammad Nabi Mohammadi, a theologian of the Harakat-i Inqilab-i Islami; and Professor Sibghatullah Mojadidi of the Afghan National Liberation Front, a largely Pashtun-backed group from Helmand province near Kandahar.[68] Fractious and disunited, the Islamists' campaign was further burdened from the start by a conflicted American strategy between "bleeders" like Brzezinski who wanted the Soviets held down and punished, and "dealers" like Secretary of State Cyrus Vance, who wanted only enough military pressure applied to get them out.[69]

Adding to the confusion was the media's generally unanimous decision to drop the controversial story altogether, leaving the American public out of the loop in regard to the secret operation. It also left a handful of critics wondering what had happened to the American media. "When the U.S.

government began a covert operation to send weapons to Afghanistan last year, it hit on a novel way to keep the operation secret: it told the press. Most reporters were unable to confirm initial leaks about weapons supplies and did not report on them. Others confirmed them, printed them, and moved on to other issues."[70]

With the expulsion of the entire western press corps from Kabul shortly after the Soviet occupation began in January 1980,[71] just getting stories out of Afghanistan or attempting to report on what was going on there soon became as controversial as the story itself.

Looking to locate the source of the problem, Jay Peterzell, an associate at the Center for National Security Studies in Washington pointed to Dan Rather of CBS News as setting the strange tone for Afghan stories, following the famous "Inside Afghanistan" broadcast he had given on April 6, a few months after the Soviet invasion.[72] "By relying almost entirely on the statements of Afghan rebels and a Pakistani information officer, Rather managed to consolidate popular misconceptions about the war into one high-impact, coast-to-coast broadcast. He accepted at face value claims that, in the words of the Pakistani, 'no country is providing arms and ammunition to the mujahideen freedom fighters.' The officer's statement was understandable given Pakistan's fear of Soviet retaliation. Rather's credulity was not."[73]

Adding that "the broadcast seemed to mark a watershed," Peterzell went on to cite a post-broadcast survey of news accounts that appeared to prove that Rather's appearance had significantly reversed journalistic opinion about Afghanistan, with three-quarters of the articles either dismissing U.S. assistance or downplaying its importance.[74]

To make matters worse, questions later arose whether Dan Rather had actually snuck across the Pakistan border for an inside look at the Soviet occupation or just pretended to. Standing by as a mujahideen fighter executed a captured Afghan army soldier for the camera, Rather would later be tried in absentia in Afghanistan and found guilty of complicity in the murder.[75] But in retelling his story to a prime-time audience, he had established a radically new pro-military standard for post-Vietnam American reporters. Questioning the overtly propagandized nature of the Rather expedition, author Peterzell asked why the "hard" questions about Afghanistan weren't being asked and, more ominously, "whether, in fact, the U.S. wants the Soviets out of Afghanistan, or prefers to make the country Russia's Vietnam."[76]

Peterzell's question only scratched the surface. Accused by neoconservatives and right-wing hawks of aiding the enemy in Vietnam by slanting new stories against the U.S. war effort, the "Russia's Vietnam" theme was to be the media's covert, collective mea culpa. Conceived directly from within the intelligence community and propagated through friendly members of the media like Rather, the entire Afghan enterprise so reeked of a CIA counterintelligence operation that most legitimate media outlets simply turned on the story and walked away. Others tread the delicate line, choosing their information carefully from CIA press releases issued from Pakistan and sanitizing the bulk of what was left. "Some reporters may also be inhibited by a reluctance to give succor to the Soviets, who have been banging the drum of CIA interference in Afghanistan since long before their own invasion. When asked about *Newsweek*'s January 5 story, Fred Coleman, one of several reporters contributing to the article, observed that 'obviously, people on this side don't want to give credence to [the Soviet claim], so that makes it sensitive.'"[77]

Cynical in the extreme, from its inception, media coverage of the events leading up to the Soviet invasion had been carefully managed to avoid any hint of the plan at work. Vital to maintaining the illusion that the Soviet action was purely the result of Soviet aggression and *not* in reaction to American subversion, a ring of silence had been prophylactically applied. Fearing accusations from back home that they would be providing "aid and comfort to the enemy," most American reporters either fudged the details, turned a blind eye to the darker implications of the covert operation, or simply lied. Only a few stories found their way out from under the self-imposed veil of secrecy, but the few that did spoke only of the "nightmare," that was being constructed for the hapless Russians. Writing from Pakistan in the Canadian weekly *MacLean's* eight months before the Soviet invasion, author Peter Niesewand described with amazement the presence of "Chinese army officers and instructors. They are there to train and equip right-wing Afghan Muslim guerillas for their 'holy war' against the Moscow-backed regime." But even more disconcerting was Niesewand's speculation that the "holy war by proxy" was being fueled by the proceeds from the sale of illegal opium in a deal with China to finance the long-sought Pakistani nuclear weapon.[78]

Following the Soviet invasion, not a shred of this background would reach the ears of the American public. Harangued by the Iranian hostage crisis and barraged by renewed pressure for massive defense spending to counter Soviet aggression, Americans would be feted to a smokescreen of slogans, news stories, and films. Designed to transform Afghanistan into Russia's Vietnam in the minds of America—any chance for a negotiated settlement would be kept off the airwaves and, as a result, off the national agenda.

GOOD OLD-FASHIONED PROPAGANDA

Almost immediately, a World War II–style public relations campaign to dismantle the media image of the Soviet Union in Afghanistan began, with London financier Lord Nicholas Bethell taking the lead with his Radio Free Kabul. A career British intelligence official with a specialization in Iranian and Arab affairs, Lord Bethell had served in the Mideast and Soviet sections of official British intelligence, MI6.[79] As a virulent anti-Soviet, Bethell had been accused in 1971 of being a "KGB stooge" and forced to resign as a Tory government whip. Reported in a Sunday, May 26, 2002 article in the *Observer,* Bethell had managed to clear his name but his murky connections to Soviet counterintelligence operations remained unclear.[80] From London, Bethell organized a who's who of the British establishment on behalf of the Afghan holy warriors, bringing on Soviet dissident Vladimir Bukovsky to take full advantage of the Soviet's indiscretion.[81]

In the United States, John C. Whitehead's International Rescue Committee and Leo Cherne's Freedom House quickly followed, pulling together key people in New York society along with Washington's neoconservative, anticommunist elite to assist lawyer John Train in forming the

Afghanistan Relief Committee (ARC).[82] As a result of these and other efforts, coverage of the war in Afghanistan was limited to official press releases drafted in Washington and London, while later in the war it would come under the direct supervision of the United States Information Agency.

Bethell's group also operated in the United States under the name of the Committee for a Free Afghanistan (CFA). Headed by U.S. Army Major Karen McKay, CFA was an odd assortment of extreme anticommunist right Republican and liberal Democrat, but representative of the wild coalition of interests brought together by Team-B and held there by Afghanistan, including General John Singlaub, former president of the World Anti-communist League (WACL), Team-B member General Daniel Graham, Senators John McCain, Claiborne Pell, Paul Tsongas, and Paul Simon, and Representatives Barney Frank, Gerald Solomon, Mickey Edwards, and Charlie Wilson as principles.[83]

Backing a class of mullahs and land owners that had been fighting any social reform for generations, the United States began a process that drove social evolution in Afghanistan back to the Stone Age. Willfully targeting any vestiges of modernity with old Soviet weapons shipped in from Egypt by Anwar Sadat to disguise the American support, the mujahideen "freedom fighters" targeted power plants, factories and schools, especially schools for women.

The covert war against the Soviet Union in Afghanistan resembled the old British "Great Game" in name only. Billions of dollars and high-tech weapons poured in from the United States and Arab states eager to establish a foothold at the gateway to oil-rich Eurasia. Many of the U.S. media signed on to the campaign, killing stories that lent credence to Afghan and Soviet complaints of a secret U.S. war while lionizing Gulbuddin Hekmatyar's heroin-dealing mujahideen. But without any U.S. supervision and with ISI's help, Hekmatyar managed to stockpile much of the weaponry and money for a future war to control Afghanistan, after the Soviets had fled.[84]

8.

Summer 1980

Even by the summer of 1980, the Soviet leadership failed to recognize the emergence of the coalition forming against it and the effect they were having on American political life. On a trip to Moscow for the U.S.- boycotted Olympics that summer, we spoke with Soviet officials unable to grasp what seemed a sudden change in American attitudes. Convinced that the U.S. government understood that Afghanistan rested well within Moscow's sphere of influence, that SALT II would be passed and détente continue, Soviet observers failed to understand the apocalypticism of America's new right and its willingness to fit the Soviets' move into Afghanistan into the coming of "End Times" biblical prophecy. Even after spending the previous three years in and out of the studios of Pat Robertson's Christian Broadcasting Network affiliate WXNE (Christ for New England), listening to America's televangelists streaming their prophecies of Armageddon across the nation, we could not find the language to explain to these officials the eschatological bent that had emerged in U.S. politics.

Mired in a geriatric haze and blinded by their own ideology, the Soviet leadership also failed to grasp that their presence in Afghanistan was feeding Team-B's campaign to alter the fundamental assumptions on the use of America's nuclear force, a campaign which was growing stronger with every day they remained there.

That summer Brzezinski pushed through a succession of presidential directives designed to wage a nuclear war. Rejecting the proof of the failure of the counterforce doctrine in Vietnam as well as the principle of Mutual Assured Destruction (MAD), Presidential Directives 58 and 59 accelerated the arms race in keeping with the warnings of the Team-B report.[1] "'For the first time,' wrote Carter's national security advisor, Zbigniew Brzezinski, 'The United States deliberately sought for itself the capability to manage a protracted nuclear conflict.' And Presidential Directive 59, signed July 24, 1980, required the U.S. to develop the capability to fight and win a nuclear war that would last for months, not an hour or a day."[2]

As a former presidential science advisor and MIT president, Jerome Wiesner knew the game well. "The public is now being exposed to terrifying exaggerations of military dangers not for the second time but at least for the *fifth* time," Wiesner wrote that year. "So far this season, we have had the following pro-war initiatives all in the name of insuring peace: Presidential Directive 59 (substituting a nuclear-war-fighting strategy for the previous deterrent strategy), binary nerve gas, the sidetracking of the strategic-arms treaty, the neutron bomb, a call for re-establishing strategic nuclear superiority (really a call for an open-ended arms race), added support for the MX-missile system."[3]

Chastising the Carter administration for election-year warmongering, Wiesner pleaded with the public to not allow itself to be fooled yet another time.[4] Yet his warnings fell on deaf ears, due largely to the media's unquestioning acceptance of exaggerated Soviet strength and their overreaction to the Soviet invasion of Afghanistan.

Writing that summer of 1980 in the *Columbia Journalism Review*, author Roger Morris—a contributing editor to the *New Republic*—attempted to put the newly induced Cold War hysteria into perspective:

> The mass of articles on national security since last summer was premised on an assumption journalists seemed to take for granted: the huge size and menacing nature of the Soviet threat. Wherever readers turned, the awesome dimensions of Moscow's military budget defined the danger, and, of course, justified the need for more Pentagon spending. . . . So also this winter did the media see the Russian military machine in Afghanistan as larger than life, or at least larger than its underfunded Pentagon counterpart. To [Drew] Middleton [in the *New York Times*], the invasion clearly demonstrated "Russia's capability to project military power rapidly and efficiently" (January 7) with fateful implications for the Persian Gulf and beyond. The January 21 *Time* found "elite" troops, "a

line-up of one of the meanest looking, deadliest vehicles in the world's arsenal of armor," and cited anonymous experts who warned of a Soviet strike into Iran or onward that "no force could stop."[5]

Missing from most accounts was the fact that by early that spring, the Soviet effort to seal their southern border and prop up the Afghan communists had already been bogged down in a bloody Vietnam-like quagmire. One of the few exceptions was the firsthand report by British reporter Robert Fisk, whose prominent, front-page article in the March 4 *Christian Science Monitor* presented the sad story of Russia's invasion of Afghanistan through a clearer lens. "They look for all the world like figures from a World War II movie. And their actions may indeed have been prompted by some distant general's fading memories of how old wars were fought. . . . It has been a harrowing experience for them. And despite their overwhelming technical superiority and their immense fire-power, things are not likelier to get any easier."[6]

AGAINST THIS BACKDROP

That fall we applied to the Afghan legation at the United Nations for permission to bring a film crew to Kabul to capture the untold story from the Afghan perspective. Receiving permission from the PDPA government in Kabul, the following spring we became the first Americans to acquire authorized travel visas to Afghanistan since the Soviet expulsion of the western media in January 1980. Under contract with CBS News, the images of Afghan life in Kabul and Jalalabad that we filmed showed an Afghan picture far more complex and nuanced than the dualistic black and white established by Rather and the rest of the mainstream media. Afghanistan was a complicated story to tell, where "progressive" Islam and women's rights stood side by side with a strong nationalist movement and a fractious but highly committed Marxist party. Despite the presence of seventy-five thousand Soviet troops, the Khalq-Parcham split had only widened, with the Soviets increasingly unwilling to support the divisive feud. With a U.S.- and Saudi-financed insurgency from Pakistan burning schools, toppling power lines and murdering any and all elected officials they could find, Communist or otherwise, the Afghan PDPA, chaired by Babrak Karmal, could do little but maintain social reforms made under Zahir Shah and Daoud. Battered by public opinion for his inability to escape the label of "Soviet-installed puppet," Babrak Karmal faced our camera at the Arg Palace to tell the "noble, hardworking, peace-loving people of America" that "any time a reliable and [convincing] guarantee is given on the part of the neighboring countries—Pakistan and Iran and the United States of America and China—that there will be no recurrence or any sign of aggression, provocation and interference into the internal affairs of Afghanistan, the limited contingent of the Soviet troops will return to their lands; otherwise, if these interferences, provocations and aggressions, particularly from the Pakistani soil, continue to exist, then the limited contingents of the Soviet troops will remain in the country."

It was a message that *CBS Evening News*, with Dan Rather, was not interested in delivering. Instead of advancing the dialogue for a negotiated settlement or even correcting the broken lens that framed Afghanistan as a hypothetical Soviet chess move in the Great Game for Central Asia, their exclusive report (filed four weeks after our return) focused only on the presence of Soviet troops *that we did not see,* while not even bothering to air the conditions, laid out by Afghan President Babrak Karmal in person, by which those Soviet troops might be withdrawn. It was a theme we were to experience repeatedly over the next decade, as efforts to bring an end to the fighting in Afghanistan became increasingly subservient to the destruction of the Soviet Union.

That December, at a preview of our WGBH-sponsored PBS documentary account of the experience, titled *Afghanistan Between Three Worlds*, we were treated firsthand to the Cold War chill, operating just below the surface of the media's coverage of Afghanistan. There, with the local and national media as witness (including the *Time* magazine correspondent), Theodore Eliot, former U.S. ambassador to Afghanistan and dean of the Tufts Fletcher School of Law and Diplomacy, rose to his feet to protest the very presence of any view on the Afghan story not authorized by the U.S. government.

Last seen on *MacNeil/Lehrer* beside Richard Pipes on January 2, 1980, espousing the Team-B view of Soviet aggression in Afghanistan,[7] there was little wonder that the eminent dean should oppose any talk of negotiation or Soviet withdrawal. To Theodore Eliot, along with Richard Pipes, Zbigniew Brzezinski and a resuscitated class of defense intellectuals, the Soviet Union was in Afghanistan for only one thing, to move the Team-B agenda forward, and there was nothing that was going to stand in their way.

Attending that same event was the director of the Harvard Negotiation Project, Roger Fisher. Fisher complimented our presentation as an example of what he had written about with coauthor William Ury in his best seller *Getting to Yes*, and offered his assistance. When we suggested he might be helpful in getting the Soviets to withdraw their forces by going back with us to Afghanistan, a deal was struck.

9.

The Reagan Era

The aggressive position first put forth by Brzezinski and then carried forward into the Reagan administration destabilized U.S.-Soviet relations far more seriously than press accounts of the day were allowed to reveal. With the Soviets in Afghanistan, the entire force structure of the United States had gone on alert and would stay that way throughout the Reagan era. Covert and overt wars would be fought in Grenada, Panama, El Salvador and Nicaragua. Accepting the neoconservative proposition that Soviet action in Afghanistan was the first step in a march to the Persian Gulf, Carter's overplayed militaristic stance had broken prior restraints and elevated the United States as close to a nuclear "first-strike" scenario as we had yet to come. Predicated entirely on the mistaken assumption that the Soviets were running out of oil, as summed up in a secret 1977 CIA memo titled, "The Impending Soviet Oil Crisis," an apocalyptic Third World War fantasy was being dreamed into reality,[1] and by 1981 the Reagan White House was getting ready to act on it. In 1986 KGB defector Oleg Gordievsky revealed that Soviet Union had gone on an extraordinary intelligence alert in early 1981 and remained so until late in 1983, convinced that the United States was preparing a surprise nuclear attack to forestall a Soviet attack on the Middle East.[2]

Having played a critical but unheralded, back-channel negotiating role in the Iran hostage release, Roger Fisher's involvement at that critical moment in time—when Afghanistan threatened to cause the Cold War to escalate to nuclear war—wasn't hard to fathom.

Following the death of the Soviet general secretary of the Communist Party, Leonid Brezhnev, in the fall of 1982, his successor, former KGB chairman Yuri Andropov, opened the door to the possibility of a Soviet withdrawal. A hardened realist and former chief spy, Andropov grasped the widening implications of the Soviet stalemate in Afghanistan and moved quickly to cut his losses. Feared more in Reagan's Washington and Thatcher's London for his ability to actually *lessen* tensions than to aggravate them following his offer to reduce intermediate-range nuclear missiles in Europe, the powers-that-be driving the new Cold War viewed Andropov with the deepest suspicion.[3]

Paul Warnke told us, "Look back sometime . . . at some of the articles when Andropov took over. They refer to him as 'Scary Yuri'—you know, the product of the KGB, bad days are here again, that Chernienko was a slob but this guy's a sneak. And there's nothing to support that. He was put into the KGB because the civilians wanted to control the KGB and he was one of them."[4]

Landing with us in Kabul that spring of 1983, Roger Fisher's ability to put both the Russians and the Afghans at ease was immediately apparent, and his revelations coming away from meetings at the sandbagged Soviet embassy with Soviet Afghan specialist Stanislav Gavrilov were no less than shocking. The Soviets wanted out, Gavrilov informed Fisher in no uncertain terms. The Soviet soldiers were unprepared to fight in such a war and were losing their will as well as their belief in the Soviet system. Drugs, typhoid, dysentery, and malaria were exacting an enormous toll for a political outcome that was far less than clear. Should the Americans hold back their support for the rebels long enough to save face, Soviet troops could withdraw from the front lines, then, following a short hiatus, retreat across the Amu Darya River. "We make mistakes," Gavrilov admitted. "But we're not stupid. We want to go home."

Contracted to ABC News *Nightline* before we left the United States, we were greeted with blank stares by the *Nightline* staff upon our return. Held as a closely guarded secret by top management during our absence, our successful return with surprising news from the Afghan front was once again a cause for concern. By 1983, the mistaken and exaggerated Team-B assumptions of Soviet intentions had become so ingrained in the mainstream media that the very idea that they might be wrong was itself a controversial if not heretical point of view. The entire Reagan defense buildup rested on the erroneous assumption of a Soviet drive to the Middle East. Word had filtered down through the standard and approved mouthpieces that Andropov was on a "charm offensive." Falling prey to Soviet propaganda was career suicide. What was to be done?

Rejected out of hand as a worthy news story by the staff of ABC's *World News Tonight* with Peter Jennings, we were granted one Thursday evening after midnight to tell our story and make the case for a negotiated Soviet withdrawal. Interviewed live by Ted Koppel alongside Soviet dissident Vladimir Bukovsky, Roger Fisher's effort to explain the war's deepening cost to the Soviets was taken politely but not seriously, with Bukovsky's deadening delivery of the Team-B line coming down on Roger's high-level, back-channel communication like a bludgeon.

> KOPPEL: Vladimir Bukovsky. Do you believe that that kind of a cost to the Soviet Union is the sort of thing that would ever cause them to withdraw?
>
> BUKOVSKY: No I don't believe in that; in fact, unlike the United States, the Soviet Union is not very apprehensive of the casualties. They probably lost about twenty thousand by now, but they wouldn't be giving any consideration to that. What is important for them is the strategic advantage of their moving toward the Persian Gulf and to all accounts we have right now they do keep certain bases inside, the equipment, the planes capable to project force into the Persian Gulf.[5]

Intent on painting the Soviets as bloodless killers driven to seize Middle East oil, Bukovsky's statement stood in stark contrast to the RAND Fukuyama trip report in which the Soviet expert repeatedly cited the Soviet's "sensitivity to casualties" as a sure sign that they were unlikely to escalate the conflict. It also stands in stark contrast to what we now know the U.S. government actually believed about the reasons for the Soviet invasion at the time, but kept concealed for the benefits of propaganda. "It is unlikely that the Soviet occupation is a preplanned first step in the implementation of a highly articulated grand design for the rapid establishment of hegemonic control over all of south Asia. The occupation may have been a reluctantly authorized response to what was perceived by the Kremlin as an imminent and otherwise irreversible deterioration of its already established position in a country within the Soviets' legitimate sphere of influence."[6] Continuing along that line, Bukovsky went on to further dismiss Fisher's discussions in Kabul as just so much Soviet cleverness—"which is why they now try to persuade people that they are ready to withdraw if they are given a chance to save the face, which is not true. From all the accounts we have of that country, the Soviets have no intentions of withdrawing."

Koppel allowed Bukovsky to finish off by plugging Radio Free Kabul and Karen McKay's Committee for a Free Afghanistan. Then he went on to present, in his New York studio, Abdul Rahim, a political officer of Rabbani's Jamaat-i Islami, which Koppel described as "an anti-communist resistance group based in Pakistan. He is here in the United States under the auspices of two American organizations, concerned with democracy in Afghanistan, the Afghan Relief Committee and Freedom House."[7]

Had the Afghan Relief Committee and Freedom House really been concerned about democracy in Afghanistan, their choice of the Jamaat-i Islami could not be viewed as anything but the darkest of inside jokes. Originally founded by Abul Ala Maudidi in 1941, the goal of the Jamaat-i Islami was more than just that of gaining political representation for radical Islamists in a pluralist, democratic government. The Jamaat was to be an all-embracing, extremist Islamic Society, crafted through the strictest interpretation of Islamic law, as a *replacement* for a modern western-style democracy.[8] Supported by right-wing Pakistani, Saudi, and Arab interests, throughout the 1970s the Jamaat-i Islami had mauled secular, democratic political interests in Pakistan and solidified its extreme right-wing political dominance through the iron fist of the military dictator Zia-ul-Haq.[9]

Certainly concerned more with advancing Saudi and Arab interests in establishing an extremist Wahhabist presence in Afghanistan than with democracy, the Afghan Relief Committee and Freedom House represented the cream of the right-wing, neoconservative, Team-B, defense-intellectual class, controlling public opinion of the Afghan war.

Connected via interlocking boards of directors and trusteeships, Leo

Cherne's Freedom House alone connected Zbigniew Brzezinski to the Afghan propaganda effort, while CIA Director William Casey had served in 1979 as chairman of the executive committee of Whitehead and Cherne's International Rescue Committee.[10] It was Leo Cherne's Research Institute of America (RIA) that had served as America's unofficial CIA long before there was a CIA or even OSS.[11] It was Leo Cherne who originally formulated the mechanism for transforming the depressed American economy of 1939 by proposing to convert it into a military-industrial "arsenal."[12] Together with future CIA director Bill Casey, Cherne produced *The Business and Defense Coordinator* as a guide to the coming war economy, pronouncing that "war has become a conflict of economics in which financial and material resources are the chief weapons."[13] It was Leo Cherne who prophesied in 1941 that the United States could not become involved in the war in Europe "until a triggering event occurs in the Pacific."[14] Cherne's ability to predict the future made him a wealthy and influential man. Cherne had good reason to champion the CIA's war in Afghanistan while doing all he could to revive America's faith in the benefits of armed conflict. As a key member of the Vietnam lobby, Leo Cherne had been personally involved in recommending Ngo Dinh Diem to President Eisenhower as a solution to America's problem there.[15] And it was Leo Cherne, as chairman of President Ford's Foreign Intelligence Advisory Board (PFIAB) who convinced CIA Director George H. W. Bush in 1976 to allow a group of outsiders known as Team-B to lay the groundwork for a new Cold War.[16]

In the studio at ABC that May 26, 1983, Team-B, Leo Cherne, Bill Casey, and the whole neoconservative agenda going back to 1941, put their cards for killing Russians and not negotiating with them on the table—and they won. A few months later, a call from Karen McKay summed up what we had been up against all along. When I informed her that she could make a stronger case for her claim of Soviet use of poison gas and other atrocities if she just produced conclusive evidence, her reply—"we don't need evidence, we know they're guilty"—said it all. The Russians were not going to be allowed to leave Afghanistan until enough blood, treasure, and bad public relations had been extracted to repay the humiliation of Vietnam. While making repeated pronouncements that the Soviets must leave Afghanistan at the earliest possible moment, the Reagan administration and the U.S. Congress did everything in their power to prolong the war and keep them there. It would be that way for the next six years.

"Was there a lost opportunity for the Soviets to withdraw in 1983?" Cordovez and Harrison asked in their comprehensive analysis of the Soviet dilemma, *Out of Afghanistan*. "Ironically, during the very period when Andropov was groping for a way to disengage from Afghanistan, supporters of stepped-up American involvement were on the ascendant in the Reagan Administration."[17]

By that spring of 1983, Washington was already striking back at Andropov's "peace offensive." In ill health and with not long to live, the clever Kremlin bureaucrat was everything Trotsky's Fourth Internationalists and Brian Crozier's Sixth Internationalists lived to despise.

Intent that no middle ground of mutual interest be reached between the United States and the Soviet Union, Assistant Secretary for Policy Richard Perle began to press Congress for more and better funding to the Afghan "freedom fighters." In a preview of the tactics used to justify the 2003 Iraq war, Perle isolated dissenting State Department views by selecting his own intelligence team, then used the one-sided results of perceived dire Soviet intentions to lobby members of Congress and private interest groups for the need to increase the pressure. It was a process of creating self-fulfilling prophecies: "Perle and his staff 'came in with a definite agenda relating to Afghanistan,' recalled [Army Chief of Staff] General [Edward C.] Meyer. 'They were anxious to increase the Pentagon's role in providing more and better equipment to the Afghans as well as people to assist with the transfer of the equipment. It was clearly unusual for them to have their own separate intelligence network by which they were gathering information of Soviet activities in the region.'"[18] Perle's ideologically motivated efforts to seize control of the Afghan campaign for the Pentagon from well-entrenched CIA Director William Casey fell short of the mark. Yet in the end it inspired Casey to accelerate his own plan.

Disconnected from any fixed foreign-policy objective and already technically beyond the CIA's direct purview, Afghanistan was on the verge of becoming Christmas Day every day for Washington's old right wing, like Cherne and Casey and its reminted, self-invented, neoconservative defense intellectuals like Richard Perle. Between 1983 and 1985, a fierce battle ensued inside the CIA between Casey and the agency's deputy director, John McMahon, over what kind of advanced technology and how much more money the mujahideen would be allowed to receive. "My objection was that we didn't have a foreign policy to back it up," McMahon said, quoted by Cordonez and Harrison. "I made it clear at the highest levels throughout 1983 and afterward that I felt we had to have a political settlement. If covert action is not based in foreign policy objectives, it's pure fun and games, it's no basis for achieving anything."[19]

McMahon's problem stemmed directly from Casey's conflicting desire to *hold* the Russians in Afghanistan as long as possible while claiming he was doing it to *expel* them. According to Army Chief Meyer, "Casey would *say* [Cordovez and Harrison emphasis] that he wanted to get them out, but he actually wanted them to send more and more Russians down there and take casualties."[20]

Juggling an equally ideological motive with his own private financial interests, Texas Democrat Charlie Wilson spearheaded the drive to make keeping the Russians in Afghanistan a quasi-religious bipartisan lovefest, while marrying the Hezb-i Islami's vicious Gulbuddin Hekmatyar to the American cause. Backed by an intense behind-the-scenes lobbying campaign by Dick Cheney—then a congressman from Wyoming—Wilson's duel assignment to both the House Appropriations Committee and the House Permanent Select Committee on Intelligence guaranteed him direct control over the congressional component of the Afghan war.[21] Intent on inflicting as much humiliation on the Soviets as possible, Wilson's stage managing turned Bill Casey's "fun and games" into a comedy of the absurd, with a Kiplingesque Wilson in mufti staging mock raids from Pakistan into Afghanistan brandishing a sword while riding a white stallion.[22] Working closely with the Pakistani ISI chief, General Abdul Rahman Akhtar, Wilson managed to transform the war from a dirty, low-key, covert operation on the Soviet Union's southern border into a Washington cocktail-circuit cause célèbre.[23] With Congress giddy to pick up the bill to arm and train the world's most notorious Muslim terrorists and the press generally cheering them on, even the most diehard of congressional liberals found it impossible to comprehend, let alone defeat, Wilson's seemingly magical strategy. "Meanwhile, Democratic liberals and reporters, who might ordinarily have questioned the wisdom of these programs, simply couldn't figure out how to overcome the impression left by right-wing critics that the CIA's crime in this case was not doing too much but too little—that McMahon and the Agency were subverting the President's clear mandate."[24] But the danger of Wilson's absurdist campaign was not lost on those who better understood the real nature of the crime in progress. As former CBS newsman George Crile noted, "Wilson invited [Sibghatullah] Mojadeddi to join him and Joanne [Herring] for lunch at the Democratic Club. Almost immediately Joanne began to sing the praises of an Afghan leader she had gotten to know when making her documentary with Charles Fawcett. Gulbuddin Hekmatyar was his name, and she had found him marvelous beyond words. The meek-looking professor became instantly agitated and began, in a most remarkable fashion, to denounce Gulbuddin as a *true monster* and an enemy of Afghanistan. He accused Gulbuddin of being a dangerous fundamentalist, busy assassinating moderate Afghans, a man no self-respecting nation should support."[25]

Milt Bearden, who was chosen by Casey to run the CIA's operation from Pakistan in the spring of 1985 following a growing surge of congressional complaints about ISI's corruption and monopoly over weapons distribution, found Hekmatyar uncooperative and ungrateful. "He began his great controversy with the Reagan administration when he accompanied the other resistance leaders to the UN to make their case and refused to travel on down to Washington with the others to be the guests of the president at the White House. So he decided to personally insult the president of the United States."[26] Well versed in the history of the Pashtunistan issue and of tribal independence movements "in the lands of the Wazirs, the Mahsuds, and the Ahmadzis," Bearden is candid about his U.S. military role and its commercial objectives as a man who considered himself "a twentieth-century American version of the British East India Company political agent and quartermaster"[27] to the legendary Pashtun fighters.

Despite concerns voiced to Bearden, Casey went ahead and upped the jeopardy, providing ISI with American frontline Stinger missiles, greatly expanding Hekmatyar and ISI's prestige as well as their control over the illegal drug trade helping to finance the ISI. Hushed up in American media accounts, the combination of Stingers and heroin trafficking quickly laid the basis for a monstrous new kind of privatized drug industry, outside the purview of any elected authority.[28] Alfred McCoy writes, "During the decade-long covert war, the American press published positive reports about Hekmatyar, the leading recipient of U.S. arms shipments, ignoring his heroin dealing and human rights abuses. A year after the Soviet withdrawal in 1989 stripped the Afghan war of its national security imperatives, the *New York Times* finally reported what it called 'the sinister nature of Mr. Hekmatyar' and the *Washington Post* published a page 1 expose about his heroin syndicate."[29]

The events of 9/11 finally turned the American military against Hekmatyar, a hero to congressman Charlie Wilson during the war against the Russians, making him one of the first targets of American missile attacks. But according to George Crile, during the war against the Russians it was a different story, with Wilson dismissing criticism of Hekmatyar, figuring that "he had just stumbled into some ancient tribal rivalry and that it made no sense to try to figure out who was right and who was wrong. The only relevant question, in the face of the great Soviet evil, was whether they both were trying to kill Russians."[30]

Whether it was killing Russians or not, the not-so-secret war and the rationale for overlooking the consequences of it produced a strange, almost surreal effect on Reagan's Washington during the 1980s, with senators, representatives, other policy makers, and government staffers who were in on the dirtier secrets of U.S. involvement suspending any moral disbelief over what they had signed on for.

Intentionally privatized at the outset by groups like the Safari Club and Crozier's "The 61" to avoid any stain of CIA involvement, and managed completely (and corruptly) on the ground by Zia-ul-Haq's Inter-Services Intelligence, until 1983 the three-billion-dollar U.S. contribution[31] to the jihad had no overarching purpose but to generate mayhem on the Soviets' southern border. But as the war dragged on, with Moscow's decrepit leadership in a state of near collapse and the Soviets clearly suffering, the ever-mystical imperialist Bill Casey's plan drifted into something far more dangerous. Drawing on plans drawn up by Brzezinski and Paul Henze during the Carter administration, Casey's idea was as close to a first-strike scenario against the Soviet Union as he could get with all the potential of triggering a nuclear war. Robert Dreyfuss reports, "Starting in 1984, Casey pushed the Saudi-Pakistan alliance to undertake a much more explosive strategy, launching propaganda, sabotage, and guerrilla activity across the Amu River into the Soviet Union's Muslim republics. . . . A CIA official who worked with Casey at the time says: There were occasional forays that took place within the territory of the Soviet Union, which scared the crap out of Moscow."[32]

According to Stanford's Peter Schweizer in his book *Victory: The Reagan Administration's Secret Strategy*, Casey's plan to "ship arms, to encourage local uprisings" in the "soft underbelly of the Soviet Union" was initially greeted with shock by his Pakistani partners. "Putting together a military operation and carrying it into the Soviet Union had never been done. There had been no combat on Soviet territory since the Second World War. The diplomatic and military repercussions could be colossal. Pakistan as a sponsor of the mujahideen could be a target for military retaliation. But so could its sponsor, particularly if it became known in the Kremlin that this was a Reagan initiative."[33]

Milt Bearden was the one to take the call from the CIA's deputy director of operations, Clair George, when the shock wave caused by Casey's holy war inside the Soviet Union finally broke over Washington. "Were you in any way involved in an attack on an industrial site deep inside the Soviet Union . . . in Uzbekistan . . . anytime in the last month?"[34] George asked. Bearden responded that by the rules of the game, even if the attackers had used weapons provided by the United States, it wouldn't prove American involvement. "We stand by our position that once the stuff's delivered to the Paks, we lose all control over it," Bearden responded.[35] Absolved of responsibility, Bearden's ability to distance himself from the consequences of the American weapons might have added a technical layer of protection for the CIA, but it also added to the growing and dangerous institutional surreality of supporting extremist Muslim killers—so long as the Soviets were being defeated.

Adding to the danger of intended or unintended consequences of U.S. weapon supplies was the amount of weapons being siphoned off or simply stolen from the pipeline. Conservative estimates put the number at 20 percent in 1986. Stansfield Turner, Carter's CIA director, estimated that if only 20 percent *got through*, he wouldn't have been surprised.[36]

Exacting a heavy toll on Soviet morale, the entire Afghan countryside was now alive in opposition to Soviet forces as the KGB had predicted in the fall of 1979. Despite a long history of involvement in Afghan politics, Soviet support for Babrak Karmal doomed him from the start as an Afghan president. As feuding continued between Parcham and Khalq, typhoid, hepatitis and Alexandre de Marenches' drug-addiction scheme (see below) wracked Soviet troops. Early in 1983 Yuri Andropov had ordered a high-level policy review that concluded that Afghanistan could not be resolved through military means.[37] His young protégée Mikhail Gorbachev, on a visit to Canada, remarked early that year that the invasion "was a mistake."[38] In March Andropov informed the UN that a settlement was needed. Less ideological and far more practical than fellow Kremlin leaders, he floated proposals for a Soviet withdrawal, but by February of 1984 he too had died.[39] Cordovez and Harrison write, "It all began in 1983. The reason that Gorbachev was able to act so much more decisively in foreign affairs than in domestic policy was largely because of the reappraisal set in motion under Andropov."[40] Replaced by the comparably aged and ailing Brezhnev aide Konstantin Chernenko,[41] Soviet policy on Afghanistan resumed a hard, but increasingly delusional line. "[D]espite the conventional wisdom that has coalesced in the West, the new Soviet leadership does not believe that its Army is bogged down in Afghanistan.[42]

CASEY'S BRAND OF MYSTICAL IMPERIALISM

William Casey began a life of intelligence work in London during World War II.[43] Groomed under OSS founder Bill Donovan, who referred to his men as Knights Templar,[44] Casey's passion for the Afghan jihad has sometimes been described as messianic. An ultra-conservative Catholic, Casey saw little difference in the antimodernist beliefs of the Wahhabist House of Saud and the antimodernist, anti-enlightenment views of the newly installed Polish Pope, John Paul II.[45] Pope Pius X had mandated against the heretical influences of modernism on Catholic dogma in his 1910 "Oath Against Modernism" and all but forty members of the clergy had signed it.[46] The document was rescinded only in 1967[47] and many conservative Catholics continued to believe that modernism and the "true faith" were diametrically opposed. Active as a Knight of Malta—an eleventh-century knighthood originally established to guard Christian pilgrims on the their visits to the Holy Lands—Casey maintained close ties to the Vatican.[48] There, among fellow Knights of Malta such as former CIA director John McCone, French intelligence director Alexandre de Marenches, and W. R. Grace and Company CEO Peter Grace, he would indulge his fondness for the past and the trappings that went with it, as they played "at nineteenth-century-style royalty, wearing fancy ribbons and medals and calling each other 'Prince' and 'High Eminence.'"[49] Whether carrying a religious holy war into Soviet territory or into the halls of Congress, Casey's ultimate objectives were far closer to those of the radical Islamists than any Afghan nationalists attempting to establish a broad-based democratic state. According to Steve Coll, "Casey saw political Islam and the Catholic Church as natural allies in the realistic counter-strategy of covert action he was forging at the CIA to thwart Soviet imperialism."[50]

Criticized for what appeared at times a crude and careless attitude toward an Afghan jihad whose ultimate goal was the destruction of the modern world, it might better be said that in the end destruction was exactly what his "care" was. And in this he was not alone. Coll cites a meeting in 1985, when Fred Ikle, under-secretary of defense for policy, was told that his suggestion for skipping the Pakistanis all together and dropping weapons directly to the mujahideen might start World War III, his response was, "World War III? That's not such a bad idea."[51]

Interviewed in 1982 by Robert Scheer for his book on Team-B and first-strike nuclear war, *With Enough Shovels*, Jerome Wiesner grappled with the mad dynamic that he thought drove this kind of apocalyptic thinking inside the American government: "The arms race . . . has acquired a psychology—Kennan called it a genetic code—which rides through all kinds of things. The U.S., I eventually became convinced, was fighting a bogeyman. That doesn't mean that [the Soviets] don't have weapons, but on the whole we were racing with ourselves. We'd invent a weapon, then we'd invent a defense against it, then we'd defend the next weapon because the Russians would have built what we'd invented. We've really been pacing the thing, and we've been doing it for thirty years."[52]

Whether conscious of it or not, by 1987 the United States was racing madly with itself to create a new kind of bogeyman, a dark messiah that would wipe the world clean of modernity by destroying the institutions that supported it. But this time, instead of it being a nuclear missile stored in some deep silo in the heart of the Urals, the bogeyman would emerge in human form in the mountains of Afghanistan and the nearby tribal areas of Pakistan's North-West Frontier Province.

PRIVATIZING THE HOLY WAR

"If you want to move arms around, you don't want your bankers to talk about it," journalist Peter Truell told filmmaker Samira Goetschel. "Yet, if you're involved in those kinds of activities you need access to finance. You want to be unregulated and you've also got to make foreign exchange transactions and so on and you want the people who are doing that for you to be complicit with you and not tell the authorities anything and so on. And if you're looking for that kind of Service, BCCI was pretty much top of the list."[53]

Following Ronald Reagan's election in the fall of 1980, French intelligence chief Alexandre de Marenches had visited with an old friend from World War II, future CIA director William Casey, and suggested bringing the drug operation for Afghanistan inside the CIA. Code-naming it Operation Mosquito, to "sting" the Russians, de Marenches suggested stimulating the narcotics trade near Soviet bases to addict Russian soldiers as the French had done in Indo-China during the colonial period, and the Vietcong had done to Americans during their war there. According to de

Marenches' biography, Casey liked the plan but insisted that since it could never be accomplished in secret, the United States could not be directly involved.[54]

Already privatized by independent, ad hoc intelligence groups, in order to avoid laws, and—in Brian Crozier's words—"recent legislation (as in the U.S.) or because political circumstances made such inquiries difficult or potentially embarrassing,"[55] within a year of initiating U.S. support for the war, Afghan heroin began flooding the markets of Europe and America. "Before 1979 Pakistan was not a major exporter of drugs. . . . In 1984, it was estimated that 80 percent of all the heroin consumed in Britain and 30 percent of the American imports came from Pakistan.[56] Financed through a little-known bank, the Bank of Credit and Commerce International, BCCI acted as a go-between for Washington, Hong Kong, Peshawar, and Switzerland, laundering money for drugs and facilitating arms sales to Nicaraguan Contras and Afghan mujahideen groups.[57] Although only a small part of the Iran-Contra hearings that found Reagan's national security advisors Robert "Bud" McFarlane, Admiral John Poindexter, and Colonel Oliver North guilty of illegal acts, its role as a financing tool for the Afghan mujahideen was never fully disclosed. But according to John K. Cooley, the CIA used BCCI as a paymaster, extensively financing mujahideen operations through its numerous branches throughout the world:

> The CIA took the unusual step of flatly denying the media reports about CIA-BCCI links. The denial backfired. The British media and American investigative reporters for ABC News and others published a series of damaging revelations about CIA accounts in London branches of BCCI, chiefly the Cromwell Road branch. . . . The *Financial Times* reported that Pakistan's finance minister had confirmed that the CIA used BCCI branches in Pakistan to channel money, presumably through the ISI, to the Afghan jihad. Further it disclosed the CIA and other agencies used "slush funds" at BCCI branches to pay off Pakistani army officers and Afghan resistance leaders.[58]

Derided as the "Bank of Crooks and Criminals,"[59] BCCI was so successful at brokering the CIA's off-the-books operation in Afghanistan that it created an entire new class of privatized international terrorist, capable of striking around the world at will. Jack Blum, former special counsel to the 1987 "Kerry" Senate Foreign Relations Subcommittee on Terrorism, Narcotics and International Relations, told filmmaker Samira Goetschel, "They did money laundering, they financed arms trading, financed smuggling operations, assisted various people in looting their countries. . . . The CIA used them, the Mossad used them, various Arab intelligence agencies used them, the Russians used them, the British used them, everybody used them. They were wonderful; sometimes they traded information from one intelligence agency to the other. If it wasn't as serious and as deadly as it turned out to be, it would be damn comical."[60]

With BCCI secretly tasked with facilitating the resources to the CIA's covert arms program, by 1987 the amount of drugs reaching the world from their operations would stagger the world's law enforcement agencies. According to Blum, "The amounts of heroin were staggering; the amounts of money involved were staggering. There was a seizure of a ship off the coast of Turkey that had come from the Makran coast of Pakistan, that had twelve tons—metric tons—of heroin and heroin derivatives on it. That is such a startlingly large number, it's sort of like the world's supply for a year."[61]

10.

Moscow's New Regime

Hobbled by the accuracy of the Stinger missiles, plagued by disease, desertion, and low morale, the Soviet will to support Kabul's communists broke. In Moscow, the 1985 succession of the young and dynamic Mikhail Gorbachev to Communist Party chair following the death of Konstantin Chernenko heralded the end of a Kremlin era.[1] Born well beyond the window of the old World War II Communist Party structure, Gorbachev had not participated in the vote to invade Afghanistan. Aware that time was running out, he used the occasion of Chernenko's funeral to scare Pakistan's Zia-ul-Haq into backing down.[2]

Supporting his threat with air strikes and artillery bombardments, Gorbachev's move was merely a bluff. Just as he began deliberations on plans to evacuate Soviet troops, President Reagan ratcheted up the campaign to defeat the Russians. Giving his generals one last year to turn the situation around, Gorbachev deposed Babrak Karmal and replaced him with the head of the Afghan secret police, Dr. Mohammad Najibullah.[3] But by then Casey's holy war had taken on a life of its own.

Rebel groups lead by Burhanuddin Rabani's military commander, the Tajik Ahmed Shah Massoud, the "Lion of the Panjshir," consistently repelled Soviet and Afghan efforts to control the Panjshir Valley in northeastern Afghanistan.[4]

Describing Afghanistan as a "bleeding wound," Gorbachev decided to remove Soviet troops.[5] Dedicated to restructuring the Soviet Union (perestroika), the new Soviet leader brought a surprising pre-Bolshevik quality to his leadership, attempting to awaken the ossified Soviet bureaucracy by setting out realistic goals with humanist themes. A revolutionary within Soviet society, Gorbachev's efforts at refocusing Russia away from nuclear competition and war itself toward peaceful cooperation, shocked the world.

Reviving traditional Russian themes that had been mostly forgotten in the West by his time, Gorbachev invoked the work of Theosophist Nicholas Roerich as an inspiration for the kind of society that a modern Russia could become. Bernice Glatzer Rosenthal wrote, "Gorbachev himself endorsed the 'Rerikh idea' (a kind of spiritual communism) in 1987 and helped to establish a center for Rerikh studies, conferences, and exhibitions in Moscow. There are at least five hundred Rerikh societies in Russia today."[6]

Unfortunately the "Rerikh idea" had little impact on the politics surrounding Afghanistan where the situation remained a bleeding wound, now worse than what had prompted the 1979 invasion. Internal Soviet justifications for the Afghan incursion—as a defense of its southern border against Islamic terrorism—had been borne out. Plagued by a growing number of cross-border attacks from radical Islamists into Soviet territory, the KGB and GRU vehemently opposed troop withdrawals from Afghanistan.[7]

The Soviet power structure was riven over what to do, torn between old-guard hard-liners and Gorbachev's reformers. In January 1988, the chairman of the Presidium of the Supreme Soviet, Andre Gromyko, publicly praised Stalin's 1945 effort to keep Poland under Soviet control. Struggling to leave Afghanistan and reform his country's crumbling political structure that February, Gorbachev announced in a nationwide address that Soviet troop withdrawals would begin on May 15, and be completed by March 1989.[8]

Presented with the opportunity to lay out a solid structure for peace in Afghanistan following a decade of war, the final agreement for a Soviet withdrawal, hammered out between Kabul, Islamabad, Washington, and Moscow was instead a diplomatic farce. In March, meetings between Secretary of State George Schultz and Foreign Minister Eduard Shevardnadze resulted in a virtual capitulation of the Soviet position, with Schultz refusing to stop aid to the rebels as a condition for Soviet withdrawal. The final UN-mediated Geneva agreement requiring a complete cessation of activities from Pakistan even posed legal problems for the United States when Pakistan's President Zia-ul-Haq phoned Ronald Reagan to tell him that "it is permissible to lie in a just cause."[9]

ZIA'S TIMELY DEATH RAISES QUESTIONS

On August 17, 1988, Zia was killed in the crash of a C-130 Hercules aircraft, along with the U.S. ambassador to Pakistan, Arnold Raphel. An investigation revealed that the plane had been sabotaged. Numerous theories were put forward, blaming the KGB, Mossad, Afghan communists, the Indian secret service, radical Iranian Shiites, rivals inside the ISI, and the CIA itself, with Milton Bearden as the "executioner."[10] The previous April, the Pakistani ammunition dump supplying the Afghan rebels at Ojhri Camp near Islamabad had exploded and burned, destroying ten thousand tons of weapons and supplies intended for the war.[11] Suspecting that the United States had deliberately detonated the ordnance in a secret protocol with the retreating Soviets, high-level Pakistanis were convinced now that the death of General Zia, Akhtar, and most of the Pakistani high command had been arranged by Bearden. Bearden writes,

> There was an impeccable South Asian logic in the suggestion that the United States was involved in Zia's death. According to the growing conspiracy theory, the elaborate U.S. endgame in Pakistan and Afghanistan had begun with the destruction of Ojhri Camp in the spring, followed by the killing of the president and his generals in August, as they were now "in the way of bigger things," thus the CIA had arranged for the destruction of the ordnance depot at Ojhri. And to be sure the plans Zia and Akhtar had put in place for a post-Soviet Afghanistan a decade earlier failed, both men had to be liquidated.[12]

Whatever plans Zia had for Afghanistan following the Soviets' departure, his death would barely slow the course of radicalization established over his decade in power nor lessen his successor's desire for the total elimination of Afghan sovereignty. Trained in the United States from 1962–1964 at the U.S. Army Command and General Staff College at Fort Leavenworth, Kansas, and aided by the CIA, the Pentagon and the State Department, Zia left the battle for Afghanistan having altered the course of his own Pakistan from a western model of national development to a radical religious model known as Nizam-i Islam (Islamic System). Steve Coll writes, "In 1971 there had been only nine hundred madrassas in all of Pakistan. By the summer of 1988 there were about eight thousand official religious schools and an estimated twenty five thousand unregistered ones."[13]

A DARK VICTORY IN PERSPECTIVE

On February 15, 1989, ten years and a day after the killing of U.S. Ambassador Adolph Dubs, the last units of the Soviet Fortieth Infantry left Afghanistan. At the CIA headquarters in Langley a celebration broke out.[14] In the CIA's eyes, the secret war—actually begun after Mohammed Daoud's coup of 1973 but accelerated after the Taraki-Amin coup of 1978—had badly shaken America's Cold War nemesis, avenged Vietnam, and proved to themselves that the methods employed by America's defense intellectuals were after all, sound. Like the Team-B report itself, it was a delusion—a self-fulfilling prophecy built on lies, exaggeration, and the bodies of a million dead Afghans. But neither the Russians nor the Afghans were in any position to argue with it nor did the American people have a clue as to what was to follow.

A cynical account of why the U.S. people never gained an accurate picture of the deluded mind-set driving the decade-long Afghan conflict and were subsequently left unprepared for the World Trade Center attacks of 1993 and 2001, was provided by Alvin A. Synder in his 1995 book *Warriors of Disinformation*. "The war in Afghanistan was the American government's 'made-for-TV' movie. It was the first war in which both AK-47's and video cams were standard infantry issue. It was a war in which media coverage was purchased from a mail order catalogue, and Uncle Sam owned the warehouse."[15] Snyder referred to Afghanistan as a "public relations nightmare for Moscow," but "a public relations dream come true" for Washington.[16] A former CBS and NBC senior executive and ranking communications official in the Ford and Reagan administrations, Snyder was an enthusiastic advocate of the use of disinformation to manipulate public opinion.[17] One of his more famous victories had been at the UN presentation of the Soviet shoot-down of Korean Airlines flight 007 in 1983. "The stunning impact our KE-007 videotape had at the United Nations showed how dramatically television could manipulate world opinion," he writes. "It was clear to all of us that it would henceforth influence the way in which America conducted its foreign affairs."[18] Snyder apologized in a *Washington Post* op-ed in 1996, admitting that the intercepted audio communications of the Soviet fighter pilot had been intentionally edited to deceive the public.[19] The bad publicity generated from the shoot-down and its manipulation had put the last nail in Andropov's efforts to end the Cold War in Afghanistan in 1983. But Synder's success with the KAL propaganda only boosted his desire to organize an Afghan disinformation campaign. "The problem for American propagandists was that the conflict was getting scant media coverage. . . . During all of 1986, the combined American TV network coverage of the war totaled less than one hour."[20] Under the direction of Reagan's Hollywood crony Charles Z. Wick[21] at the U.S. Information Agency (USIA), Snyder's proposal for a new approach to news gathering by training Afghan "freedom fighters" in propaganda techniques and giving them cameras filled the void left by the major networks in providing the grist for anti-Soviet propaganda stories.[22]

Writing a memorandum to Wick in March 1985, Snyder had outlined the potential benefits of the program. "Just as the Russians could not face the 'video document' we presented at the United Nations to expose them on KE-007, they would again be in a position to have to dispute proof positive of the horrors they inflict on Afghanistan."[23]

As the Soviets rolled across their border and out of Afghanistan after their ten-year war, Snyder's public relations dream had indeed showed how dramatically world opinion could be manipulated against Soviet Russia. Left unsaid was the overall effect of the Afghan propaganda campaign on the American media, which had allowed themselves to miss the real war and been snowed under by the make-believe struggle of good versus evil manufactured by a *Three Stooges* producer and an unholy alliance of liberal Democrats, neoconservatives and right-wing Washington insiders. But for the Afghans, there was no mistaking the end of the ten-year Soviet occupation, as a new kind of horror replaced the anti-Soviet jihad with a new kind of war and a new purpose, this one intended to benefit Pakistani and American business interests.

NAJIBULLAH SURPRISES

Unwilling to share power with any of the rebel organizations in order to form some kind of coalition government, no one, least of all the Russians, expected the remains of Dr. Najibullah's People's Democratic Party of Afghanistan to survive for long. But with the CIA's Islamist proxies as torn by tribal and political factionalism as the PDPA, Najibullah surprised the experts.

In May 1989, the newly elected government of Oxford- and Radcliffe-educated Benazir Bhutto moved to finish off the Afghan nationalists by launching an assault on Jalalabad on the Pakistani border.[24] Chasing her father's dream of an Afghan conquest, Bhutto wished to secure Jalalabad as a trophy victory prior to her appearance at the Organization of the Islamic Conference. Pushed ahead by the ISI and the Americans,[25] but opposed by the seven Afghan rebel groups, the poorly planned and executed assault was turned back by Najibullah's forces. Henry S. Bradsher writes, "Jalalabad was a proxy battle by ISI—maybe not even proxy, because there were reports of Pakistani Army units being involved. The decision to launch the attack was taken in Islamabad on 5 March at a meeting of Pakistani officials attended by United States Ambassador Robert B. Oakley but not by any mujahideen officials."[26]

The defeat disproved the decade-long claims that the Afghan communists would break and run without Russian firepower behind them. It also prolonged the war by three years while weakening Bhutto's influence with Pakistan's all-powerful military establishment.

Robert Gates wrote, "The Soviets and the CIA both were to be proven wrong about the staying power of the Afghan government after the Soviet troops left. Najibullah would remain in power for another three years, as the United States and USSR continued to aid their respective sides. On December 31, 1991, both Moscow and Washington cut off all assistance, and Najibullah's government fell four months later. He had outlasted both Gorbachev and the Soviet Union itself."[27]

Summarizing his feelings, former CIA director Gates's narrow view of the Afghan war as a bipolar struggle between the United States and the Soviet Union typified the myopic mind-set that had become the standard mode of thought for Washington's Cold War bureaucrats. Rigid, simplistic, and focused only on defeating the Soviet Union, it would lead, within a very short time, to further disaster for the Afghan people while opening the door to an ancient terrorism whose next target would be the United States itself. "It was a great victory. Afghanistan was at last free of the foreign invader," Gates said in his book. "Now Afghans could resume fighting among themselves—and hardly anybody cared."[28]

11.

A New Decade: A New and More Dangerous Afghanistan

By 1990 it was clear that Gates's "great victory" had only replaced one foreign invader for another. In the hands of Pakistan's gloating and rapacious ISI, Afghanistan was now home to a host of foreign invaders from every Muslim country in the world. Realizing that the war had left Afghanistan in an even more dangerous state than it had been under Soviet control, a handful of American experts set out to issue a warning. On May 3, 1990, Barnett Rubin, former director of the Center for Preventive Action at the Council on Foreign Relations, delivered an address on the situation in Afghanistan before the Commission on Security and Cooperation in Europe. Arguing that "it would be wrong simply to end our involvement and effectively abandon Afghanistan to fragmentation and civil war," Rubin pleaded with the United States and the international community to understand that the world had changed and to revise accordingly the thinking that had appeared to succeed in Afghanistan. "A strategy which succeeded in the past—supplying more and more sophisticated weapons through exiled leaders in Pakistan to uncoordinated resistance fronts inside the country—will lead our policy, as well as Afghanistan, to disaster."[1]

Citing the apparent confusion over exactly what the American goals were now that the Soviets had been defeated, he specifically pointed to the bipolar conceptual framework as having outlived its usefulness. "First the policy is confused in its goals. . . . Second, the policy is based on a mistaken conceptual framework derived from an outdated image of bi-polar conflict. . . . Third, the policy is inconsistent in its execution . . . [p]artly because the conflict is complex and multilateral . . . and partly because [since] there is no unified political leadership of the resistance, neither we nor anyone else can coordinate military activity of the mujahideen with political objectives, which Clausewitz singled out as the major determinant of success in war."[2]

Having established that without clear political objectives and U.S. assistance in reaching them any further war in Afghanistan could not be won, Rubin revealed his fears that the hidden hands of Pakistan and Saudi Arabia could be at work, continuing to use Afghanistan as a springboard for a Sunni Islamist assault on Soviet Central Asia and nearby Shiite Iran. Nevertheless, policy makers in the United States seemed oblivious to the problems about to erupt and the central role they had played in creating them. "Still," said Rubin,

> the debate about policy in Afghanistan continues to unfold within a bi-polar conceptual framework derived from the Cold War, which is true to the realities neither of Afghanistan nor the contemporary international system. According to this framework there are two sides in Afghanistan: the Communist government, supported by the Soviet Union, and the patriotic, Islamic resistance, supported by the U.S. and its allies. The reality is different. There are not two, but many sides in Afghanistan. The country has indeed undergone a certain ideological polarization, but even more fundamental, and becoming stronger since the Soviet troop withdrawal, is that it has undergone a process of tribal, ethnic, sectarian, political, geographical, economic, urban/rural, cultural, and generational fragmentation. . . . A military solution cannot work not only because neither side can defeat the other, but, more fundamentally, because there are not two sides one or the other of which could win.[3]

More than willing to indulge the bipolar view against a negotiated withdrawal during the Soviet occupation, Rubin and his desire to establish a new conceptual framework for dealing with the Afghan conflict would garner much the same enthusiasm from the powers that be as Yuri Andropov's "charm offensive" had seven years before. Suddenly apparent to those observers bothering to look was an alternate agenda lying just below the surface. Left in place by the departing superpowers, it would resemble more the nineteenth-century pseudo-religious imperialism of Britain's old "Forward Policy" than any late-twentieth-century Cold War counterinsurgency. Only this time the "Forward Policy" would contain a radical strain of Wahhabism, and the mystical imperialists forwarding it would be Islamic extremists.

Former special envoy to the mujahideen Peter Tomsen summed up what he referred to as "Afghanistan's second nightmare" in a 1999 interview with exiled Afghan journalist Omar Samad: "While the Soviets were in Afghanistan, the ISI sort of became an interior ministry for Afghanistan. The political and even military leadership of Pakistan could not control its own military intelligence organization. The prime minister, the foreign minister and even the president often did not know what ISI was doing: it was a kind of state within a state, and it is still operating like that. . . . Their intelligence gathering and operations spread into every region of Afghanistan. . . . This also involved a joint effort between ISI and radical Islamic groups in the Gulf and the Mid-East. . . . Their objective has been to exploit Afghanistan for their own purposes."[4]

Testifying before Congress that the United States must help the Aghan people take back their country from the Islamic extremists now that the Russians were gone, like so many other American administrators, Peter Tomsen found that his warnings fell on deaf ears.[5] According to CBS stringer Kurt Lohbeck, Tomsen's efforts were doomed from the start, as he found himself positioned between hostile political interests that—like those Adolph Dubs had faced a decade before him—had no interest in advancing a negotiated settlement. Tomsen, wrote Lohbeck, "tried unsuccessfully to close the deepening divisions among the various factions. It was a futile effort since his mission worked at cross-purposes with the covert actions of the CIA and ISI, which were supplying Massood and Gulbaddin and pushing them to attack Kabul—just as the feud between the two erupted into open deadly warfare."[6]

With no military and less Soviet financial support, by 1991 Kabul had finally been pushed to the breaking point. Without its coequal in the bipolar framework—the Soviet Union—U.S. congressional support for the Afghan mujahideen began to crumble as well. Having spent uncounted billions to train and equip an army of "holy warriors" to inflict as much terror as possible on the Soviets and their supporters, the United States now left Afghanistan in the hands of Pakistan and its ISI. As predicted, catastrophe brewed as mujahideen groups splintered into heavily armed factions. Engorged with victory and successfully "privatized" by the multibillion-dollar arms-for-drugs business, scores of rival chieftains vied for control. Splintered from the start, the Peshawar seven-mujahideen leadership now found itself further fractionalized, with CIA-sponsored Hekmatyar, Abdul Sayyaf, and Burhanuddin Rabbani on the same side as Najibullah in denouncing the January 17, 1991, U.S. war in Iraq.

Respected by people like the CIA's Bearden for his toughness and intelligence, Dr. Najibullah's attempts to hold power were dealt a death blow by Moscow in August when the same hard-line Soviet generals that supported him failed in their effort to overthrow Mikhail Gorbachev.[7] In September, James Baker III signed an agreement with the new post-coup Russian foreign minister Boris Dimitrievich Pankin to cease weapons deliveries on January 1, 1992.[8] Soviet deliveries ended before the deadline, on December 15.[9] Eleven days later, the Union of Soviet Socialist Republics was dissolved. Failing economically and militarily, Moscow could no longer continue financial support. In one final and perhaps supreme irony of the Afghan conflict, in mid-November an official mujahideen delegation led by Burhanuddin Rabbani (despite opposition from Hekmatyar) was received in Moscow by Pankin and Russia's vice president, Alexander Rutskoy, and issued a joint statement that, Bradsher writes, "condemned the Soviet invasion and wartime role in Afghanistan. This remarkable—indeed, only a short time before unthinkable—position of a Soviet foreign minister completed the transition from Brezhnevian bluster in 1979 through Andropov's incomplete reassessment to Gorbachev's discrediting of the invasion decision."[10]

1992

By April 15, defections within the PDPA had left Najibullah powerless and Kabul defenseless. Massoud advanced toward Kabul but stopped just shy at the abandoned Soviet airbase in Bagram.[11] Having operated as a mercenary for years, demanding payment in dollars for his men's service, Gen. Rashid Dostum, head of the Uzbek PDPA armored division, made an agreement with Massoud not to fight against him.[12] Supported by units of Pakistan's ISI, Hekmatyar moved on Kabul from the south.[13]

During the PDPA's final hours, old tribal lines emerged once again, causing diehard Ghilzai Pashtun Khalqis in the PDPA to side with the Pashtun Hekmatyar and align with him.[14] Najibullah attempted to flee to India, but was stopped on his way to the airport and escaped to the UN compound.[15] On April 24, 450 of Hekmatyar's Hezb-i Islami fighters snuck into Kabul and infiltrated Dostum's units. As the sun rose, hell broke loose and Red Kabul collapsed.[16]

The next day, the Peshawar leadership of the Afghan mujahaideen convened a council and declared that a coalition of mujahideen groups would lead the new Afghanistan. With his own agenda finally revealed as an ISI-front operation, on that same day Hekmatyar claimed military control of Kabul.[17] In a fresh show of disunity, Hekmatyar insisted that there was no need for any government but his own and announced that he would shoot down any plane approaching Kabul in order to to keep it that way.

In reaction to Hekmatyar's threats, Massoud moved on Kabul to join with the remnants of Dostum's tank corps and over the next three days fought Hekmatyar and his troops out of the city and into the hills. On April 28, Sibghatullah Mojadeddi was driven by car from Peshawar to Kabul and assumed the presidency of the new Islamic state of Afghanistan. With no base of popular support and no U.S. oversight or pressure, the event stood only as a glaring reminder that the U.S. policy for the radical Islamists' holy war in Afghanistan had never been more than "fun and games."[18]

In a now-declassified memo that Peter Tomsen wrote to his State Department superiors, he argued for American engagement. "U.S. perseverance in maintaining our already established position in Afghanistan—at little cost—could significantly contribute to (a) favorable moderate outcome which would sideline the extremists. The danger is that we will lose interest and abandon our investment/assets in Afghanistan, which straddles a region where we have precious few levers."[19] It was a fateful argument that he did not win.

Over the next three years Hekmatyar and Massoud would level the city of Kabul in a seesaw battle to control it, while the remainder of Afghanistan's large cities—Kandahar, Herat and Jalalabad—would fall to local chieftains.[20] Once alien to Afghanistan, Saudi- and U.S.-supported warlordism would turn these local chieftains into power brokers supported by the thriving narcotics industry. Armed with satellite phones, Stinger missiles and Swiss bank accounts, they now possessed the ability to project their raw power and primitive mentality far beyond their medieval villages.

NUCLEAR FEARS

After fourteen years of war, the existence of an autonomous, modern Afghanistan functioning as a fragile "buffer" between rival empires had finally been reduced to dust and rubble. With Afghanistan once dismissed by India's nineteenth-century British viceroy Lord Curzon as "a purely accidental geographic unit,"[21] the U.S.-backed campaign to pin the Soviets in their own Vietnam devalued the country from being a unit at all. Afghanistan was now effectively the new scientific frontier of the severed remnant of British India's purely intentional geographic unit, originally known as West Pakistan.

In a constant state of readiness for war with India over the divided province of Kashmir, Pakistan's pursuit of nuclear weaponry had remained a constant for much of its brief history. Driven on by such men as Zulfikar Ali Bhutto who vowed that Pakistan would sacrifice anything to attain a nuclear weapon,[22] it was no surprise that by 1992 it had achieved its goal. According to Tim Weiner in the *New York Times*, "It required more than three decades, a global network of theft and espionage, and uncounted millions for Pakistan, one of the poorest countries, to explode that bomb. But it could not have happened without smuggled Chinese technology and contradictory shifts in U.S. policy, according to present and former U.S. officials."[23]

Protected by the State Department and CIA since the Soviet invasion of Afghanistan, while overlooked by a compliant, militarized U.S. press during the Soviet occupation, the issue now burst onto the scene as word came of Pakistan's preparation for a nuclear war with India. With the White House having failed to report the nuclear developments to Congress during the Reagan era for fear that America's legislative body would interfere with the prosecution of the war in Afghanistan, drastic diplomatic measures had to be taken by the Bush administration to stop the imminent outbreak of a nuclear exchange.[24] It was the first of what the United States would come to know as "blowback" for its secret Cold War adventure in Afghanistan. But the worst for Afghanistan, the rest of South Asia and the United States had yet to come.

THE SOVIET COLLAPSE

The surprise collapse of the Soviet Union on December 25, 1991, was greeted with shocked bemusement throughout the corridors of official Washington. The threat, real or imagined, of Soviet military power and their philosophy of world conquest had defined the imaginations of succeeding generations of U.S. defense intellectuals. The Cold War provided a meaning for the country's financial commitment to a range of defense industries that had slowly seeped into the American subconscious as wholly natural to a civilian economy. During the 1950s, electronics, computers, superhighways, commercial aviation, nuclear energy, high-speed telecommunications, and a multitude of related industries sprang from defense research. One estimate saw 66 percent of all federal research and development funds and almost 70 percent of the Energy Department's budget[25] go directly to the military. Worse than that, as Robert L. Borosage wrote in *Rolling Stone*, "the forty-five-year war was exacting an ever more burdensome toll in debts incurred and investments not made. In less than a decade, the United States went from being the world's leading creditor nation to its greatest debtor."[26] Hidden in plain view, most people didn't see it. With great fanfare, by the 1990s defense research and related industries had become the high-tech backbone of the U.S. economy. Even the media, both print and electronic, deferred to the cross-breeding of defense and civilian, often functioning (even after Vietnam) as cheerleaders for the unprecedented Carter and then Reagan buildup, without ever questioning some of the more bizarre assumptions supporting it.

But the surprise Soviet capitulation threatened to change all that. Suddenly, for the first time since Munich in 1938, the world could look to a future without war as the main driving force and look to the past for ways to keep it from happening again. Yet in the United States it didn't happen.

A cynical David Nyhan of the *Boston Globe* echoed the despair of a savvy reporter who'd seen the illusion makers of the perpetual war machine at work over and over again, each time with the same result:

> Calling all cars, calling all cars. . . . Whatever happened to the 10-foot Russian? The one who was going to "bury you." Sneak an A-bomb into the White House during a guided tour. Gobble up Nicaragua, El Salvador, Mexico and Texas, be gnawing on Kansas City before you knew it. . . . It was to fend off the hated Russkies that Ronald Reagan tripled our national debt. Remember "Star Wars"? The 600-ship Navy? The $600 toilet seat? We needed all that, and more, to lick the Russians [so] Reagan just whistled up a Team B to put a little heat on the CIA's A-Team. Surprise, surprise. Team B came in with the scary fantasies Reagan needed. So off we went on the binge that's put our economy over the barrel we're straddling right now.[27]

Like Jerome Wiesner a decade earlier, Nyhan warned his readers that the pending war in Iraq (the first) was just another "bogeyman" being sold by the same Team-B defense intellectuals who'd sold America the ten-foot Russian.[28] Yet the iron triangle of corporations, Congress, and the Pentagon moved along to the next enemy without a hitch, as if living in its own reality where empirical observation and criticism mattered for nothing.

For former West Pointer and Vietnam veteran Andrew Bacevich—who now teaches at Boston University's Department of International Relations—the U.S. response to the Soviet collapse led him to question the premise of the entire Cold War military enterprise. "The Cold War essentially ends in 1989 when the [Berlin] Wall goes down; in '91, the Soviet Union collapses. I get out of the Army in 1992 and I'm waiting with bated breath to see what impact the end of the Cold War is going to have on U.S. policy, particularly military policy. The answer is essentially none. We come out even more firmly committed to the notion of U.S. military global supremacy. Not because there was an enemy—in 1992, '93, '94, there's no enemy—but because we've come to see military supremacy and global hegemony as good in and of themselves."[29]

Out of the army and unblinkered to Cold War rhetoric and Cold War assumptions for the first time, Bacevich came to realize that the "orthodox narrative" he had subscribed to, which mandated that "the U.S. behaved as it did because of *them*, because of external threats," was in the end the result of "some deep-seated defects in the way we see ourselves and see the world."[30]

But those defects would never be addressed, let alone resolved, following the collapse of the Soviet Union. Instead that year the small group of neoconservatives left over from the Reagan White House—who had been given jobs in the original Bush White House—were tasked by Defense Secretary Dick Cheney with extending them to another generation. Comparable to a Team-B-style analysis but now done from within the Defense Department, I. Lewis (Scooter) Libby, Paul Wolfowitz and Zalmay Khalilzad (a neoconservative Afghan whose worldview had been shaped by Albert Wohlstetter) drafted a startling post–Cold War plan that shocked the realist-dominated establishment of George H. W. Bush's administration in its sheer scope and audacity.[31]

Influenced directly by Richard Perle and Albert Wohlstetter, the recommendations called for regular and staggering increases in defense spending, the projection of lone superpower status, the prevention of the emergence of any regional competitors, the use of preventive or preemptive force, and the forsaking of multilateralism when it served American interests. In essence, the plan was more than just typical defense guidance;

it was a historical document calling for the creation of an American empire.

Immediately denounced and retracted by the White House, the 1992 draft "Defense Planning Guidance" (DPG) was to the twenty-first century what the 1976 Team-B report had been to the 1980s—and what the 1957 Gaither report had been to the 1960s and what the original 1950 NSC 68 had been to the Cold War. Establishing a new set of goals for a new world order and a new and aggressive mind-set by which to attain them, all that was needed to justify them was a national security crisis of suitable proportions. But even without that crisis, the end of the Cold War caused barely a ripple on Capitol Hill.

As the Bush presidency brought twelve years of Republican rule and the Cold War to a close, Congress could see no way to cut more than ten billion dollars from a $300-billion defense budget. Incoming Clinton administration secretary of defense Les Aspen saw even less, proposing "substantially smaller defense spending cuts," in a speech to the American Defense Preparedness Association. The *Los Angeles Times* reported, "Aspin said the actual reductions will be smaller because he plans to increase spending for other defense programs, such as fast-sealift ships, high-technology research, environmental cleanup and aid for defense industries that have been hurt by previous spending cuts."[32]

After all was said and done, it was determined by the General Accounting Office that the CIA had indeed overstated the size of Soviet military expenditures as well as the struggling Soviet economy that supported them. Instead of being 51 percent the size of the American GNP, the Soviets were at best 17 percent and perhaps less, depending on the vagaries of the Soviets' own accounting practices and how the ruble-to-dollar exchange was valued.[33] To careful observers, none of this was a surprise. "As early as 1966 a study prepared for the Congressional Economic Committee reported that 'both official Soviet data and Western estimates show a marked decline in the rate of growth of industrial production in the USSR,'"[34] a rate which had only deteriorated throughout the seventies and eighties.

Yet the incoming Clinton administration expressed no interest in correcting for the faulty assumptions of the past nor their consequences for

Afghanistan. Instead American policy for the next decade would be built on those mistakes while relying on Benazir Bhutto's Pakistan to compound and exploit them. It would be the Clinton administration's most glaring foreign policy mistake. It would also provide the opportunity for Team-B's defense intellectuals to use Afghanistan to take another step into the mirror—a step that would remove them from the reality-based community completely, detaching their defense budgets and their policies from any notion of discernible reality.

THE WORLD TRADE TOWERS—BOMBING #1

The first step into the new reality brought about by America's foray into Afghanistan emerged in New York City in the spring of 1993. Sponsored and protected by the CIA,[35] radical Islamists living in New York and New Jersey, led by radical Egyptian cleric Sheik Omar Abdel Rahman, nearly brought down the symbol of U.S. capitalism, the World Trade Towers, with a gigantic truck bomb.[36] Connected to a vast international network of Islamic fighters funded and trained for the war in Afghanistan, the bombing—which had aimed to kill 250,000 New Yorkers—brought the first taste of the destructive capacity of Bill Casey's jihad home to the United States.

Thomas Lippman reported in the *Washington Post*, "The roundup of Sheik Omar Abdel Rahman and other Islamic militants in the New York area is writing a sour last chapter to one of the great U.S. foreign policy success stories of the 1980s: U.S. support for the Islamic insurgency that drove Soviet troops out of Afghanistan. Many current and former government officials, independent analysts and Arab diplomats are now saying Washington 'created a monster' by encouraging a rebellion based on religious zealotry without stopping to analyze what would happen if the zealots triumphed."[37]

Suffering from tribal, ethnic, sectarian, political, geographical, economic, urban-rural, cultural, and generational fragmentation due to the war, "the sour last chapter to one of the great U.S. foreign policy success stories of the 1980s" was only just beginning.

Amid constant fighting, forces tied to Massoud and Hekmatyar continued to reduce Afghanistan to a state of complete anarchy. Centuries of efforts by Afghanistan's leaders to bring the country into the modern age and unite the various tribes through intermarriage and a strong central government had been aborted by the increasingly toxic mix of Soviet bureaucrats, Afghan communists, RAND defense intellectuals, Wall Street brokers, and religious fanatics on both sides of the Pakistani border. On the ground, atrocities and "ethnic cleansing" became the rule as all sides vied for ancient tribal lands with ancient tribal grudges, now armed to the teeth with the latest in modern weaponry.

Refusing to allow Washington to buy back Stinger missiles given to him during the war against the Russians, Afghanistan's new Islamic prime minister, Gulbuddin Hekmatyar, told reporters, "The Afghan government does not intend to allow even a round of ammunition to be taken out of Afghanistan."[38] Tiring of his bravado but more of his inability to achieve a decisive victory, Hekmatyar's Pakistani sponsors abandoned him in 1994 for the Taliban.[39] Without support from the United States, Massoud turned to his former enemy, Russia, and received military support. But his loose Northern Alliance coalition of Tajik, Uzbek, Turkmen, and Hazara tribes in northern Afghanistan was too weak to overcome their own tribal rivalries.

Despite Hekmatyar's failure, his bid for leadership reignited the centuries-old Pashtun claim to dominance over Afghanistan's other ethnic groups. For the first time in over two centuries, the Pashtun Durrani had lost control of the country to the Ghilzai Pashtuns. Now the appearance of a new Pakistan-based Pashtun group drew Afghan as well as Pakistani sympathies.

12.

1995–2001: The Taliban

Referred to as "the Seekers," the Taliban were Lt. Gen. Naseerullah Babar's answer to Hekmatyar's failure to secure Afghanistan for the Muslim Brotherhood.[1] Now, as the seventysomething interior minister to Prime Minister Benazir Bhutto, Babar's closeness to the ISI enabled him to exact a grand plan. Inspired by Bhutto's desire to "market Pakistan internationally" as the gateway to ancient and lucrative trade routes, Babar's plan was textbook 1840s British Great Game, bypassing Kabul completely while cutting a path to Central Asia through Kandahar and Herat. Steve Coll writes, "Babar spearheaded the effort. In October 1994 he arranged a heavily publicized trial convoy carrying Pakistani textiles that he hoped to drive from Quetta to Turkmenistan, to demonstrate Pakistan's new ambitions. The convoy arrived on the Afghan border above Kandahar just as Mullah Omar and his Taliban *shura* opened their preaching campaign in the area."[2]

Drawing from the orphans of displaced Afghan Pashtun tribal groups living in refugee camps in the North-West Frontier Province in the summer of 1994, funded by wealthy Saudi businessmen like Osama bin Laden and trained by the Jamaat-i Ulema Islam in religious madrassas, the Taliban—"my boys," as Babar referred to them[3]—represented a new and virulent hybrid of Islamist extremism.

Referred to by more objective observers as "a kind of experimental Frankenstein monster"[4] to outdo Iran's extreme Shiite mullahs, the Taliban initially numbered around 2,000 recruits from Kandahar.[5] For Pakistan there were a multitude of benefits. In addition to securing trade routes to and from Central Asia, Pakistan's generals also saw the Taliban as a means of reestablishing Pashtun dominance in the region, hoping the force would act to permanently neutralize the Durand Line issue. John Cooley writes, "This would mean that ethnic Pashtuns on both sides of the frontier might drop their historic plans to unite in a single Pashtun nation, or at least would not focus these revindications on Pakistan."[6]

The captured Afghan territory would also provide safe haven for Pakistan's counterstrike nuclear force in its never-ending feud with India, a strategy referred to as "strategic depth."[7] Added to the incentive was Pakistan's 1993 agreement with Turkmenistan to construct a pipeline between the two countries through Afghanistan with the help of the Argentinian energy company, Bridas.[8] That year California-based oil giant Unocal also joined the game, paying ten million dollars to the former Soviet republic for a one-year study that was anticipated to yield a massive $8-billion project.[9] According to Benazir Bhutto, the U.S. embassy was quick to jump on her plan for the pipeline just as long as she dropped her Argentine partner Bridas in favor of Unocal. "Bridas said 'We want to get this thing through Afghanistan.' We said fine. But everybody in my cabinet laughed. When I called them over they said 'Ha, ha, ha. Look at them thinking they're going to build this.' But anyway, we'll keep them on board, because fighting was still going on in parts of Afghanistan. And then suddenly one day Unocal arrived. And then we were under enormous pressure by . . . the American embassy in Islamabad to break off the Bridas contract. We didn't know what was happening."[10]

The question was, did Washington? For fifty years, policy centering on South Central Asia had been driven through Iran and Pakistan by dualist Cold War thinking and Cold War practices. Without a new conceptual framework that put Afghanistan in the picture, the Clinton regime foundered. "The USA dealt with issues as they came up, in a haphazard, piecemeal fashion, rather than applying a coherent, strategic vision to the region." wrote Pakistani authority Ahmed Rashid in his 1999 analysis *Taliban: Militant Islam, Oil and Fundamentalism in Central Asia.* "Between 1994 and 1996 the USA supported the Taliban politically through its allies Pakistan and Saudi Arabia, essentially because Washington viewed the Taliban as anti-Iranian, anti-Shia and pro-Western. . . . Between 1995 and 1997 US support was even more driven because of its backing for the Unocal project."[11]

In a tribute to former CIA director Bill Casey, some Washington bureaucrats blindly identified with the Taliban "as messianic do-gooders—like born-again Christians from the American Bible Belt," Rashid wrote. "There was not a word of criticism after the Taliban captured Herat in 1995 and threw out thousands of girls from schools. In fact the USA, along with Pakistan's ISI, considered Herat's fall as a help to Unocal and tightening the noose around Iran."[12]

Was the United States actively sponsoring the Taliban or just acting as cheerleader? John K. Cooley wrote in 1999 what most careful observers knew at the time to be true: "Pakistan's ISI and Saudi Arabia, the former with arms and logistical support, the latter with its seemingly inexhaustible supply of money which had flowed during and since the CIA's jihad against Russia, supported the Taliban advance. Many regional observers believed that the U.S. did too."[13]

After capturing Herat and driving Gulbuddin Hekmatyar from his base outside Kabul in February 1995, the Taliban appeared to be all that Unocal, Islamabad, and Washington needed to wrap up the Afghan saga once and for all. Steve Coll writes in his book *Ghost Wars*, "The relatively small number of American officials at the White House, the CIA, and the State Department who followed Afghanistan tended to accept the Taliban's own narrative: They were a cleansing, transitional force that would unite Pashtuns and create a new basis for peace."[14]

The few news stories that trickled out painted the Taliban as a salvation to the Afghan capital's war-weary population; they were welcomed as liberators, carried pictures of the deposed King Zahir Shah, and treated their conquered enemies with "mercy."[15] Originally claiming that they would disarm and support an elected government once Afghanistan was returned to peace, numerous Pashtun rebel groups threw down their weapons or joined them. But as their hold on the countryside reached beyond Pashtun regions into Uzbek and Tajik territory, their true role as the vanguard for an ISI–Al Qaeda sweep into Central Asia became apparent.

In May 1996, Osama bin Laden returned to Afghanistan, maintaining contact with Hekmatyar and other anti-Taliban forces. By September, bin Laden had forged ties with the Taliban. The 9/11 Commission would conclude "it is unlikely that Bin Laden could have returned to Afghanistan had

Pakistan disapproved. The Pakistani military intelligence service probably had advance knowledge of his coming, and his officers may have facilitated his travel. . . . Pakistani intelligence officers reportedly introduced bin Laden to Taliban leaders in Kandahar, their main base of power, to aid his reassertion of control over camps near Kowst, out of an apparent hope that he would now expand the camps and make them available for training Kashmiri militants."[16]

According to Milt Bearden, the United States was complicit in bin Laden's return to Afghanistan. "We were involved in sending bin Laden to Afghanistan when we told the Sudanese, 'Kick him out.' They said 'Somalia'? We said no! They said 'Afghanistan'? We said okay."[17]

Reinforced by Pakistani regulars and militia, the Taliban finally conquered Kabul in September 1996. One of their first victims was former PDPA president Najibullah. Reportedly beaten to death by the Taliban in revenge, word leaked to the Afghan community that Najibullah had been killed by the ISI for refusing to sign a document agreeing to the Durand Line as Pakistan's permanent boundary. Castrated and dragged from the UN compound together with his brother, their bodies were hanged from a lamppost "with his [Najibullah's] genitals stuffed in his mouth"as a display of the new intolerant Islamic order that had come to Afghanistan.[18]

Fearing for their lives, both Hekmatyar and Rabbani fled the city, wisely deciding to forego Taliban offers of clemency. According to a Reuters report, "The Taleban described Rabbani, Prime Minister Gulbuddin Hekmatyar and Masood as 'national criminals' for not accepting Taleban amnesty in return for their surrender."[19]

Recently released U.S. documents indicate that the U.S. embassy in Islamabad had full knowledge that Pakistanis were fighting in Afghanistan as well as knowledge of the involvement of Pakistan's senior officer corps in directing the operation.[20] Cables also reveal Islamabad's knowledge of the Taliban's "harsh and oppressive rule," as well as their support for Osama bin Laden and organizations like the Pakistani-supported Harakat ul-Ansar (HUA), a Kashmiri terrorist organization.[21] Though admitting that "for Pakistan, a Taliban based government in Kabul would be as good as it can get in Afghanistan," the U.S. ambassador to Islamabad, Tom Simons, questioned whether at some point it might prove to be more of a problem for Pakistan than their creators had anticipated. "Many Pakistanis claim they detest the Taliban brand of Islam, noting that it might infect Pakistan, but this apparently is a problem for another day."[22]

Also clearly indicated in cables is the Taliban's growing disaffection with the West's futile efforts to impose standards of behavior on their antediluvian practices. "The Taliban leadership are developing an attitude problem about the West and especially the UN and the NGOs—the organizations they deal with on a daily basis, and the source of the media criticism of their policies. . . . We've also heard bucketfuls from the Taliban that they, as the rulers of Kabul, have not been recognized as Afghanistan's government."[23]

Conflicted by the challenge the Taliban posed, the veteran Ambassador Simons tried to draw a fine line for Assistant Secretary of State Robin Raphel (divorced wife of slain U.S. ambassador to Pakistan, Arnold Raphel) between a "movement we find repugnant" and the hope that a limited engagement might "moderate and modernize" the Taliban, in one case trying to put a happy face on the problem by providing a history lesson. "Amid this swirl of events, it is important to recognize the historic context we are dealing in and understand that the type of problem that the U.S. faces in a Taliban-dominated Afghanistan is not a new one in our diplomatic history. We faced similar problems in dealing with the French revolution (remember citizen Genet?), the Bolshevik revolution, and most recently, the Iranian revolution (remember trying to find the Iranian moderates?). The basic issue is how the U.S. should react to the rise of radical movements, which are committed to the imposition of their beliefs on every strata of society."[24]

It is hard to imagine how Simons's "historic context" could fail to include any mention of how American policy itself had laid the groundwork for these most extreme radical Islamic movements. It is also hard to imagine what exactly a seasoned diplomat like Simons was doing by calling Bhutto an extortionist—to her face—for resisting his pressure to drop the Bridas contract in favor of Unocal. Steve Coll writes, "Simons said directly that Bhutto should cancel her memo of understanding with Bridas and sign with Unocal instead. Bhutto didn't like his tone. Members of her government had been under U.S. pressure over the Unocal pipeline for months. Simons seemed to be issuing a demand, not a request. 'We could never do that because that's breaking the contract,' she told him. 'But that's extortion!' Simons shot back forcefully."[25]

During this period, talk surfaced that the CIA secretly supported Taliban aims, with Raphel meeting with Taliban representatives in Kandahar. The meeting produced a rosy assessment of Taliban intentions. Both Raphel and Ambassador Simons aggressively supported the Unocal pipeline, accepted Bhutto's lies that she was not behind the Taliban's military campaign, and angrily derogated Massoud's plans for a representative democracy in Afghanistan after meeting with him in Kabul. So inflexible was Raphel's position that Massoud's camp came to believe that Raphel and Simons had marked Massoud as an enemy of the United States for signing a $1-million agreement with Unocal rival Bridas.[26]

Coll writes, "It was a tawdry season in American diplomacy. After years of withdrawal and disengagement American policy had been captured by the language of corporate dealmaking. In the absence of alternatives the State Department had taken up Unocal's agenda as its own."[27]

Unocal also pressured Turkmenistan's ruler, Saparmurat Niyazov, to drop Bridas as well.[28] All that was left before Unocal went ahead with its massive oil and natural gas project through Afghan territory was the Taliban's cooperation and a Taliban victory. If not publicly, Raphel's meeting was viewed by outside observers as U.S. approval for a strategic encirclement of radical Shiite Iran and a vote for Unocal. But the truth was far more complex, with the Clinton administration appearing confused and divided on the issue.

Coll writes, "It was unclear during the fall of 1996 whether the United States regarded the Taliban as friend or foe. . . . The Taliban themselves, worried about rumors that they received support from the CIA and were a pro-American force. . . . U.S. ambassador to the United Nations Madeleine Albright denounced the Taliban decrees in Kabul as 'impossible to justify or defend.' . . . But just three weeks after that Robin Raphel outlined the Taliban's claims to legitimacy before the U.N. Security Council and pleaded that they not be isolated."[29]

The truth was that the United States really had no conception of what to do or even what to expect for its sponsorship of the Taliban, with some American diplomats benignly visualizing that a Taliban victory would simply turn Afghanistan into a miniature Saudi Arabia. Rashid quotes one as saying, "The Taliban will probably develop like the Saudis did. There will be Aramco, pipelines, an emir, no parliament and lots of Sharia law. We can live with that."[30]

Unable to live with a Taliban-controlled Afghanistan was the Lion of the Panjshir, Ahmed Shah Massood, whose twenty-five-year campaign to oust the Russians and establish an Islamic democracy from the ground up was grinding painfully to a close.

With the increasingly well-financed Pashtun Taliban pressing on his northern enclaves and the post-Soviet Russian military drained by the breakup of the Soviet states, the desperate Tajik fighter turned to an alternate supplier for the spare parts and weapons needed to maintain his war. Pakistan's military-drug mafia had fueled the war against Russia, now Russia's mafia would supply the war against Pakistan. "Ahmed Shah Massoud acknowledged that he received much equipment from the Russian Mafia arms merchants, rather than the Russian army or Defense Ministry. Western intelligence officials admitted this, but insisted that both governments in Moscow and Tehran were involved."[31]

Headlines screamed: *Afghan Militia Executes Fighters; Taliban Obstruct Food Aid from UN; Taliban Seeks Destruction of Art; Taliban Forces Women Out of Jobs; Taliban Cracks Down on Women; Taliban Imprison Seven for Singing.*[32]

By the end of 1997, the black project designed to bleed the Soviet Union in Afghanistan had taken on an insane inverted logic of its own, with atrocity after atrocity filling the daily papers and not just those committed by the Taliban. That December the UN announced that up to 4,000 Pashtun Taliban militia had been massacred by a former Rashid Dostum ally following their failed effort to seize Sheberghan in the North.[33] Investigators also claimed that evidence had been found of a mass slaughter of Uzbeks by Taliban troops in a fit of ethnic cleansing. "It appears that everybody was butchering everybody up there,"[34] according to one official. Unfettered by the bad publicity, Unocal turned its attention toward Washington—hiring neoconservative RAND expert Zalmay Khalilzad and former U.S. ambassador to Pakistan Robert Oakley as advisors, as well as the University of Nebraska's Afghan specialist Thomas Gouttierre to establish a job-training program in Kandahar.[35] Hoping to move political support for its pipeline project into line with the growing likelihood of a Taliban victory, the lavishly financed effort ran up against a surprising political obstacle.

Coll writes, "By the autumn of 1997 persistent lobbying against the Taliban by the Feminist Majority had influenced the two most important women in the Clinton administration, Madeleine Albright and Hillary Clinton. When Albright visited a refugee camp in Peshawar that November, she departed from her prepared script and denounced the Taliban's policies toward women as 'despicable.'"[36] Grabbing the entertainment media's attention, Eleanor Smeal's Feminist Majority finally broke the trance imposed by Ronald Reagan's anti-Soviet Hollywood imagery machine during the 1980s and replaced it with a vivid new image of female enslavement in Afghanistan. Calling it "gender apartheid," Smeal surprised herself at the worldwide reception, telling interviewers that she could not remember organizing on an international issue of this size and importance before.[37]

As media awareness grew, Smeal's Feminist Majority and other women's organizations found themselves locked in an unprecedented battle with Unocal's team of wealthy and well-connected lobbyists. It was hardly an even playing field. With a corps of seasoned veterans of the Afghan campaign, Ambassador Oakley's team was more than suited to controlling the debate from the inside and out. Coll writes, "Oakley's wife, Phyllis, was at the time the chief of the State Department's intelligence wing, the Bureau of Intelligence and Research. She had access to virtually all of the U.S. government's most sensitive intelligence reporting."[38]

In the opinion of one prominent member of the Afghan royal family long involved in the issue, Robert Oakley was—along with the CIA—the *creator* of the Taliban.[39]

Interviews we conducted at the time with Afghan sources in Washington insisted that the Oakleys were playing the stalking horse for Unocal—holding out for a Republican administration—while the Clinton administration floundered helplessly, unable to formulate a coherent policy. At the time, the Clinton administration assistant secretary of state for South Asian affairs, Karl F. Inderfurth, stated publicly that the door was still open to negotiations if the Taliban could mitigate their draconian policies, saying, "The Taliban will not change their spots, but we do believe they can modify their behavior and take into account certain international standards with respect to women's rights to education and employment."[40] But few outside the inner circle realized how little grasp and even less control the Clinton administration had of the facts on the ground in either Pakistan or Afghanistan.

One example of how little oversight the administration asserted over its own military's agenda emerged in the summer of 1998 during Operation Inspired Venture. A Joint Combined Exchange Training operation (JCET), Inspired Venture was due to take place with Pakistan that August despite sanctions imposed after the testing of five underground nuclear devices that May. Authorized by Section 2011 of Title 10 of the U.S. Code, the 1991 law specifically allowed U.S. training operations to sidestep the U.S. government's own restrictions on numerous occasions, "unencumbered by public debate, effective civilian oversight or the consistent involvement of senior U.S. foreign affairs officials," according to the *Washington Post*.[41] Having sidestepped sanctions on Pakistan since 1993, Operation Inspired Venture was to "bring together 60 American and 200 Pakistani special operations forces for small unit exercises outside Peshawar near Afghanistan and for scuba attacks on mock targets in Mangla Lake, on the edge of the contested mountain region of Kashmir."[42]

Given their support for Osama bin Laden and the numerous terrorist training camps under his supervision near Peshawar and Kandahar, including the Kashmiri terrorist group Harakat ul-Ansar, the operation to further train Pakistani military—in what could only be regarded as up-to-date terrorist techniques—raised some additional unpleasant questions about the real nature of the U.S.-Pakistani relationship. Put on hold following the *Washington Post* exposé, Clinton's national security staff were stunned by the revelation—apparently unaware that such a program existed. Sandy Berger, Clinton's national security advisor, responsible for coordinating the president's diplomatic and military policy, at first admitted that he was "not familiar with the program's details," then later refused to talk about it.[43] Secretary of Defense William Cohen finally defended the JCET program, issuing a terse, one-paragraph statement saying that "JCET's are the backbone of training for Special Operations Forces, preparing them to operate throughout the world . . . they encourage democratic values and regional stability."[44]

The controversy would die out quickly, soon to be overshadowed by the immediate threat posed by Osama bin Laden and his Pashtun-based terrorist training camps. But the exposé left unsettling questions regarding the growth of special operations units inside the Pentagon as well as the lack of oversight into who these units were and what they were actually engaged in. Blowback from the CIA's lack of oversight of the covert training program of the mujahideen during the Afghan war was already a major problem for the administration. Having made Afghanistan the most dangerous country in the world during the anti-Soviet crusade, the United States abandoned the country to a fanatical Taliban that carried over Pentagon training techniques to train Islamic terrorists who threatened to spark a nuclear war with India, sequestered women in their homes, and publicly executed men, women or children for the slightest violations of their arcane rules.

Formerly a politically and religiously moderate constitutional monarchy, Afghanistan had been turned inside out into a land-mined, shell-pocked, bullet-riddled, antimodernist nightmare of an Islamic emirate. And all this under the official sobriquet of "regional stability."

But with Al Qaeda linked to the bombing of American embassies in Kenya and Tanzania that August 7,[45] the Clinton administration was faced with an Afghanistan problem it could no longer mitigate or ignore.

The son of Saudi Arabia's wealthiest construction magnate, Osama bin Laden was by now a well-entrenched benefactor to the Taliban cause. Best known to the U.S. for his support of the war against the Soviets, bin Laden had turned against the U.S. for their continued presence in Saudi Arabia following the first Persian Gulf War in 1992.[46] In February 1998, bin Laden and a fugitive Egyptian doctor, Ayman al-Zawahiri, had issued a decree (fatwa) declaring that since America had claimed war on God and his messenger, it was a Muslim's individual duty to murder any American anywhere on earth.[47] Holding him responsible for the bloody embassy bombings in Africa that killed nearly three hundred people and injured over four thousand, the Clinton administration attacked his mountain training camps on the border with Pakistan.[48] The action did little to alter bin Laden's support for international terror operations, except to announce to the world that bin Laden and Al Qaeda had arrived.

Posed like a bearded Lee Harvey Oswald with loaded AK-47 at the ready for a *Newsweek* magazine spread,[49] America's new poster boy of Islamic extremism slipped into the empty picture frame of Cold War Manichean dualism as if he had been tailored for it. In many ways he had been. As the largest construction company in Saudi Arabia, bin Laden Brothers Construction knew the workings of the U.S. corporate-military economy by heart, having shared a sizeable portion of the construction for the top-secret $200-billion U.S. military basing system buried under the Saudi desert.[50]

Though contractual arrangements with NATO, bin Laden's engineers had overseen construction of high-tech, bomb-proof Afghan "caves" to protect his forces during the war against the Soviets[51] and was now using those facilities and his inside knowledge of the U.S. defense establishment to direct a campaign of terror against his former American sponsors.

In an August 24, 1998, *New York Times* article, Tim Weiner reminded his readers of the quality construction attributed to bin Laden's NATO-trained engineers. "During their nine-year occupation of Afghanistan, the Soviets attacked the camps outside the town of Khost with Scud missiles, 500-pound bombs dropped from jets, barrages of artillery, flights of helicopter gunships and their crack special forces. . . . But neither carpet bombing nor commandos drove the Afghan holy warriors from the mountains."[52]

On November 4, a U.S. federal grand jury indicted bin Laden in the bombings of the two U.S. embassies in Africa. Attempting to drive a wedge between the Taliban's Pashtun leadership and the predominantly Arab Al Qaeda, the United States attempted to negotiate his surrender.[53] The Taliban openly refused, maintaining that bin Laden "was an honored guest and a friend who fought with it against invading Soviet soldiers in the

1980s."[54] Taliban leader Mullah Mohammad Omar claimed ignorance as to his whereabouts, saying "We don't know whether he is in Afghanistan or whether he left the country."[55] One supposedly well-connected Pakistani source claimed that bin Laden had fled to Chechnya.[56] The Associated Press reported that following a meeting with U.S. and British government officials, "The Taliban said . . . that it had imposed restrictions on bin Laden, denying him access to his satellite telephone and ordering him not to make any public statements."[57] Few, if any knew what to believe.

Still locked into the Cold War, anti-Soviet mind-set that guaranteed big defense bureaucracies, high-tech weaponry and job security, Washington's defense intellectuals seemed at a loss.

Gen. Rashid Dostum, now leader of the Uzbek militia, visited Turkey, asking for financial support against the Taliban.[58] Together with Ahmed Shah Massoud's collaboration with the Russian mafia[59] and former CIA darling Gulbuddin Hekmatyar's embrace of Iran's Shia regime,[60] the disturbing picture from South Asia was of a United States walking into something it did not comprehend, just the way the Soviets had.

A January 11, 1999, *Newsweek* magazine interview with Osama bin Laden in his Afghan hideout revealed as much:

> QUESTION: What is your status in Afghanistan, and what is your relationship with the Taliban?"
>
> ANSWER: We support the Taliban, and we consider ourselves part of them. Our blood is mixed with the blood of our Afghan brothers. For us, there is only one government in Afghanistan. It is the Taliban government. We obey all its orders. Afghanistan was the place where we buried the Soviet Union, and it will be the place to bury the Americans for their designs on the Muslims.[61]

In response to the cruise missile strike, Taliban leader Mullah Mohammad Omar remarked that under his version of Islamic law (Sharia) President Clinton should be stoned to death as an adulterer.[62] While some in the United States lamented the creation of the "Frankenstein monster,"[63] a coherent policy for dealing with the bin Laden phenomenon failed to materialize.

Having eschewed diplomacy in Afghanistan for the business of building a pipeline that was now moribund, the Clinton administration sent the CIA to carry out what some thought was a fool's errand. Hoping to snatch bin Laden from under the Taliban's nose without ruffling the Taliban, Clinton's NSC advisor Sandy Berger dispatched a CIA covert action team. Code-named Jawbreaker-5, the team's mission was to grab—or if necessary kill—bin Laden, with the help of Ahmed Shah Massoud.[64] Nearly spent in his efforts to stave off the Taliban's complete takeover of Afghanistan, Massoud warned the CIA that the Clinton national security team was seriously missing the larger picture. Steve Coll wrote in the *Washington Post*, "Massoud also told the CIA delegation that US policy toward bin Laden and Afghanistan was doomed to fail. The Americans directed all of their efforts against bin Laden and a handful of his senior aides, but they failed to see the larger context in which al Qaeda thrived. What about the Taliban? What about the Taliban's supporters in Pakistani intelligence? What about its financiers in Saudi Arabia and the United Arab Emirates?"[65]

Hobbled by an obsession to help Massoud capture bin Laden but at the same time keep him from using CIA money to fight the Taliban, the Clinton effort would fail. Unable to fashion a coherent policy for dealing with the Taliban, they would continue to flounder until it was too late.

INCOMPETENCE, BLINDNESS AND SELF-DECEPTION

With Democrats seemingly blind to the big picture, conservatives began formulating a grand strategy of their own. A Washington group known as the Afghanistan Foundation, headed by Zbigniew Brzezinski, former Pennsylvania congressman Don Ritter, and Zalmay Khalilzad, issued a white paper. Urging the United States to help in the creation of "a popularly based, legitimate government that does not threaten regional and international peace and stability,"[66] it represented the first serious attempt in the long history of U.S.-Afghan relations to formulate a coherent policy for Afghanistan that was not merely fun and games. Featuring the Afghan "brain trust" of official Washington, the lengthy document painted the larger picture missing from the Clinton playbook. But in a reflection of the strange special relationship that had ruled Pakistani-U.S. relations since its creation in 1947, it inverted that picture, expressing its main concern for the welfare of Pakistan and how Afghan radicalization was destabilizing it. "The Taliban's ties to Pakistani Islamists combined with Islamabad's other internal problems increases the possibility that Pakistan might become a failed state and turn further away from the West," the report stated, while recommending, "[i]n its Afghanistan policy, the United States should seek to prevent the emergence of a rogue state in the region, to counter the spread of 'Talibanism'—an extreme, backward and oppressive version of radical Islam—to Pakistan and Central Asia, to improve human rights, and to facilitate a lasting peace."[67]

Had the white paper emanated from a group unfamiliar with the problem, the effort to confuse Afghanistan with the spread of Talibanism to Pakistan could be described as badly misinformed. With names of experts such as General Brent Scowcroft, Zalmay Khalilzad of the RAND Corporation, Tom Gouttierre, Barnett Rubin of the Council on Foreign Relations, and former congressman Charles Wilson attached to the document, the recommendation flipped the reality on its head.[68]

That year foreign press reports painted a clearer picture than ever of Pakistan's command and control of Talibanism, with Pakistani fighting units made up of thirty men, "each commanded by older men with military experience," Anthony Davis wrote in *AsiaWeek*. "Often ex-regular non-commissioned officers, officially retired—so Islamabad could deny supporting them—these men form the backbone of Pakistan's Limited Contingent in Afghanistan."[69]

According to Davis, who'd followed the flow of Pakistanis and Arabs from Pakistani madrassas onto the Afghan battlefield, "no fewer than 8,000 Pakistani citizens in Afghanistan are serving in combat and support roles. As the Taliban prepare for a final offensive, hundreds more young Pakistanis have been crossing the border in recent weeks."[70]

Recently declassified documents paint the white paper's fallacious assumptions in even starker terms, revealing once and for all that "Pakistan's paramilitary Frontier Corps was operating across the border"[71] and that the

U.S. embassy in Islamabad and the Pentagon's Defense Intelligence Agency knew it.

Special emissary Peter Tomsen knew it as well, warning, "There is a danger that the ISI and others in Pakistan will infuse more and more troops and material. . . . Pakistan may attempt to more directly control Afghanistan, especially along the frontier. Eventually there is the fear that I have heard among Afghans that they might try to get the Taliban just to sign a piece of paper creating a confederation with Pakistan. There is the danger that things might go in that direction as the Taliban fail to reach the objective, which was predicted by the Pakistani military head."[72]

Guided by private foundations, wealthy conservatives and oil interests lobbied behind the scenes for military action on behalf of Massoud. By 2000, published sources inside Pakistan claimed that the CIA would soon move on the Taliban, replacing them with a more "friendly" regime. One such source was Colorado rancher and commodities trader James Ritchie and his brother Joseph. Devout Christians, the Ritchies' interest was partly driven by missionary zeal and partly by their father's involvement there as a civil engineer during the 1950s. James had been born there. His father was buried there. Having established a furniture factory in Pakistan to employ Afghan refugees during the mid-'90s, the Ritchies hired former Reagan national security advisor Robert "Bud" McFarlane to help organize a putsch.[73]

When we met with James Ritchie at his Colorado outpost, he described a plan that was as daring, outrageous, and improbable as it was genuinely heartfelt. "King Zahir Shah is an old family friend. We have maintained contact with him in Rome," Ritchie said. "Until recently he had no interest in returning to Afghanistan. But he had a dream in which his father appeared to him and told him he must return to help his people."

With the king's blessing, the Ritchies and McFarlane set out to organize opposition to the Taliban from within Pakistan, finally settling on one of Gulbuddin Hekmatyar's ablest lieutenants, Abdul Haq, as its leader. Having split with Hekmatyar for the hard-line Younas Khalis faction early in the war, Haq had earned a reputation for bravery and political skill. Now a successful businessman with an office in Dubai, Haq seemed a perfect rallying figure for a relatively more moderate Pashtun political resurgence.

Then word leaked out about the plan. In a silent, nighttime attack in January 1999, Haq's wife and children were murdered in their sleep inside their Peshawar compound by ISI-trained agents.[74] As Abdul Haq's family were close to the highly regarded Pashtun political family of Abdul Ahad Karzai (Hamid Karzai's father),[75] the murders proved even more of a reason for the moderate Pashtuns to seek an alliance with Massoud. But the twisted path between U.S. and Pakistani political objectives remained treacherous. Elements of the CIA and State Department still clearly favored ISI over Massoud despite bin Laden, while Clinton's antiterror chief Richard Clarke disparaged Massoud as a drug runner, human rights abuser and ethnic minority.[76] In his opinion, Massoud was not the kind of man on which to build a multiethnic Afghan nation.[77] As political tensions grew between Washington and the Taliban, the U.S. relationship to Islamabad and ISI began to mirror the Byzantine experience of Ambassador Adolph Dubs twenty years before, when the State Department had worked at cross purposes to the CIA. With the American defense establishment unable to escape the hidebound assumptions of the Cold War and bedazzled by the powers of its own technology, its self-created perception of itself as invulnerable was its greatest weakness.

Having clung to the century-old position that the United States had no vital interests in Afghanistan, the bombing of the billion-dollar USS *Cole* in Aden harbor in October 2000 by Al Qaeda agents came as a wake-up call.[78] The United States had misjudged the seriousness of its Afghanistan problem. Two White House counterterrorism aides to Richard Clarke accused the navy of outright ignoring the Al Qaeda threat. "'A more telling display of the persistent disbelief' that bin Laden and his network posed a danger 'would be hard to imagine.' they wrote."[79] Not imagined either was the lasting effect of the bombing on the minds of a million potential jihadists, who saw three of their own nearly sink a billion-dollar symbol of American technological infallibility with nothing more than a barrel of explosives and a motorboat.

Adding to the emerging crisis, on July 14, Abdul Ahad Karzai was assassinated. Hamid Karzai swore to avenge his father's death.[80] That same fall, Massoud's military position grew even more tenuous as the Taliban seized the northern city of Taloqan, severing his overland supply routes to Tajikistan.[81] Although losing popularity and declining in numbers, these decisive late-in-the-game Taliban victories were increasingly seen by western military observers as further proof Pakistan's military involvement. According to an article published in the *Fletcher Forum of World Affairs* by Peter Tomsen in April 2001, "Jane's Defense Weekly cited Western military sources as estimating that combined Pakistani army regular troops, Pakistani religious students, bin Laden's 'Arab Brigade,' and a medley of other foreign radicals comprised over 30 percent of the 20,000-man force that overran Masood's northern base at Taloqan in September 2000."[82]

A political solution appeared impossible, with the Taliban immune to criticism and unwilling to even discuss the possibility of surrendering bin Laden. By the fall of 2000 the Clinton administration had run out of ideas and out of time. The problem would be left for the next president of the United States to resolve—George W. Bush.

PART III

AFGHANISTAN FROM 2001 TO 2008

13.

Countdown to 9/11

In an effort to finalize the complete rejection of modernism in the lands it controlled, in March 2001 the Taliban announced their intentions to begin destroying any depiction of the human form. What statues that had survived the twenty years of war and looting at the Kabul Museum were dragged outside and blown to pieces with rocket grenades. At Bamiyan the famous sixth-century Buddhas, that had survived countless wars and invasions, were packed with explosives and destroyed.[1]

As news reports mounted, it was growing increasingly clear that the Taliban were something the world had not seen before, in their vengeance against the material world and their desire to return that world to dust. The war against the Soviet Union in Afghanistan had awakened a dark messiah in the guise of Osama bin Laden. His minions—the Taliban—would bring on the end of the civilized world, and the more the United States did to stop them, the better it fit the plan. Bin Laden wanted the United States to attack and bin Laden chose Afghanistan as the place. He "complained frequently that the United States had not yet attacked [in response to the *Cole*]. . . . Bin Laden wanted the United States to attack, and if it did not he would launch something bigger."[2]

In control of all but Ahmed Shah Massoud's small mountainous sector of northeast Afghanistan, the Sunni Taliban had spread their terror far and wide over the Afghan landscape. At this late date Tajiks, Uzbeks, and Turkmen had all been subjected to ethnic cleansing, especially the Hazaras, who, as Shiites aligned with Iran, were subject to a special wrath. With word of their atrocities spreading throughout the Afghan countryside, the appeal of the Taliban vanished. Talibs captured by Massoud's fighters confessed that their soldiers were increasingly drawn from the ranks of Pakistan's military.[3] Supplemented by impoverished young Afghan orphans who knew nothing of Afghan's history or culture, dissatisfaction with their rule inside Afghanistan grew.

Bush's secretary of state, Colin Powell, engaged Taliban leaders on the issue of illicit narcotics—offering $25 million to cease opium production in the lands under their control.[4] By summer the project seemed to be paying off. But Powell's success was deceiving. Enriched by a bumper crop of opium the previous year, Taliban growers had seen profits decline, as cheap opium flooded world markets.[5] Accepting a subsidy to work down inventory and drive up prices was good business.

In April Massoud addressed the European Parliament and warned that Al Qaeda was planning an important terrorist attack. That summer James Ritchie and Peter Tomsen traveled to Tajikistan for meetings with Massoud to coordinate a linkup with Abdul Haq and Hamid Karzai. Massoud agreed to drop old grievances in favor of an alliance. Steve Coll writes, "Massoud appealed to Tomsen to bring the king into his alliance. 'Talk to Zahir Shah,' he urged. 'Tell him that I accept him as head of state.'"[6] According to McFarlane, Haq returned in mid-August to Peshawar to prepare for operations in Afghanistan.

WASHINGTON 2001

In Washington, the new Bush administration was already triggering alarms as it implemented aggressive new policies dreamed up by its brain trust of neoconservative defense intellectuals.

The constitutional crisis caused by the hung election had set nerves on edge, but the administration seemed bent on doing nothing to allay fears. Instead the president took every opportunity to heighten tensions by overturning the accepted conventions of past administrations.

George Bush had been in power for less than three months when Anthony Lewis of the *New York Times* wrote in "The Feeling of a Coup" on March 31, 2001, "Without a popular mandate, George W. Bush is making radical changes that will have long-term consequences for this country and the world. He is making them in a hurry, and for the moment there are no checks or balances to stop him. . . . Day after day headlines tell us of fundamental policy reversals. Mr. Bush spurns the global effort, going back to the first Bush presidency, to reduce global warming. He calls off talks with North Korea about its missiles, casting doubt on the whole attempt to ease relations between South and North. He proposes to rethink U.S. aid programs that help dismantle former Soviet nuclear, chemical and biological weapons. . . . Contempt for public opinion as well as for science is evident. . . . This is the most radical administration in living American memory. . . . George Bush and his people are driven by right-wing ideology to an extent not remotely touched by even the Reagan administration. And we haven't seen the half of it."[7]

With the destruction of bin Laden and Al Qaeda as Bush's foreign policy priority number one, Lewis and the rest of the American public would not have to wait long to see the other half. But the complexities of separating Al Qaeda from the Taliban from the ISI, without bringing down the perennially shaky Pakistani state, continued to cause policy gridlock. In August, Republican congressman Porter Goss, Democratic senator Bob Graham, and Republican senator Jon Kyl visited Islamabad for talks with President Pervez Musharraf and the ISI chief, Gen. Mahmoud Ahmad, regarding the possible extradition of Osama bin Laden. By September 4, a plan had finally emerged from Bush's national security council that saw the CIA supporting Massoud in a full-scale support operation with trucks, guns, ammunition and helicopters. The Bush administration was taking the United States back into the covert war for Afghanistan for the first time in ten years. The Ritchie-financed plan that Tomsen, McFarlane, and a small core of concerned senators and representatives had been lobbying the Clinton White House for, for three years, was about to come into being.[8] All that was left to do was to inform Massoud that the United States was back on his side.

On September 9, at Massoud's headquarters in the Panjshir Valley, two men posing as visiting Arab journalists who had traveled from Kabul were allowed an audience. As one man read the questions aloud, the second detonated a bomb hidden inside the television camera he'd brought for the interview. Within an hour, Massoud, the Lion of the Panjshir and the sole remaining opponent of Taliban–ISI–Al Qaeda control of Afghanistan, was dead. "A 2002 Asia Times Online investigation would later establish that Masoud was killed as a gift from al-Qaeda to the Taliban, with heavy involvement by Abdul Sayyaf, an Afghan mujahideen commander very close to ISI and the Saudis."[9]

On September 10, the Pakistani daily *News* reported that ISI chief Mahmoud Ahmad was visiting Washington, which "triggered speculation about the agenda of his mysterious meetings at the Pentagon and National Security Council."[10] Shortly before his visit Ahmad had ordered British-born Pakistani militant Ahmed Omar Saeed Sheikh (using the alias Mustafa Muhammad Ahmad) to wire one hundred thousand dollars from an account in the United Arab Emirates to the Florida bank account of one Mohammad Atta.[11] Saeed Sheikh would later be arrested in Pakistan for the 2002 murder of *Wall Street Journal* reporter Daniel Pearl.[12] Writing in his memoirs *In the Line of Fire*, Pakistani president Pervez Musharraf would state that Ahmed Omar Saeed Sheikh had been recruited by Britain's spy agency MI6 while a student at the London School of economics.[13]

On the morning of September 11, 2001, Gen. Mahmoud Ahmad sat down for breakfast with Republican congressman Porter Goss and Democratic senator Bob Graham in Washington.[14] Neither Mahmoud Ahmad nor Saeed Sheikh would be held accountable for what was about to happen.

Only a veteran observer of the Afghan conflict could fully anticipate the effect that September 11 would have on the self-created reality of the American defense intellectual as the spectacle unfolded before a worldwide television audience. Having found Afghanistan fundamental to triggering the last massive military upgrade anticipated by the 1976 Team-B report, it would be impossible for Afghanistan not to trigger the next massive upgrade as foreseen in Scooter Libby, Paul Wolfowitz, and Zalmay Khalilzad's 1992 draft "Defense Planning Guidance" (DPG) document. "There are other potential nations or coalitions that could, in the future, develop strategic aims and a defense posture of region-wide or global domination. Our strategy must now refocus on precluding the emergence of any potential future global competitor."[15] In fact the spectacle would so bludgeon public opinion that it would enable them to enact the entire scenario for American empire. Warned repeatedly of the "monster" that had been created by Pakistan's ISI with the full knowledge, consent and assistance of Washington's small and exceptionally inbred collection of men, the attack on the World Trade Towers was greeted as if the largest and most powerful national security bureaucracy in the world had been completely without a clue as to its origin.

On three separate occasions since World War II, the same like-minded corps of defense intellectuals, led by Nitze, Wohlstetter, Perle and their protégés, had used such opportunities to radically expand the role of the American military, while coaxing the entire economy further onto a permanent wartime platform. Backed by powerful interests in Congress, labor, industry, academia, finance, and the media, their recommendations had created the Cold War, kept it alive, and then brought it back from the dead following the debacle of Vietnam. With the Soviet invasion of Afghanistan in 1979 they had reclaimed their reputations by building an army of holy warriors to defeat, in President Reagan's terms, "the Evil Empire." Now, with the destruction of the World Trade Towers, America was told that those same, ungrateful holy warriors had become "evildoers" themselves. Like a perpetual-motion machine that generated both cause and effect, Afghanistan had managed to transform the process of action and reaction into a permanent war-making machine. Thanks to neoconservatives in the Bush administration like I. Lewis (Scooter) Libby and Zalmay Khalilzad, the machine was already warming up on the runway.

Even as the World Trade Towers burned, old faces connected to the Afghan debacle materialized, with Dan Rather of CBS News on the air live, talking to reporter Mika Brzezinski.[16] It had been Dan Rather who had set the chilling tone with his first trip to Afghanistan in 1980 by consolidating popular misconceptions about the war while serving up the execution of an Afghan army conscript. Rather had again focused on Afghanistan in a 1987 CBS special report, *The Battle for Afghanistan*, an Emmy-winning program designed to undermine a U.S.-Soviet diplomatic effort then underway. "In foreign affairs, the story the Soviets most want suppressed is Afghanistan. . . . In turn, American diplomacy contributes very little but rhetoric to this conflict. The U.S. is on the verge of an arms agreement with the Soviets and that's why our protests are muted and our aid is clandestine."[17] According to the organization Fairness & Accuracy in Reporting (FAIR), Rather was criticized for the show in a series of 1989 articles by the *New York Post*'s Janet Wilson, who charged that "Dan Rather's CBS newscasts had repeatedly 'aired fake battle footage and false news accounts' of the Afghan war."[18] Among many, the charges also included the use of "actors" as Afghan rebels, describing a Pakistani Air Force jet on a training mission as a "Soviet jet bombing Afghan villages," and the stalking of "enemy positions and blowing up a mine," as being "acted out and filmed in the safety of a Pakistani training camp."[19]

Now as the World Trade Towers burned, Rather spoke on camera to the daughter of the man—Zbigniew Brzezinski—whose black operation had made the rise of radical Islam in Afghanistan a reality. The first Bush administration's failure to engage Afghanistan at a critical moment in 1992, had left the country in the hands of the Pakistani ISI and rebel drug lords that the U.S. had armed and trained during the war with the Soviets. The World Trade Tower attack was the casus belli of casus belli—the latest self-fulfilling prophecy in a long line of self-fulfilling prophecies. But how could this have happened with the ISI's own chief in high-level talks in Washington at the moment the towers were hit, having been on record as recently sending the lead hijacker one hundred thousand dollars?

As the fires in New York continued to burn, tortured explanations emerged. In a September 26 UPI interview with former ISI director Hamid Gul by famed French journalist Arnaud De Borchgrave, cousin to former French intelligence chief Alexandre de Marenches, Gul diverted blame from Pakistan to Israel and the United States. "The U.S. spends $40 billion a year on its 11 intelligence agencies. That's $400 billion in ten years. Yet the Bush administration says it was taken by surprise. I don't believe it. Within 10 minutes of the second tower being hit in the World Trade Center, CNN said Osama bin Laden had done it. That was a planned piece of disinformation by the real perpetrators. It created an instant mind-set and put public opinion into a trance." Asked by the incredulous De Borchgrave what he'd been smoking, Gul explained that from his perspective, it was the West and particularly the United States that was hallucinating by continuing to consume 32 percent of the world's resources with only 4 percent of its population.[20]

Summing up, the former ISI chief believed the mathematics of consumption alone spelled the end for the West while signaling that the Taliban were the divine model for the coming of the "postmodern state." "It's a clean sheet. And they were also moving in the right direction when this crisis was cooked up by the U.S. Until September 11, they had perfect law and order with no formal police force, only traffic cops without sidearms. Now, in less than two weeks, they have mobilized some 320,000 volunteers to fight American and British invaders if they come."[21]

And come they did. Engaging in an equally Orwellian conceptual drama by declaring a "war on terror" (terror of course being the concept), in less than a month the Bush administration's battle plans to seize Osama bin Laden, destroy Al Qaeda and drive the Taliban from power were under way, with B-52s pounding Taliban positions throughout Afghanistan. In Pakistan, James Ritchie's more down-to-earth plan kicked into gear, with Afghan war veteran Abdul Haq sneaking over the border from Pakistan into southern Afghanistan to organize a Pashtun resistance movement. "Wounded 17 times and minus his right foot, the portly Abdul Haq had 5,000 armed followers in 1989, when the Soviets withdrew. A darling of Western media at the time, the English-speaking commander was dubbed 'Hollywood Haq' by the CIA and ISI."[22]

Lightly armed, but with a satellite phone and lots of the Ritchies' cash, Haq had been advised by the CIA against going and was refused tactical support. By the time a member of his beleaguered unit sat-phoned Ritchie with a panicked plea for help, it was already too late.[23] Finally gaining Washington's attention but for all the wrong reason's, Haq's bloody death raised further questions about the continuing relationship between the CIA and the ISI. Barbara Slavin and Jonathan Weisman wrote in *USA Today*, "The crux of the criticism over his death is the CIA's relationship with Pakistan's Inter-Services-Intelligence (ISI). Abdul ran afoul of the ISI more than a decade ago when he was a commander of Afghan freedom fighters battling the Soviet army. The ISI sided with other factions that wanted to create an Islamic fundamentalist state.[24] The CIA went along with the ISI, including the ISI's creation of the Taliban, critics say. 'The CIA was hoodwinked by the ISI in the Soviet Afghan war,' says Peter Tomsen, the former State Department envoy to the Afghan fighters. 'I fear this is happening again.'"[25]

How or why the chief intelligence organization of the most powerful country on Earth could allow itself to be "hoodwinked" by a foreign power is something on which Tomsen did not speculate. But the pattern of questionable CIA alliances in Afghanistan stemming back to the 1970s could not be overlooked.

The Ritchies were not left unscathed by the incident; the death of Haq raised questions about the underlying motivations for their freelance Afghan foreign policy, turning up a connection between the brothers and the lobbying firm for Delta Oil, a Saudi Arabian company vying to build a gas pipeline across Afghanistan.[26] Accused of rushing Abdul Haq into battle against the CIA's advice, in the end the Ritchies were awarded a clean bill of health, with a State Department official remarking, "To the extent they are working to get Afghans involved with each other to help create a broad-based government, we have no objections at all."[27]

Still, the Ritchies' efforts brought to light the darker side of what some in Washington were beginning to sense if not outright see: that the United States was up against more than just the Taliban or Al Qaeda in Afghanistan. Lack of oversight, a privatized proprietary foreign policy, and secret alliances, even within its own CIA, had so eroded the U.S. government's control over events that it had lost sight of its own mission. In this environment, the United States could not hope to defeat a phantom Islamic movement aided by the ISI that would neutralize any and all efforts to subdue it. It would be a lesson that the organizers of the U.S. big-budget "war on terror" would fail to fully account for as they rushed to exploit it.

14.

Kabul, October 7, 2001

The first stage of the second Afghan-American war was brief, as rumors of the Taliban's weakened popularity proved true. Kabul, that once vibrant city with a burgeoning middle class and tolerant Muslim population, had little use for the narrow-minded Taliban purists and their sadistic tactics.

With reassurance from global public opinion, Afghanistan admitted U.S. special forces and airborne troops. Despite the killing of thousands of additional innocent Afghans by U.S. bombing, the Americans were welcomed. The monstrous product of Pakistan's ISI dissolved as quickly into the countryside as they had appeared. Osama bin Laden, the Taliban, and Al Qaeda retreated back over the Durand Line into the Pashtun tribal homelands of Pakistan's North-West Frontier Province (NWFP) and the Federally Administered Tribal Areas (FATA) and vanished.[1] For a brief moment, it seemed that the long Afghan nightmare had come to a close.

In Bonn, Germany, that December, a conference was quickly cobbled together to form a new and legitimate government, one that included a role for women. At the meeting, Hamid Karzai was brought forward and named chairman of the twenty-nine-member governing committee.[2] Billions of dollars in reconstruction and emergency aid were promised by leading nations.[3] It was a promising and rational beginning to the formulation of a new Afghanistan. But the high hopes of bringing a semblance of reform and democracy to a shattered Afghan landscape were quickly dashed. Unimaginable from a five-star hotel in Germany was the situation on the ground in Kabul and the rest of the country. Ten years of brutal Soviet occupation and ten additional years of internecine strife and Taliban rule had caused the old monarch-centered, multiethnic Afghanistan of Zahir Shah to simply cease to exist.

Kabul Museum, the home to some of the world's most famous Buddhist,

Hindu and Indo-European relics had been laid waste, with statues and artifacts either stolen by thieves or blasted to pieces by the Taliban's religious fanatics. Seventy-five percent of Kabul had been reduced to rubble, with the remainder badly damaged. One of the world's least developed countries prior to the Marxist coup of 1978,[4] the country's infrastructure (where it still existed) had been rendered useless. Power plants and water facilities lacking spare parts produced electricity for only part of the day, if at all. Clean water was barely available.

THE PEACE CREATES NEW PROBLEMS

One major reason for the Taliban's initial success beginning in 1994 had been the senseless brutality of the Saudi-Pakistani and U.S.-backed warlords. With the Taliban driven out, these fugitive Pashtun, Tajik, Uzbek, and Hazara bandits returned, armed and ready for the spoils of victory. Not a traditional part of Afghanistan's social and political structure, since 1992 warlords had become a fixture of Afghan life. Set loose on the countryside as enforcers of the U.S. occupation as well as hunting parties for Al Qaeda and bin Laden, Washington failed to see the problem it was creating from the outset.

Ahmed Rashid, the legendary Pakistani journalist, bitterly recalled the wasted opportunity in an August 2007 interview with Amar C. Bakshi, who wrote, "The administration has 'actively rejected expertise and embraced ignorance,' Ahmed told me inside his fortress." Following the Taliban defeat, Rashid had been embraced in Washington for his understanding of the complexities of Afghan and Pakistani politics. Yet instead of implementing what Rashid calls his "common sense line" of recommendations, official Washington smiled, winked, and went about doing its business as usual. "In Afghanistan you have 'a population on its knees, with nothing there, absolutely livid with the Taliban and the Arabs of Al Qaeda . . . willing to take anything.' The U.S. could 'rebuild Afghanistan very quickly, very cheaply and make it a showcase in the Muslim world that says 'Look U.S. intervention is not all about killing and bombing; it's also about rebuilding and reconstruction, about American goodness and largesse.'"[5]

With little understanding and even less conceptual framework with which to address Afghan rebuilding, the positive strides that had been made at Bonn for women and democratic reform in a post-Taliban Afghanistan quickly sank into a sea of unfulfilled promises, arrogantly brushed aside in the mad rush to project power and seize control. Deferring to its old and corrupted warlord allies in the war against the Soviets, the Bush administration embarked on its twenty-first-century Afghan enterprise by laying a foundation for failure. Ann Jones writes, "Critics of American Afghan policy agree that the Bush administration, in its haste to take out Saddam's Iraq, did things backward. After bombing the Taliban into the boondocks in 2001, it set up a government without first making peace—a scenario later to be repeated in Iraq. Instead of pressing for peace negotiations among rival Afghan parties, the victorious Americans handed power to Islamists and militia commanders who had served as America's stand-in soldiers in its Afghan proxy war against the Soviet Union in the 1980s. Then the Bush administration staged elections for these candidates and touted the result as democracy. It also confined an International Security Assistance Force, made up largely of European troops, to the capital, creating an island of safety for the government, while dispatching warlords of its choice to hunt for Osama bin Laden in the countryside."[6]

At the core of the problem lay at least three fundamental flaws in the Bush administration's approach. First: under a non-nation-building president, the administration's reconstruction plans were placed in the hands of free-market ideologues. In addition to the free-for-all of waste, fraud, and corruption that this created, their completely unrealistic objectives favored privatization of Afghanistan's resources with only a figurehead role for Afghanistan's official government. One Afghan-American highway engineer, who'd volunteered his time to inventory the government's road-building equipment and the parts necessary to get it up and running, hit a brick wall when told by USAID that the Afghan government was not going to be competing with private contractors.[7] Other Afghan-Americans who'd returned to help with reconstruction met with similar experiences, watching American companies burn up precious reconstruction money on beefed-up security while padding their bottom line with little if anything to show for it. The problems encountered in the first vital years stemmed from the very structure of the American approach. Ann Jones writes:

> In 2001, Andrew Natsios, then head of USAID, cited foreign aid as "a key foreign policy instrument" designed to help other countries "become better markets for U.S. exports." To guarantee that mission, the State Department recently took over the formerly semi-autonomous aid agency. And since the aim of American aid is to make the world safe for American business, USAID now cuts in business from the start. It sends out requests for proposals to a short list of the usual suspects and awards contracts to those bidders currently in favor. (Election-time kickbacks influence the list of favorites.)[8]

A second fundamental flaw in the Bush administration's approach: by empowering corrupted tribal leaders who had gained power through brutality and trafficking in illegal narcotics during the war against the Russians, the administration immediately set itself against the vast majority of the civilian population. Even Hamid Karzai, the well-known and respected Pashtun politician from Kandahar could do little to interfere with this arrangement as interim president. With no political base and no real power to rule, he survived only at the sufferance of his U.S. Special Forces bodyguards.[9]

Finally, the administration continued to believe its own fabricated press releases, a habit its neoconservative managers had picked up from the Reagan administration's war against the Russians. Deluded by a simplistic ideology, and unable and unwilling to distinguish its own propaganda from the facts on the ground, it convinced itself that it had achieved a decisive victory, when in fact the enemy was only laying in wait. So deluded, it turned its eyes to its main objective—the conquest of Iraq—thereby dooming a job that it had just begun.

In this environment, the elderly king of Afghanistan, Zahir Shah, was invited to return. Forbidden in a last-minute frenzy from functioning as head of state by Bush envoy Zalmay Khalilzad, the long-awaited return of the king as a symbol of a new, united Afghanistan was wasted. Without the king as the traditional center of Afghan life and politics, any hope of binding the multiethnic Afghan personality together once again, as one nation, would prove a pointless enterprise.

15.

Afghanistan Redux

As a pretext for resurrecting the Cold War against the Soviet Union following Vietnam and justifying a historic new era of defense spending, Afghanistan had proved a powerful reactant. Accepting it as a pretext for resuscitating it once again—while undoing constitutional protections and shifting the United States into a permanent warlike engagement with an amorphous concept (terrorism)—required an entirely new level of what is referred to in drama as suspension of disbelief.

Like the Soviet tanks rolling into Kabul at Christmastime in 1979, Osama bin Laden's September spectacle had coincidentally opened a floodgate of pent-up Pentagon plans and desires reminiscent of the fabulous fifties. Presented as an outgrowth of the war on terrorism in Afghanistan but actually self-initiated, that September of 2002 the Bush administration presented to the world its imperial project, or what has since come to be known as the "Bush doctrine." Espousing a policy of "preventive war," the imperial project advocated the use of unilateral military intervention wherever and whenever it was deemed necessary. Known officially as the "National Security Strategy of the United States," it was in reality a final draft version of Paul Wolfowitz's 1992 Defense Planning Guidance document and known around Washington as the "Wolfowitz doctrine."[1]

F. William Engdahl wrote in *Asia Times*, "The Bush Doctrine was and is a neo-conservative doctrine of preventive war. It has proved a strategic catastrophe for the US role as sole superpower. That is the background to comprehend all events today as they are unfolding in and around Washington."[2]

Hard-pressed to ignore the obvious, the *Guardian*'s Mark Tran commented on the new Bush policy's striking resemblance to NSC 68: "It is a safe bet that Bush's present national security advisor, Condoleezza Rice, pored over NSC 68 for inspiration in preparation for this new Bush doctrine. In fact, with a bit of tweaking here and there, substituting terrorism, or axis of evil, or rogue states for Kremlin, much that was written in 1950 could easily be applied to the present. The new twist is the emphasis on pre-emptive action."[3]

With barely a terrorist in sight here at home, a large part of that preemptive action coincidentally took aim at the U.S. Constitution and the Bill of Rights. Raising the issue of the Bush administration's aggressive efforts to undo centuries of legal precedents and juridical principles in order to catch an elusive Osama bin Laden, *New York Times* columnist Anthony Lewis joined the ranks of Jerome Wiesner and David Nyhan in trying to get U.S. citizens to wake up to the dangers of the Pentagon's most recent national-security scam. "It is the broadest move in American history to sweep aside constitutional protections. Yet President Bush's order creating military tribunals to try those suspected of terrorism has aroused little public uproar. Why? Because, I am convinced, people do not understand the order's dangerous breadth—and its defenders have done their best to conceal its true character."[4]

Nor were most Americans aware of the true character of dozens of other doings surrounding America's engagement with the now infamous bin Laden and his phantom terror organ Al Qaeda.

In a BBC *Newsnight* interview with former head of the U.S. visa bureau at the U.S. consulate in Jeddah, Saudi Arabia, Michael Springman explained how bin Laden and his organization had become proficient at terror and how he'd lost his job trying to report it: "What I was reporting was, in reality, an effort to bring recruits, rounded up by Osama bin Laden, to the U.S. for terror training by the CIA. They would then be returned to Afghanistan to fight against the . . . Soviets. The attack on the World Trade Center in 1993 did not shake the State Department's faith in the Saudis, nor did the attack on the American barracks at Khobar Towers in Saudi Arabia three years later, in which nineteen Americans died."[5]

DRUGS, NUCLEAR WEAPONS AND 9/11

Neither was the American public particularly well informed about the complex and dirty business of Afghan heroin, which by February 2002 had seen a huge leap in production following the U.S. invasion. According to the *Financial Times*, "The US and United Nations have ignored repeated calls by the international anti-drugs community to address the increasing menace of Afghanistan's opium cultivation, threatening a rift between Europe and the US as they begin to reconstruct the country. . . . European governments believe one of the reasons the US is 'out to lunch on the issue', as one diplomat put it, is that Afghan heroin is not a significant player in the U.S. market."[6]

Another reason why the United States might have been "out to lunch" on the heroin problem went back to its original involvement with the ISI during the war against the Russians. Fully informed of mujahideen drug dealing at least as early as 1984, the House Select Committee on Narcotics Abuse and Control pleaded with their Afghan mujahideen clients to curtail their opium-smuggling operation. "It is time the United States, Canada, Western Europe and the Arab countries begin to demand that the Mujahideen leadership, through their *mystical* tribal communications networks, put an end to the production of opium, morphine base and heroin in their territory so tragically affecting the countries which are their friends and benefactors."[7] But with U.S. concerns focused on Latin American cocaine and with opium fueling the war against the Russians,[8] Congress understood its action amounted to little more than a request for a token of appreciation.

Author and activist Rob Schultheis, who'd covered the mujahideen for *Time* magazine during the war against the Russians, continued to hold very strong opinions on how the Afghan heroin problem went global. "My theory is that a lot of the policy decisions that were made here that were so inexplicable were produced by corruption on a local level by CIA station chiefs and lower. I actually know some things about that. Somebody I know in Washington told me . . . 'This is all I'm going to say to you; the planes flew in full and they flew out full, that's all I'm going to say.' You know a lot of fortunes have been made in Langley. I think a lot of dirty things went on at that level and a lot of what's happening today is being done by friends of those people covering for them at this point because they don't want to see old Colonel Klutz or [whomever] going to prison. And I think the stuff's probably still going on because of that."[9]

Schultheis minced no words about CIA culpability for 9/11 and the hideous betrayal of both American and Afghan lives being covered up by the blanket secrecy imposed by the war on terror. "I worked for the agency briefly on my way out of college. My father was a lifer at the agency. Now I find them morally repulsive. The majority of them should be in prison who were in charge of the Afghan-Pakistani [operation]. They're directly responsible for 9/11 happening. They were getting paid a lot of money to make sure that wasn't going to happen and they didn't do anything. But there were a lot of shady deals having to do with Arab money and drug money and weapons money and there were kickbacks, I'm sure. And I think a lot of the evils in the policy can be traced back to a lot of individual actors, because individual actors out here have a lot of power. I think [there are] people out hunting foxes in Leesburg on the backs of dead Afghans because Gulbuddin and ISI kicked X amount to them. I'll bet any amount of money on that because there's no other reason for a lot of this."[10]

As a reason for disaster, one had to look no further that year than the streets of Kabul where U.S. troops painted a vivid picture of the bizarre state of isolation the United States had adopted for itself under the neoconservative Bush doctrine. Accompanying human-rights expert Sima Wali back to Kabul in October of 2002, we found Afghanistan to be in a twilight realm, with local Afghan nongovernmental organizations providing a broad array of vital services on shoestring budgets. All this while the Bush administration struggled to fashion a viable reconstruction policy in the midst of a Taliban resurgence that everyone expected to grow worse.

Despite sharing duties with the UN's International Security and Assistance Force (ISAF), the United States maintained an estrangement from the rest of the world's forces. Conducting its own search-and-destroy missions in various parts of the country, the United States seemed preoccupied with the nearby border with Pakistan. The go-it-alone stance produced a growing wonderment within the international community, with foreign soldiers curiously asking what exactly it was the United States was in Afghanistan to do. One reason for the concern was the ongoing conflict in the south, below Kandahar, where 5,000 marines still struggled to establish control in the midst of an overt, ISI-backed campaign to regroup Al Qaeda.[11]

Rob Schultheis addressed the glaring inconsistencies in the American campaign. "I talked to a woman last night from an aid agency who said everything south of Kandahar is just rife with ISI people. There are villages full of Pakistanis trying to revive Al Qaeda. We do have the means here to wipe out everything like that. But there seems to be a kind of funny . . . there are areas where we're very active but there are others where—" Schultheis tried to broach the subject as delicately as possible. "It could be our intelligence. It could be incompetence could play a role . . . but some people are still getting money. Probably not from Pakistan, probably, to be frank, probably from Saudi Arabia. I always thought they were the prime movers. I've said that publicly before and they know I've said it so I'm not putting myself in any increased danger. But who knows. But I think they are still heavily involved in backing this stuff. I haven't seen any sign they're not."[12]

Just as strange was the U.S. reaction to humanitarian assistance where the Pentagon was rewriting the rulebook on a wide range of time-worn and time-tested methods.

Writing in their journal *Crosslines*, noted foreign correspondents Edward Girardet and William Dowell cited a kind of schizophrenia ruling the U.S. military's behavior, which was making the already dangerous business of providing medical aid and assistance to needy villagers even more dangerous. "The blurring of humanitarian roles" they wrote, "has exacerbated the recent rise of violence against relief volunteers in Afghanistan. While aid agencies have a long tradition of staying out of combat, the US and British military have been dabbling in humanitarian action since Coalition forces first intervened in Afghanistan last October. Trouble is, a soldier may act as a humanitarian, but at any moment he can revert to his original function, which is to threaten or apply deadly force in order to bend an opponent to his will."[13]

According to the report, well-known international aid agencies like Médecins sans Frontières, CARE, and Mercy Corps were seriously questioning "how the Americans in Afghanistan can be involved in a military war against the Taliban and Al Qaeda elements, and at the same time expect to have credibility when they conduct 'humanitarian' operations through their military-based Civilian Affairs teams."[14] Closer to the truth was the role the Civilian Affairs teams were actually playing as intelligence operatives for the so-called "Chickmotif" (Coalition Joint Civil-Military Operations Task Force). Dressed as civilian aid workers, the soldiers were often spotted in rural villages near the Iranian border, promising to return with aid, but were never seen or heard from again.

But the surreal nature of the occupation didn't end with intelligence officers compromising humanitarian aid workers. Inside the sandbagged and bunkered U.S. embassy, the impression was of a tension not only generated by the real potential for an imminent terrorist attack, but by an internal dissension that divided career diplomats from the political appointees sent from President Bush's ideological White House.

The American reporters we interviewed in Kabul were at a loss to explain the strange atmosphere that permeated the streets and the lack of progress at reconstruction. Some voiced frustration at finding a way to convey an authentic picture of the country when most Americans lacked even the language to understand. Chris Hondros of Getty Images said, "I think people aren't dealing with the important issues. And one of the reasons is because they're complicated. And the American public has not been educated in such a way in the last generation or so to start understanding some of these nuances. So things get oversimplified. . . . Half of the Taliban is running around still in the country and is back to farming. Do you send them to Hague for war crimes or do you let them get back on with their lives? All these kind of issues are difficult to understand from an American point of view. That makes it hard to convey what's going on here; to really somehow report from here in a way that really makes people back in the states understand in a good way what's happening."[15]

Others, like *USA Today* correspondent Steve Komarow, who'd ridden in on horseback from Tajikistan with U.S. Special Forces during the invasion, were more cynical. "What you see is more traffic, more cars," Komarow said. "What you don't see are the big infrastructure improvements. The things that would make the power reliable, make the water safe. . . . Once you get out of town you see much less. None of the big projects are underway."[16]

When asked what he thought of America's Afghan allies in the war on terror, he was blunt. "This is a country full of very charming killers. You know, you meet a fellow who commands a—the classic term here is 'warlord.' I mean [there are] some big, big guys in this country under investigation for war crimes but they've got charisma. . . . Massoud is deified here in Kabul and it's a town he destroyed or took part in destroying."[17]

That same year, the former commander of NATO forces in Europe, Gen. Wesley Clark, warned of the danger that Afghanistan could ensnare American forces in an unwinnable guerrilla war in exactly the same fashion as it had the Soviets, but expressed no objections to aligning with Kabul's charming killers. Ben Fenton reported for the *Telegraph*, "General Clark said it was necessary to win the support of the Afghan warlords by persuasion rather than intimidation. . . . 'We have to reach accommodations with the warlords. At the moment, I have to say, there are worrisome signs.'"[18] But the warlords would soon prove to be more liability than asset as Washington struggled to define its Afghan mission. By October 2002, with little more than the broken, bullet-riddled city of Kabul under control and an immense reconstruction job yet to begin, the U.S. focus both in terms of military and media had already shifted from solving Afghanistan's problems toward invading Iraq. By the spring of 2003 the grand victory over the Taliban and Al Qaeda in the good war to liberate Afghanistan was looking more and more like a scene from *Apocalypse Now*: monies allocated for reconstruction had failed to arrive due to a lack of security while security could not be established due to the raping and pillaging of the warlords. As Washington shifted focus from the Afghan countryside to conquering Baghdad, the overall impression of the American commitment echoed former CIA director Robert Gates's comment about the end of the Soviet occupation in 1989—"hardly anyone cared."[19]

With U.S. influence in reshaping a new Afghanistan crumbling, the *Washington Post* published a stark outline—by Hamid Karzai's brother, Mahmood, former New York Congressman Jack Kemp, and Hamed Wardak, son of an Afghan general—of the mounting catastrophe. "Instead of facilitating political openness and economic growth, the [Afghan] government is proving to be an obstacle to political and economic reform. . . . Even more disconcerting is the lack of a comprehensive vision. . . . To make matters worse, Afghanistan's politics and stability are beholden to warlords who were in power before the rise of the Taliban. These warlords are despised as the main cause of corruption and tyranny. Democracy and free markets will never take root in an environment dominated by them. Unfortunately the reemergence of these warlords is directly related to U.S. financial and military support, which is the sole source of their power."[20]

Warning that the best the United States could hope for from this arrangement was the alienation of the common Afghan citizen, the article took pains to predict that a "worst-case scenario is that Afghans will associate U.S. involvement with tyranny and become vulnerable to political manipulation by the Taliban and al Qaeda. . . . This is a dangerous path, as the public good is controlled and consumed by the few, while the masses are deprived of subsistence and basic needs."[21]

But even as congressional leaders began to realize they had authorized the wrong war, Afghanistan's pleas would again be ignored in Washington as the U.S. conquest of Iraq grew into a blind, all-encompassing obsession.

By summer, Rob Schultheis's suspicions about ISI's Al Qaeda recruiting near Kandahar were coming into bloom. Mullahs aligned with the government were under attack. In July a remote-controlled bomb exploded at the Abdurrad Akhunzada mosque, injuring the chief mullah and twenty-four worshippers as they prayed. April Witt reported in the *Washington Post*, "Two days later, a mullah who had hung the Afghan flag in his mosque and said good Muslims support the nation's central government was shot to death as he sat praying, a book open in his hand. A third Kandahar mullah was attacked this week, executed outside his mosque by gunmen on a motorcycle."[22]

After a one-day stop in Afghanistan, the chairman of the joint chiefs, Gen. Richard B. Myers, found no reason for concern over Taliban attacks, declaring that "security and stability are increasing." But reports from the countryside told the opposite story. With local officials, humanitarian aid workers, engineers, and mine clearers under constant attack, some were predicting that the country was slipping into anarchy. Robyn Dixon reported for the *Los Angeles Times*, "Already there are signs there—a boom in opium production, rampant banditry and huge swaths of territory unsafe for Western aid workers. The central government has almost no power over regional warlords who control roads and extort money from truck drivers, choking commerce and trade. If the country slips into anarchy, it risks becoming a haven for resurgent Taliban and Al Qaeda fighters. And the point of U.S. military action here could be lost—a major setback in the war against terrorism."[23]

The growing parallels between the Soviet and U.S. Afghan experience were hard to overlook. A November 2003 article in the *Guardian* by Jonathan Steele, titled "Red Kabul Revisted," cited the similarity between the Soviet and U.S. wars, while correcting some of the more outrageous fantasies governing the West's assumptions of the evil empire's conquest. "Two years after Kabul was freed from the Taliban there's a sense of déjà vu about Afghanistan. . . . Kabul today bears a strong resemblance to the Kabul of 1981. This time the men setting the model are American rather than Russian, but the project for secular modernization which Washington has embarked on is eerily reminiscent of what the Soviet Union tried to do."[24]

While admitting that "the Soviet's did not run a pretty war," Steele also admitted that the western press had missed the real reason for the war, a fact that made understanding the current U.S. war in Afghanistan nearly impossible to understand: "This was not a war of Russia vs. Afghanistan, but a civil war in which the Russians supported secular, urban Afghans against Islamic traditionalists and their Arab and western backers. For a foreign journalist to make that case at the time was a lonely, unpopular business. Had the PDPA given more visas, they might have done better. Instead they got a diet of romantic stuff about treks with the mujahedin."[25]

Further spooked by evidence that U.S. ally Pakistan had allowed or perhaps even encouraged the spread of its nuclear technology to Iran, North Korea, and Libya,[26] by February 2004 Washington's growing fears of a terrorist threat were changing the physical appearance of the U.S. capital city as well as the character of its government. That February the *New York*

Times reported the striking changes, citing the presence of antiaircraft missiles on buildings surrounding the White House, devices that sampled the air for chemical and biological substances, bomb-containment trash bins situated at subway stops, and the rerouting of a major highway away from the Pentagon. "Day by day, the nation's capital is becoming a fortress, turning a city known for graceful beauty into a virtual armed camp."[27]

Member of the British Parliament Michael Meacher raised further disturbing questions about the ISI-CIA connection to the 9/11 hijackings that July in an article in the *Guardian.* Citing glaring deficiencies in Washington's pre-9/11 intelligence, he asked how three of the most obvious Pakistani perpetrators of the crime had managed to escape justice: "[Gen. Mahmoud] Ahmed, the paymaster for the hijackers, was actually in Washington on 9/11, and had a series of pre-9/11 top-level meetings in the White House, the Pentagon, the national security council, and with George Tenet, then head of the CIA, and Marc Grossman, the undersecretary of state for political affairs. When Ahmed was exposed by the *Wall Street Journal* as having sent the money to the hijackers, he was forced to 'retire' by President Pervez Musharraf. Why hasn't the US demanded that he be questioned and tried in court?"[28]

Adding to the growing concern over the CIA's institutional responsibility for 9/11, Meacher cited the strange case of Sibel Edmonds. A thirty-three-year-old Turkish-American former FBI intelligence translator, Edmonds had been put under two gag orders to keep her from testifying in court or even mentioning the names of the suspects or the countries involved in the hijackings cited in pre-9/11 CIA reports. "My translations of the 9/11 intercepts included [terrorist] money laundering, detailed and date specific information . . . if they were to do real investigations, we would see several significant high-level criminal prosecutions in this country [the US] . . . and believe me, they would do everything to cover this up." According to Meacher, "The report was sent from the CIA to the FBI, but neither agency apparently recognized the significance of a Bin Laden lieutenant sending terrorists to the US and asking them to establish contacts with colleagues already there."[29]

That year investigative journalist Seymour Hersh had his own revelations about the strange state of America's effort to quash terror in its war on Afghanistan. "At the end of 2002," he wrote for the *New Yorker*, "somebody in the office of Special Operations and Low Intensity Conflict asked Hy Rothstein, an expert in unconventional warfare and a veteran of the Special Forces, who now teaches at the Navy Postgraduate School, in Monterey, California, to do a military study of what happened in Afghanistan. . . . As part of his research, he went to Afghanistan, and spent a lot of time in the field with various commanders and troops."[30]

Rothstein's report came as a shock to everyone at the Pentagon who thought they knew what was going on. "And his report, when it was delivered in January," Hersh continued, "was a quite devastating account of a war that wasn't won, and why it wasn't won, and why it's not going to be won unless significant changes are made by the leadership of the Pentagon."[31] According to Secretary of Defense Donald Rumsfeld, Afghanistan was to be a model for a whole new kind of war. What Rothstein discovered was "that Donald Rumsfeld and the President kept on talking about waging this new kind of war, an unconventional war, and using Special Forces in a new way, but, in reality, it was just the same old thing."[32]

Hersh went on to cite the growing heroin problem, which by 2003 had already grown to twenty times the size of the problem under the Taliban's control. "The fact is that the U.N. Office of Drugs and Crime recently reported that not only did the number of fields used to cultivate poppies—the raw ingredient for heroin—grow to near-record levels in 2003, but, according to surveys of farmers, seventy per cent expect to grow even more next year. Much of that is taking place in areas in which the U.S. has a major military presence."[33]

By summer 2004 the situation in all of Afghanistan had become so dangerous, Médecins sans Frontières withdrew its eighty foreign staff after five of its members were assassinated in northern Afghanistan. The Taliban took the credit. After working in the country for twenty-four years under Soviet and Taliban occupation, bringing aid to refugees and remote Afghan communities by packhorse and mule, the dismissal of 1,400 local staff represented more than just the failure to provide security in rural Afghanistan.[34] What the Médecins sans Frontières withdrawal signified was the collapse of the moral code that had guided the modern era. Just as the atom bomb had atomized traditional concepts for waging war, the so-called Bush war on terror had atomized time-worn and time-respected rules governing noncombatants and the traditional assumptions of civilian innocence.

In a piece written for the *Guardian* titled "For Whom the Bell Tolls," Yale University professor Paul Kennedy inferred that the final victim of this travesty would be the United States itself:

> The MSF deaths, and the organization's decision to withdraw from Afghanistan point to two big questions about international peace and security in the 21st century. The first is whether any international relief group (devoted to human rights, women's issues, the environment, childcare) that has its headquarters in New York, Geneva or Vienna can avoid the suspicion that it is just another form of western intrusion. . . . Are not German religious and relief workers in distraught Kosovo part of a NATO plot? . . . To many of us, these seem totally absurd suspicions. Yet, when one learns of MSF's complaints that the US military had badly mixed its role in Afghanistan with those of the civilian aid groups . . . one cannot be surprised at the local response.[35]

Amidst the tragedy and Kennedy's ominous for-whom-the-bell-tolls warnings came a fateful reminder from northern Afghanistan that other civilizations had once passed this way, as the Kabul Museum's officials revealed that more than twenty-two thousand items from the legendary Bactrian hoard had been found.[36] Excavated in 1978 by Soviet archaeologist Viktor Sarianidi, the hoard of elaborate golden objects dating back two thousand years had been safely stored by the Marxist government behind a complex shield of seven locks in bank vaults under the Arg palace.[37] In conformity with the "Evil Empire" propaganda of the day, some western historians voiced fears that the Russians had carried it off and melted it down along with other treasures. They, of course, hadn't. But some Afghans had a better idea as to where Afghanistan's other precious treasures had gone that same year, demanding the return of ancient manuscripts that had found their way to London. "The Afghan government is to request the return of the 'Dead Sea Scrolls of Buddhism' from the British Library, amid concerns the priceless manuscripts were looted during the civil war in the early nineties. Afghanistan's Minister of Culture will formally ask for the 2000-year-old scrolls to be sent from London to the newly restored Kabul Museum in the next few weeks as part of a campaign to bring home stolen treasure from foreign collections."[38]

That December, on a visit to London, Pakistani president Pervez Musharraf denounced the war on terror, claiming it made the world a more dangerous place. Speaking after talks with Tony Blair at 10 Downing Street, Musharraf expressed frustration at the West's insistence on using military force alone when the long-term causes of the terror went unaddressed. "That is getting at the core of what creates terrorists, what creates an extremist, militant environment which then leads on to terrorism. . . . That is the resolution of political disputes."[39]

Chastising Musharraf ever so condescendingly, Blair responded by saying,"Most sensible people looking at the world today know that since September 11 we have got to take every action that we can to fight terrorism militarily." But then he conceded, "We would be foolish to ignore the causes upon which terrorism preys. And that is why it is also important to address those political disputes as well."[40] Left unsaid was the continuing failure of U.S. and western powers to address those political disputes, the failure of British and American military policy which made peace with warlords and war on civilians, or even the impact of the historic resurrection of the opium trade which financed the growing sophistication and presence of the Al Qaeda–Taliban resurgence.

The political implications of the drug explosion alone were not lost on Zalmay Khalilzad who said in a speech from Paktika Province that same month, "The narcotics trade poses a mortal threat to Afghanistan. Narcotics pose a threat to Afghanistan's political future: drug dealers could take over the political system. Narcotics pose a threat to the economy: criminal gangs and mafia can bring the economy under their control."[41]

With one-third of the Afghan economy (estimated by the UN to be at

$2.8 billion that year) already in the hands of narcoterrorists, having risen 64 percent in just one year, Khalilzad's statement was a prophecy of what was soon to come. In 2005 the figure would set another record, at 4,500 tons, and another record in 2006, at 6,700, making Afghanistan accountable for 92 percent of global illicit opium production. Now in a self-described "war on drugs" as well as a self-described "war on terror," the United States was losing both in Afghanistan, and losing them badly. But none of it seemed to matter to Washington where Congress continued to rubber stamp the administration's requests for the highest military budgets in history, despite a lack of evidence that any of it was working. Around this time *New York Times* columnist Ron Suskind wrote of a meeting with a high-level White House official who he felt embodied the Bush administration's surreal ambivalence to the consequences of their actions. "The aide said that guys like me were 'in the reality-based community,' which he defined as people who 'believe that solutions emerge from your judicious study of discernible reality.' I nodded and murmured something about enlightenment principles and empiricism. He cut me off. 'That's not the way the world works anymore,' he continued. 'We're an empire now, and when we act, we create our own reality. And while you're studying that reality—judiciously as you will—we'll act again, creating other new realities, which you can study too, and that's how things will sort out. We're history's actors . . . and you, all of you, will be left to just study what we do.'"[42]

In the spring of 2005, Cold War architect George Kennan died at the age of 101. A *Washington Post* obituary provided an insight into the mind of one of the foremost figures of post–World War II U.S. foreign policy and his antipathy for the modern world. "Walter Isaacson and Evan Thomas reported in their book 'The Wise Men' that he suggested in an unpublished work that women, blacks and immigrants be disenfranchised. He deplored the automobile, computers, commercialism, environmental degradation and other manifestations of modern life. He loathed popular American culture. In his memoirs, he described himself as a 'guest of one's time and not a member of its household.'"[43]

Despite having created the framework for U.S. intervention around the globe, Kennan testified before the Senate Foreign Relations Committee against the Vietnam War and campaigned for nuclear disarmament. He firmly believed that his policy of containing the Soviet Union had been turned on its head while trying to convince the powers that be in Washington that military pressure increased the danger of war rather than reducing it. Although correct in his assumptions that the Soviet Union would eventually mellow, in this he failed. Nor did his efforts succeed in keeping U.S. hubris out of foreign policy decisions and foreign wars. "A touchstone of his worldview was the conviction that the United States cannot reshape other countries in its own image and that, with a few exceptions, its efforts to police the world are neither in its interests nor within the scope of its resources. 'This whole tendency to see ourselves as the center of political enlightenment and as teachers to a great part of the rest of the world strikes me as unthought-through, vainglorious and undesirable,' he said in an interview with the *New York Review of Books* in 1999."[44]

As vainglorious and undesirable as the war on terror appeared and despite the overwhelming wealth of empirical evidence that it was failing, America's defense intellectuals had by 2005 moved well beyond discernible reality into their own freakish Valhalla of war without end. Following the terrorist bombings in London that summer, former secretary of state for foreign and commonwealth affairs of the United Kingdom and former leader of the House of Commons Robin Cook tried to set the record straight on Islamic extremism, stripping bin Laden and Al Qaeda of their propaganda value by establishing exactly who had created the terrorist organization. "Osama bin Laden is no more a true representative of Islam than General Mladic, who commanded the Serbian force, could be held up as an example of Christianity. . . . Bin Laden was, though, a product of a monumental miscalculation by western security agencies. Throughout the 80s he was armed by the CIA and funded by the Saudis to wage jihad against the Russian occupation in Afghanistan. Al-Qaida, literally 'the database', was originally the computer file of the thousands of mujahideen who were recruited and trained with the help of the CIA to defeat the Russians."[45]

Warning that the war on terror could not be won by military means, Cook ended by making an appeal to the G8 summit. "The breeding grounds of terrorism are to be found in the poverty of back streets, where fundamentalism offers a false, easy sense of pride and identity to young men who feel denied of any hope or any economic opportunity for themselves. A war on world poverty may well do more for security of the west than a war on terror."[46]

In less than a month Robin Cook was dead, the victim either of a heart attack or a broken neck after falling while hiking in the Scottish Highlands with his wife.[47] But in Washington, neither his death nor his warning would barely raise an eyebrow.

Now a besieged, forbidden city of frightened mandarins, Washington appeared momentarily distracted by a domestic terror threat, with the president evacuated from the White House over the approach of a private plane into restricted airspace. Numerous threats that year added to the aura of heightened fear, but upon investigation proved to be empty of any substance.

The *New York Times* reported that summer of 2005 that Afghans were beginning to feel uneasy about the future after a U.S. military helicopter crash near the Pakistani border took the lives of seventeen Americans: "Violence has increased sharply in recent months, with a resurgent Taliban movement mounting daily attacks in southern Afghanistan. . . . The steady stream of violence has dealt a new blow to this still traumatized nation of 25 million. In dozens of interviews conducted in recent weeks around the country, Afghans voiced concern that things were not improving, and that the Taliban and other dangerous players were gaining strength."[48]

Reports also surfaced that summer of protests by Afghans, angry at the United States for not treating them with dignity. That year Washington tried its hand at changing the name of the "war on terror" to the "global struggle against violent extremism," in the hopes that people would start thinking about the threat of terrorism as more than just a war. The chairman of the joint chiefs, Richard Myers, said that he "objected to the use of the term 'war on terrorism' before, because if you call it a war, then you think of people in uniform as being the solution." A stickler for the Queen's English, the general told the National Press Club that the threat was really "violent extremism" and not terror itself, because "terror is the method they use."[49]

That fall a BBC Two television series on the Middle East, titled "Elusive Peace: Israel and the Arabs," revealed that President Bush had informed Palestinian Prime Minister Abu Mazen and Nabil Shaath, his foreign minister, that God had told him to invade Afghanistan. "Nabil Shaath says: 'President Bush said to all of us:' 'I'm driven with a mission from God. God would tell me,' 'George, go and fight those terrorists in Afghanistan.' And I did."[50]

That year marked the completion of the Bonn process, which had established the new Afghan government.[51] The United States and Europe trumpeted the successful presidential and parliamentary elections while the Bush administration cited Afghanistan as a great victory in its "Global War on Terror" (GWOT). Such talk was a frightening self-delusion. In the fall, Afghan police discovered a mass grave of hundreds of communist troops in Paktika Province, murdered after surrendering to the mujahideen in 1989. Reports stated that at least two of the candidates for the national election were implicated.[52]

A Sidney Bloomenthal interview with the Bush administration's first emissary to Afghanistan removed any hint of truth from the administration's rhetoric:

> "I was horrified by the president's last speech [on the war on terror], so much unsaid, so . . . disingenuous, so many half truths," said James Dobbins, Bush's first envoy to Afghanistan, now director of international programmes at the Rand Corporation. Afghanistan is now the scene of a Taliban revival, chronic Pashtun violence, dominance by US-supported warlords who have become narco-lords, and a human rights black hole. From the start, he said, the effort in Afghanistan was "grossly underfunded and undermanned." The military doctrine was the first error. "The US focus on force protection and substitution of firepower for manpower creates significant collateral damage." But the faith in firepower sustained the illusion that the mission could be "quicker, cheaper, easier." And that justification fitted with Afghanistan being relegated into a sideshow to Iraq. According to Dobbins, there was also "a generally negative appreciation of peacekeeping and nation

> building as components of US policy, a disinclination to learn anything from . . . Bosnia and Kosovo."[53]

By February 2006 the new chairman of the joint chiefs of staff at the Pentagon, Gen. Peter Pace, was calling for an even newer name for the Global War on Terror, which he now described as "the Long War." Explaining that "the struggle . . . may well be fought in dozens of other countries simultaneously and for years to come," Pace asked Congress for a whole new array of weapons and military increases, including new, high-speed naval capabilities, more aerial drones and a new long-range bomber fleet to combat terrorism. Requesting also the conversion of sub-launched Trident nuclear missiles to conventional warheads,[54] the general hearkened back to another era, when U.S. B-52s had been reconfigured from nuclear to conventional bombs to carpet bomb North Vietnam back to the Stone Age. Having failed in its Iraq adventure and failing to make a dent in Osama bin Laden's phantom-like organization after five years of trying, with the largest military budget in the world's history, the general was asking Congress for more.

And still, the press and most of the president's political opposition in Congress maintained their suspension of disbelief that the general's requests were justified, increasingly cowed by their fear of looking soft on terror and right-wing charges that labeled any criticism of the president's policies as treasonous. In July, *New York Times* columnist Paul Krugman declared he'd had enough. "Over the last few months a series of revelations have confirmed what should have been obvious a long time ago: the Bush administration and the movement it leads have been engaged in an authoritarian project, an effort to remove all the checks and balances that have heretofore constrained the executive branch. . . . Those of us who tried to call attention to this authoritarian project years ago have long marveled over the reluctance of many of our colleagues to acknowledge what was going on."[55]

That summer fourteen people were killed and 142 injured in violent rioting against U.S. forces in Kabul following a traffic accident. Police cars were set on fire, foreigners were attacked and the compound of CARE International was set ablaze. According the *Telegraph*, a Kabul police chief said one other person was killed when U.S. troops fired into a crowd of stone-throwing protesters soon after the accident.[56]

Freed from any serious criticism as well as constitutional restraints, the Bush administration continued to plunge headlong into disaster, as the Afghan sideshow become the main show with the war shifting away from Iraq. Sebastian Rotella wrote in the *Los Angeles Times*, "The conflict in Iraq is drawing fewer foreign fighters as Muslim extremists aspiring to battle the West turn their attention back to the symbolically important and increasingly violent turf of Afghanistan. . . . Al Qaeda and its allies, armed with new tactics honed in Iraq, are coming full circle five years after U.S. led-forces ousted the Taliban mullahs."[57]

Seen as a resumption of the war in which Islam defeated the Soviet Union, the calling to the "hallowed ground" of Afghanistan was now viewed within the Islamist community as the completion of the holy cause, offering the opportunity to get a shot at the "Great Satan"[58] without the inconvenience of a Sunni-Shia civil war getting in the way. "In contrast," Rotella wrote, "an accelerating Afghan offensive by the resurgent Taliban offers a clearer battleground and a wealth of targets: U.S. and other North Atlantic Treaty Organization troops, and the Western-backed government."[59]

As the media caught wind of the resurgent Taliban in Afghanistan, the sudden increase in activity in America's war-on-terror ally Pakistan was an even greater cause for alarm. In the tribal areas of North and South Waziristan on the Afghan border, the military government of President Pervez Musharraf had reportedly lost control of events. Self-described Pakistani Taliban patrolled the village bazaars in Toyota pickups, free to eliminate anyone accused of being anti-Islamic or suspected of spying for the Americans. According to a report by Declan Walsh of the *San Francisco Chronicle* Foreign Service, as of April 2006 over a hundred pro-government politicians and elders had been killed in the previous nine months, with the most recent victims being a former militant who'd gone over to the government and a local mullah, Maulana Zahir Shah, accused of being a spy.[60]

Walsh wrote, "The chaos is spreading to nearby areas administered by the provincial government. On March 20, a remote-controlled bomb—similar to those used against U.S. forces in Afghanistan—ripped through a police vehicle in Dera Ismail Khan, just outside South Waziristan, killing seven people. Efforts by the Pakistani military, which has deployed 70,000 soldiers and paramilitaries to Waziristan, are faltering. An army strike against an alleged al Qaeda training camp March 1, three days before President Bush visited Islamabad, sparked a bloody battle for control of Miran Shah between the army and the rebels that left more than 100 people dead."[61]

Echoing the catalog of failures racked up by more than a century of British attempts at pacifying the Wazirs, many of the local tribes joined the Taliban insurgents exactly *because* of Islamabad's brutal efforts at suppression. Maiming and killing hundreds of innocent civilians in an effort to destroy a handful of Taliban or Al Qaeda, the war on terror was causing the entire province of Waziristan to rise up in defiance. Nor was responsibility for the deaths falling on the Pakistani military alone, with the Pentagon in one incident blamed for killing thirteen innocents with a Hellfire missile fired from a remote-controlled drone in the ongoing going hunt for Al Qaeda's number-two man, Ayman al-Zawahiri.[62]

Meanwhile, in the United States, the Pentagon continued to eavesdrop on American citizens—freed as well from constitutional restrictions by the necessities of winning a war on a method (terrorism), a war that could not be won. Having declared the United States a theater of military operations as part of the 2002 Bush doctrine,[63] the Pentagon had succeeded in reaching into layers of civilian authority specifically forbidden by the Constitution. Now, the president's new nominee for director of the Central Intelligence Agency, Air Force general Michael Hayden, had to explain why the Pentagon should be allowed to continue eavesdropping and why they had been collecting data on peaceful political protests. (One such report focused on a protest against Halliburton for war profiteering).[64]

By the fall of 2006, the absurd disconnections, ambiguities, phony justifications, failures and just plain lies about America's war in Afghanistan provoked author and women's rights activist Ann Jones to comment. "So you see what I mean about the weird policies a government such as ours can develop when it can't talk about real facts. When it cozies up to people it professes to be against. When it attacks people whose hearts and minds it hopes to win. When it pays experts to report false conclusions it wants to hear. When it spends billions to tear down the lives of poor Afghans even as our NATO allies pray for a break in battling the Taliban so that—with time running out—they can rebuild."[65]

Increasingly viewed as masters of illusion and little else, an October 16 article titled "Who's Running Afghan Policy?" by the *Nation*'s Washington editor, David Corn, suggested that the administration may never have had a clue as to what to do in Afghanistan:

> Several months ago a leading American expert on Afghanistan was meeting with Meghan O'Sullivan, a deputy national security adviser in the Bush White House. . . . The expert explained that many factors shape the difficult Pakistani-Afghan relationship. He pointed to the decades-long conflict between Afghanistan and Pakistan and mentioned the Durand Line, the supposed border between Afghanistan and Pakistan. . . . By referring to the Durand Line, the expert was noting that US efforts in the region are complicated by pre-9/11 history. O'Sullivan, according to this expert (who wishes not to be named), didn't know what the Durand Line was. The expert was stunned. O'Sullivan is the most senior Bush Administration official handling Afghanistan policy. If she wasn't familiar with this basic point, US policy-making on Afghanistan was in trouble.[66]

Corn cited long-time expert Barnett Rubin's congressional testimony that Afghanistan was ripe for fundamentalism, and quoted Rubin who said that "the most sensible conversations I have are with three- and four-star generals on the ground there. . . . The diplomats—they recycle through and have no experience in the area. Everyone in the region assumes that the United States is not serious about succeeding in Afghanistan."[67]

With the United States having used up both its diplomatic and military credibility, and with time clearly running out, former CIA officer Milt Bearden stepped forward in February 2007 with a dire warning to the Bush administration against opening still another front in the "Long War."

"As the drumbeat for war with Iran grows more insistent, the search for a 'casus belli' compelling enough to calm a newly assertive Congress and convince an increasingly questioning American public intensifies. . . . But before Americans get sent off to a third war in a Muslim country, it is worth recalling that in the past century, no nation that has started a major war has ended up winning it." Knowing that a war with Iran "will most certainly have a bad outcome," Bearden added that it would be "delusional to suggest that Iran would remain a spectator to a foreign invasion of a part of 'Greater Iran'" and called for the administration to start talking to Tehran.[68] With the administration besieged on all sides and willing only to play its military card, it could be argued that it would be delusional to think they wouldn't.

The prelude to the complete unwinding of the Bush administration's Afghan strategy was visible as early as January to anyone bothering to look beyond the rosy press briefings. Once the capital of a tolerant Muslim country bent on democratization and modernization under international supervision and British military control, Kabul had taken on the sad look and rancid smell of a nineteenth-century imperial project in its final hours. Terrorism specialist and senior fellow at the New America Foundation Peter Bergen told a tale of occupied Kabul "as David Lynch might imagine it": "Kabul 2006 has a distinctly *fin de siècle* air. The hotel I stay at plays loungey house music at night and serves beer discreetly. It also has a makeshift bunker surrounded by sandbags in the event the hotel is attacked, a reasonable precaution given that in May an angry anti-American mob shot out the ground-floor windows of another Kabul hotel. Suicide attacks are now a weekly event in the Capital, while an economy steeped in corruption and driven by the heroin/opium trade and foreign aid enriches an elite who party into the night."[69]

Sounding a death knell for the American effort, Bergen observed, "Between the rising Taliban insurgency, the epidemic of attacks by suicide bombers and improvised explosive devices (IEDs), and spiraling criminal activity fueled by the drug trade, Afghanistan today looks something like Iraq in the summer of 2003, when descent into violent conflict began. As a former senior Afghan Cabinet member told me in September, 'If international forces leave, the Taliban will take over in an hour.'"[70] Going so far as to quote Kant, "Out of the crooked timber of humanity, no straight thing was ever made,"[71] in order to paint the West's most recent failure in Afghanistan as purely Afghanistan's fault, Bergen cleverly set the stage for the Bush administration's fallback position.

Determined to salvage something from its investment in Afghanistan, early in the year the White House renewed its commitment, earmarking billions of dollars for the U.S. military's provincial reconstruction projects. But the attention was too little and too late. With the air long-poisoned by anti-Muslim rhetoric, the abandonment of human rights, and international law represented by Guantánamo, Abu Ghraib, and extraordinary rendition, by 2007 everything the United States did in Afghanistan would be viewed by the local population with suspicion or in bad faith. In February a roadside bomb in Pakistan claimed the life of Dr. Abdul Ghani, the chief surgeon at the main hospital in Khar, near the Afghan border. In charge of a polio immunization campaign, Ghani was targeted by Islamists who claimed the campaign was a U.S. plot to sterilize Muslims. In January alone the parents of twenty-four thousand children in areas bordering Afghanistan refused to allow their children to be vaccinated.[72]

On February 18 the *New York Times* reported that Al Qaeda, operating from their bases in Pakistan, had "re-established significant control over their once-battered worldwide terror network. . . . American officials said there was mounting evidence that Osama bin Laden and his deputy, Ayman al-Zawahiri, had been steadily building an operations hub in the mountainous Pakistani tribal area of North Waziristan."[73]

According to the German magazine *Der Spiegel* one week later, a powerful bomb exploded at the entrance to the U.S. military base at Bagram airfield during a visit by Vice President Dick Cheney. According to the report, knowledge of Cheney's movements, the sophistication of the bomb, and the ability of the attacker to reach the gate of the highly secure facility indicated the Taliban possessed a "disconcerting" level of capability.[74]

Throughout the spring and into the summer reports surfaced of the growing resurgence of the well-financed and well-armed Taliban and Al Qaeda taking over virtual control of the perennially turbulent border regions between Afghanistan and Pakistan. In July the Pakistani army's elite Special Services Group stormed Islamabad's radical Red Mosque, the Lal Masjid, in a bloody siege that killed ten soldiers and over a hundred militants after a thirty-five-hour gun battle. Located near the headquarters of Pakistan's Inter Services Intelligence (ISI) and once a favored mosque of Gen. Zia-ul-Haq, the Red Mosque remains at the center of Pashtun extremist sentiment as well as calls for the assassination of General Musharraf.[75] That same month King Zahir Shah died in Kabul at ninety-two, following a long illness.[76] Eulogized with his symbolic title—given to him by Hamid Karzai—Father of the Nation (but not "king"), Afghanistan lost the only figure capable of uniting Afghans under one flag.[77]

The *New York Times* published an article that month revealing the Bush administration's approval of a $20-billion arms package to Saudi Arabia, including satellite-guided bombs. The move was criticized by some American officials who claimed the Saudis were "playing a counterproductive role in Iraq."[78] Their role in Afghanistan and Pakistan was not mentioned. That summer London's *Daily Mail* published an article headlined "Britain Is Protecting the Biggest Heroin Crop of All Time," raising the question: what are our servicemen dying for?[79] On July 24, the government of Pakistan told the BBC that it would oppose any attempt by the United States to strike at bin Laden should his whereabouts be discovered inside the country. Washington responded that nothing could be ruled out in hunting down the Al Qaeda leader.

A new threat assessment issued by U.S. counterterrorism experts that July revealed that Al Qaeda had somehow managed to restore their operational capabilities to pre-9/11 levels right under the nose of Pakistan's Gen. Pervez Musharraf. Unfazed by the six-year "war on terror," Al Qaeda was now—according to the White House—not only able to assist the Taliban in undermining NATO and U.S. control over the Afghan countryside, but was on the verge of seizing control of Pakistan and launching attacks on the U.S. "homeland," as well.

PASHTUNISTAN NOW

Citing Al Qaeda as the number-one threat in Iraq, White House press secretary Tony Snow used the opportunity to call for a renewed commitment to the war there. But as the month wore on it became clear that it was Iraq that had become the sideshow to history, as Afghan expert Selig Harrison reported a shocking new twist to a centuries-old conflict: "The alarming growth of Al Qaeda and the Taliban in the Pashtun tribal region of northwest Pakistan and southern Afghanistan is usually attributed to the popularity of their messianic brand of Islam and to covert help from Pakistani intelligence agencies. But another, more ominous reason also explains their success: their symbiotic relationship with a simmering Pashtun separatist movement that could lead to the unification of the estimated 41 million Pashtuns on both sides of the border, the breakup of Pakistan and Afghanistan, and the emergence of a new national entity, 'Pashtunistan,' under radical Islamist leadership."[80]

Divided by Britain's 1893 Durand Line edict and maintained as a front line in the Cold War for almost fifty years by Pakistan and the United States, the entire region of South Central Asia, in only six years of the misconceived and incompetently managed "war on terror," now stood on the verge of a radical extremist–backed transformation.

16.

Afghanistan and the Region

At the end of Soviet involvement in the Afghan conflict in 1989, U.S. defense intellectuals disconnected politically from the Afghan scene. As they turned their attention back to the Middle East, China, Eastern Europe and Iraq, the strategic importance of a broken Afghanistan as the gateway to Central Asia was left for others to calculate. As the United States deferred direct involvement, the Taliban rose to power, supported by a Saudi Arabian–inspired vision of a greater Islamic Central Asia. With no effective policy of its own and lacking any sophisticated understanding of the region outside of its geographic importance to Eurasian oil and gas reserves, Washington's deferral of responsibility opened the door to a host of special interests. The Mecca for Islamic jihadists the world over during the 1980s, the first problem was the existence of Al Qaeda. Named for the database of extremists used by American, British and Saudi Arabian intelligence officials to terrorize the Soviet effort in Afghanistan, by the mid-1990s the organization had become a powerful political player with a plan of its own. Antimodernist and backward looking, its extreme Wahhabist social orientation stood in sharp contrast to Afghanistan's traditionally moderate and tolerant brand of Islam. It also stood sharply profiled against a century of progressive political movements in Afghan politics which saw the Afghan monarchy breaking centuries of class and ethnic imbalances and moving toward women's equality with men. As an example, during Amanullah's reign in the 1920s a new constitution (had it been implemented) would have provided women with the right to vote. Article 25 of the 1964 constitution under King Zahir Shah stated that "the people of Afghanistan, without any discrimination or preference, have equal rights and obligations before the law."[1] This was clarified in Article 27 of Mohammad Daoud's 1976 constitution to read: "All the people of

Afghanistan, both women and men, without discrimination and privilege, have equal rights and obligations before the law."[2]

Publicly opposed to American power and interests in the world, but privately connected through a network of financial interests, Al Qaeda's radical-conservative politics and its backing of a Taliban-controlled Afghanistan at first found approval from an influential core of U.S. conservative and neoconservative intellectuals. It was these American antimodernist and anti-enlightenment elements which found more in common with the flowing robes and misogynist salons of the Middle East than with a progressive Islamic Afghanistan. And it was these antimodernist and anti-enlightenment elements in the U.S. government that held back attempts to form an effective U.S. Afghan policy.

Lulled by a philosophical commonality and the bonds of mutual self-interest imposed by America's oil dependency, the growing problem of Al Qaeda and its connection to the Taliban movement went largely overlooked; when seen, profoundly underestimated; and when understood, ignored. A report on the CIA's handling of the terrorist threat in the 1990s released in August 2007 by the CIA's inspector general noted specifically that the intelligence community "was hampered by insufficient analytic focus," causing vital problem areas to be "covered insufficiently or not at all."[3] "For instance," stated a *Washington Post* article on the report, "the CIA had made no comprehensive report on Osama bin Laden since 1993, had not examined the potential for terrorists to use aircraft as weapons, and had done only limited analysis on the potential of the United States as a target."[4] Only when publicly embarrassed by the 1998 U.S. embassy bombings and the 2000 bombing of the USS *Cole* did the United States seek to finally engage Afghanistan. But when separating Al Qaeda from the dozen other terrorist organs now based there, U.S. defense intellectuals came up against their own self-invented reality. As recounted in earlier chapters, the legacy of this process originated in 1945 with the dropping of the atomic bomb and the creation of the national security state whereby threats—both imagined and real—formed the basis of the U.S. posture against the Soviet Union. Revived and extended to the U.S. covert war against the Russians in the 1980s, an entire faux nineteenth-century Afghanistan had been hodgepodged together and used as a stage prop to win U.S. public support for war. Now it was America's turn to reconcile the staged Afghanistan of legend with the real Afghanistan. But the real Afghanistan was lacking one important ingredient. In the words of Cheryl Bernard, a RAND analyst and expert on the Middle East who is married to Zalmay Khalilzad, "'In Afghanistan we made a deliberate choice. . . . At first, everyone thought, There's no way to beat the Soviets. So what we have to do is throw the worst crazies against them that we can find, and there was a lot of collateral damage. We knew exactly who these people were, and what their organizations were like and we didn't care,' she says. 'Then we allowed them to get rid of, just kill all the moderate leaders. The reason we don't have moderate leaders in Afghanistan today is because we let the nuts kill them all. They killed the leftists, the moderates, the middle-of-the-roaders. They were just eliminated, during the 1980s and afterward.'"[5]

Following the chaos that wracked Afghanistan after Soviet forces withdrew, there had been a concerted effort by western intelligence elites, particularly in Britain and the United States, to advance the Taliban in the U.S. public's mind as a natural and "cleansing" outgrowth of Afghan society. A worldwide publicity campaign conducted on behalf of the Taliban by Leili Helms, niece of former CIA director Richard Helms, went so far as to brand any Afghan woman who complained about the Taliban's policies against women as a communist, miraculously transforming any woman educated under the communist regime into a communist herself.[6]

After Osama bin Laden and Al Qaeda became enemies of the United States, the United States maintained an open line to the Taliban into July 2001 in the clear hope that they would continue on in their pacification of the Afghan countryside while delivering bin Laden to American counterterrorism officials. Their failure to do so was a major contributing factor to the U.S. invasion in October of that year.

Even after the invasion, efforts were made by Hamid Karzai—who originally supported the Taliban—to open a dialogue with them and bring them into the reconstructed Afghan government. Exclusively of Pashtun descent, the Taliban movement remains the product of Pakistan's madrassas and ISI, the vanguard of a radical pan-Islamic movement trained by Al

Qaeda and funded by Saudi money and money from other Arab countries. According to Afghan human rights expert Sima Wali, "Over the years, due to the dismal economic condition in Afghanistan, many young Afghan men were either forcibly recruited or volunteered to join the Taliban forces. While I was in Pakistan, Afghans confirmed that the only way for their boys to receive education was through the madrassa system and by joining the Taliban. In most cases they were housed, clothed and fed in madrassas in Pakistan and lectured in anti-Americanism with the full knowledge of the American authorities."[7]

On the verge of losing its war in Afghanistan and with its anti-Taliban campaign back-firing on Pakistan, by the fall of 2007 the Bush administration hinted at a renewed effort at conciliation with the Taliban in order to stave off defeat. Calling on the services of a veteran hard-liner, Deputy Secretary of State John Negroponte, the plan entailed creating an intra-Afghan dialogue by bringing 117 tribal leaders together in a Jirga, while anticipating that the more moderate elements of the Taliban could at some point in the future participate without threat of retribution.[8]

Once again attempting to parse between the merely extreme and the most-extreme elements as they had prior to 9/11, the UN secretary general's special envoy, Tom Koenigs, informed a German newspaper, "So far many have said we do not negotiate with terrorists, meaning also the Taliban. However, the Taliban movement is multi-faceted. You cannot lump all of them together."[9]

Surprisingly, numerous radical Islamists seemed to agree, with the Tajik Burhanuddin Rabbani recommending the inclusion of both the Taliban and Gulbuddin Hekmatyar's Hezb-i Islami in any future talks.[10] But though a split in the extremist movement might benefit a U.S. and NATO military effort whose time and plan was used up, the fear of a renewed Talibanized Afghanistan—no matter how moderate—was anathema to democracy advocates, especially women's groups whose temporary gains under the existing regime were barely adequate as it was. Ann Jones wrote, "The fact is that the 'liberation' of Afghan women is mostly theoretical. The Afghan Constitution adopted in 2004 declares that the Citizens of Afghanistan—whether man or woman—have equal rights and duties before the law. But what law? The judicial system—ultra-conservative, inadequate, incompetent, and notoriously corrupt—usually bases decisions on idiosyncratic interpretations of Islamic Sharia, tribal customary codes, or simple bribery. And legal scholars instruct women that having equal rights and duties is not the same as being equal to men."[11]

Neither would Sima Wali accept the legitimacy of a Taliban resurgence, having warned cadets at West Point in 2006 of what she feared was either a fallback position or even a long-term strategy underlying the administration's willful incompetence. "As an Afghan woman who firmly believes in the power of the people, especially women—who constitute the majority of post-war Afghanistan, I remain highly concerned about the Taliban mentality that reigns among those in powerful posts. The world community must not be acquiescent with rhetoric, tokenism, or symbolic assurances. We, as women of the world who are concerned about the fate of our Afghan sisters, must challenge developments in Afghanistan."[12]

But with developments in Afghanistan hidden behind the wall of an increasingly desperate administration's rhetoric and still confused by misleading assumptions about Afghanistan's past, a successful resolution to the continuing Afghan crisis continued to be made to appear far more difficult than it really was.

As noted Pakistani scholar Ahmed Rashid wrote in August 2007, the path to winning over the Afghan countryside in 2001 had been straight and narrow to anyone familiar with the Afghan debacle.[13] "Many lifelong bureaucrats specializing in the region shared Ahmed's enthusiasm, and they agreed that after decades of violence America could finally turn Afghanistan around through aid."[14]

But Rashid's vision, like that of Sima Wali and a host of knowing professionals, was thwarted by political appointees in Washington who overruled the U.S. foreign policy bureaucracy in their effort to carry out their own personal policy goals for the Middle East, while denying Afghanistan the basics needed to recover. As James Rupert writes, "While Bosnia was stabilized by the deployment of 60,000 foreign troops (about one for every 50 local citizens), Afghanistan for two years had only 5,000 peacekeepers in Kabul (one per 5,600 Afghan citizens), all based in Kabul. The security vacuum let the Taliban re-ignite an insurgency."[15]

Now focused on extending the war to Iran and facing a severe deadline in the 2008 presidential elections, these political appointees were at work again, preparing to offer the olive branch to Taliban extremists they had been fighting for six years, and making it look as if there was no alternative. Given the dire history of U.S. involvement, it appeared a natural outgrowth of events, but the preparation for the legitimization of the Taliban and an Islamic offensive on South Asia had been in the works for decades.

THE AFGHAN-PAKISTAN SPLIT

If the United States had wanted to establish a vehicle for advancing Pashtun nationalism at the expense of both the Pakistani and Afghan governments, they could not have created a better, more motivated vehicle than the state-destroying, antimodernist Taliban. Feared by American diplomats in the 1990s to have the potential for undermining Pakistan's fragile politics, by 2007 Washington had realized those fears. A Pashtunistan-centered insurgency, the Taliban's influence as representatives of Afghanistan's majority ethnic group appealed to both the Pashtun's fierce pride and the long-suppressed dream of returning Afghanistan to a pre–Durand Line existence.

Historically Afghanistan's dominant ethnic group (providing Afghanistan with its kings and amirs for over two centuries), Pashtuns had been marginalized in the minority Tajik-dominated government of Hamid Karzai, bombed indiscriminately, and subjected to excessive force that had claimed more than 5,000 civilian casualties since 2001.[16] Demonized by the broad brush of the war on terror, by the fall of 2007 they were a unified, well-armed, and radical opposition to both the U.S.-supported governments of Pervez Musharraf and Hamid Karzai, and according to Selig Harrison "seething with anger" throughout Pakistan's Federally Administered Tribal Areas. "At a Washington seminar March 1, convened by the Pakistan Embassy, the Pakistani ambassador, Mahmud Al Durrani, a Pashtun, commented that 'I hope the Taliban and Pashtun nationalism don't merge. If that happens, we've had it, and we're on the verge of that.'"[17]

Some members of the Afghan parliament felt the Taliban-Pashtun nationalist merger was already well underway, with Pashtunistan and Baluchistan becoming more and more trouble for Pakistan in the next year. To these Afghans, the idea that the Taliban should join the Afghan government was a positive development, with Pashtunistan and Baluchistan peacefully joining a "greater Afghanistan," in a renewed Durrani empire, opening a gateway for Kabul to the Arabian Sea regardless of whether U.S. and British overseers liked it or not. In their minds, the foreign armies imposed following the U.S. invasion should vacate Afghanistan immediately. Seen from their extremist viewpoint, it was the Taliban who had put the country back together after the mujahideen destroyed it and it was the United States who had stopped their progress and handed them over to Al Qaeda and Pakistan.

Even to moderate Afghans, the U.S. indiscriminate bombing campaign, support for warlordism, and crop-eradication efforts provided enough evidence that the United States was not on their side. Afghans wondered what they had done as pawns in the Cold War to deserve being ethnically cleansed by the United States in order to keep a Punjabi-dominated regime in Islamabad from dealing with its own vast corruption, suppression of democracy, and support for terrorism.

By the fall of 2007 virtually everyone outside the Bush administration accepted that the western-created government of Hamid Karzai was broken, held together by NATO and U.S. forces, and that it would fall in an hour without their support. According to one high-level Afghan close to the scene, "Karzai loses popularity every day. He is now surrounded with dangerous people like Rasul Sayaf, Yunus Qanuni and Rashid Dostum who have taken power in the house and Parliament. He is so isolated that almost everyone is standing against him, even the general public. Everyone says that he had the best opportunity to get rid of the warlords and build a clean and healthy government. But everywhere you go you find corruption. Everyone steals and they steal more and more because they think the Americans are not going to stay and last much longer."[18]

Had the United States and NATO provided more troops early on, and had those troops disarmed the warlords and provided security, and had that security enabled reconstruction teams to rebuild the roads, schools, power grids and irrigation projects necessary to get the rural economy up and running, then the western effort to stop opium production and keep the war-beaten Afghan people on their side could have succeeded. But as recounted in these pages, even as the United States was declaring "mission accomplished" and packing up for Iraq, the tide was turning, as Pakistan's ISI helped Al Qaeda regroup in Kandahar, in plain view for all to see.

Although downplayed if not altogether missing from the mainstream U.S. media's coverage of the Afghan debacle, among U.S. allies the cause of the Bush administration's policy failures in Afghanistan is increasingly impossible to hide. Hamid Karzai's few remaining defenders point the finger back to the White House, blaming "an array of government officials, . . . 'These people have hijacked a weak system,' says a senior member of President Hamid Karzai's staff, who spoke on condition of anonymity. 'People here initially welcomed diaspora Afghans with open arms and looked to them for guidance. But that's changed. It's clear that too many Afghan-Americans paraded their patriotism only to promote their careers, or to advance ethnic agendas."[19]

Central to both agendas is a Reagan-doctrine architect—RAND director, UN ambassador and fellow Afghan-American Zalmay Khalilzad—whose pivotal, three-decade-long role in advancing the Islamic extremist cause in Afghanistan remains unexamined, underappreciated and generally invisible to this day. Arthur Kent writes:

> When Khalilzad served the Reagan administration in the 1980s, he backed anti-Soviet Afghan resistance figures of his own Pashtun ethnicity—despite their extremist views. He favored fundamentalists like Gulbuddin Hekmatyar, and allied himself to Pakistan's campaign against the Afghan nationalist leader, Ahmed Shah Massoud, an ethnic Tajik. Today, Hekmatyar is among America's most-wanted Afghan terrorists. . . . As a director of the RAND Corporation, he lobbied the Clinton administration to recognize the Taliban regime. . . . Says a source close to the

> Presidential Palace: "He encouraged Karzai to rid his government of Tajiks, and except for a few positions, he has succeeded. Ethnic fascism is not too strong a label for Zal and his friends."[20]

In the hands of a purported ethnic fascist and unabashed supporter of terrorists, it should come as no surprise that the U.S. effort to establish a modern, pluralist democracy in Afghanistan has struck bottom. But Khalilzad's personal failure and the more general failure of the Bush administration's efforts to cope with the reality on the ground in Afghanistan should not rest on him alone. The fatal flaw in today's "war on terror" philosophy and its arcane, self-defeating logic suffers a long history reaching back to the origins of the Cold War, to the worldview of the people who created it, and especially to the machinations of the Trotskyist philosopher mentor who shaped it as a weapon of war against Soviet Russia, Albert Wohlstetter.

Having lost (with the end of the Cold War) the central motivating factor driving Wohlstetter's expansive theorems on the vulnerability of the United States to nuclear attack, articulated in his landmark 1959 *Foreign Affairs* magazine article "The Delicate Balance of Terror," today's frustrated defense intellectuals press on, undeterred by the oppressive reality of a strategic *imbalance* of terror. As Eric Schmitt and Thom Shanker write in the *New York Times*: "After piecing together a more nuanced portrait of terrorist organizations, they say [administration, military and intelligence officials], there is reason to believe that a combination of efforts could in fact establish something akin to the posture of deterrence, the strategy that helped protect the United States from a Soviet nuclear attack during the cold war."[21]

Even with the illusion of deterrence obliterated by the events of 9/11, today's crop of defense intellectuals persist in claiming their obsolete and unproven "balance of terror" models can be adapted to counter the fundamentally ineffective, out-of-balance models of their "war on terror."

Using the old standby that failed in Vietnam, Iraq and Afghanistan—that complex systems and expensive technology can do what politics, diplomacy and even armies cannot—they quietly leak to a more-than-credulous press that, as Schmitt and Shanker write, "[m]uch effort is being spent on perfecting technical systems that can identify the source of unconventional weapons or their components regardless of where they are found—and letting nations around the world know the United States has this ability."[22]

Yet nearly seven years after the "war on terror" began, and with an overwhelming balance of nuclear and conventional terror still on the side of the United States, the end is nowhere in sight and the enemy remains a phantom in the Afghan mountains, as illusive in his defiance to the president of the United States as he was to Alexander the Great.

As Wohlstetter's protégé, Khalilzad's presence in Iraq, at the United Nations, and as a rumored candidate for president of Afghanistan[23] puts what Fred Kaplan described as the new self-created power elite put in place after World War II, "whose power would come . . . from their having conceived and elaborated a set of ideas,"[24] right at the center of the world's oldest civilization, completing a circle that began with the Team-B report, found its midway point at the end of the Soviet empire, and finishes with the end of the American republic.

It also puts the terrifying, doomsday nuclear-war-fighting theories of Wohlstetter and the nuclear priesthood back into the control room, as the United States and its NATO allies struggle to come to grips with a persistent failure to prevail in a ground war that numerous military and intelligence experts now consider to be unwinnable.

As Ian Traynor wrote in the *Guardian*, "The west must be ready to resort to a pre-emptive nuclear attack to try to halt the 'imminent' spread of nuclear and other weapons of mass destruction, according to a radical manifesto for a new NATO by five of the west's most senior military officers and strategists."[25]

Once again embracing the arcane, "mirror-imaging" logic once described by Jerome Wiesner as a self-serving explanation for the Cold War arms race, the five authors,[26] all NATO commanders, see no other way to stop the first use of nuclear weapons in the twenty-first century than to use them first themselves. "The risk of further [nuclear] proliferation is imminent and, with it, the danger that nuclear war fighting, albeit limited in scope, might become possible. . . . The first use of nuclear weapons must remain in the quiver of escalation as the ultimate instrument to prevent the use of weapons of mass destruction."[27]

With Arab militants once again pouring into Afghanistan and Pakistan, and Washington's neoconservative defense intellectuals distracted by yet another war—this time against Iran—the smell of a colossal American defeat is in the air. Associated Press reporter Kathy Gannon wrote, "In both Iraq and Afghanistan, young militants feel that 'Allah's victory seems to be drawing near' and see parallels with the stalemating of the Soviet army in Afghanistan in the 1980s and its ultimate withdrawal, said Michael Scheuer, a former CIA official who until 2004 headed a team that searched for Osama bin Laden."[28]

To Afghan expert Sima Wali, even at this late date Washington's recommendations continue to miss the mark. Instead of addressing what the war-weary Afghan people desperately need and want, the solutions offered so far only pit Taliban warlords against Tajik warlords without addressing the complex issues of ethnic identity driving the regional problem. "The Afghan people don't want any warlords at all in the government. The Karzai plan to replace Tajik warlords with Pashtun-Taliban warlords is all about ethnic rivalry. Karzai's power base is Pashtun. He believes that if he can get Pashtun ethnic Taliban into his government he will be able to run the country which is out of control. The Afghan people don't want any warlords at all, no matter what the ethnicity."[29]

Making the all-vital distinction between Afghan Taliban and Pakistani Taliban, Wali believes that the Afghan people would accept the Afghan Taliban back as citizens of the country, but putting them back into government would solve nothing, either for the United States or the Afghan people. "Pakistani Taliban made sure the Afghan Taliban had limited influence. That means the Afghan Taliban are not *as* responsible for the atrocities as the Pakistani Taliban. But the Afghan people still hold them accountable by carrying out the orders especially against women. Afghans would accept Afghan Taliban back as citizens but they should not be rewarded with government positions for what they did on behalf of the Pakistani Taliban."[30]

One of the only three women invited to the Bonn conference establishing the new Afghan government, Wali once believed that the United States was serious about implementing a straightforward plan to aid Afghanistan, only to realize—like Ahmed Rashid—that a separate and flawed agenda lay beneath the surface. "Karzai thinks that bringing the Taliban into his government will save him. Afghans do not accept his plans and are outraged that he is offering them positions. Only Afghans with direct ties to the government or special interests—many of them Afghan-Americans who never suffered under the Taliban—support the idea of Afghan Taliban being invited to join the government. This would be a slap in the face to the majority of Afghans."[31]

The issue of ethnicity in any successful policy employed by the United States is not limited to the ethnic Pashtun-Tajik competition. In Pakistan, the ethnicity issue compounds the pressure put by the United States on the government of Pervez Musharraf. As observed by Selig Harrison, "Pakistan and Afghanistan are fragile, multiethnic states. Ironically, by ignoring ethnic factors and defining the struggle with jihadists mainly in military terms, the United States is inadvertently helping al Qaeda and the Taliban capture the leadership of Pashtun nationalism."[32]

According to Harrison, Afghanistan's Pashtun mountain tribes have resisted Punjabi domination for centuries. With Musharraf's regime dominated by the Punjabi ethnic majority, any effort to bring the tribal areas under control will produce more chaos. "Yet the United States is pushing Musharraf to bring the autonomous tribal areas under central government control and is threatening unilateral air strikes against suspected Al Qaeda hideouts"[33] if he doesn't.

To make matters worse, U.S. efforts to eradicate Afghan opium strengthen Al Qaeda's hold on the civilian population, as they align with poor Afghan farmers against U.S. efforts to destroy the only cash crop they rely on for their livelihood: poppies.

A July 2007 article in the *Daily Mail* by Britain's former ambassador to Uzbekistan, Craig Murray, explained how the West's short-sighted favoritism for Northern Alliance warlords acts against the war's stated objectives of rooting out terror, instead turning Afghanistan from a mere grower of opium into the biggest heroin exporter in the world: "It [Afghanistan] has succeeded in what our international aid efforts urge every developing country to do. Afghanistan has gone into manufacturing and 'value-added' operations. It now exports not opium, but heroin. Opium is converted into heroin on an industrial scale, not in kitchens but in factories. Millions of the gallons of the chemicals needed for this process are shipped into Afghanistan by tanker. The tankers and bulk opium lorries on the way to factories share roads, improved by American aid, with NATO troops."[34]

"How could this have happened, on this scale?" Murray asked. "The answer is simple. The four largest players in the heroin business are all senior members of the Afghan government. The government that our soldiers are fighting and dying to protect."[35]

Murray's testimony might seem like a contradiction, given Britain and America's much-publicized efforts to destroy Afghanistan's opium crop. But a careful look at the operation reveals that the program targets largely Pashtun farmers in the South near Kandahar—stoking the flames of Pashtun anger—while inadvertently protecting northern warlords like Gen. Rashid Dostum, who as head of the Afghan armed forces operates around the interdiction without interference.

Murray writes, "Dostum is an Uzbek, and heroin passes over the Friendship Bridge from Afghanistan to Uzbekistan, where it is taken over by President Islam Karimov's people. It is then shipped up the railway line, in bales of cotton, to St. Petersburg and Riga. The heroin Jeeps run from General Dostum to President Karimov. The UK, United States and Germany have all invested large sums in donating the most sophisticated detection and screening equipment to the Uzbek customs center at Termez to stop the heroin coming through. But the convoys of Jeeps running between Dostum and Karimov are simply waved around the side of the facility."[36]

SHANGHAI COOPERATION AGREEMENT

With the potential for short-circuiting any future U.S. ambitions to control oil and gas routes from Eurasia, the massive contagion of Afghan heroin reaching Europe and Russia, plus the possibility of an increasingly radicalized Afghanistan, are provoking an anti-American backlash in the larger region. M. K. Bhadrakumar writes in *Asia Times*, "Russia and Central Asian states would worry that once the radical movement is allowed into mainstream political life, Afghanistan could get 'Talibanized'. The ground reality is that the Taliban today are by far the best-organized force in Afghanistan. They could easily eclipse other groups and establish their dominance. From Moscow's point of view, such fears will surely push Russia and Central Asian countries closer together."[37]

An example of this togetherness is the Shanghai Cooperation Organization (SCO). Founded in June 2001 as an intergovernmental organization by Russia, China, Kazakhstan, Kyrgyzstan, Tajikistan, and Uzbekistan, the SCO and its military counterpart, the Collective Security Treaty Organization (CSTO), represent more than a billion and a half people, covering an area of over thirty million kilometers or almost nineteen thousand miles.[38] Viewed by western analysts as Beijing's and Moscow's attempt to challenge Washington's influence in the region while locking in the area's vast oil and gas reserves, the SCO's lesser members originally preferred to play the United States against the China-Russia axis. As U.S.-inspired political upheavals developed in nearby Georgia and the Ukraine, the small Central Asian regimes realized their vulnerability.

With the United States failing to discuss a Taliban revival within a regional context and threatening intervention in Iran, SCO members Russia and China have become vocal in their objections to talk of a Taliban rebirth. Vladimir Socor writes, "The Russian Foreign Ministry's major survey on foreign policy in March singled out that an objective basis existed 'for arriving at an agreed option of de-monopolization of the political settlement in the country, and at the enlistment of all Afghanistan's neighbors without exception in it . . .' Russian commentators have warned about the futility of summarily re-establishing Pashtun dominance in Afghanistan."[39]

China too has taken a strong stand against any Taliban legitimacy in Afghanistan, viewing the situation there as increasingly destabilizing with all the potential of developing into another Iraq-style war.[40] But as Afghanistan's U.S.-backed warlords struggle to hold onto their gains in the midst of a new swarm of Al Qaeda and Taliban fighters, the resolution to the country's problems may have less to do with these regional players than with the threadbare legacy of British India's colonial objectives, dressed in the trappings of radical Islam.

17.

Geopolitical Realities vs. Osama bin Laden, Superstar

"The American and international media went nuts over the year 2000. Two things were going to happen. Your computer was going to crash at one second after midnight and bin Laden was going to blow up your New Year's Eve party whether it was in Toronto or Sidney harbor or Times Square or Jerusalem and so bin Laden, bin Laden, bin Laden. The myth was created and you've never been able to turn it back."

—Milt Bearden

If we rely on the perspectives mapped out in foreign policy journals or Washington think tanks, we can surmise that the war in Afghanistan has had little to do with establishing democracy, freeing women from the chador ("burka" is the Pakistani word) or even making Afghanistan safe for a Unocal pipeline—which at this point would be far better for the Afghan people than dropping more bombs on them.

Nevertheless, the U.S. news media and the politicians who are funding the war tell us that Afghanistan is about protecting America, American lives and American interests from hardened Islamic terrorists bent on destroying our peace and security.

Throughout the term of the second Bush administration, the invocation of Winston Churchill and comparisons to World War II, the threats of (Islamo) fascism and references to Pearl Harbor have served to make this war as laden with nostalgia and meaning as possible. Osama bin Laden and Ayman al Zawahiri have been dutifully cast as the next Hitlers and are trotted out whenever the president's advisors wish to place more of the nation's security into private hands or ask for more money for a war in Iraq, where bin Laden and Zawahiri are *not* hiding. But what the spectacular Fox News specials and more subtle PBS World War II documentaries omit in their patriotic accounts is the two centuries of British military pressure on the "soft underbelly" of Eurasia and how the United States is now providing the money and the muscle for another century of such pressure under the guise of the war on terror.

As the drama of Afghanistan, "The Good War, Still to Be Won," plays out in the pages of the *New York Times*,[1] and as the pundits at the *Los Angeles Times* wring their hands over whether democracy and power sharing in Pakistan will "deprive [President] Musharraf of the dictatorial power" he needs to carry out counter-terrorism operations at the behest of the United States,[2] a growing number of critics are questioning whether the United States is in Afghanistan to win the war against Al Qaeda at all. "America is investing nowhere near the troops and money needed to confront the Taliban and other insurgents. Nearly six years on, the total of troops and police backing the Afghan government remains less than ten percent of what leading counter-insurgency analysts say is needed."[3]

Added to America's curious lack of due-diligence is ally Pakistan's dual role in the war on terror "that has made it a sanctuary where jihadist guerrillas can recruit and train fighters, raise money and infiltrate Afghanistan," while at the same time "it tolerates a broad support network for Taliban and other guerrillas that includes active-duty members of Pakistan's security forces."[4]

Used as a weapon to undermine Soviet influence in Central Asia by CIA director William Casey and Pakistan's ISI during the 1980s, in actuality the new wave of Saudi-supported Islamist extremism incubating under Pakistani supervision and protection represents the same game under a different name. Utilizing a policy whereby Musharraf *pretends* to hunt for extremists while the U.S. *pretends* to believe him, the U.S. repeats a practice that turned a blind eye to the Hekmatyar/ISI abuses in the war against the Soviets. But as the White House presses Pervez Musharraf and his ISI to help in the destabilization of Iran as it did the destabilization of Soviet-occupied

Afghanistan under Zia-ul-Haq, that game may be backfiring on its protagonists. According to Ahmed Rashid, the White House is panicking as the growing unrest threatens the cohesion of Pakistan's military. "Then there is the crumbling morale in the army. Two weeks ago US and Nato forces in Afghanistan were shocked to discover that 300 Pakistani soldiers—their erstwhile partners in the war on terrorism—had surrendered to the Taliban in Waziristan without firing a shot. Soldiers in the badlands controlled by the Taliban and al-Qa'eda are deserting or refusing to open fire. The White House is panic-stricken. That is because Gen. Musharraf in his hubris has utterly failed to convince Pakistanis or the army that Pakistan has to fight not America's war, but its own war against ever-expanding extremism."[5]

Pressing a twenty-first-century version of the same old Wahhabist jihad into India, China, Russia and South Asia through radical groups in Kashmir, Uzbekistan, Tajikistan, Turkmenistan[6] and Chechnya, Al Qaeda's base in Pakistan has become a complex dynamic for radical change. At the same time a new development—the growth of a "Pakistani Taliban"—threatens to push the country into civil war. "Pakistan's own Taliban are running wild in large parts of the country, beheading women, burning video shops, launching suicide bombers against army convoys and taking over law and order in towns just 100 miles from Islamabad."[7]

When U.S.-backed Benazir Bhutto returned to Pakistan in late October to challenge the military government after being granted an amnesty on corruption charges, it was believed an arrangement could be made to share power with Musharraf in a new government. Yet, her glaringly pro-American tilt and her long legacy of corruption and political manipulation were not forgiven or overlooked by her opponents. With her assassination on December 27, 2007, the already heated political environment boiled over with global implications. At the time it remained to be seen what kind of solution to Pakistan's many problems could be found within the swirl of events. But with talk surfacing of the real chance that the current crisis could escalate beyond the borders of Pakistan and rebound on other pro-western Muslim states like Saudi Arabia, it was unlikely that any lasting solution to the current impasse would be found within the framework of what the United States could or would find acceptable.

With Bhutto gone and Musharraf facing an election while embroiled in an unpopular war, the United States entered 2008 with few options and little time to rework a failed strategy.

In a January hearing on Afghanistan in the U.S. Senate, chaired by Sen. Joseph Biden, official after official testified to the fact that as of January 31, 2008, after six years of fighting, the United States had yet to actually come to grips with the political and historical complexities of the situation or to have developed a strategy at all.[8]

Biden: "Security is probably at its lowest ebb since 2001. Much of the country is only nominally under the control of Kabul. The US and coalition forces win every pitched battle, but the Taliban still grow stronger day by day."[9]

Testifying before the committee, Thomas Pickering, former undersecretary for political affairs at the Department of State, expressed what numerous Afghan leaders had been trying to get the United States leadership to hear for much of the last century when the United States hadn't been paying attention. "Afghanistan can no longer be considered as a kind of island state in the middle of nowhere. It is in fact deeply linked with what goes on around it and particularly with what is happening in Pakistan. And as we have seen, that porous and ungoverned border region is a source of continued difficulty, that there is no question at all that Pakistan itself has serious problems in coming to grips with governing that piece of its own territory, and it has been a historical legacy that has not been, in my view certainly, dealt with in the way it needs to be done. We believe overall that the effort to come together on an assessment and a strategy for Afghanistan is way overdue."[10]

But an assessment based on a military strategy that relies mainly on cross-border raids from Afghanistan into Pakistan and unilateral air strikes on unsuspecting villages—aside from further alienating an already alienated population—is hardly likely to prove any more effective against Pashtun nationalism and a century and a half of unaddressed grievances than Soviet or British efforts did in previous eras.

As the winter wore on, the dominoes continued to pile up. Mistake upon mistake in the field, compounded by misjudgment and incompetence in Washington, added up to a shocking level of political paralysis. Divisions within the NATO coalition helping to pacify the countryside continued to grow. As the Pakistani military faltered and Pashtun tribal groups merged with Arab and Al Qaeda fighters to form what Pakistani political scientist Husain Haqqani called "one seamless whole," most observers found little to agree about except "that the Bush administration bears much of the blame for the worsening crisis."[11]

In February 2008, Pakistan's Gen. Musharraf suffered a stunning defeat in the general election forcing Pakistan's Parliament to form a coalition government uniting the assassinated Bhutto's Pakistan's People's Party (now led by her widower, Asif Aki Zardari) with conservative Islamist Nawaz Sharif's Pakistan Muslim League.[12] Generally hostile to Musharraf and the war on terror, the democratically elected coalition was immediately viewed by the elite of U.S. experts like Graham Allison as a blow to American interests in both Afghanistan and Pakistan. "Eighty-nine percent of Pakistanis said they disapprove of the US war on terrorism. Eight in ten Pakistanis oppose allowing the United States to pursue Al Qaeda terrorists in their country. A similar percentage rejects US pursuit of Taliban forces in Pakistan. In opposing Musharraf, opposition parties called him 'Busharraf' and accused him of being a 'lackey' of the United States in the 'so-called war on terrorism,' which they say is a US-led war on Islam."[13]

Painting a grim picture of the fruits of Pakistani democracy, Allison pointed out that "critics of Musharraf's limited cooperation with the US-NATO campaign should recognize that a government that more closely followed the wishes of its people would be less cooperative in combating the Taliban," warning ominously that "advocates of instant democracy should be careful what they wish for."[14] Yet it was America's blind support for dictators Zia-ul-Haq and Pervez Musharraf that kept Pakistan's democracy on hold for three decades while helping to facilitate the nightmare of Al Qaeda and the Taliban which former Pentagon planner and RAND advisor Allison now seems to have forgotten.

It should also be noted when mentioning U.S. support for Musharraf, that most of what has been claimed he was doing for the United States—as an ally in the war on terror—has been revealed as little more than public relations, with up to 70 percent of the $5.4 billion dollars in military assistance provided to him since 2002, gone missing. "The official said that he did not know what had happened to the remaining 70 percent of the funds—amounting to approximately $3.8.bn—but suspected that some of the money might have been spent on F-16 fighter jets or 'a new house for an army general.'"[15]

In fairness, not all the blame for the failure of the war on terror in Afghanistan can be blamed on Pakistani corruption. Since 2006, Washington has supplied the Afghan government with ammunition to fight Washington's war on terror from a Miami Beach, Florida, company run by a twenty-two-year-old "whose vice president is a licensed masseur," the *New York Times* reported. Much of the ammunition comes from aging stockpiles of the old Communist Bloc, including stockpiles that the State Department and NATO have determined to be unreliable and obsolete, and have spent millions of dollars to have destroyed."[16]

Meanwhile, in Kabul the political tensions grew as Karzai showed his displeasure with London and Washington, expelling diplomats Michael Semple (deputy head of the European Union mission in Afghanistan) and Mervyn Patterson (a political officer for the UN) for helping the British enact a secret plan to train former Taliban fighters in Helmand province.[17] Chafing under the misguided patronage of his Anglo-American sponsors Karzai had no choice but to rebuff the plot (revealed by one of his own intelligence operatives) in another jaw-dropping example of a U.S. policy failing to come to grips with reality. "Given the backlog of history in the region, Britain should never have cast itself in a lead role in the Afghan war, howsoever compelling the geopolitical compulsions of containing Russia or China might be. Afghans still take pride in the Anglo-Afghan wars. Equally, it is a gross error of judgment on Washington's part to have overlooked this fact."[18]

The gross errors compounded. As winter came to a close, Defense Secretary Robert Gates finally addressed the collateral impact of America's Iraq policy on NATO's failure in Afghanistan, warning that a NATO military defeat would have far reaching consequences for Europe. "I worry that for many Europeans the missions in Iraq and Afghanistan are confused," the *New York Times* quoted him as saying. "Many of them, I think have a problem with our involvement in Iraq and project that to Afghanistan, and do not understand the very different—for them—the very different kind of threat."[19]

But the time for parsing between the good American war in Afghanistan and the bad American war in Iraq may have already passed, given the harsh political realities that member states—originally supportive of the U.S.—have been asked to endure.

"The intra-NATO resentments have gotten so bitter that Canada's prime minister, Stephen Harper, has said that he will withdraw his 2,500 troops—the Canadians have suffered heavy losses—as scheduled next year, unless other members ante-up another 1,000 troops."[20]

As spring arrived, U.S. diplomatic efforts continued, with U.S. Deputy Secretary of State John Negroponte suggesting U.S. efforts against Al Qaeda on Pakistani soil would not take place without the new government's approval, saying the fighting should be done "through cooperation and not through unilateral measures."[21]

Yet only the previous day, the *Washington Post* reported that the United States had stepped up unilateral strikes at least partly because of concerns that Pakistan's new government would interfere in the American mission. "The United States has escalated its unilateral strikes against al-Qaeda members and fighters operating in Pakistan's tribal areas, partly because of anxieties that Pakistan's new leaders will insist on scaling back military operations in that country, according to U.S. officials."[22]

As the months wore on, these anxieties were borne out. On April 27, 2008, in an unparalleled breakdown in security, President Hamid Karzai, alongside members of his government, foreign diplomats, ISAF commanders and UN directors, was attacked in Kabul by Taliban assassins at what the *New York Times* curiously identified in its first paragraph as "the Afghan national day military parade."[23] The German magazine *Der Spiegel* identified the occasion more accurately—perhaps more embarrassingly for acolytes of America's "war on terror," theme—by its real name, Mujahideen Day.[24] The event was intended to celebrate the sixteenth anniversary of the calamitous fall of the Moscow-backed Marxist PDPA government. Instead, the scene quickly degenerated into a calamity of its own as officials scrambled for cover with "hundreds of soldiers running off the parade ground in disarray."[25]

According to an official statement issued by U.S. ambassador William B. Wood, the incident was handled quickly and efficiently by the Afghan security forces. "The security institutions of Afghanistan defeated the attack within 120 seconds of the first shot and performed in a skilled, professional, and disciplined way during the attack."[26] But *Der Spiegel* reporter Ullrich Fichtner explained how the American ambassador's comments were little more than candy for the western media's consumption. "'The whole thing was over within 120 seconds.' This is the sugarcoated version for the Western public. The people in Afghanistan, however, know that in reality the shooting continued for 25 or 30 minutes, and that the attackers used bazookas, machine guns and grenades. Soon there were helicopters in the air and the assassination attempt turned into a battle, with the presidential guard returning fire, eventually killing three attackers and chasing three of their accomplices through the city."[27]

As feared by western officials, throughout April and May, the new government of Pakistan moved quickly to expedite deals with tribal militants, often at the expense of U.S. and NATO operations on the other side of the border. Pakistani authorities assured the West that it remained committed to the war on terror, but western analysts insisted that the deals were just another example of Pakistan's determined self-interest. "North Atlantic Treaty Organization and U.S. officials have voiced increasing concern over the nature and scope of such negotiations and the resulting agreements. Under them, the militant factions have received significant concessions, including the release of dozens of prisoners and the granting of what is in effect amnesty to fugitive commanders who were on the most-wanted lists . . . NATO says it has tracked a notable increase in cross-border insurgent attacks in Afghanistan since the truce negotiations began."[28]

Still, NATO refused to bow to the growing uncertainty, insisting in their early April report to the Bucharest Summit that the "broad international effort to help Afghanistan build a more stable and secure future is achievable, and is being achieved."[29] The April NATO report painted a reassuring picture of success, where "the Afghan government, in cooperation with its international partners, is working to develop fully functioning state institutions at the national level and to expand its ability to provide basic services to its population throughout the country by establishing subnational institutions, including civil administration, police, prisons and judiciary, in each province."[30] In this confident and harmonious world of international partnership, ISAF, the International Security and Assistance Force provides "quick humanitarian assistance, such as food, water and shelter," and "repair[s] buildings immediately following sizeable ISAF military operations."[31] ISAF helps to coordinate projects "covering fields such as vocational training, female literacy, the eradication of tuberculosis and the construction of primary, middle and secondary schools."[32]

But in the extensive German *Der Spiegel* news article, "The Third World War, Why NATO Troops Can't Deliver Peace in Afghanistan," reporter Ullrich Fichtner separates fact from the fantasy. "Anyone standing in front of a map of Afghanistan, with shading delineating the five ISAF regional commands, must conclude that the country is under control. Colorful little flags identify the NATO troops' presence throughout the country, with Germany's colors flying in the northeast, Italy's in the far west, the Stars and Stripes covering the east, and the Union Jack and Canada's Maple Leaf blanketing the south. . . . But the flags are an illusion. . . . Last year 1,469 bombs exploded along Afghan roads, a number five times as high as in 2004. There were 8,950 armed attacks on troops and civilian support personnel, 10 times more than only three years ago. There is no peace anywhere in Afghanistan, not even in the north, which officials repeatedly insist has been pacified."[33]

One major criticism of NATO's operation concerns the policy of disproportionate responsibilities called "national caveats," where some member states' troops find themselves embroiled in daily firefights with Taliban and Al Qaeda insurgents, while others perform little more than routine police work in the quieter provinces.[34] There is also the question of the size of NATO's commitment, which by internationally accepted standards barely addresses the most basic needs. "ISAF Commander [Dan] McNeill has said himself that according to the current counterterrorism doctrine, it would take 400,000 troops to pacify Afghanistan in the long term. But the reality is that he has only 47,000 soldiers under his command, together with another 18,000 troops fighting at their sides as part of Operation Enduring Freedom."[35]

In an interview published in the March 31, 2008 issue of *Der Spiegel*, McNeill expressed his desire to see German troops do more of the fighting, but admitted that political realities were pushing that idea in the opposite direction. "I know that in some European capitals the debate is raging about this mission. I can only give high marks to Chancellor Angela Merkel because of her leadership. . . . It would be good if the German government would allow the QRF [Quick Reaction Force] to act outside the north. I would be happy to use them."[36] But with fighting all over Afghanistan growing worse by the day and May's casualty count surpassing Iraq's, the chances for a significantly larger NATO commitment or allowing German soldiers to join their U.S., British and Canadian counterparts in the east, appeared increasingly doubtful. Still, despite Europe's nearly unanimous rejection of U.S. leadership over the Iraq war, the United States used the opportunity to pressure NATO to bail them out in Afghanistan. On June 13, 2008, the Associated Press reported, "It's a grim gauge of U.S. wars going in the opposite direction: American and allied combat deaths in Afghanistan passed the toll in Iraq for the first time, last month. Defense Secretary Robert Gates used the statistical comparison to dramatize his point to NATO defense ministers that they need to do more to get Afghanistan moving in a better direction. He wants more allied combat troops, more trainers and more public commitment."[37]

But more commitment from a European public that has developed a fundamental mistrust of the entire U.S. enterprise—especially with its overt reliance on military solutions—will remain difficult, if not impossible to achieve.

Defense Secretary Robert Gates's appeal to Europe exceeded three degrees of irony. As one of the architects of the covert war against the Soviet Union in the 1970s and early '80s, Gates helped to set into motion a chain of events that would permanently shatter the relative peace and normalcy of life in Afghanistan by luring the Soviets into a war they knew they couldn't win.[38] Now it was Gates who faced the legacy of the mujahideen and Pakistan's Inter-Services Intelligence (ISI) whom he had once helped to empower, while hoping to convince audiences in Europe and the United States that his plan to make Afghanistan a barrier to Islamic terrorism would work where the Soviets had failed. At nearly the same moment, the United States–Russia Working Group on Counterterrorism (CTWG), meeting in Moscow, "revealed that the two sides [Russia and the U.S.] had reached 'agreement in principle over the supply of Russian weaponry to the Afghanistan National Army' in its fight against the Taliban insurgency."[39]

Since beginning the war in 2001, the United States had strongly resisted Russian involvement. But with the war going badly, NATO showing little stomach for a larger commitment and with Pakistan looking more like an enemy and less like an ally,[40] the United States had been forced to accept the unthinkable and embrace Russia's help.

"The deterioration of the war is undoubtedly a factor behind the shift. (Incidentally, in a similar shift, Washington recently approached China and India also for the dispatch of troops to Afghanistan.) Britain's *Telegraph* newspaper reported last week on a growing 'despair' in Washington over the NATO allies' perceived failings in Afghanistan. The gung-ho attitude—'have-gun-will-travel'—is no more there."[41]

The latest thinking on the war by conservative think tanks like the Heritage Foundation combines some practical common-sense recommendations with a hefty dose of naiveté and chutzpah. While recognizing the importance of "providing security for Afghan civilians, rooting out the Taliban and other Islamic extremists, boosting the Afghan economy and helping the Afghans to build a responsive government,"[42] the April 2008 Heritage Foundation report titled *The War in Afghanistan: More Help Needed* shifts most of the responsibility for transforming the situation onto the backs of others to make it happen. Authors James Phillips and Lisa Curtis wrote, "[T]he United States and the young Afghan government need more international support in their efforts to secure and stabilize Afghanistan, which is a crucial front in the global war against al-Qaeda and its radical allies. Washington and Kabul need greater cooperation from Pakistan in controlling the border and from NATO, which is leading the International Security and Assistance Force (ISAF)."[43]

On the positive side, suggestions for streamlining the international reconstruction effort, pressing NATO allies for more troops, removing the national caveats on fighting forces, inducing Pakistani cooperation in combating Taliban and constraining Islamic radicalism and ruling out a peace agreement with top Taliban leaders, are all good ideas. If anything, the reconstruction effort has been hamstrung from the beginning by "global interest-driven politics,"[44] lack of coordination, lack of a defined vision, a duplicitous Pakistani involvement, and a creeping, subversive form of extreme Islamism referred to as "Taliban-Lite."[45] But the foundation's recommendations to: Substantially increase aid to the North-West Frontier Province in tandem with Pakistani military, expedite counterinsurgency training of Pakistan's Frontier Corps and pursue deradicalization programs to delegitimize suicide bombings, are things that fly in the face of reality. As recounted in these pages, the radicalization of the North-West Frontier Province tribes, the recruitment of Arab Al Qaeda fighters and the very creation of the Taliban itself were all part of a grand plan by the Central Intelligence Agency and Pakistan's Inter-Services Intelligence agency to conquer South Central Asia. As documented by noted Afghan expert Selig Harrison, "General Zia spoke to me about expanding Pakistan's sphere of influence to control Afghanistan, then Uzbekistan and Tajikistan and then Iran and Turkey."[46] Never the indigenous, Afghan fighting force that they claimed to be, by 2001 they had metamorphosized into a well-financed, agenda-driven vanguard of the Pakistani military. Never just "recruits" from the madrassas (Muslim theological schools), from the beginning the Taliban were on the payroll of the ISI (Inter-Services Intelligence, the intelligence wing of the Pakistani government) and "making a living out of terrorism."[47]

According to a June 2008 RAND study by Seth G. Jones, they continue on in that relationship under cover of the "war on terror." The Associated Press quoted Jones: "Every successful insurgency in Afghanistan since 1979 enjoyed safe haven in neighboring countries, and the current insurgency is no different. Right now, the Taliban and other groups are getting help from individuals within Pakistan's government, and until that ends, the region's long term security is in jeopardy."[48]

The Pashtun tribal areas bordering Afghanistan have never come under anything more than nominal control by either the British in India nor their Pakistani successors. They remain to this day, intrinsically tied to the Pashtun tribal areas of what is today Afghanistan, whose residents harbor long-standing memories of a precolonial Afghan Durrani empire that extended over most of what is today Pakistan.[49]

An additional Heritage Foundation proposal also requires a fact check with reality: "Tackling the Taliban/al-Qaeda threat in Pakistan's Tribal Areas will require a multifaceted effort that includes close U.S.-Pakistan coordination and cooperation, large-scale economic assistance, precision military operations against terrorist leaders, a comprehensive effort to undermine the extremist ideologies that drive the various groups in the region, and a new political arrangement that incorporates the region into Pakistan proper."[50]

State-based solutions that require "large-scale economic assistance," combined with U.S.-Pakistan coordination and cooperation require a viable state to work with as a partner. Today, not only is that partnership in trouble, but the reality of the Pakistani state itself remains in question. No less a factor is that state's ability to work with or control Pakistan's military establishment which has been described as an even more powerful state within a state.[51] To mandate a military operation against terrorist leaders who work hand in hand with Pakistan's military to subvert American and NATO operations[52] as well as to establish "a new political arrangement that incorporates the region into Pakistan proper," would require a political reality in both Pakistan and Afghanistan that has not only never existed, but is rapidly moving in the opposite direction. In other words, it would be more realistic for the United States and Europe to advocate a restoration of the Afghan-based Durrani empire, than to imagine Pakistan's failed and divided government ever consolidating control over former Afghan territory on their side of the Durand Line.

As of late May 2008, Pakistan showed further signs of disintegration as its newly elected leadership struggled to formulate a policy from within a "political quagmire."[53] With tensions running high, former premier Nawaz Sharif warned President Pervez Musharraf that he would not be forgiven for selling out to foreign powers, for implementing the Lal Masjid massacre,[54] or for imprisoning Dr. Abdul Khan, the founder of Pakistan's nuclear program.[55] Days later, Jane Perlez reported for the *New York Times* on the growing confidence of the Pakistani Taliban and their leader Baitullah Mehsud, whose "jaunty appearance in his home base, South Waziristan, a particularly unruly region of Pakistan's tribal areas, underscored the wide latitude Pakistan's government has granted the militants under a new series of peace deals."[56]

Accused by both U.S. and Pakistani officials of masterminding the assassination of Benazir Bhutto last December, some in Pakistan fear the usually reclusive Mehsud's newfound stridency may indicate that he and his Taliban–Al Qaeda alliance sense an impending victory in their war on the West. "The spread of the Pakistani Taliban threatens even Peshawar, the capital of the North-West Frontier Province bordering the tribal areas, the inspector general of police, Malik Naveed Khan, warned. 'They are now on the periphery,' Mr. Khan said in an interview. If nothing else is done, it could be 'a matter of months' before Peshawar falls, he said."[57]

Should Mr. Khan's prophecy prove true, and the Pakistani Taliban achieve even a symbolic takeover of Peshawar, the victory would prove a further devastating blow to the Washington beltway's dystopian leadership. From the East it would be seen as a major turning point in the jihad against the West and a rallying cry for a larger and far more serious phase of fighting to begin.

Yet, in the haze of Washington's election-year politics it was impossible to know whether the gathering storm over the Hindu Kush was even on the radar.

Despite the mounting evidence that some form of civil war was about to spread throughout the region, in a May 2008 interview with the *Washington Post*, CIA Director Michael V. Hayden claimed Al Qaeda was down for the count, outright defeated in Saudi Arabia and Iraq "and on the defensive throughout much of the rest of the world, including in its presumed haven along the Afghanistan-Pakistan border."[58] A day later, Principal Deputy Director of National Intelligence Donald M. Kerr contradicted Hayden, reasserting that little progress has been made against Al

Qaeda in the Afghan-Pakistan border regions, admitting that it was "the number one thing we worry about."[59] The question remained however, with Pentagon accounting so careless, and the administration's priorities so profoundly incoherent, would it even be possible for Washington to know whether they were winning a war against Al Qaeda and the Taliban or not? According to one General Accountability Office report issued in June 2008,[60] "[a]fter six years and $16.5 billion in spending, the Defense and State departments still lack a 'sustainable' strategy for developing Afghanistan's army and police force."[61] According to another General Accountability Office report issued in late June 2008, the Bush administration had paid Pakistan more than $2 billion without even knowing how or where the money was spent.[62] "$20 million for army road construction and $15 million to build bunkers in Pakistan, but there's no evidence that the roads or bunkers were ever constructed."[63]

On the ground, the strained relationship between the coalition forces and the Pakistani army reached a breaking point on June 10, 2008, when U.S. aircraft opened fire on a Pakistani border post at Goraprai, bordering Afghanistan's Kunar province, killing eleven members of the Mohmand Rifles, including a major.[64]

The Pakistani government reportedly stunned the Bush administration by calling the airstrikes "unprovoked and cowardly."[65] Days later, the newly appointed Pakistani ambassador Husain Haqqani issued a more diplomatic response, but tensions were soon to increase as the Taliban's spring offensive got underway.

Despite Pakistani intransigence, both NATO and American commanders had expressed confidence earlier in the month that they were gaining the upper hand, convinced that the Taliban's ability to strike at will had been severely curtailed. "The new 'precise, surgical' tactics have killed scores of insurgent leaders and made it extremely difficult for Pakistan-based Taliban leaders to prosecute the campaign, according to Brig Mark Carleton-Smith. In the past two years an estimated 7,000 Taliban have been killed, the majority in southern and eastern Afghanistan. But it's the 'very effective targeted decapitation operations' that have removed 'several echelons of commanders.'"[66]

As if to reprimand the British for their hubris, within days the Taliban delivered another shocking blow to western confidence by attacking the main prison in Kandahar, freeing over 1,000 prisoners, and setting the stage for a major assault on that city.[67]

The prison attack provoked Afghan President Hamid Karzai to call for a retaliatory raid on Pakistan, threatening Beitullah Mehsud personally, "to go after him and hit him in his house."[68]

Accused by even his best friends of being feckless,[69] this time Karzai wasted no words in stating his anger. "If these people in Pakistan give themselves the right to come and fight in Afghanistan, as was continuing for the last 30 years, so Afghanistan has the right to cross the border and destroy terrorist nests, spying, extremism, and killing, in order to defend itself, its schools, its people and its life."[70]

By June 17, 2008, the fighters of Pakistani and Arab origin were reported to have seized seven villages, sweeping into the Arghandab district and causing more than 4,000 residents to flee.[71]

"A Taliban commander named Mullah Ahmedullah said that around 400 Taliban moved into Arghandab from Kharkrez, one district to the north. He said some of the militants released in Friday's mass prison break had joined the assault." "They told us, 'We want to fight until the death,' Ahmedullah said."[72]

And so they did. By June 20, 2008, the Afghan Defense Ministry was reporting that more than fifty-six Taliban had been killed while Kandahar's governor put the number of killed and wounded in the hundreds.[73] But the telltale signs of mission-fatigue in the seven-year conflict shown through the victorious rhetoric. In summing up the battle, *Los Angeles Times* reporter M. Karim Faiez stated,"In fewer than 48 hours, they [Afghan and western soldiers] had driven the insurgents away. But the brief Taliban incursion near Kandahar that authorities declared yesterday had been repelled illustrated the ease with which even a handful of militants could tie up large numbers of coalition troops and heavy weaponry to counter what NATO repeatedly describes as a not particularly serious threat."[74]

He also hinted at a growing discord between Afghan and coalition forces, stating: "public statements by coalition and Afghan authorities were out of sync, suggesting that the Afghans and their Western allies might not be fully sharing intelligence or conferring closely with one another."[75]

With Pakistan failing as a state and ally, NATO in a political crisis over continuing support, the United States still tied down in Iraq, and President Karzai's office asserting that Pakistan's Inter-Services Intelligence agency was the "main organizer of the terrorist acts," and attempted assassination at the sixteenth anniversary Mujahideen Day celebration,[76] experts began to question whether the long-anticipated "tipping point" had finally been reached. "There has been a sharp rise in violence along Afghanistan's eastern frontier in recent months. . . . The top US general in Afghanistan said that insurgent attacks have increased 40 percent this year over 2007 in the east of the country . . . attacking civic centers and schools—killing teachers, students, road crews and others working to improve life in Afghanistan."[77]

As June came to a close the prevailing sentiment held that the fall of Peshawar was only a matter of time and with it America's most important "war on terror" ally, as the entire Pakistani state teetered on the brink of collapse. "'The government is helpless,' said Arbab Hidyat Ullah, a former senior police officer here. 'It has lost its wits. The police have lost so many men at hands of the Taliban they are scared.' Mr. Ullah said that the police of Peshawar had a considerable budget, but that the money had little impact and that the void allowed the brute force of the Taliban to flourish."[78]

Financial Times chief foreign affairs commentator Gideon Rachman observed the continuing conundrum with distress. "It is also becoming increasingly obvious that this is not just some sort of policing operation, with a bit of fighting thrown in. British troops are firing 11,000 bullets every day. . . . The trouble is that whenever I talk to experts in private they usually say three irreconciliable things: 1) Our current strategy isn't working 2) There are no real alternative strategies 3) We cannot afford to lose."[79]

In a June 6, 2008 interview with National Public Radio's *All Things Considered*,[80] Moscow's veteran ambassador to Afghanistan, Zamir Kabulov, mused on his own country's failure in Afghanistan. "We underestimated the Afghan allergy to foreign invaders because we didn't see ourselves as invaders at the time. . . . We tried to bring forcefully, artificially, social justice to the country."[81]

And so, after seven years and a billion bullets later, the United States, Britain, and the western alliance sit at the edge of Eurasia without a victory, or a strategy for victory or even a credible definition of what a victory might be.

CONCLUSION

With the Russians back in Afghanistan, this time to help the western effort, it is time for the West and especially the United States to recognize its mirror image in the Soviet experience. It is also time to reconsider Afghanistan's invisible history and the underlying assumptions that have not been factored into the West's solutions. It took ten years for the Soviets to accept why they were losing in Afghanistan. The local population viewed them as invaders. Regardless of how the United States and their NATO allies see their role, they must learn that lesson now and adjust their policies to assist the Afghans in regaining their independence, before it is too late.

18.

What Can President Barack Obama Do?

President Obama will face the toughest foreign policy decisions of any president since Franklin Roosevelt. But among the toughest of those tough decisions will be how to handle the ongoing battle for Afghanistan.

Lest he fall prey to the popular misconceptions and the self-fulfilling delusions of Washington's current Beltway wisdom, he should be well advised that today's Afghanistan is more a creation of Washington, Islamabad and London than it is of Kabul. He should also be advised that achieving anything resembling a real victory will require much more than just additional troops or taking the battle into Taliban- and Al Qaeda–controlled areas of neighboring Pakistan. It will require rethinking some basic assumptions about both Afghanistan, and Pakistan and America's goals in the region.

When we first entered directly into the Afghan story, a year after the Soviet invasion, we encountered a country frozen between its feudal past and one hundred years of gradual social modernization. We found schools that had been burned to the ground, factories destroyed and Afghan communities bordering Pakistan, terrorized. What was left of the Afghan state was a product of Soviet influence accrued over thirty years of socialist assistance to Afghanistan's uniquely "progressive" Islam.

Today's Afghanistan suffers no such legacy or even a trace of its progressive social and Islamic past. Having been culturally erased by the U.S.- and Saudi Arabian–backed war from Pakistan, today's Afghanistan is a neo-feudal, corporatized playground of international greed, warlords, NATO troops, private military companies and radicalized Islamists. Kabul's traffic-congested streets are a vision from hell where "liberated" chadorclad women beg desperately for handouts at the darkened windows of local drug lords' Japanese SUVs. For thousands of years a hub for trade and a melting pot of cultures, Afghanistan is now the world's largest exporter of heroin, a culture of unbridled exploitation and the most radical and extreme forms of Islam.

Afghanistan deserves to be rebuilt socially, psychologically and economically from the ground up, but after seven years and billions spent, little of that has happened. The new constitution guarantees women's rights. More women work and vote, girls can go to school. But press releases and statistics don't tell the story. Without enforcement or oversight in the countryside outside Kabul, without solid guarantees of security and without officials being held accountable, hard-fought women's rights are meaningless. According to Ullrich Fichtner in *Der Spiegel*, "More nine- and ten-year-old girls are being forced into arranged marriages once again . . . Outside Kabul, almost all women over thirteen are required to wear the burqa . . . girls do not go to school, and no one reports kidnappings and rapes."[1]

President Obama must reverse this process by remaking U.S. policy. That policy will have to be radical, implemented quickly, and designed to address the needs of the Afghan people, not the people in Washington who are making it. This may seem a simple truth, but it has not been understood. The president's options will be severely limited. With a new government in Pakistan negotiating in its own self-interest with Al Qaeda and Taliban extremists and with Pakistan's army actively training insurgents to fight against U.S. and NATO troops,[2] the transformation of the war is well underway. In the event that a regional war has not already eclipsed the combined U.S.-NATO effort in Afghanistan and that Pakistan continues to function as some kind of ally in efforts to roll back the influence of Al Qaeda and the Taliban, President Obama must first change the tone of the American engagement. He can do this by first establishing a revised set of rules by which the United States must play, stressing a return to the old values of international law and respect for civil and human rights. The president could then initiate these rules by announcing the first priority of their foreign policy in Afghanistan is the preservation of human life. In other words:

1. Stop killing Afghans. According to the United Nations humanitarian affairs chief, John Holmes, the number of Afghan civilians killed in the first half of 2008 rose 62 percent from that of the year before. Since September 11, 2001 the United States has behaved as if it is at war with the Afghan people. It is not. American fighter jets and drones firing Hellfire missiles on rural mud-walled villages and killing innocent Afghans is more than just ineffective. Its cartoon-like simplicity paints a grotesque image of the devolution of the American political process and the ineffectiveness of high-tech, precise and surgical tactics. Even William Casey was said to have regretted the slaughter of the Afghan people in his bid to hurt the Russians. Now the United States does it without blinking. A June 30, 2008, *New York Times* report on a secret CIA operation to hunt Al Qaeda in Pakistan, code-named Operation Cannonball, indicated that even CIA field officers in Islamabad derided the use of Predator drone missile strikes "as the work of 'boys with toys.'"[3] If Washington's bureaucrats don't remember the history of the region, the Afghans do. Bitterly. The British used air power to bomb these same Pashtun villages after World War I and were condemned for it. When the Soviets used MIGS and the "dreaded" MI-24 HIND helicopter gunships to do it during the 1980s they were called criminals.[4] For America to use its overwhelming firepower in the same reckless and indiscriminate manner defies the world's sense of justice and morality while turning the Afghan people and the Islamic world even further against the United States.

2. Stop humiliating Afghan men and desecrating their homes. Whoever introduced Rafael Patai's book *The Arab Mind* as a guide for interrogating Muslim men through sexual humiliation[5] should be put on trial for inciting terrorism. Anyone vaguely aware of the military's behavior while on search-and-destroy missions in rural Afghan villages would not wonder why the countryside has turned en masse against the U.S. presence.

3. Call in people with a better understanding of the problem from a diversity of the Afghan political perspective and take their advice seriously. Washington's think tanks and a handful of elite eastern universities dom-

inate U.S. planning in Afghanistan. Hundreds of veteran CIA and State Department personnel responsible for creating and overseeing the creative destruction of Afghan civil society during the 1980s now share the virtues of that creative destruction with a whole new crop of eager young students. Without exception these "experts" mimic to one degree or another, an Anglo-centric view of Afghanistan that remains firmly rooted in a nineteenth-century Victorian view of colonial virtue while advancing failed "free market" ideologies common to the Reagan era as solutions to the country's problems. In a column written for the *Asia Times* on September 27, 2007, even former CIA bin Laden hunter Michael Scheuer cited Rudyard Kipling and *The Man Who Would Be King* as an excuse for why it's so difficult catching Osama bin Laden in the mountains of Waziristan.[6] As roadside bombs emulate the Iraqi quagmire, Taliban fighters surround Kabul and record amounts of heroin spill from the seams of Afghanistan's porous borders, the U.S. continues to look at a British-led effort designed in London in the 1830s to expand her Indian Empire into Central Asia as a model. It should be remembered that as long ago as 1870 that model was referred to by British statesman Sir John W. Kaye as "a folly and a crime."[7]

4. Start helping Afghans in a way they can understand, see, and appreciate. The way humanitarian aid is now delivered appears designed to fail. A June 2008 article in *Prospect* magazine by Clare Lockhart, cofounder of the Institute of State Effectiveness with former Afghan finance minister Ashraf Ghani, described one story "of $150m going up in smoke," saying that "the money was received by an agency in Geneva, who took 20 per cent and subcontracted the job to another agency in Washington DC, who also took 20 percent. Again it was subcontracted and another 20 per cent was taken; and this happened again when the money arrived in Kabul. By this time there was very little money left." The young Afghan man telling the story summed up his opinion this way: "We may be illiterate, but we are not stupid."[8]

According to Oxfam, the per capita expenditure for rebuilding Afghanistan after the Taliban defeat was $57 compared to $679 per capita in Bosnia.[9] Despite being absurdly inadequate, "Only approximately 25–

30% of all aid coming into the country is routed through the government, eroding its legitimacy, planning capacity and authority."[10]

Redirect the focus of U.S. government policy to serving local needs. Roads and irrigation to start, a viable secular education program to compete with Pakistan's free madrassas. This is not the way Washington has been operating. As one aid person who recently worked in Afghanistan for a year explained. "The U.S. government would be more effective if they just took the money and threw it out the helicopter window. At least that way it might have *some* chance of getting to the people who need it."[11] Either re-governmentalize foreign aid or make U.S. contractors accountable for their actions. Contractors must be chosen based on competence not ideology or loyalty to a political party. Success must be defined by local needs, not Washington's. Help the Afghans clean up their new government and rid the country of corruption. Military victory is meaningless without the political backup to support it and the government delivery systems necessary to support growth. Afghanistan could use a core of mature American civilian experts, (retirees) and lots of them, to help the country rebuild. Under normal conditions Afghanistan's climate and culture had much to recommend it. Cosmopolitan and friendly, the people are beautiful, funny, proud and smart. Think of them that way and how they can be helped to make their country safe again. Empower Afghanistan's women. Safeguarding women's rights in Afghanistan under equal protection under the law will bring about Afghanistan's economic recovery faster.

5. Declare the "global war on terror," the "Long War" and the "global struggle against violent extremism" to be over. This will be greeted by a collective sigh of relief by most of the world, especially the American public. The "war on terror" is the "sub-prime loan" of U.S. foreign policy (a phony bubble waiting to burst). Although Washington remains clueless, the American people already know it. So does most of the world. Six years and billions of dollars later Osama bin Laden has barely noticed. In fact, declare all the wars to be over including the war on drugs and the war on poverty. Wars are failed policy by other means. By definition, making war is failure—the making of failure on failure. According to Sarah Sewall, director of Har-

vard University's Carr Center for Human Rights Policy, "The West's use of military power in Afghanistan has been a combustible and confusing mix of doctrine and tools. Along with our NATO allies, we must think through the conceptual blurring of counterterrorism and counterinsurgency in Afghanistan. . . . Hunting high-value targets in Afghanistan is important, but we must align that goal with our broader political aims in Afghanistan and beyond."[12]

6. Address the conceptual blurring. Determine exactly what the United States hopes to accomplish and settle on one foreign policy as opposed to many competing goals. From the 1980s on the United States has at once fostered Pakistan's strategic goals for controlling Afghanistan, Saudi Arabia's extreme religious goals for converting Asia to Islam and Unocal's financial goals of building pipelines. Is the United States interested in a peaceful settlement to the Afghan question or just controlling Shiite-Iranian oil for Saudi/American oil executives?

7. Get everybody on the same page. If the goal is regional stability then everyone must have a role in stabilizing it. Make normalization of relations between India and Pakistan a priority. Traditional Hindu/Muslim antagonisms fuel the jihad inclination, not to mention the nuclear ambitions of both nations. Unfortunately, the United States has used up its good offices. The U.S. military has been wounded deeply by imperial overreach. The U.S. economy is in deep debt to China and Saudi Arabia—severely weakening American leverage. Russia is becoming resurgent and increasingly friendly with China. Even America's closest ally, Britain, sees America's use of unmitigated force as a conceptual failure and counter-productive. The United States cannot continue on this path indefinitely and U.S. foreign policy must be adjusted to deal with the impending reality of a global meltdown of influence and prestige.

8. Promote a regional dialogue and invest whatever political currency Washington has left in it before it's too late. Regional and Afghan sentiment for expelling the American/NATO military presence grows. Calls for

a regional summit which includes Pakistan, India, Russia and Iran but excludes the United States are making the rounds. The Russians have recently offered to open a transit corridor through their territory to NATO in return for full participation in the Afghan reconstruction effort. This could very well be the watershed that will determine victory or defeat for the United States. Russia's ambassador to NATO, Dmitri Rogozin, told *Der Spiegel* magazine in an interview in March, "We support the anti-terror campaign against the Taliban and al-Qaida. I hope we can manage to reach a series of very important agreements with our Western partners at the Bucharest summit."[13] At the April 3 summit, France and Germany combined to thwart a Bush administration plan to allow the Ukraine and Georgia to join NATO.[14] This can only be seen as a victory for Russia. In terminology all too reminiscent of the 1930s, Georgia's President Mikhail Saakashvili had already warned "that a rebuff would amount to 'an appeasement of Russia.'"[15] But with dissension rising within NATO and the Afghan campaign on the brink of a Soviet-style defeat, the United States must rethink its rusty, old mandate for Eurasian conquest or risk losing its European allies to long-standing Eurasian realities. The United States must also free itself of its pre–World War II mind-set that transforms all diplomacy into a Munich-style appeasement and every nationalist leader into the next Hitler. Times have changed. It's time for the United States to enter the twenty-first century and finally eschew the influence of Washington's would-be nineteenth-century imperialists. If not, the United States risks losing its place in the game altogether to Europe's older and more experienced players. The logic is simple. Time is not on America's side. Pakistan can no longer be counted on to do America's bidding, even half-heartedly. The Pakistanis continue to lobby for a neutralized Afghanistan and undermine the NATO effort, turning the country into a federation of disconnected states akin to nineteenth-century British plans for colonial domination. From the Pakistani point of view, India is the problem. One gets the impression that most Pakistanis don't even see Afghanistan out of their obsession with India over Kashmir. In the eyes of many in the ISI, it needs Afghanistan to provide what they call "strategic depth"—a place to hide its retaliatory nuclear weapons cache in case of an Indian first-strike.

Should the United States wish to remain in the region this should provide all the more reason for helping Afghanistan establish itself and freeing itself from Pakistani domination. As recounted in these pages, from the Afghan point of view, Pakistan has always been the problem.

9. Address the issue of illegal narcotics from where they originate and not to suit Washington's needs: To the poor Afghan farmer, the decision to grow opium poppy is a matter of economics. Without adequate roads to carry farm produce to market and without adequate security to police what roads there are, planting poppy is his only chance for survival. Subjected to crop eradication by chemical spraying that sicken his children and kill his livestock he is easily recruited by Al Qaeda and the Taliban to fight the central government and its American backers. Intent on reestablishing themselves as the single most powerful force in the government, Pashtun Taliban will continue to fight and poor Afghan farmers in the tribal areas will continue to support them. As long as the United States continues to legitimize Tajik, Uzbek and Hazara warlords at the expense of Pashtun goals, the Taliban will continue to be viewed by the injured Pashtun population as an army of national pride. Unless the West adapts to this local reality, it will lose.

To the West and particularly the United States, the problem of opium poppy and heroin is an issue of law enforcement. The object of four decades and a trillion-dollar bureaucracy, the "war on drugs," like the "war on terror," has failed conceptually to stop the problem of drug addiction and related crime but has turned the United States into the world's largest jailer. The United States has 4.6 percent of the world's population and 22.5 percent of its prisoners.

A proposal by the Senlis Council, an international policy think tank which operates in Afghanistan as a nongovernmental organization, would see the conversion of Afghan opium into medicine, with the ultimate beneficiary being the rural Afghan villager. According to their proposal, the Senlis Council "would see village-cultivated poppy transformed into morphine tablets in the rural communities of Afghanistan by bringing the important added value of the transformation of poppy into medicine at the local level. This would address the current world shortage of these pain-relieving medicines."[16]

Together with programs to legally purchase Afghan opium directly from growers for international pharmaceutical use, engage professional organizations like LEAP, Law Enforcement Against Prohibition for advice in creating a system of regulation and control of production and distribution.

10. Much has been written about negotiating with the Taliban insurgents as a way to stop the fighting. Well-meaning peace activists have recommended reviving the practice of parsing between Al Qaeda and the Taliban. Some recommend engaging the Taliban as the United States engaged the Soviet Union, Communist China, or Tony Blair engaged the Irish Republican Army.[17] Aside from not delineating between Pakistani Taliban and Afghan Taliban and that both use terrorist methods, such recommendations ignore the reality that the Taliban were expressly created "as a kind of experimental Frankenstein monster,"[18] by the CIA and Pakistani ISI to invade Afghanistan. That mission has not changed. More importantly, such recommendations wrongly paint the Taliban as an indigenous tribal force bent on bringing peace to a troubled land. If the Taliban's pre-9/11 reputation for murder, drug dealing, assassinations, child kidnapping and mass abuse of women were not enough, a recent peace-making effort in Pakistan's Northwest Frontier Province provided an up-to-date assessment of the consequences of negotiating with the Taliban: "The bodies of 22 members of a government-sponsored peace committee were found dumped near South Waziristan yesterday. . . . The peace committee was attacked by supporters of Baitullah Mehsud, the head of the Pakistani Taliban. . . . The killings occurred after the Pakistani Army negotiated a cease-fire with Mehsud's forces earlier this year and pulled its soldiers back from Mehsud's territory in South Waziristan."[19]

Another view currently making the rounds in Europe lays the groundwork for a NATO pullout of Afghanistan by arguing that since "no government put in place by foreign troops . . . can be considered a legitimate government," and since "other Pathans, inside Afghanistan, who are not religious fundamentalists, and the Tajiks, Hazaras, and Uzbeks . . . will not defend themselves, there is nothing the foreigners can do to save them from their countrymen."[20] "The Taliban in Afghanistan are not the Russian army, overrunning Afghanistan with tanks and helicopters, or an invading British colonial army. If they were, the problem would be simple."[21]

As any level of reflection on the history of Afghanistan will demonstrate, at least from the Afghan perspective, the answer to a century and a half of British and Russian attempts to overrun Afghanistan is anything but simple. The Taliban's first assault on Afghanistan in the 1990s did include tanks and helicopters operated by Pakistan's military. Today's dilemma for the Afghans, be they anti-extremist Pashtuns, Tajiks, Hazaras or Uzbeks, is rooted deeply in the history of czarist, Napoleonic, Kaiserian, Nazi, British, Soviet, Chinese, Iranian, American and Pakistani efforts to use Afghanistan for their own grand designs. Any solution that does not recognize the need for those nations to counter the legacy of foreign-supported extremism with an extended commitment to civil society and nation building, cannot hope to formulate a successful policy.

If any negotiations are to be conducted, they must begin with the state within the state sponsors of this Taliban terror, Pakistan's army and its Inter-Services Intelligence branch. It is this institution, which from 1973 on has played the key role in funding and directing first the mujahideen battle plan and then the Taliban. It is Pakistan's army that controls its nuclear weapons, constrains the development of democratic institutions, trains Taliban fighters in suicide attacks and orders them to fight American and NATO soldiers protecting the Afghan government. Nothing can be accomplished without neutralizing them as a subversive influence and turning them toward the task of nation building.

President Obama must restore belief in civil society and protect the mechanisms by which civil society is grown and maintained. In Afghanistan that means reaching out to moderate Afghans to oppose anti-statist Islamist authority. Given the history of U.S. involvement, this will not be easy. But the conceptual framework must be built for a radically new kind of engagement away from the Islamist extremism of Taliban-like organizations. This may be easier to do than expected in Afghanistan where no one suffers illusions. Getting support in the United

States may be harder. The U.S. government remains torn between continuing a policy of destabilization and implementing a policy of nation-building. According to numerous authorities, over the last 30 years the United States has not done a good job at nation building anywhere. Destabilization of foreign countries comes home to America as war and terrorism. War and terrorism weaken our own democracy by requiring urgent measures that strip the majority of Americans of their rights. Already disenfranchised and deeply suspicious of Washington's motives, inventions like the USA PATRIOT Act, no-fly lists and Homeland Security alerts blur reality and fantasy while numbing Americans to real dangers and real solutions.

11. If President Obama is to save Afghanistan and the United States itself from the impending tipping point, it would be wise to follow the advice of David Walker, comptroller general of the United States. Warning that the United States government was paralleling the decline and fall of the Roman empire, Walker described the country in an August 2007 interview with the *Financial Times* as being on a "'burning platform,' of unsustainable policies and practices with fiscal deficits, chronic healthcare under-funding, immigration and overseas commitments threatening a crisis if action is not taken soon."[22]

Action does not mean more military action. Set the record straight. According to a September 11, 2007 CBS News/New York Times poll, 1 in 3 Americans still believed Saddam Hussein was personally involved in the 9/11 attacks on the World Trade Towers—despite Bush administration denials.[23]

Another poll gave George Bush his lowest approval rating yet at 29 percent and Congress a "paltry" 11 percent approval rating.[24] An April 21, 2008 poll by the American Research Group rated president Bush's approval as "holding steady at 22%."[25]

The American people have lost faith in the government's ability to tell the truth. They now believe whatever they want to believe. Suspension of disbelief and the creation of alternate realities may work for theme parks and Hollywood movies, but not for U.S. foreign policy. Sustaining unreality will not fix Afghanistan or the United States. We are fast reaching the point of no return for both.

12. Finally, reopen the national debate on U.S. identity and its future, a debate that was silenced on December 7, 1941, when the Japanese attacked Pearl Harbor. Resumption of this debate was overruled by the creation of the Cold War and the national security state and edited out of the script by the events of 9/11. If we are to restore our nation to health, this debate must begin now. Enlist the people from within the institutions of government who best understand this to be the problem. There are many who have the courage to help. Milt Bearden said, "We better at some point feel it's not unpatriotic or weak to say why did these guys do it? That debate or dialogue has not yet begun in this country. We're just having a war against terrorism whether it takes us to Afghanistan or it takes us to Iraq rather than saying 'time out—why did those guys do it?' . . . If we proceed on a straight line from where we are today [we'll] wind up fighting the birthrate of the Islamic world."[26] Andrew Bacevich, former West Pointer, now professor of international relations at Boston University, has said, "If you're like me and you're quite skeptical about this imperial project, the stresses imposed on the military and the obvious limits of our power simply serve to emphasize the imperative of rethinking our role in the world so we can back away from this unsustainable notion of global hegemony."[27]

The United States is in a fight for its life—not because of what happened on that September 11, 2001, but because of the way America responded to it. That response was at once wildly exaggerated, dangerously reckless and, in the end, ineffective, putting more control into the hands of the very same people who had allowed it to happen. Imperial presidency aside, the roots of this dilemma stem from the reality-creation machine dreamed up by Dean Acheson, George Kennan, Paul Nitze and James Forrestal at the beginning of the Cold War. But the continuing problem lies in the psychology of the people who were given the authority to drop the first atomic bomb and fantasize a horrific new reality of their own: that "small and exceptionally inbred collection of men. . . . a new elite that would eventually emerge as a power elite, and whose power would come not from wealth or family or brass stripe, but from their having conceived and elaborated a set of ideas."[28]

Today those men, their ideas and their legacy are destroying the United States—not willfully, but by their sheer inability to live within the framework of the observable world. Demystify their process and end the nightmare. It's not complicated. The future father of the hydrogen bomb, Edward Teller, gambled with his fellow physicists in the New Mexico desert on whether the first atomic explosion would ignite the earth's atmosphere and end life on the planet.[29] Physicist John Von Neumann suggested covering the polar icecaps with dye to reduce their reflectivity and "jiggle the entire planet" into a semitropical paradise.[30] Free market proponent, futurist and RAND analyst Herman Kahn (Dr. Strangelove) referred to the Strategic Air Command's battle plan for nuclear conflict as a "war orgasm,"[31] and worked up a scale of forty-four "rungs of escalation," to make nuclear war not only possible, but desirable.[32] Hailed by science and glorified by the American media these are the class of men whom our leaders have looked to for guidance for three quarters of a century. In the process they have made our politics meaningless, transformed our democracy into a ritualistic, procedural farce and turned us all into clockwork oranges to sign on to our own destruction.

As if looking in a darkened mirror, when they emerged in the Team-B of 1976, their backward-looking focus saw the Soviet Union as a dangerous and expanding empire instead of the decaying and imploding prison it had become. When they looked to Afghanistan, they saw a primitive, feudal country of no particular significance, not the independent, democratic republic it was striving to be.

The new president will find himself in a comparable period to that of the Carter administration of thirty years ago. A devastating loss in a foreign war sparked an economic crisis, which released uncontrolled inflation, debased the American ideal, and proved the ruination of the military. Instead of being corrected internally by righting a failed course, that original crisis of American identity caused by policy failure in Vietnam was terminated by a Soviet invasion of Afghanistan and a restoration of the Cold War. With the help of Paul Nitze and the group known as Team-B, a revisionist idea took hold that replaced the bruised mythology of Vietnam with an older, more comforting mythology forged somewhere between the Munich Agreement and Victory in Europe Day in 1945. Today, that mythology clings to life as the ghost of Neville Chamberlain stalks the halls of the White House.[33] But as Nitze's Team-B protégés rewrite their failures with themselves as the victims,[34] the new president should be warned that leading the country by the rear-view mirror as a guide to the future will no longer work. We are two countries, perhaps, still defined by the boundaries of our own civil war. One wishes to live in an American confederacy of states rooted in a nineteenth-century religious duality of black and white, good versus evil, while the other wishes to live in a multipolar world. President Obama must find a way for the two to live together if we are to remain a nation. But remember: Osama bin Laden didn't beat the Soviet Union; the Soviet Union undid itself because it did not possess the political will to change. Osama just took the credit. Osama is not beating the United States and NATO in Afghanistan. The United States is beating itself and beating itself badly.

If our government has no other purpose than to serve the fantasies of its own defense intellectuals in their desire to create new ways of making endless war, then we are in serious trouble and like the Soviet Union, Afghanistan will be our final test.

EPILOGUE

The Twenty-first Chapter

We began this book by telling of an Afghan artist painting icons on the stairwell of a Kabul hotel in 2002. That man inspired us to see Afghanistan as a metaphor for our own dilemma as a free people, once bursting with the spirit of democracy, now reduced to spiritually drained "clockwork oranges"; subjected to airport no-fly lists, warrantless eavesdropping and blank-check defense budgets while our government engages in an Orwellian cycle of mind-numbing *ultraviolence* on enemies who were both trained and financed in Afghanistan by that very same government in the uses of *ultra violence.*

That violence had been delivered by Boeing B-52 Stratofortresses to the Taliban and Al Qaeda at the Tora Bora alleged hideout of Osama bin Laden only a few months before our visit. The destructive capacity awed the ragged Tajik fighters of the Northern Alliance who watched attentively as the engines of the huge flying machine carved mile-wide spirals in the sky and mile-wide craters on the ground, vaporizing whatever hapless fighters had dared to stay behind. Designed to incinerate communist armies or level Soviet and Chinese cities on the vast Eurasian plain during the Cold War, the planes were now a generation older then the men who flew them. The ultimate killing machines, designed to fight and win a nuclear apocalypse, they had flown from the mid-twentieth century into the twenty-first: another century and another war. Now we know, they worked no better at ridding America of her enemies than they had in the past.

Upon our return, we reread Anthony Burgess's *A Clockwork Orange.* Burgess wrote *A Clockwork Orange* in the early 1960s when the B-52s were new. His original book, published in Britain and around the world, contained twenty-one chapters.[1] The book published in the United States contained twenty.[2] It was this book that Stanley Kubrick made into a film and this book that burned the image of the unreformable, endlessly violent

English villain Alex into the more impressionable minds of the planet. But it was not the image that Burgess had intended to prevail. In the introduction to his 1986 new edition, Burgess explained and apologized, noting that there is more to literature and life than often meets the eye.

"21 is the symbol of human maturity, or used to be, since at 21 you got the vote and assumed adult responsibility. Whatever its symbology, the number 21 was the number I started out with. Novelists of my stamp are interested in what is called arithmology, meaning that number has to mean something in human terms when they handle it. The number of chapters is never entirely arbitrary. . . . Those 21 chapters were important to me. But they were not important to my New York publisher. . . . The Americans, he said in effect, were tougher than the British and could face up to reality. Soon they were facing up to it in Vietnam. My book was Kennedyan and accepted the notion of moral progress. What was really wanted was a Nixonian book with no shred of optimism in it. Let us have evil prancing on the page and up to the very last line, sneering in the face of all inherited beliefs, Jewish, Christian, Muslim and Holy Roller, about people being able to make themselves better."[3]

According to Burgess, the twenty-first chapter gives the story its humanity, its truth in the assumption that human beings can learn and change, "There is, in fact, not much point in writing a novel unless you can show the possibility of moral transformation, or an increase in wisdom, operating in your chief character or characters."[4]

Anthony Burgess died on November 22, 1993, seven years before the turn of the twenty-first century, eight years before the events of 9/11.[5] Yet his revised 1986 introduction to a *Clockwork Orange* explained more about the mentality of those White House officials caught in the endless convolutions of their permanent war on terror than most of the commentaries yet written. In the end of course, the B-52s did not kill Osama bin Laden or Mullah Omar nor did they stop the violence or counter the terrorism. Instead, the response to America's B-52s has only brought more terror, with a resurgent Taliban and Al Qaeda, "prancing on the page and up to the very last line, sneering in the face of all inherited beliefs."[6] Yet calls for more and better versions of its violent-but-impotent solutions grow shriller.

It was the influential nineteenth-century Russian Orthodox Christian philosopher, Nikolai Fyodorovich Fyodorov who believed the Hindu Kush/Pamir region to have been the original Eden of biblical lore, and to be central to the spiritual and physical evolution of the human race. Living during the height of the Great Game between czarist Russia and imperial Britain, he saw in the great-power competition for the region, the seeds of a new kind of cooperation and proposed a joint Anglo-Russian archaeological expedition to the region, "as a first step toward restoring the wasteland to a garden."[7]

However far-fetched Fyodorov's philosophies may seem to us today, his prophecies that the Pamirs and the Hindu Kush region of Afghanistan would emerge from behind their veil of invisibility to become the central focus of the world's concern, may finally be at hand.

Afghanistan cracked the Soviet Union's old Stalinist mind-set and brought it to its knees, not in a lightning battlefield victory, but in a slow process of disintegration and awakening. That process emboldened the Islamists' vision while dimming the Soviets' illusion of establishing a progressive socialist state. Today that process is reversed as the United States exchanges places with the Soviets in claiming to establish democracy. But as the illusion of that democracy fades and is replaced by the brutality and greed of medieval warlords and the *ultra violence* of U.S. Predator drone attacks, Al Qaeda suicide bombers and the Pakistani and Afghan Taliban guerrillas, the time has come to move away from violence and to a new kind of international cooperation as a solution.

APPENDIX

MAPS OF AFGHANISTAN

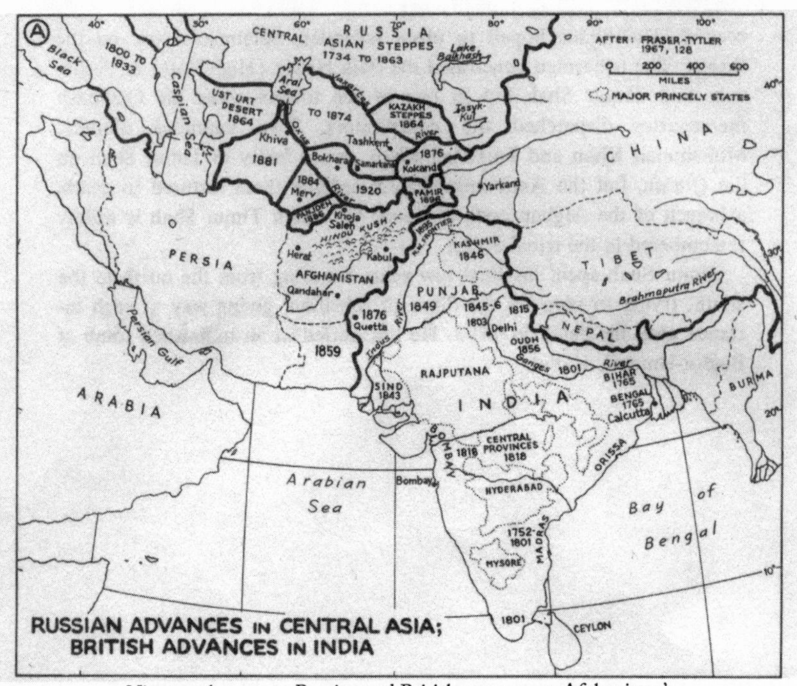

Nineteenth-century Russian and British pressure on Afghanistan's borders set the stage for Cold War confrontation.

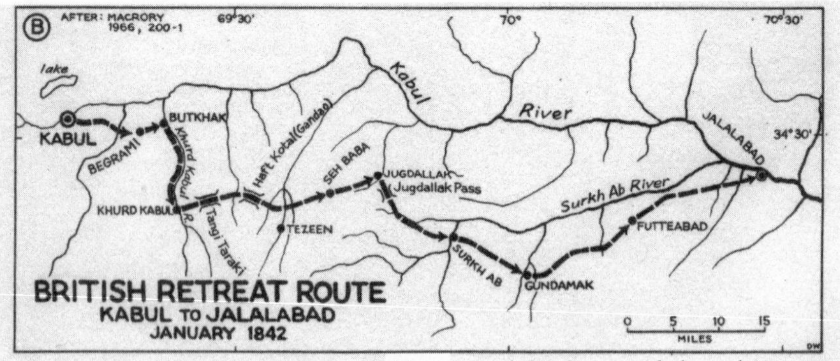

Britain's first attempt to conquer Afghanistan ended in disaster with the total annihilation of Britain's army of the Indus in 1842.

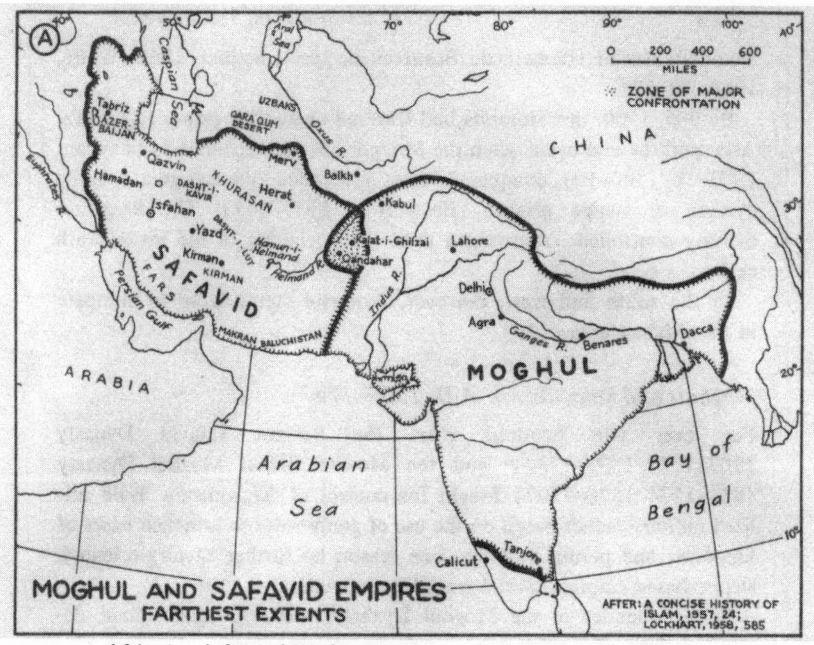

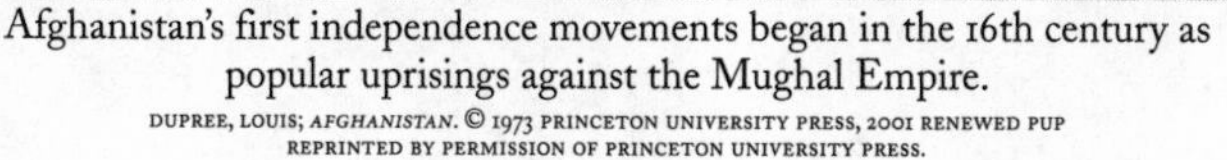
Afghanistan's first independence movements began in the 16th century as popular uprisings against the Mughal Empire.

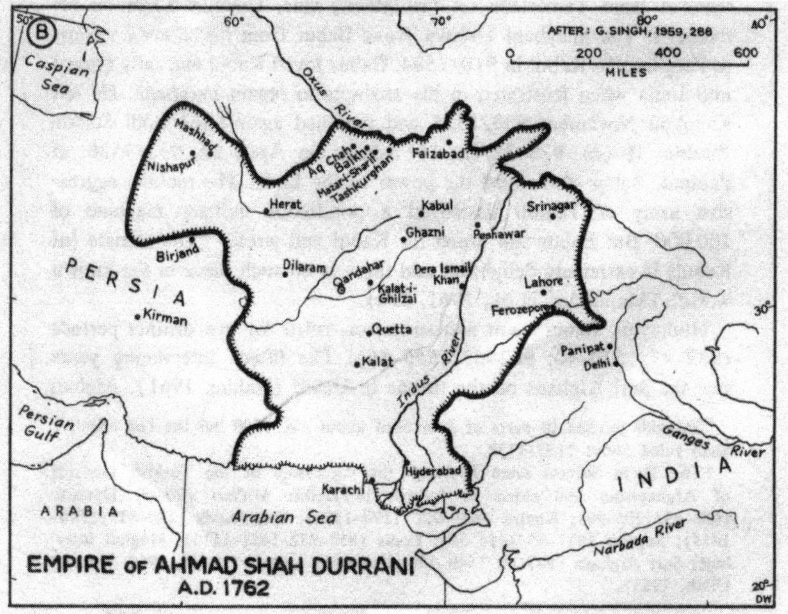

At its height, Ahmad Shah Durrani's Afghan Empire rivaled the size and influence of the Ottoman Empire and ruled Afghanistan until the Marxist coup of 1978.

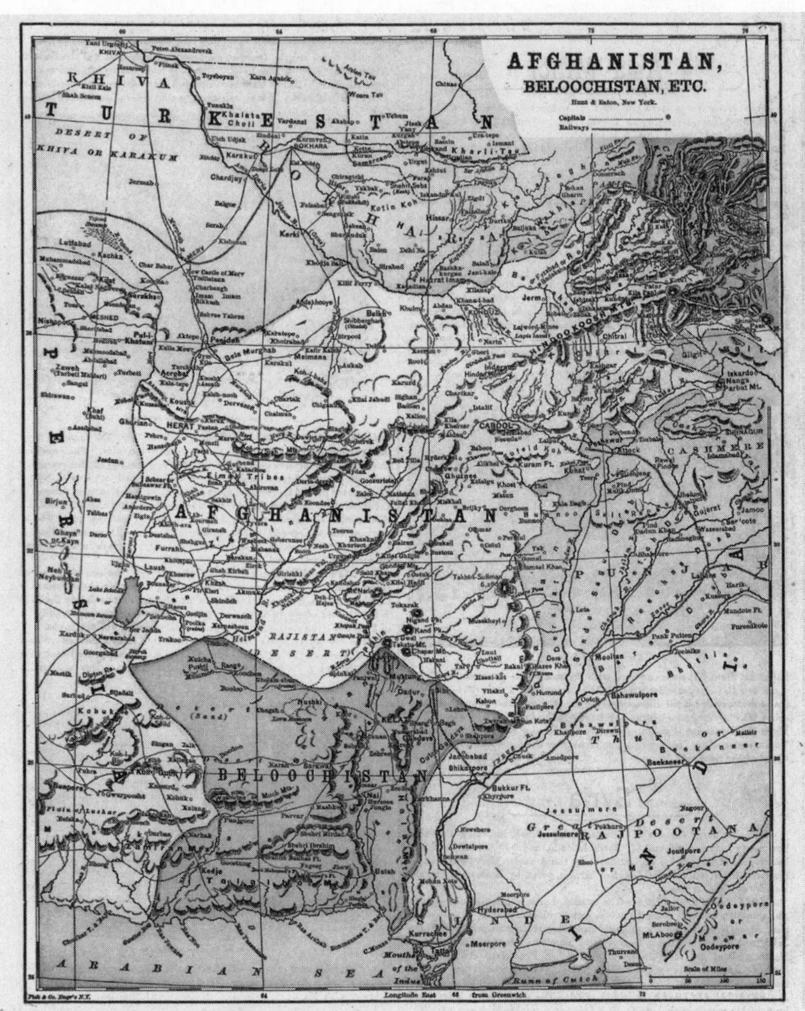

Afghanistan at the time of the establishment of the Durand line which cut Afghanistan's access to the Arabian Sea and severed it from its Indus River Valley territories.

LIBRARY OF CONGRESS. HTTP://WWW.LOC.GOV/RR/GEOGMAP/PUB/AFGHANISTAN.HTML (ACCESSED OCTOBER 24, 2008).

Notes

PROLOGUE—A CLOCKWORK AFGHANISTAN

1. Anthony Burgess, "Introduction: *A Clockwork Orange* Resucked," in *A Clockword Orange* (New York: W. W. Norton, 1986), p. ix.
2. Anthony Burgess, *A Clockwork Orange*, chap. 4, p. 39.
3. Fred Kaplan, *Wizards of Armageddon* (Palo Alto, CA: Stanford University Press, 1983), p. 5.

CHAPTER 1—PROBLEMS WITH THE HISTORICAL RECORD

1. Louis Dupree, *Afghanistan* (Oxford: Oxford University Press, 1997); "Afghanistan," *The New Encyclopedia Britannica*, vol. 13, 15th ed. (Chicago: Encylopaedia Britannica, 1993), p. 31.
2. Ibid.
3. Louis Dupree, *Afghanistan* (Oxford: Oxford University Press, 1997).
4. Bowersox, Gary W. & Chamberlin, Bonita E., *Gemstones of Afghanistan* (Tucson, AZ: Geoscience Press, 1995).
5. Correspondence with Central Asian expert Beatrice F. Manz. Manz considers the name "Aryana" to apply to the Afghan/Iranian region.
6. Afghanan.net, http://www.afghanan.net/pashto/pashtunwali/afghan.htm citing Olaf Caroe, *The Pathans, 550 B.C.–A.D. 1957* (London: Macmillon, 1958).
7. *Asiatick Researches; or Transactions of the Society Instituted in Bengal for Inquiring into the Histories and Antiquities, the Arts, Sciences, and Literature of Asia* 2, London: 1807, p. 69.
8. Abd al-Rahman Khan, *The Life of Abdur Rahman* (London: J. Murray, 1900), p. 213.
9. "Afghanistan, History," *The New Encyclopaedia Britannica*, vol. 13, 15th ed., p. 31.
10. Dupree, p. 276.
11. Ibid.
12. Dupree, pp. 277–278.
13. Frank L. Holt, *Into the Land of Bones* (Berkeley, CA: University of California Press, 2005), p. 98.
14. A stone containing these precepts resides at the Kabul Museum, one of the few artifacts to survive post-Soviet looting and the Taliban's campaign of cultural savagery.
15. Holt, p. 105.
16. Dupree, pp. 280–282.
17. Richard F. Nyrop and Donald M. Seekins, *Afghanistan a Country Study* (Washington, DC: For sale by the Supt. of Docs., U.S. G.P.O., 1986, p. 6.
18. Dupree, p. 285.
19. "Afghanistan, History," *The New Encyclopaedia Britannica*, vol. 13, 15th ed, p. 32.
20. Ibid.
21. Edward Sachau, *Alberuni's India*, vol. 2 (London: Kegan Paul, Trench, Trubner & Co., 1910), p. 253.
22. "Sassanid Empire," Wikipedia.org, http://en.wikipedia.org/wiki/Sassanid_Empire (accessed July 20, 2008).

23. Dupree, p. 301.
24. "Iran, The Sasanian Period," *The New Encyclopaedia Britannica*, vol. 21, 15th ed, p. 955.
25. Ibid.
26. Dupree, p. 302.
27. Ibid.
28. Correspondence with Beatrice F. Manz
29. Xuanzang's *Record of the Western Regions*, Book One, translated by Samuel Beal (1884).
30. "Xuanzang," Wikipedia.org, http://en.wikipedia.org/wiki/Xuanzang (accessed June 28, 2008).
31. Dupree, p. 303.
32. "Afghanistan, History," *The New Encyclopaedia Britannica*, vol. 13, 15th ed, p. 32. Dupree, p. 110.
33. Manz.
34. Dupree, p. 312
35. Ibid., p. 313.
36. Ibid., p. 314.
37. "Afghanistan, History," *The New Encyclopaedia Britannica*, vol. 13, 15th ed, p. 32.
38. Dupree, p. 315.
39. "Afghanistan, History," *The New Encyclopaedia Britannica*, vol. 13, 15th ed, p. 32.
40. Ibid.
41. Dupree, p. 316.
42. Richard F. Nyrop and Donald M. Seekins, *Afghanistan a Country Study* (Washington, DC: For sale by the Supt. of Docs., U.S. G.P.O., 1986), p. 11.
43. Manz maintains that the formal breakup of the Mongol Empire only occurred after the death of Genghis Kahn's grandson, the Great Khan Mongke, in 1259.
44. Britannica.
45. Charles William Heckethorn, *The Secret Societies Of All Ages and Countries*, vol. 1 (London, George Redway, 1897), pp. 123–124.
46. Sher Alam Shinwari, "Remembering great Pakhtoon Sufi, writer revolutionary, political visionary, Bayazid Ansari," KhyberWatch, Feb. 26, 2007, http://khyberwatch.com/nandara/index.php?option=com_content&task=view&id=276 (accessed June 28, 2008).
47. Arkon Daraul, *A History of Secret Societies* (New York: MJF Books, 1989), p. 220.
48. Ibid.
49. Ibid., p. 221.
50. "Bayazid Ansari," Encyclopedia of Pakistan, Overseas Pakistani Foundation, http://www.opf.org.pk/almanac/S/sufis.htm (accessed June 28, 2008).
51. Colin A. Ross, *Satanic Ritual Abuse, Principles of Treatment* (Toronto: University of Toronto Press, 1995), p. 10.
52. Dupree, p. 319.
53. Ibid.
54. "Afghanistan, History," *The New Encyclopaedia Britannica*, vol. 13, 15th ed, p. 32.
55. Dupree, p. 322.
56. Dupree, p. 324.
57. Ibid., p. 328.
58. "Afghanistan, History," *The New Encyclopaedia Britannica*, vol. 13, 15th ed, p. 32.
59. Dupree, p. 333.
60. "Afghanistan, History," *The New Encyclopaedia Britannica*, vol. 13, 15th ed, p. 33.
61. Dupree p. 334. (Originally published in 1973, Dupree's assessment of the Durrani kings' future seems particularly ironic given that the last Durrani King, Zahair Shah, was overthrown that very year by his cousin Mohammed Daoud, who was in turn overthrown in 1978 by Ghilzai Pashtun Hafizullah Amin.)
62. "Afghanistan, History," *The New Encyclopaedia Britannica*, vol. 13, 15th ed, p. 33.

CHAPTER 2—THE BRITISH ARE COMING

1. Alfred W. McCoy, *The Politics of Heroin: CIA Complicity in the Global Drug Trade* (Chicago: Lawrence Hill Books, 1991), p. 80.
2. Ibid., p. 83.
3. "Afghanistan, History," *The New Encyclopaedia Britannica*, vol. 13, 15th ed, p. 33.
4. Ibid.
5. Yu. V. Gankovsky, *A History of Afghanistan*, translated by Vitaly Baskakov (Moscow: Progress Publishers, 1985), p. 131.
6. Manz.
7. Gankovsky, pp. 136–137.
8. "Afghanistan, History," *The New Encyclopaedia Britannica*, vol. 13, 15th ed, p. 33.
9. Gankovsky, p. 136.
10. John H. Waller, *Beyond the Khyber Pass* (New York: Random House, 1990), p. 123.
11. Nyrop and Seekins, p. 25
12. Ibid., p. 28.
13. Dupree, p. 377, citing Kaye, 1874.
14. Waller, p. 45. "Burnes concluded prophetically that the dynasty of the Saddozai [rule of the British puppet Shah Shoja] was finished. . . . The British must look for another family to rule Afghanistan."
15. Waller, p. 278.
16. "No modern liberal historian could be as harsh as a contemporary British analysis (Extract from Report of the East India Committee on the Causes and Consequences of the First Afghan War, written before its conclusion, quoted in Hanna, 1899, I:I) of the 1838-42 Afghan adventure: 'This war of robbery is waged by the English Government through the intervention of the Government of India (without the knowledge of England, or of Parliament and the Court of Directors); thereby evading the check placed by the Constitution on the exercise of the prerogative of the Crown in declaring war. It presents, therefore, a new crime in the annals of nations—*a secret war!* [emphasis theirs] It has been made by a people without their knowledge, against another people who had committed no offence.'" Cited by Dupree, p. 400.

CHAPTER 3—THE GREAT GAME

1. Nyrop and Seekins, p. 27.
2. Ibid.
3. Ibid., p. 30.
4. Ibid.
5. Nyrop and Seekins.
6. Ibid., p. 32.
7. Ibid.
8. Karl E. Meyer and Shareen Blair Brysac, *Tournament of Shadows* (Washington, DC: Counterpoint, 1999), p. 182. This quote is found in Romesh Dutt, C.I.E., *The Economic History of India in the Victorian Age,* 3rd ed. (London: Kegan Paul, Trench, Trubner and Co. 1908), p. 422.
9. Dupree, p. 408.
10. Ibid.
11. Nyrop and Seekins, p. 33.
12. Ibid.
13. Dupree, p. 410.
14. Ibid., p. 411.
15. Meyer and Brysac, p. 244.
16. Dupree, p. 272.

17. Vartan Gregorian, *Emergence of Modern Afghanistan,* pp. 43, 421 note 49. "The Roshania movement included elements from both Isma'ilism and Sufism intermingled with a belief in the transmigration of souls, which was borrowed from Hinduism, and in the manifestation of divinity in the persons of the *pirs* [his emphasis] (holy men)."
18. Karl E. Meyer and Shareen Blair Brysac, *Tournament of Shadows,* p. 449.
19. Ibid., p. 244.
20. Robert Dreyfuss, *Devil's Game* (New York: Metropolitan Books, 2005), p. 32.
21. Meyer and Brysac, p. 244.
22. Frances Yates, *The Occult Philosophy in the Elizabethan Age*, Routledge Classics (London: Routledge, 2003), pp. 100–101.
23. Ibid., p. 127.
24. Karl E. Meyer, *The Dust of Empire: The Race for Mastery in the Asian Heartland* (New York: Public Affairs, 2004), p. 34.
25. Meyer and Brysac, p. 566.
26. Ibid., pp. 246–247.
27. H .P. Blavatsky, *The Secret Doctrine, The Synthesis of Science Religion, and Philosophy* (London: Theosophical Publishing House, 1897).
28. Meyer and Brysac, p. 483.
29. Bernice Glatzer Rosenthal, ed., *The Occult in Russian and Soviet Culture* (Ithaca, NY: Cornell University Press, 1997), p. 182.
30. Ibid. "Federov proposed a joint Anglo-Russian archaeological expedition to the Pamirs in search of common ancestral remains as a first step toward restoring the wasteland to a garden."
31. Dupree, p. 425.
32. Meyer and Brysac, p. 199.
33. Abdul Samad Ghaus, *The Fall of Afghanistan: An Insider's Account* (Washington, DC: Pergamon-Brassey's International Defense Publishers, 1988), pp. 6–7.
34. E. J. Rapson, et al., *Cambridge History of India*, vol. 6 (Cambridge University Press, 1962), p. 408, as quoted by Munawwar Khan, *Anglo-Afghan relations, 1798–1878* (Peshawar: University Book Agency, 1965?), pp. 104–105. Cited by Ghaus, 8–9.
35. Ghaus, p. 11.
36. Ibid.
37. Peter Hopkirk, *The Great Game: The Struggle for Empire in Central Asia* (New York: Kodansha International, 1992), p. 398.
38. Ibid., p. 415.
39. Ibid., pp. 420–421.
40. Correspondence with Beatrice F. Manz.
41. Meyer and Brysac, p. 200.
42. Dupree, p. 417.
43. Ghaus, p. 14.
44. Dupree, p. 419.
45. Correspondence with Beatrice F. Manz
46. Seekins and Nyrop, p. 35.
47. "Afghanistan," in Karl Marx and Frederick Engels, *Collected Works*, Volume 18 (Moscow: Progress Publishers, 1982), p. 42.
48. Ghaus, p. 15.
49. Dupree, p. 426.
50. Ibid., p. 427.
51. Ghaus, p. 16.
52. Ghaus, p. 17.

CHAPTER 4—TWENTIETH-CENTURY AFGHANISTAN

1. Ghaus pp. 21–22.
2. Dupree, p. 432.
3. Ghaus, p. 21.
4. Ghaus, p. 23.
5. Ghaus, p. 24.
6. Peter Hopkirk, *Like Hidden Fire*, p. 2.
7. Ibid., p. 62.
8. Ibid.
9. Ibid., p. 63.
10. Ibid., p.62.
11. Ibid., p. 165.
12. Ghaus, p. 26.
13. Peter Hopkirk, *Like Hidden Fire*, p. 192.
14. Ghaus, p. 27.
15. Ibid.
16. Ibid., p. 27.
17. Ibid., p. 25.
18. Ibid., p. 31.
19. Dupree, p. 442.
20. Ghaus, pp. 32–33.
21. Adamec, Ludwig W. *Afghanistan 1900-1923: A Diplomatic History* (Berkeley, CA: University of California Press, 1967), p. 124. Cited by Ghaus, p. 33.
22. Ghaus, p. 35.
23. Ibid., p. 31.
24. C. Collin Davies, *The Problem of the North-west Frontier*, 1890–1908 (New York: Barnes & Noble, 1975), pp. 26–28. Cited by McCoy, p. 442.
25. Ghaus, p. 35.
26. A term used by Ghaus, p. 43, to describe the Pashtun tribes on both sides of the Durand Line.
27. Ghaus, p. 36.
28. Ibid., p. 35, citing Charles Miller, *Khyber: British India's North West Frontier* (New York: Macmillan Publishing Co., 1977), p. 106.
29. Nyrop and Seekins, pp. 43–44.
30. Ghaus, p. 42.
31. Dreyfuss, pp. 48–49.
32. Ibid., p. 20.
33. Ibid., p. 21.
34. Nyrop and Seekins, p. 45.
35. Ibid.
36. Ibid., p. 46, citing Leon Poullada.
37. Ghaus, p. 45.
38. Ibid., p. 44.
39. Ibid., p. 45.
40. Ibid.
41. Ibid.
42. Nyrop and Seekins, p. 47.
43. Leon B. Poullada, *Reform and Rebellion in Afghanistan, 1919–1929* (Ithaca, NY: Cornell University Press, 1973), p. 251, as cited by Ghaus, p. 47.

44. Leon B. Poullada and Leila D. J. Poullada, *The Kingdom of Afghanistan and the United States* (Lincoln, NE: Center for Afghanistan Studies at the University of Nebraska at Omaha and Dageforde Publishing), p. 16.
45. Ibid., p. 18.
46. Ghaus, p. 47.
47. Ibid., pp. 47–48.
48. Ibid, p. 49.
49. Ibid.
50. Noam Chomsky, *Year 501: The Conquest Continues* (Boston: South End Press, 1993), p. 9.
51. Added to the complex mix of imperial, tribal and political forces vying for control of Afghanistan were the beginnings of a quasi-religious "nonviolent" progressive movement in the contested Pashtun tribal areas of the North-West Frontier. Named the Khudai Khidmatgaran ("Servants of God"), it was founded by Abdul Ghaffar Khan, who sought to reorganize the fractious, divided Pashtun tribes into a powerful state, hoping that by linking his organization to the Gandhian movement and Afghan independence, a peaceful solution to the persistent encroachment of the British could be found. Dressing in red shirts and promising independence and equal rights for men, women, Hindus and Muslims, the group was initially thought to be pro-Soviet. By 1931, the movement's links to Gandhi's Congress Party and its political goals would draw charges of bourgeois liberalism from Moscow, the suspicion of the British, and the denial of Nadir Shah who wished to anger neither. The Red Shirts found allies in the progressive followers of Amanullah and were often sheltered by them when forced to flee from British persecution. Influential as an organizational tool for Indian independence throughout most of the 1930s, the coming of World War II and the partition of India into Hindu and Muslim states would eventually render their methods unserviceable and their ideology irrelevant to Cold War politics. See Dupree, pp. 487–89.
52. Nyrop and Seekins p. 48.
53. Ibid., 49.
54. Ghaus, p. 49, citing William Kerr Fraser-Tytler, *Afghanistan* (New York: Oxford University Press, 1997), p. 231.
55. Ghaus, p. 52.
56. "Biography: Nadir Shah," Afghanistan Online, http://www.afghan-web.com/bios/yest/nadir.html (accessed July 2, 2008).
57. Ghaus, p. 49.
58. Ibid., p. 52.
59. Dupree, p. 477.
60. Leon B. Poullada, *Reform and Rebellion in Afghanistan*, 1919–1929, p 251 as cited by Ghaus, p. 47.
61. Ghaus, p. 64, footnote 11.
62. A famous clock tower, named after Sir George Cunningham and dedicted to the "Commemoration of the Diamond Jubilee of Her Majesty the Queen Empress," remains a tourist attraction in the streets of Peshawar.
63. Dreyfuss, pp. 47–48.
64. "Mohammed Zahir Shah, Last Afghan King, Dies at 92," *New York Times*, July 24, 2007.
65. Dupree, p. 477.
66. Ghaus, p. 51.
67. Ghaus recalls the incident (p. 57, footnote 6, citing Ludwig Adamec, *Afghanistan's Foreign Affairs*, 303), stating that, according to accounts primarily by Afghan foreign minister Faiz Mohammed, "the deal was cancelled because of British pressures."
68. Poullada, *Afghanistan and the United States*, p. 66.
69. Ibid.
70. Ghaus, p. 58.
71. Meyer and Brysac, pp. 509–510.
72. Ibid.

73. Ibid.
74. Nicholas Goodrick-Clarke, *The Occult Roots of Nazism* (New York: New York University Press, 1992), p. 220, citing Louis Pauwels and Jacques Bergier's *Morning of the Magicians.*
75. "Rosenberg Explains," *Time*, September 26, 1938, http://www.time.com/time/magazine/article/0,9171,788810,00.html (accessed July 20, 2008).
76. Vartan Gregorian, *Emergence of Modern Afghanistan* p. 385 cited by Ghaus p. 60.
77. R. J. Sontag and J. S. Beddie, eds., *Nazi-Soviet Relations 1939–1941* (New York: Didier, 1948), p. 250. Cited by Ghaus, p. 61.
78. Leon Poullada, *Afghanistan and the United States*, p. 68, citing Ludwig W. Adamec, *Afghanistan's Foreign Affairs to Mid-Twentieth Century,* pp. 213–260.
79. Ghaus, pp. 62–63.
80. Nyrop and Seekins, p. 51.
81. *Foreign Relations of the United States: Diplomatic Papers*, The Near East and Africa, Volume IV, 1942, p. 52.
82. Ibid.
83. Ibid.
84. Ibid., p. 53
85. Ibid., p. 55.
86. Ibid.
87. Ibid.
88. Ibid.
89. "Under no conditions would the use of air or land routes be granted; and that an attempt to establish such routes might undermine the present regime in Afghanistan and lead to serious disorders." *Foreign Relations of the United States: Diplomatic Papers*, China, 1943, p. 616, in Foreign Relations of the United States, University of Wisconsin Digital Collections, http://digital.library.wisc.edu/1711.dl/FRUS (accessed July 20, 2008).
90. Leon Poullada *Afghanistan and the United States* p. 72.
91. *Foreign Relations of the United States: Diplomatic Papers*, The Near East and Africa, Volume IV, 1942, p.23, in Foreign Relations of the United States, University of Wisconsin Digital Collections, http://digital.library.wisc.edu/1711.dl/FRUS (accessed July 20,2008).
92. Ibid.
93. The Minister in Afghanistan (Engert) to the Secretary of State Kabul, May 16, 1943, in ibid.
94. *Foreign Relations of the United States: Diplomatic Papers*, The Near East and Africa, Volume IV, 1942, p. 34, in ibid.
95. The Secretary of State to the Minister in Afghanistan (Engert) No. 69 Washington, November 23, 1943, in ibid.
96. *Foreign Relations of the United States: Diplomatic Papers*, The Near East and Africa, Volume IV, 1942, p. 53, in ibid.
97. "It is the kind of work which has made itself felt, slowly but surely throughout the world by the example set by unselfish Christians whose personal integrity, clean lives, and intellectual honesty have 'converted' thousands of men to the western (i.e. Christian) concept of life without outwardly changing their religion." Ibid., p. 54.
98. Henry S. Bradsher, *Afghanistan and the Soviet Union*, Durham: 1985, p. 17.
99. Nyrop and Seekins, p. 51
100. Ibid., p. 37.
101. Ghaus, pp. 67–70; Nyrop and Seekins, p. 54.
102. Hassan Abbas, *Pakistan's Drift into Extremism: Allah, the Army, and America's War on Terror* (Armonk, NY: M. E. Sharpe, 2005), p.16.
103. Ghaus, p. 69.
104. Ibid.
105. Ibid.

106. Ibid.
107. Ibid., p. 71.
108. Dupree, p. 492.
109. U.S. Dept. of State/Foreign Relations of the U.S. diplomatic papers, 1948, Near East and Africa, Vol. V p.490, in Foreign Relations of the United States, University of Wisconsin Digital Collections, http://digital.library.wisc.edu/1711.dl/FRUS (accessed July 20,2008).
110. Ibid., p. 492.
111. Ibid., p. 493.
112. Bradsher, *Afghanistan and the Soviet Union*, p. 38. Bradsher maintains Taraki played only a minor role in the organization while Taraki's official biography claimed he had founded the organization.
113. Meyer and Brysac, p. 569.
114. Memorandum of Conversation, by Mr. Richard S. Leach of the Division of South Asian Affairs (Washington) December 8, 1948 (1948 Vol. I page 492), in Foreign Relations of the United States, University of Wisconsin Digital Collections, http://digital.library.wisc.edu/1711.dl/FRUS (accessed July 20,2008).
115. *Foreign Relations of the United States: Diplomatic Papers*, Near East, South Asia and Africa, Vol. V, 1950, p. 1496, in ibid.
116. Ibid., p. 1490.
117. Ibid., p. 1502.
118. Ibid., p. 1502.
119. Ibid., p. 448.
120. Ghaus, citing a study prepared by the National Security Council, Index of Declassified Documents, No. 3, 377A (Arlington, VA, 1978).
121. Dreyfuss, p. 2.

CHAPTER 5—A BACKGROUND TO COLD WAR POLICY

1. Bernice Glatzer Rosenthal, *The Occult in Russian and Soviet Culture* (Ithaca, NY: Cornell University Press, 1997), p. 391.
2. Ibid., citing Lynn Mally, *Culture of the Future: The Prolekult Movement in Revolutionary Russia* (Berkeley, CA: University of California Press, 1990), p. xxix.
3. Ibid., pp. 24, 400, 407. See also Meyer and Brysac, pp. 486–490.
4. See Meyer and Brysac, pp. 480–481.
5. Ibid., 566–569.
6. David Greenberg, "The Choice," *Boston Globe,* May 21, 2006.
7. Ibid.
8. Fred Kaplan, "Paul Nitze: The Man Who Brought Us the Cold War," *Slate*, October 21, 2004.
9. "NSC 68: United States Objectives and Programs for National Security (April 14, 1950)," Federation of American Scientists, http://www.fas.org/irp/offdocs/nsc-hst/nsc-68.htm (accessed July 2, 2008).
10. Ibid.
11. Quoted in Fred Kaplan, *Wizards of Armageddon* (New York: Simon and Schuster, 1983), p. 140.
12. Ibid., p. 11.
13. See ibid., pp. 67–68, 91, 178, 214.
14. Ibid., p. 10.
15. Ibid., p. 13.
16. See Meyer and Brysac pages, 569–573; George Orwell's essay, "James Burnham and the Managerial Revolution," http://www.george-orwell.org/James_Burnham_and_the_Managerial_Revolution/0.html (accessed July 2, 2008); and Daniel Kelly, *James Burnham and the Struggle for the World* (Wilmington, DE: ISI Books, 2002).

17. Michael Lind, "A Tragedy of Errors," *Nation*, February 23, 2004.
18. See Michael Lind, "Right and Wrong," *Boston Globe*, January 13, 2003; John B. Judis, "Trotskyism to Anarchism: The Neoconservative Revolution," *Foreign Affairs*, July/August 1995.
19. Meyer and Brysac, p. 569.
20. Ghaus, p. 78.
21. Ibid., pp. 74–75.
22. Ibid., pp. 77–78.
23. Poullada, *Afghanistan and the United States* pp. 103–104.
24. Ibid., p. 104.
25. Nancy and Richard S. Newell, *The Struggle for Afghanistan* (Ithaca, NY: Cornell University Press, 1981), p. 62.
26. Ibid., pp. 59–60.
27. Ibid.
28. Archie Roosevelt, *For Lust of Knowing: Memoirs of an Intelligence Officer* (Boston: Little, Brown, 1988), p. 435.
29. Daoud's tough, outspoken Pashtun nationalism and his willingness to use the Soviet Union to balance the impasse with Pakistan was a major reason for his ascent to prime minister as well as his demonization by the United States.
30. Isaac Cronin, ed. *Confronting Fear: A History of Terrorism* (New York: Thunder's Mouth Press, 2002), p. 365.
31. Ghaus, pp. 86–87.
32. Ibid., p. 80.
33. Ghaus relates (p. 80) that instead of responding to Naim's confidential request, Dulles betrayed the information to Afghanistan's opponent Pakistan, then informed both the Afghans and the Pakistani ambassador in Washington that the Afghan request had been rejected.
34. "The Frontiersman," *Time*, April 2, 1956, http://www.time.com/time/magazine/article/0,9171,862050,00.html (accessed July 20, 2008).
35. Bradsher, *Afghanistan and the Soviet Union*, p. 23.
36. "The Frontiersman," *Time*, April 2, 1956.
37. Ghaus, p. 82.
38. Ibid., pp. 83–84.
39. Marshall I. Goldman, *Soviet Foreign Aid* (New York: Praeger, 1967), p. 122.
40. Nikita Khrushchev, *Khrushchev Remembers* (Boston: Little Brown, 1970), pp. 560–62.
41. Henry S. Bradsher, *Afghanistan and the Soviet Union*, p. 28, citing International Institute for Strategic Studies, The Military Balance, 1977-1978 (London, 1977), pp 55–56.
42. Ibid.
43. Ibid.
44. Ibid., p. 28.
45. Ibid., p. 29. Bradsher quotes W. R. Polk, "Elements of U.S. Policy Towards Afghanistan" (1962), in *Declassified Documents 1978*, no. 65B.
46. Ibid., p. 30.
47. Ibid., summarizing Poullada, *Afghanistan and the United States,* pp. 185–86.
48. Poullada, *Afghanistan and the United States*, p. 157.
49. Dreyfuss, p. 257.
50. Ibid.
51. Victor Marchetti and John D. Marks, *The CIA and the Cult of Intelligence* (New York: Dell, 1980), pp. 150–151.
52. Muhammed Hisham Kabbani, *Classical Islam and the Naqshbandi Sufi Tradition* (Washington, DC: Islamic Supreme Council of America, 2004).
53. Dupree, p. 460; Newell and Newell, p. 93.
54. Newell and Newell, p. 93.

55. Beverley Male, *Revolutionary Afghanistan* (New York: St. Martin's Press, 1982), p. 172.
56. Milt Bearden and James Risen, *The Main Enemy* (New York: Random House, 2003), p. 230.
57. Beverley Male, p. 172.
58. Dreyfuss, p. 252.
59. Alexandre Bennigsen and Marie Broxup, *The Islamic Threat to the Soviet State* (New York: St. Martin's Press, 1983), p. 64.
60. Dreyfuss, p. 253.
61. Ibid., p. 252.
62. Newell, *The Struggle for Afghanistan*, p. 61.
63. Brzezinski came to Columbia in 1961 to join the new Institute on Communist Affairs.
64. Male, p. 28–29.
65. Ibid., p. 30; Newell, *The Struggle for Afghanistan*, p. 61.
66. Newell, *The Struggle for Afghanistan*, p. 61.
67. Diego Cordovez and Selig S. Harrison, *Out of Afghanistan* (New York: Oxford University Press, 1995), p. 19.
68. Marchetti and Marks, p. 197.
69. Newell, *The Struggle for Afghanistan*, p. 61.
70. Steve Coll, *Ghost Wars* (New York: Penguin, 2004), p. 47, cites Amin's reputed connection to the Asia Foundation, a known CIA creation. In conversation, another source cited Amin's ties to the World Bank through a family connection.
71. "Coups at the Crossroads," *Time*, July 30, 1973, p. 34.
72. Seekins and Nyrop, p. 58.
73. Ghaus, p. 90.
74. Geoffrey Francis Hudson, Richard Lowenthal, and Roderick Farquhar, *The Sino-Soviet Dispute* (New York: Praeger, 1961), p. 15, *Marchetti and Marks*, pp. 26–27.
75. Roger S. Whitcomb, *The Cold War in Retrospect: The Formative Years* (Westport, CT: Praeger, 1998), p. 161.
76. Fred Kaplan, pp. 249–250.
77. "Report of Meeting Between Secretary of State Herter and Pakistani Foreign Minister Mansur Qadir, June 2, 1960," *Foreign Relations of the United States*, 1958–60, vol. 15, p. 812.
78. Abbas, p. 39.
79. Ghaus, p. 93; Dupree, p. 541.
80. Abbas, p. 40.
81. Ghaus, p. 90.
82. Dupree, p. 539.
83. Ghaus, p. 91.
84. Ibid., p. 92.
85. Ibid., p. 91.
86. Ibid., p. 93.
87. Ibid., p. 94.
88. Ibid.
89. Ibid., p. 93.
90. See Bradsher, *Afghanistan and the Soviet Union*, p. 29.
91. Ghaus, p. 95–97.
92. John K. Cooley, *Unholy Wars* (London: Pluto Press, 2000), p. 12.
93. Ibid., p. 34.
94. One young Afghan high school student recruited under this plan, by a Peace Corps volunteer named Thomas Gouttierre, was Zalmay Khalilzad. Khalilzad would go on to receive a doctorate under Albert Wohlstetter at the University of Chicago and from there find fame and fortune as a national security manager at RAND, becoming what one American Afghan hand described as the "Reagan Doctrine architect" following the Soviet invasion of 1979.

95. See Dupree, chapter 24, pp. 558-658.
96. Nyrop and Seekins, p. 64.
97. See Dupree, chapter 24, pp. 558-658.
98. This mislabeling would create serious confusion following the PDPA's violent rise to power.
99. Male, p. 37.
100. Ibid., p. 47.
101. Khalq and Parcham split in 1967, with Khalq virtually disappearing off the Afghan political radar. In 1973 Parcham would use its political influence in the military to assist Mohammed Daoud's comeback.
102. Bradsher, op cit., p. 50, citing Dupree, *Red Flag over the Hindu Kush: Part I: Leftist Movements in Afghanistan* (Hanover, NH: American Universities Field Staff, 1979), p. 8.
103. Male, p. 39.
104. Ibid., p. 38. Male gives a detailed account of the mystery of Hafizullah Amin's expulsion.
105. Ibid., p. 39.
106. Ghaus, p. 97.
107. Vasiliy Mitrokhin, *The KGB in Afghanistan*, Cold War International History Project Working Paper No. 40 (Washington, DC: Woodrow Wilson International Center for Scholars, 2002), p. 20.
108. Ibid., p. 18.
109. Ibid., p. 19.
110. Ibid., p. 22.
111. Ibid., p. 22.
112. Ibid.
113. Newell, *The Struggle for Afghanistan*, p. 62, Bradsher, p. 51.
114. Male, pp. 43–47.
115. Mitrokhin, p. 21.
116. Male, p. 46.
117. Ibid., p. 47.
118. Ibid. ABC's Athens bureau chief, John K. Cooley, eventually placed the Afghan Maoists at the center of a Chinese-Iranian-Pakistani destabilization of Afghanistan prior to the Soviet invasion.
119. Dupree, p. 565, cited by Ghaus, p. 98.
120. *New York Times*, September 6, 1963, as cited by Ghaus, p. 98.
121. Male, pp. 47–48.
122. Male, p. 52. The king's weakness at implementing reforms "secured the ascendancy of the feudal tribal ruling class."
123. Dreyfuss, p. 258.
124. Ibid.
125. Ibid.
126. Steve Coll, *Ghost Wars* (New York: Penguin, 2004), pp. 110–111.
127. Olivier Roy, *Afghanistan: From Holy War to Civil War* (Princeton, NJ: Darwin Press, 1995), p. 38.
128. Arnaud de Borchgrave, "Al Qaedism and communism," *Washington Times*, June 17, 2006.
129. Coll, p. 113.
130. Dreyfuss, p. 138, citing Sylvain Besson, *Le Temps*, October 26, 2004.
131. Ibid., p. 259.
132. Dreyfuss, p. 260.
133. Authors' personal correspondence, April 2008.
134. Nyrop and Seekins, p. 67.
135. Male, p. 49.
136. Ghaus, p. 98.
137. Alastair Iain Johnston, Robert S. Ross, ed., *New Directions in the Study of China's Foreign Policy* (Palo Alto, CA: Stanford University Press, 2006), p. 69.
138. Bradsher, *Afghanistan and the Soviet Union*, pp. 51–52.

139. EYES ONLY MEMORANDUM FOR THE PRESIDENT, January 21, 1970, p. 1, from authors' files.
140. SECRET MEMORANDUM FOR THE PRESIDENT from Henry Kissinger re Private Conversations with the king and prime minister, January 26, 1970, in FROM THE SECRET FILES ON KING ZAHIR'S REIGN IN AFGHANISTAN, 1970–1973, National Security Archive Electronic Briefing Book No. 59, edited by William Burr, October 26, 2001, p. 3; http://www.gwu.edu/~nsarchiv/NSAEBB/NSAEBB59/zahir01.pdf (accessed July 21, 2008).
141. EYES ONLY MEMORANDUM FOR THE PRESIDENT, January 21, 1970.
142. "Airgram A-90, King Zahir's Experiment: Some End-of-Tour Observations, August 1, 1970," in FROM THE SECRET FILES ON KING ZAHIR'S REIGN IN AFGHANISTAN, 1970–1973, National Security Archive Electronic Briefing Book No. 59, edited by William Burr, October 26, 2001, p. 3; http://www.gwu.edu/~nsarchiv/NSAEBB/NSAEBB59/zahir03-1.pdf (accessed July 3, 2008).
143. Ibid., pp. 3–4.
144. "Airgram A-77, Afghanistan's Clerical Unrest; a Tentative Assessment, June 24, 1970," in FROM THE SECRET FILES ON KING ZAHIR'S REIGN IN AFGHANISTAN, 1970–1973, National Security Archive Electronic Briefing Book No. 59, edited by William Burr, October 26, 2001, p. 3; http://www.gwu.edu/~nsarchiv/NSAEBB/NSAEBB59/zahir02.pdf (accessed July 3, 2008). p. 1.
145. Ibid., p. 2.
146. Ibid., p. 5.
147. Ibid., p.7.
148. Ibid.
149. Bradsher, *Afghanistan and the Soviet Union*, p. 52, citing Hasan Kakar, "The Fall of the Afghan Monarchy in 1973." *International Journal of Middle East Studies,* 9 (1978) pp.209-11; Smith, *Area Handbook,* pp. xix-xx; *Hong Kong Sunday Standard*, 16 November 1972.
150. Ibid.
151. Mohammed Hassan Kakar, *Afghanistan: The Soviet Invasion and the Afghan Response, 1879–1982* (Berkeley, CA: University of California Press, 1997), Introduction.
152. The majority of Afghanistan's middle class consisted mainly of government employees and state-subsidized businesses.
153. Authors' conversation with an American resident in Kabul at the time.
154. Community Christian Church and Related Religious Organizations, Kabul 2091, March 30, 1973, in authors' files (Nixon, Kissinger, Daoud).
155. King Zaher Travel to London for Medical Treatment, Kabul 4728, June 25, 1973, in FROM THE SECRET FILES ON KING ZAHIR'S REIGN IN AFGHANISTAN, 1970–1973, National Security Archive Electronic Briefing Book No. 59, edited by William Burr, October 26, 2001, http://www.gwu.edu/~nsarchiv/NSAEBB/NSAEBB59/zahir14.pdf (accessed July 21, 2008).
156. Ibid.
157. Bradsher, *Afghanistan and the Soviet Union*, pp. 56–57, citing Robert G. Neuman, "Afghanistan Under the Red Flag," in Z. Michael Szaz, ed., *The Impact of the Iranian Events Upon Persian Gulf and United States Security* (Washington: American Foreign Policy Institute, 1979), pp. 128–48.
158. Ghaus, p. 105.
159. Ibid., p. 106.
160. Ibid.
161. Daoud's brother, Prince Naim, visited U.S. ambassador Robert Neuman to tell him that "the king was irresponsible, that Parliament was a joke, that the king was not working hard and was leading the country into bankruptcy." Meeting with Daoud's Brother Naim, Kabul 5325, July 20, 1973 in ("Afghanistan: The Making of U.S. Policy 1973–1990,") National Security Archives, Fiche 13, item 00066.
162. Ibid.

163. Soviets Deny Role in Afghan Coup, 116529, July 23, 1973 ("Afghanistan: The Making of U.S. Policy 1973–1990") Fiche 17, item 00095.
164. Republic of Afghanistan Prospects, Kabul 5540, July 27, 1973 ("Afghanistan: The Making of U.S. Policy 1973–1990") Fiche 19, item 00109.
165. Afghan Coup: View from Quetta, Karachi 1300, July 26, 1973, ("Afghanistan: The Making of U.S. Policy 1973–1990") Fiche 20, item 00113.
166. Ibid.
167. Ibid.
168. Ghaus, p. 107.
169. According to Bradsher, p. 56, "Maiwandwal was also reported to have been starting a coup plan with support of military officers . . . but Daoud preempted him."
170. A U.S. cable on August 2 reported rumors of the Maiwandal coup as well as a third coup attempt by the king's son-in-law, General Abdul Wali, "supported by the Americans" [only to see its plan foiled prematurely by Daoud as well]. ("Afghanistan: The Making of U.S. Policy 1973-1990") Fiche 24, Item 00136
171. Diego Cordovez and Selig S. Harrison, p. 15.
172. CIA Biographic Report on Mohammed Daud, August 13, 1973. ("Afghanistan: The Making of U.S. Policy 1973–1990") Fiche 26, item 00150.
173. Afghan Coup: View from Quetta Confidential Karachi 1300.
174. "PAK Views of Afghan Coup: Two Weeks After," July 31, 1973, p. 3, ("Afghanistan: The Making of U.S. Policy 1973-1990") Fiche 22, item 00124.
175. Lutz Kleveman, *The New Great Game: Blood and Oil in Central Asia* (New York: Grove Press, 2004), pp. 239–240.
176. Cordovez and Harrison, p.14
177. Ibid.
178. Bradsher, *Afghan Communism and Soviet Intervention* (New York: Oxford University Press, 2000), p. 17.
179. According to Robert G. Wirsing, *Pakistan's Security Under Zia 1977-1998* (New York: Macmillan, 1991), p. 73; "Prime Minister Benazir Bhutto's Special Assistant Nasirullah Babar reportedly stated in a press interview in April 1989 that the United States had been financing Afghan dissidents since 1973 and that it had taken Hezb-i Islami chieftain Gulbuddin Hekmatyar 'under its umbrella' months prior to the Soviet military intervention."
180. Bradsher, *Afghanistan and the Soviet Union*, pp. 57–58, 87, citing Airgram no. A-58, U.S. Embassy, Kabul, 26 June 1978; memorandum from Peter Tarnoff, executive secretary of the State Department, to Zbigniew Brzezinski, national security advisor, dated 29 June 1978 (recommending acceptance of Nur as ambassador; Agency France-Presse [AFP] from Kabul, 5 July 1978, in Foreign Broadcast Information Service/Middle East, 6 July 1978, p. S1.
181. Kleveman, pp. 239–240.
182. Newell, pp. 45–46.
183. Cordovez and Harrison, pp. 16–17; Nyrop and Seekins, p. 68.
184. Cordovez and Harrison, pp. 16–17; Male p. 55.
185. Bradsher, *Afghanistan and the Soviet Union*, 1975.
186. Ibid., pp. 20–28.
187. Relations with Daud Government, August 7, 1973. ("Afghanistan: The Making of U.S. Policy 1973-1990") Fiche 24, item 00142.
188. Anthony Sampson, *The Arms Bazaar* (New York: Viking Press, 1977), p. 252.
189. Ibid.
190. Ibid., pp. 251–252.
191. Evaluation of Daud's Government and comments on Pashtunistan policy, Kabul 6377, August 29, 1973. ("Afghanistan: The Making of U.S. Policy 1973-1990") Fiche 28, item 00164.
192. Cordovez/Harrison, *Out of Afghanistan*, p. 16.

193. Ibid.
194. Ibid.
195. Ibid.
196. Ibid.
197. Ibid., p. 17.
198. Ibid.
199. Bradsher, *Afghanistan and the Soviet Union*, pp. 58–59.
200. Ibid.; Cordovez and Harrison, p. 22.
201. Ibid., p. 17.
202. Bradsher, *Afghanistan and the Soviet Union*, p. 71, citing various sources. This is the estimate of Dupree, ' Red Flag Over the Hindu Kush, Part V: Repressions, or Security Through Terror Purges, I-IV,' AUFS/ A, 28, 3 (1980), p. 3. See also *New York Times*, 9 September 1979, p. 3. Ulyanovsky, whose estimate of several thousand members in the late 1960s has been cited above, and who claimed 'more than 60,000 members' in 1982, does not give an estimate for 1978; see his 'The Afghan Revolution,' in USSR Report, No. 1279, 20 July 1982, p. 18. Amin claimed in 1979 that there were 15,000 members before the coup.
203. Bradsher, *Afghanistan and the Soviet Union*, p. 60; "[a]t the same time there was *growing disillusionment* [authors' emphasis] in the Third World about the benefits of Soviet aid, growing recognition that it tended in the long run to reduce flexibility of the recipients' economies, tie them to the Soviet economy, and ultimately benefit Moscow."
204. According to Cordovez and Harrison, the principle mouthpiece for Moscow on Afghan affairs.
205. Male, p. 53.
206. Cordovez and Harrison, p. 18.
207. Ibid.
208. Ibid.
209. "Intelligence (International Relations)," *The New Encyclopaedia Britannica*, 15th ed. (Chicago: Encylopaedia Britannica, 1993): "Until the Soviet Union's dissolution in the early 1990s, the KGB resembled a combination of the American CIA, FBI and Secret Service."
210. "KGB," Wikipedia.org, http://en.wikipedia.org/wiki/KGB (accessed July 5, 2008).
211. An excellent tome on the transformation of German society from a community-based culture to one based on total security is Curt Riess, *Total Espionage* (G. P. Putnam's Sons, 1941).
212. "GRU," Wikipedia.org, http//:en.wikipedia.org/wiki/GRU (accessed July 21, 2008.
213. Ibid.
214. Cordevez and Harrison, p. 19.
215. Ibid.
216. See Poullada, *Afghanistan and the United States*, p. 70; State Department Web site, http://www.state.gov.
217. Administered through Columbia University Teachers College.
218. Cordovez and Harrison, p. 19.
219. Bradsher, *Afghanistan and the Soviet Union*, p. 59.
220. Ibid., p. 62.
221. Ibid., p. 58.
222. Ibid., p. 59.
223. The equipment installed was said to aid in the detection of earthquakes. It presumably could also detect rocket launches and underground explosions due to nuclear weapons testing.
224. Ghaus, p.179.
225. Ibid., p. 180.
226. Tim Weiner, *Blank Check: The Pentagon's Black Budget* (New York: Warner Books, 1990), p. 147. Following India's nuclear test in 1974, Zulfikar Ali Bhutto exemplified the crisis mentality driving Pakistan's determination to prevail in the almost constant war with its neighbors by declaring that,

"If India builds the bomb, we will eat grass or leaves—even go hungry—but we will get one of our own."

227. Bradsher, *Afghan Communism and Soviet Intervention,* p. 22, citing Louis Dupree, "The Marxist Regimes and the Soviet Presence in Afghanistan: An Ages-Old Culture Responds to Late Twentieth–Century Aggression," in M. Nazif Shahrani and Robert Canfield, eds., *Revolutions & Rebellions in Afghanistan: Anthropological Perspectives* (Berkeley, 1984), pp. 60-61.

CHAPTER 6—TEAM-B

1. Kaplan, p. 336.
2. See Kaplan's chapter on the development of Counterforce Doctrine at RAND during the 1950s, pp. 201–220.
3. Anne Hessing Cahn, *Killing Détente: The Right Attacks the CIA* (Pennsylvania State University Press, 1998), p. 15.
4. Ibid.; Fareed Zakaria, "Exaggerating the Threats," *Newsweek*, June 16, 2003.
5. See Robert Scheer, *With Enough Shovels: Reagan, Bush & Nuclear War* (New York: Random House, 1982).
6. Report of Team "B", Intelligence Community Experiment in Competative Analysis, p. 46, in "The Master of the Game": Paul H. Nitze and U.S. Cold War Strategy from Truman to Reagan, National Security Archive Electronic Briefing Book No. 139, by William Burr and Robert Wampler, posted October 24, 2004 (accessed July 21, 2008). http://www.gwu.edu/~nsarchiv/NSAEBB/NSAEBB139/nitze10.pdf
7. A tightly knit group of RAND analysts had "surreptitiously" aided the Kennedy campaign as an "Academic Advisory Group." Brought together by Daniel Ellsberg, "[t]he group was composed mostly of Harvard and MIT professors—among them Henry Kissinger, Arthur Schlesinger, John Kenneth Galbraith, Paul Samuelson, Archibald Cox . . . as well as such outsiders as Paul Nitze and General James Gavin." Kaplan, p. 249.
8. Ibid., p. 287.
9. Cited in Noam Chomsky, *Hegemony or Survival: America's Quest for Global Dominance* (New York: Macmillan, 2004), p. 83.
10. James Bamford, *Body of Secrets* (New York: Anchor Books, 2002), p. 82.
11. Ibid., p. 89.
12. Scheer, p. 77.
13. Team-B Report, p. 3.
14. Ibid., p. 46.
15. Scheer, p. 55, citing an article by Murrey Marde, *Washington Post*, January 2, 1977.
16. Michael Lind, "A Tragedy of Errors," *Nation*, February 23, 2004.
17. Burnham served as Trotsky's secretary for a time before joining the American OSS.
18. See James Burnham, *The Suicide of the West* (New York: John Day, 1964).
19. Fred Kaplan, "Paul Nitze: The Man Who Brought Us the Cold War," *Slate,* October 21, 2004.
20. See Cahn.
21. See Kaplan.
22. Scheer, p. 54
23. Hugh Sidey, "Parting Words from President Ford," *Time*, January 10, 1977.
24. Based on the Team-B report.
25. Anthony Sampson, *The Arms Bazaar* (New York: Viking Press, 1977), p. 259.
26. Cordovez and Harrison, p. 20.
27. Ibid.
28. Ibid., pp. 22–23.
29. Ibid., p. 21.
30. Ibid.

31. Ibid., pp. 21–22.
32. Male, p. 61; Cordovez and Harrison, p. 23.
33. Cordovez and Harrison, p. 23.
34. Bradsher, p. 73; "Taraki publicly charged Daoud's 'fascist and terrorist regime' with the killing," citing Kabul Radio, 12 May 1978, in Foreign Broadcast Information Service/Middle East, 15 May 1978, pp. S1-4.
35. Ghaus, pp. 194-195.
36. Ibid., p. 194.
37. Cordovez and Harrison, pp. 23–24.
38. Ibid.
39. Louis Dupree, Red Flag Over The Hindu Kush: Part II: The Accidental Coup Or Taraki in Blunderland, September 1, 1979, Institute of Current World Affairs, http;//www.icwa.org/txtArticles/LD-89.htm (accessed July 21, 2008).
40. Cordovez and Harrison, p. 24.
41. Bradsher, p. 75. Bradsher recounts the confusion surrounding the coup.
42. Ghaus, p. 200.
43. Bradsher, p. 76, citing Kabul Radio, 27 April 1978, in Foreign Broadcast Information Service/Middle East, 28 April 1978, p. s1, and May 1978, pp. s1-2; Telegram no 3234, U.S. Embassy, Kabul, 27 April 1978.
44. Cordovez and /Harrison, pp. 27–28.
45. Ibid., p. 28.
46. Over the next year and a half Amin would consolidate his power by assuming numerous official positions. He would be supported in Moscow in his efforts by the GRU.
47. The Coup in Afghanistan from INR William G. Bowdler, May 1, 1978 in "Afghanistan: The Making of U.S. Policy 1973–1990," Fiche 59 , item 00276.
48. Ibid.
49. Ibid.
50. Ibid.
51. Cordovez and Harrison, p. 6.
52. Cooley, pp. 25–26.
53. First Conversation with Afghan president, Kabul 3619, May 6, 1978 ("Afghanistan: The Making of U.S. Policy 1973–1990") Fiche 59, item 00278.
54. Ibid.
55. Department of State, Annual Policy Assessment February 27, 1978 ("Afghanistan: The Making of U.S. Policy 1973–1990") Fiche 56, item 00261.
56. First Conversation with Afghan president, Kabul 3619, May 6, 1978 ("Afghanistan: The Making of U.S. Policy 1973–1990") Fiche 59, 00278.
57. Raymond L. Garthoff, *Detente and Confrontation* (Washington, DC: Brookings Institution, 1985), p. 715.
58. Ibid., p. 704.
59. Ibid., pp. 701–702.
60. Authors' interview with Selig Harrison, February 1993.
61. Cordovez and Harrison, p. 33.
62. Authors' interview with Selig Harrison, February 1993.
63. Ibid.
64. Cordovez and Harrison, p. 33, citing Brzezinski's *Power and Principle*, p. 73.
65. Authors' interview with Selig Harrison, February 1993.
66. Bradsher, p. 87.
67. Dilip Ganguly, PRC-Trained Pakistanis Sent to Hit Afghan Troops, April 14, 1979, contained in *Foreign Broadcast Information Service* (FBIS) Daily Report, April 18, 1979, pp. S6-7.
68. Cooley, pp. 11, 72.

69. Ibid., p. 68.
70. Cooley, pp. 64–68.
71. Ibid., p. 24.
72. Ibid., pp. 25–28, 99.
73. Cahn, pp. 139–40, 147, 149, 150, 155, 156, 157, 177; Edward Jay Epstein, *Deception The Invisible War Between the KGB and the CIA* (New York: Simon and Schuster, 1989), p. 272; William R. Corson, Susan B. Trento, and Joseph Trento, *Widows: The Explosive Truth Behind 25 Years of Western Intelligence Disasters* (New York: Crown Publishers, 1989); Dick Russell, *The Man Who Knew Too Much* (New York: Caroll and Graf, 1992).
74. Cahn, p. 187.
75. Ibid.
76. "John Paisley," Spartacus Educational, http://www.spartacus.schoolnet.co.uk/JFKpaisley.htm (accessed July 5, 2008).
77. Ibid.
78. Ibid.
79. Russell.
80. Brian Crozier, *Free Agent: The Unseen War, 1941-1991* (New York: HarperCollins, 1993), p. 134.
81. Ibid., pp. 135–36.
82. Ibid.
83. Ibid.
84. Garthoff, p. 616.

CHAPTER 7—THE 1979 WINTER NIGHTMARE

1. On this date Shah Mohammed Reza Shah Pahlavi fled his country. "Shah Flees Iran, January 16, 1979," History.com, http://www.history.com/this-day-in-history.do?action=Article&id=6778 (accessed July 5, 2008).
2. Cordovez and Harrison, p. 34.
3. "The Crescent of Crisis," *Time*, January 1, 1979.
4. Coll, p. 48.
5. "Towards an International History of the War in Afghanistan, 1979-89," panel discussion, Woodrow Wilson Center for Scholars April 29, 2002, http://www.wilsoncenter.org/index.cfm?event_id=12594&fuseaction=topics.event_summary&topic_id=1409 (accessed July 5, 2008).
6. The esoteric significance of the number 117 has long been considered mystical. Signifying the relationship between law and grace, the room may have been chosen by the kidnappers to signal that the taking of the hostage represented the beginning of a universal judgment.
7. Department Press Briefing February 14, February 15, 1979 ("Afghanistan: The Making of U.S. Policy 1973–1990") Fiche 77, item 00375.
8. See Cordovez and Harrison, pp. 34–35. A great deal of confusion surrounded the assassination of Dubs. The cable traffic between Washington and Kabul reveals a struggle between those in government trying to get at the facts and those in Washington trying to exploit it to advance an anti-Soviet agenda. The Dubs assassination came at a pivotal moment in U.S.-Soviet relations and the direction of the U.S. government The subject remains sensitive and the motives for the hostage-taking and murder obscure, thirty years on.
9. Distribution of Information RE Terrorists 0281, February 16, 1979 ("Afghanistan: The Making of U.S. Policy 1973–1990") Fiche 85, item 00431.
10. "Death Behind a Keyhole," *Time,* February 26, 1979.
11. On February 19, six journalists, including Moreau, were granted an interview with Amin to discuss the Dubs killing and grilled Amin as to his association with Setam-i Melli. At that meeting Amin referred to the kidnappers as "intellectuals." The word Muslim does not appear in the U.S. cable describing the meeting.

12. *Newsweek*, February 26, 1979, p. 27.
13. Raymond Garthoff, *Détente and Confrontation*, revised ed. (Washington, DC: Brookings Institution, 1994), p. 1057.
14. Cordovez and Harrison, pp. 35–36
15. Authors' interview with Selig Harrison, February, 1993.
16. Alfred W. McCoy, *The Politics of Heroin* (Brooklyn, NY: Lawrence Hill Books, 1991), p. 451 .
17. "US, China, Pakistan Seen Behind Afghan Rightists," *Current Digest of the Soviet Press* 31, no. 15 (May 9, 1979).
18. Ibid.
19. The Afghan Left 11652, May 22, 1973, in FROM THE SECRET FILES ON KING ZAHIR'S REIGN IN AFGHANISTAN, 1970–1973, National Security Archive Electronic Briefing Book No. 59, edited by William Burr, October 26, 2001, p. 3; http://www.gwu.edu/~nsarchiv/NSAEBB/NSAEBB59/zahir13.pdf (accessed July 21, 2008).
20. Ibid.
21. Dreyfuss, p. 265.
22. Both Hazara and Tajik minorities found political expression in the two dominant Maoist parties, Sho'la-yi Jawed and Setam-i Melli, and were open to covert Chinese political influence. Setam-i Melli (*Against National Oppression*), a Tajik nationalist movment, was specifically opposed to Pashtun nationalism.
23. Legal for centuries, but dampened by twentieth-century social mores, the off-the-books political destabilization of South Asia revived a drug trade long suppressed by the nationalist governments of India, Afghanistan and Iran. Reported by a U.S. intelligence analysis for 1979 to have reached an output of four hundred tons of opium, that year Pakistan surpassed the "Golden Triangle" as the world's leader of opium production.
24. For an in-depth study of the massive, illicit, guns-for-drugs campaign, see Peter Truell and Larry Gurwin, *False Profits* (Boston: Houghton Mifflin, 1992) and Jonathan Beaty and S.C. Gwynne, *The Outlaw Bank* (Washington, DC: Beard Books, 2004).
25. "CIA Helped Afghan Mujahideen Before 1979 Soviet Intervention: Brzezinski." Agence France-Presse, January 13, 1998.
26. See Hassan Abbas, *Pakistan's Drift into Extremism* (M. E. Sharper, 2005), pp. 94–95.
27. Cordovez and Harrison, pp. 34–49.
28. Meeting with Soviet Diplomat part I of III – Observations on the Internal Afghan Political Scene, Kabul, 4088, June 25, 1979. ("Afghanistan: The Making of U.S. Policy 1973–1990") Fiche 105, item 00569.
29. Summary of growing opposition to Khalqoi regime, Kabul 6251, August 16, 1979 ("Afghanistan: The Making of U.S. Policy 1973–1990") Fiche 112, item 00615.
30. Ibid.
31. Cordovez and Harrison, p. 39.
32. Male, p. 173, citing Kuldip Nayar, *Report on Afghanistan* (New Delhi: Allied Publishers, 1981), p. 32.
33. Cordovez and Harrison, pp. 39–42.
34. Ibid., p. 41; Bradsher, p. 117. Bradsher, citing Telegrams nos. 7444 and 7784, U.S. Embassy , Kabul 11 and 30 October 1979, maintains that the Chinese ambassador was not invited. Harrison makes a point that their invitation was a "calculated affront to Moscow."
35. 'PRC Troop Movements on Afghan Border Reported," as reported by Moscow Radio Peace and Progress in English to Asia 1331 GMT 10 Sep 79, in *USSR International Affairs South Asia*, FBIS Daily Report September 14, 1979, p. D1.
36. "Painting the Red One Green," *Economist*, September 1, 1979.
37. "Support Afghan Resistance Movement," *Guardian*, February 20, 1980.
38. Former U.S. ambassador to Kabul (1966–73), senior associate at the Center For Strategic and International Studies (CSIS) Robert G. Neumann, *Washington Review of Strategic and International Studies,* July 1978.

39. An assessment of Soviet influence and involvement in Afghanistan, Kabul 6672 September 6, 1979, ("Afghanistan: The Making of U.S. Policy 1973–1990") Fiche 114. item 00633.
40. Mitrokhin Archive.
41. "Crescent of Crisis," *Time,* January 15, 1979.
42. Unnamed Afghan official now living in the United States.
43. Cordovez and Harrison, p. 43.
44. Ibid.
45. Authors' interview with Selig Harrison, February 1993.
46. Garthoff, *Détente and Confrontation*, revised ed., p. 1067. Garthoff rightly characterizes Carter's response as "obviously a gross overstatement."
47. Cordovez and Harrison, p. 49.
48. Cooley, p. 18.
49. "U.S. Faulted on Afghan Response," Reuters, September 21, 1995.
50. Ibid.
51. Federation of American Scientists, www.fas.org/nuke/control/salt2/index.html.
52. Authors' interview with Paul Warnke, February 1993.
53. Authors' interview, February 1993.
54. Senator Edward (Ted) Kennedy's challenge for the nomination revealed the ideological crisis inside the Democratic Party.
55. "Afghanistan: UN / USSR Impact," The *MacNeil/Lehrer Report* Library #1113, Show #5133, January 2, 1980.
56. Sovietology (or Kremlinology) involves the arcane study of key phrases and words in Soviet speeches and documents, a process which has evolved over time from Vladimir Soloviev's philosophy and the Symbolists' belief in the alchemical power of words. See Rosenthal, pp. 225–226 and Bradsher, *Afghanistan and Soviet Union*, p. 64.
57. "Afghanistan: UN / USSR Impact," The *MacNeil/Lehrer Report* Library #1113, Show #5133, January 2, 1980.
58. Garthoff, revised ed., p. 1084.
59. Garthoff, first edition, p. 956.
60. Ibid.
61. *Presidential Documents* 16 (January 14, 1980), p. 40; *Meet the Press*, January 20; Garthoff, p. 957.
62. Garthoff, p. 951.
63. Cordovez and Harrison, pp. 56–57.
64. Jonathan Beaty and S. C. Gwynne, *The Outlaw Bank: A Wild Ride into The Secret Heart of BCCI* (Washington, DC: Beard Books, 2004), p. 276.
65. Dreyfuss, p. 263.
66. As governor of the NWFP, General Fazle Haq would oversee the rapid growth of the heroin refining industry which would double to 575 tons from 1982 to 1983. A close friend of General Zia, General Haq, would accumulate a multi-billion-dollar fortune managing security for the operation.
67. Francis Fukuyama, *The Future of the Soviet Role in Afghanistan: A Trip Report*, Rand Notes, RAND Corporation, September 1980.
68. Bradsher, *Afghan Communism and Soviet Intervention*, p. 187.
69. Cordovez and Harrison, p. 187; Weiner, pp. 143–171. The terms "bleeders" and "dealers" would evolve as the definition for the struggle between Washington's protagonists in the early 80s.
70. Jay Peterzell, "The New Afghanistanism," *Columbia Journalism Review*, March/April 1981, p. 5.
71. This event gave us the opportunity to acquire exclusive permission to enter Kabul via diplomatic contacts at the United Nations one year later.
72. Alvin A. Snyder, *Warriors of Disinformation* (New York: Arcade Publishing, 1995), p. 205.
73. Jay Peterzell, "The New Afghanistanism," *Columbia Journalism Review*, March/April 1981, p. 5.
74. Ibid.

75. *Kabul New Times*; authors' discussions with Afghan diplomats at the United Nations. In 1987 we were told by an Afghan diplomat that Rather could come back with us to Afghanistan if we invited him. A short time later the country was again opened to the western press.
76. Ibid.
77. Ibid.
78. Peter Niesewand, "Peking's Finest Fuel a Holy War," *MacLean's*, April 30, 1979.
79. Adam K. East, "The Anglo-American Support Apparatus behind the Afghani Mujahideen," *Executive Intelligence Review*, October 13, 1995.
80. Bethell's obituary in the London *Times* September 11, 2007 reaffirmed his anti-Soviet/Russian credentials, stating, "He traveled repeatedly to the Soviet Union, and to Agfhanistan and Poland. . . . Bethell continued to defend the rights of critics of Russia's current regime, such as the media tycoon Vladimir Gusinsky and Alexander Litvinenko."
81. Authors' personal experience with Bukovsky on ABC's *Nightline*.
82. With the ARC housed in the law offices of John Train, monies raised by it flowed to Whitehead's CIA-connected IRC.
83. The Committee for a Free Afghanistan was a who's who of the iron triangle of corporate, congressional and Pentagon support for the mujahideen.
84. Interview with journalists in Kabul with personal knowledge of Hekmatyar, 2002.

CHAPTER 8—SUMMER 1980

1. With the "trapped" Soviets mired in an Afghan war, the Team-B report became a self-fulfilling prophecy.
2. Weiner, p. 60.
3. Jerome B. Wiesner, "The Old Arms Scare Again," *Boston Globe*, October 17, 1980.
4. Ibid.
5. "Confronting the Armor Gap," *Time,* January 21, 1980.
6. Robert Fisk, *Christian Science Monitor*, March 4, 1980.
7. "Afghanistan: UN / USSR Impact," The *MacNeil/Lehrer Report* Library #1113, Show #5133, January 2, 1980.

CHAPTER 9—THE REAGAN ERA

1. Donald L. Bartlett and James B. Steele, "The Oily Americans," *Time*, May 19, 2003.
2. Christopher Andrew and Oleg Gordievski, *Top Secret Files on KGB Foreign Operations* (Palo Alto, CA: Stanford University Press 1993), p. 15.
3. Garthoff, 1985, p. 1024. Garthoff explains that the American negotiating position was a ruse "tailored to be unacceptable to the Soviet Union." Andropov's offer of missile reductions, by nearly half, exposed the American ploy.
4. Authors' interview with Paul Warnke, February 1993.
5. *ABC Nightline*, May 26, 1983.
6. Robert M. Gates, *From the Shadows* (New York: Touchstone, 1997) p. 147, quoting from an "Eyes Only" memo sent from CIA director Stansfield Turner to President Carter on January 16, 1980.
7. Ted Koppel's introduction, *ABC Nightline*, May 26, 1983.
8. Dreyfuss, pp. 258–259.
9. Ibid., p. 132.
10. International Rescue Committee Inc., Annual Report, 1979.
11. James T. Fisher, *Dr. America: The Lives of Thomas A. Dooley, 1927–1961* (Amherst: University of Massachusetts Press, 1997), p. 93.
12. Ibid., pp. 93–94.
13. Leo Cherne, *The Business and Defense Coordinator* (New York: Research Institute of America, 1941).
14. *Research Institute of America Newsletter,* Fall 1941. See also Fisher, p. 94.

15. See Robert Scheer and Warren Hinckle, "The Vietnam Lobby," *Ramparts* July 1965; Fisher; Seth Jacobs, *The Cold War Mandarin: Ngo Dinh Diem and the Origins of America's War in Vietnam, 1950–1963* (Lanham, MD: Rowman & Littlefield, 2006); John Cooney, *The American Pope: The Life and Times of Francis Cardinal Spellman* (New York: Times Books, 1984), pp. 240–245.
16. Robert Scheer, *With Enough Shovels*, pp. 59–60.
17. Cordovez and Harrison, p. 102.
18. Ibid, p. 103.
19. Ibid.
20. Ibid.
21. Milt Bearden and James Risen, *The Main Enemy* (New York: Random House, 2003), pp. 276–277. According to Bearden, Wilson's assignment to the HPSCI was engineered from behind the scenes by Congressman Dick Cheney.
22. Kurt Lohbeck, *Holy War, Unholy Victory* (Washington, DC: Regnery Gateway, 1993), p. 205.
23. See George Crile, *Charlie Wilson's War* (New York: Atlantic Monthly Press, 2003), pp. 67–75.
24. Ibid., p. 338.
25. Ibid., p. 212.
26. Samira Goetschel interview with Milt Bearden, *Our Own Private Bin Laden*, Chaste Films, 2005.
27. Milt Bearden, "Meet the Pashtuns," *Counterpunch*, March 31, 2004.
28. The tribal areas of Pakistan and Afghanistan today account for over 90 percent of the world's heroin supply, which has increased every year following the events of September 11, 2001.
29. McCoy, p. 452.
30. Crile, p. 213.
31. The total amount supplied by the United States is a much-disputed figure. Some estimates run as high as eleven billion dollars, not counting the billions in unauthorized and undisclosed drug and weapons transfers.
32. Dreyfuss, p. 284.
33. Peter Schweizer, *Victory: The Reagan Administration's Secret Strategy That Hastened the Collapse of the Soviet Union* (New York: Atlantic Monthly Press, 1994), p. 177.
34. Bearden and Risen, p. 283
35. Ibid.
36. Weiner, p. 153.
37. Sarah E. Mendelson, *Changing Course: Ideas, Politics and the Soviet Withdrawal from Afghanistan* (Princeton, NJ: Princeton University Press, 1998), p. 74; Cordovez and Harrison, pp. 96–97.
38. Ibid., p. 74n.
39. Cordovez and Harrison, pp. 97–102.
40. Ibid., p. 102, citing a personal interview with Nikolai Shishlin, a longtime Gorbachev advisor.
41. Ibid., p. 175.
42. "Big Soviet Drive in Afghanistan Reflects Tougher Chernenko Line," *Christian Science Monitor*, May 10, 1984.
43. Gates, p. 200.
44. "Wild Bill Donovan" and such men as Joseph Kennedy and J. Peter Grace were members of a rival Catholic knighthood known as the Knights of Malta.
45. Jonathan Kwitny, *Man of the Century: The Life and Times of Pope John Paul II* (New York: H. Holt, 1997), p. 334.
46. *The Oath Against Modernism, Given by His Holiness St. Pius X September 1, 1910*, Papal Encyclicals online; http://www.papalencyclicals.net/Pius10/p10moath.htm (accessed July 8, 2008).
47 See Raymond B. Marcin, *The Oath Against Modernism and the Spirit of Vatican II*, Ecclesia Militans: The Church Militant, http://www.geocities.com/militantis/oathvatican2.html (accessed July 8, 2008).
48 Kwitney, pp. 331–332.
49 Ibid., p. 332.

50 Coll, p. 98.
51 Ibid., p. 128.
52 Scheer, p.77.
53 Samira Goetschel interview with Peter Truell, in *Our Own Private Bin Laden.*
54 Cooley, pp. 126–127.
55 Crozier, p. 136.
56 Truell and Gurwin, p. 159.
57 Ibid., pp. 19, 132–133, 139, 289, 311.
58 Cooley, p.115.
59 Beaty and Gwynne, p. 346.
60 Samira Goetschel interview with Jack Blum, in *Our Own Private Bin Laden.*
61. Ibid.

CHAPTER 10—MOSCOW'S NEW REGIME

1. Gorbachev's failed attempt to reform the communist system was referred to as *perestroika* (restructuring).
2. Cordovez and Harrison, p. 182.
3. Ibid., p. 208.
4. Ibid., pp. 379–380.
5. Ibid., p. 226.
6. Bernice Glatzer Rosenthal, Introduction to *The Occult in Russian and Soviet Culture* (Ithaca, NY: Cornell University Press, 1997), p. 29.
7. Ellen Propper Mickiewics, *Changing Channels: Television and the Struggle For Power in Russia* (Durham, NC: Duke University Press, 1999), p. 57.
8. Gates, p. 431.
9. Cordovez and Harrison, p. 265.
10. Bearden and Risen, pp. 339–343.
11. Ibid., p. 346.
12. Ibid., p. 342 .
13. Coll, p. 180.
14. Crile, p. 504.
15. Alvin A. Snyder, *Warriors of Disinformation*, p. 204.
16. Ibid.
17. Ibid.
18. Ibid., p. 73
19. Alvin A. Snyder, "Flight 007: The Rest of the Story," *Washington Post*, September 1, 1996.
20. Snyder, *Warriors of Disinformation*, p. 204.
21. Wick, originally named Zwick, was a Hollywood agent, writer, and producer whose credits included the infamous 1961 box office flop *Snow White and the Three Stooges.*
22. Snyder, *Warriors of Disinformation*, p. 204
23. Ibid., p. 206.
24. Bearden and Risen, p. 353.
25. Kurt Lohbeck, a stringer for CBS News, reports in his book *Holy War, Unholy Victory* (p. 266) that he witnessed "a jeep carrying three American intelligence agents—the first time ever, to my knowledge, inside Afghanistan. Their jeep was leaving the only position occupied by Gulbaddin's forces."
26. Bradsher, *Afghan Communism and Soviet Intervention*, p. 346.
27. Gates, p. 432.
28. Ibid., p. 239.

CHAPTER 11—A NEW DECADE: A NEW AND MORE DANGEROUS AFGHANISTAN

1. Barnett R. Rubin, "The Situation in Afghanistan," testimony before the Committee on Security and Cooperation in Europe, U.S. Congress, May 3, 1990. ("Afghanistan: The Making of U.S. Policy 1973–1990,") Fiche 420, item 02313.
2. Ibid.
3. Ibid.
4. Azadi Afghan Radio interview with Ambassador Peter Tomsen, June 7, 1999.
5. Coll, p. 209; Tomsen's pleas, like those of many Americans close to the war, have been consistently ignored by U.S. neoconservative-dominated policy makers.
6. Lohbeck, p. 273.
7. Cordovez and Harrison, p. 386.
8. Ibid.
9. Bradsher, *Afghan Communism and Soviet Intervention*, p. 369
10. Ibid., p. 372.
11. Philip Corwin, *Doomed in Afghanistan: A UN Officer's Memoir* (New Brunswick, NJ: Rutgers University Press, 2003), p. 70.
12. Coll, p. 234.
13. Ibid., p. 235.
14. Ibid.
15. Cordovez and Harrison, p. 386.
16. Coll, pp. 234–237.
17. Ibid.
18. John McMahon's warning to CIA Director William Casey about the absence of policy surrounding the mujahideen buildup of the '80s.
19. Coll p. 239 citing Tomsen memos, "Afghanistan—U.S. Interests and U.S. Aid," December 18, 1992, excised and declassified April 4, 2000, author's files; and "Central Asia, Afghanistan and U.S. Policy," February 2, 1993, excised and declassified March 23, 2000, author's files.
20. See Coll, pp. 265–300.
21. Nick Cullather, "Damming Afghanistan: Modernization in a Buffer State," in *History and September 11*, ed. Joanne Meyerowitz (Philadelphia: Temple University Press, 2003), p. 25; Arif Hussain, *Pakistan: Its Ideology and Foreign Policy* (London: Routledge, 1966), p. 115.
22. Tim Weiner, "Nuclear Anxiety: The Know-How: U.S. and China Helped Pakistan Build its Bomb," *New York Times*, June 1, 1998.
23. Ibid.
24. Ibid.
25. Robert L. Borosage, "How Bush Kept the Guns," *Rolling Stone*, February 21, 1991.
26. Ibid.
27. David Nyhan, "An Old Enemy Collapses And Another Is Found," *Boston Globe*, December 6, 1990.
28. Ibid.
29. "Tomdispatch Interview: Bacevich, the Arrogance of American Power," May 25, 2006, http://tomdispatch.org/post/85882/tomdispatch_interview_bacevich_the_arrogance_of_american_power (accessed July 9, 2008).
30. Ibid.
31. "'Prevent the Reemergence of a New Rival': The Making of the Cheney Regional Defense Strategy, 1991–1992," The Nuclear Vault, http://www.gwu.edu/~nsarchiv/nukevault/ebb245/index.htm (accessed July 9, 2008).
32. "Aspin Sees Fewer Trims in Defense," *Los Angeles Times*, February 12, 1993.
33. "Soviet Economy: Assessment of How Well the CIA Has Estimated the Size of the Economy, September 30, 1991," U.S. General Accounting Office, http://archive.gao.gov/d18t9/145131.pdf (accessed July 9, 2008).

34. Cahn, p. 191.
35. James Bamford, *A Pretext for War*, pp. 95–100.
36. Ibid.
37. Thomas W. Lippman, "Aid to Afghan Rebels Returns to Haunt U.S.," *Washington Post*, July 26, 1993.
38. "Afghans Decline to Return US Stingers," Associated Press, August 20, 1993.
39. Ahmed Rashid, *Taliban: Militant Islam, Oil and Fundamentalism in Central Asia* (New Haven: Yale University Press 2000), p. 27. Rashid maintains that Pakistan assisted a Taliban attack on Hekmatyar's garrison in October 1994.

CHAPTER 12—1995–2001: THE TALIBAN

1. Coll, p. 114. Babar had been an early sponsor of Hekmatyar and Massoud, arming and assisting them from 1973.
2. Ibid., p. 291.
3. Ibid., p. 295.
4. Ibid., p. 145.
5. Ibid., p. 143.
6. Cooley, p. 145.
7. Rashid, pp. 186–187.
8. Samira Goetschel interview with Benazir Bhutto, *Our Own Private Bin Laden*, Chaste Films, 2005.
9. Coll, p. 306.
10. Samira Goetschel interview with Benazir Bhutto, *Our Own Private Bin Laden*, 2005.
11. Rashid, p. 176.
12. Ibid., p. 177.
13. Cooley, p. 144.
14. Coll, p. 299.
15. Authors' conversations with Afghan exiles, 1997.
16. *9/11 Commission Report*, National Commission on Terrorist Acts Against the United States, Chapter 2, p. 64 (http://govinfo.library.unt.edu/911/report/index.htm).
17. Samira Goetschel interview with Milt Bearden.
18. Seumas Milne, "Special Report: They Can't See Why They are Hated: Americans Can't Ignore What Their Government Does Abroad," *Guardian*, September 13, 2001.
19. "Taleban Take Kabul, Chase Afghan Force," *Reuters*, September 28, 1996.
20. "The Taliban File Part III, Pakistan provided Millions of Dollars, Arms and 'Buses Full of Adolescent Mujahid,' to the Taliban in the 1990's," National Security Archive, http://www.gwu.edu/~nsarchiv/NSAEBB/NSAEBB97/index4.htm (accessed July 9, 2008).
21. "Islama 00436, U.S. Embassy (Islamabad) Cable, 'Scenesetter for Your Visit to Islamabad: Afghan Angle,' January 16, 1997," National Security Archive, http://www.gwu.edu/~nsarchiv/NSAEBB/NSAEBB227/index.htm (accessed July 9, 2008).
22. Ibid.
23. Ibid.
24. "Islama 01873, U.S. Embassy (Islamabad) Cable, 'Official Informal for SA Assistant Secretary Robin Raphel and SA/PAB,' March 10, 1997," National Security Archive, http://www.gwu.edu/~nsarchiv/NSAEBB/NSAEBB227/index.htm (accessed July 9, 2008).
25. Coll, p. 311.
26. Ibid., p. 329, citing a declassified cable released by the National Security Archive and interviews with Massoud's aides.
27. Ibid., p. 330.
28. Ibid., p. 306.
29. Ibid., p. 338.

30. Rashid, p. 179, citing an American diplomat in 1997.
31. Cooley, p. 167.
32. News clippings from authors' files.
33. Associated Press, December 14, 1997.
34. Ibid.
35. Coll, p. 364.
36. Ibid., pp. 362–363.
37. "Afghanistan Pipeline Angers Women," *Boston Globe*, January 18, 1998; authors' interview with Eleanor Smeal, 1999.
38. Coll, p. 364.
39. Authors' interview, fall 1999.
40. "Afghanistan Pipeline Angers Women," *Boston Globe*, January 18, 1998.
41. Dana Priest, "U.S. Military Trains Foreign Troops," *Washington Post*, July 12, 1998.
42. Ibid.
43. Ibid.
44. Ibid.
45. GlobalSecurity.org, http://www.globalsecurity.org/security/ops98emb.htm.
46. Scott Macleod, "The Paladin of Jihad," *Time*, May 6, 1996; "Terrorist Most Wanted," *Newsweek*, August 24, 1998.
47. Fatwa issued in *Al-Quds al-Arabi*, an Arabic newspaper published in London on February 23, 1998.
48. On August 20, 1998, Clinton ordered a cruise missile attack on bin Laden's Afghan training camps.
49. Jamal Ismail, "I Am Not Afraid of Death", *Newsweek*, January 11, 1999, p. 36.
50. "The Arming of Saudi Arabia," PBS Frontline Show #1112 Air Date: February 16, 1993. Bin Laden Brothers Construction, now known as SBG, was sued following the events of 9/11 for its association with Osama bin Laden. See http://www.arabianbusiness.com/499165-binladin-group-files-defense-papers-in-911-suit?ln=en.
51. Tim Weiner, "Afghan Camps, Hidden in Hills, Stymied Soviet Attacks for Years," *New York Times*, August 24, 1998. Cooley, p. 223.
52. Tim Weiner, "Afghan Camps, Hidden in Hills, Stymied Soviet Attacks for Years," *New York Times*, August 24, 1998.
53. Associated Press, February 15, 1999.
54. Ibid.
55. Ibid.
56. Ibid.
57. Ibid.
58. Interviews with Afghan exiles. See Human Rights Watch, www.hrw.org/backgrounder/asia/afghan-bck1023.htm. Dostum had fled Afghanistan for Turkey in 1997 following the defection of one of his deputies. He returned weeks later and rallied his forces, but frequently returned to Turkey for aid. Owen Mathews, "Afghanistan: Another Kind of War," *Men's Journal*, August 1998
59. Cooley, p. 167.
60. Cary Gladstone, *Afghanistan Revisited* (Huntington, NY: Nova Publishers, 2001), p. 46.
61. Jamal Ismail, "I Am Not Afraid of Death," *Newsweek*, January 11, 1999.
62. Gary Young, "Bin Laden Allegedly Planned to Kill Clinton," *Guardian.co.uk*, Aug. 26, 1998. (accessed July 18, 2008)
63. Cooley, p. 145.
64. Gary Berntsen and Ralph Pezzullo, *Jawbreaker: The Attack on Bin Laden and Al Qaeda: A Personal Account by the CIA's Key Field Commander* (New York: Crown Publishers, 2005).
65. Steve Coll, "Ahmad Shah Massoud Links with CIA," *Washington Post*, February 23, 2004.
66. "U.S. Policy in Afghanistan: Challenges and Solutions," Afghanistan Foundation, July 12, 1999, http://www.bibliotecapleyades.net/sociopolitica/elite/afghanistan_foundation/foundation_Whitepaper2.htm (accessed July 9, 2008).

67. Ibid.
68. Ibid.
69. Anthony Davis, "One Man's Holy War," *AsiaWeek*, week of August 6, 1999.
70. Ibid.
71. Julian Borger, "US Documents Show Pakistan Gave Taliban Military Aid," *Guardian*, August 16, 2007.
72. Omar Samad interview with Ambassador Peter Tomsen, Azadi Afghan Radio, June 5, 1999 (transcript from authors' files).
73. Andrew Buncombe, "Millionaire Brothers Who Bankrolled the Rebels," *The Independent*, November 3, 2001.
74. Coll, p. 445.
75. Ibid., p. 285.
76. Ibid., p. 522.
77. Ibid.
78. Ibid., pp. 537, 538, 543, 556.
79. Ibid., p. 537.
80. Ibid., p. 461.
81. Ibid., p. 536.
82. Peter Tomsen, "Untying the Afghan Knot," *Fletcher Forum of World Affairs* 25 no. 1 (Winter 2001), http://fletcher.tufts.edu/forum/archives/pdf/25-1pdfs/tomsen.pdf (accessed July 9, 2008).

CHAPTER 13—COUNTDOWN TO 9/11

1. Coll, p. 554.
2. *9/11 Commission Report*, National Commission on Terrorist Acts Against the United States, Chapter 6.3, (http://govinfo.library.unt.edu/911/report/index.htm).
3. Interviews with Afghan exiles.
4. Ibid.
5. Ibid.
6. Ibid., p. 564.
7. Anthony Lewis, "The Feeling of a Coup," *New York Times*, March 31, 2001.
8. Interviews with Afghan exiles, fall 1999.
9. Pepe Escobar, "9-11 and the Smoking Gun, Part 2: A Real Smoking Gun," *Asia Times Online*, April 8, 2004.
10. Ibid.
11. Ibid.
12. Ibid.
13. Pervez Musharraf, *In the Line of Fire: A Memoir* (New York: Free Press, 2006).
14. Abid Ullah Jan, *From BCCI to ISI: The Saga of Entrapment Continues* (Ottawa: Pragmatic Publishing, 2006), pp. 156–157.
15. 1992 Draft Defense Planning Guidance (DPG) excerpt, Nuclear Vault, http://www.gwu.edu/~nsarchiv/nuclearvault/ebb245/doc03_extract_nytedit.pdf (accessed July 10, 2008).
16. CBS News correspondent and daughter of Carter national security advisor Zbigniew Brzezinski.
17. "The Battle for Afghanistan," CBS, July 9, 1987.
18. See "Biased Afghan Coverage at CBS," *Extra!*, October/November 1989, www.fair.org/extra/8910/cbs-afghan.html (accessed July 9, 2008) for Janet Wilson, *New York Post*, September 27, 1989
19. Ibid.
20. Arnaud De Borchgrave, interview with General Hamid Gul, United Press International, September 26, 2001.
21. Ibid.

22. Barbara Slavin and Jonathan Weisman, "Taliban Foe's Death Sparks Criticism of U.S. Goals," *USA Today*, October 31, 2001.
23. Stephen Kinzer, "A Nation Challenged: The Opposition: Brothers Act Behind the Scenes to Build Taliban Alternative," *New York Times*, November 1, 2001.
24. See Coll, pp. 101, 167, 206.
25. Barbara Slavin and Jonathan Weisman, "Taliban Foe's Death Sparks Criticism of U.S. Goals," *USA Today*, October 31, 2001.
26. Marc Kaufman and Robert E. Pierre, "Rich Brothers' Mission to Save Afghanistan Stirs Suspicion," Washington Post Service, November 9, 2001.
27. Ibid.

CHAPTER 14—KABUL, OCTOBER 7, 2001

1. Interviews in Kabul, October 2002.
2. Agreement On Provisional Arrangements in Afghanistan Pending the Re-Establishment of Permanent Government Institutions, http://www.afghangovernment.com/AfghanAgreementBonn.htm. (accessed July 20, 2008).
3. Toby Helm, "'We Want to Leave the Middle Ages,'" *Telegraph*, November 28, 2001.
4. The Marxist coup of 1978, known as the Saur or April Revolution by the PDPD—People's Democratic Party of Afghanistan.
5. Amar C. Bakshi, "Ahmed Rashid: Bush Didn't Listen," Post Global, August 17, 2007, http://newsweek.washingtonpost.com/postglobal/america/2007/08/ahmed_rashid_bush_pakistan.html#more (accessed July 10, 2008).
6. Ann Jones, "Why It's Not Working in Afghanistan," TomDispatch.com, August 27, 2006, http://www.tomdispatch.com/post/116512/ann_jones_on_the_road_to_taliban_land (accessed July 10, 2008).
7. Coversation with Afghan-American engineer, spring 2002.
8. Ann Jones, "Why It's Not Working in Afghanistan," TomDispatch.com, August 27, 2006, http://www.tomdispatch.com/post/116512/ann_jones_on_the_road_to_taliban_land (accessed July 10, 2008).
9. Karzai's U.S. Army bodyguards were later replaced by the private security firm DynCorp.

CHAPTER 15—AFGHANISTAN REDUX

1. 1992 Draft Defense Planning Guidance (DPG) excerpt, Nuclear Vault, http://www.gwu.edu/~nsarchiv/nuclearvault/ebb245/doc03_extract_nytedit.pdf (accessed July 10, 2008).
2. F. William Engdahl, "The US's Geopolitical Nightmare," *Asia Times*, May 8, 2006.
3. Mark Tran, "The Self Interest of National Security," *Guardian*, September 20, 2002.
4. Anthony Lewis, "Abroad at Home; Wake Up America," *New York Times*, November 30, 2001.
5. Interview with Michael Springman, BBC *Newsnight*, November 6, 2001.
6. Peter Dale Scott, "Why Is the US Letting Afghan Drug Production Resume?" http://socrates.berkeley.edu/~pdscott/qdimu.html (accessed July 10, 2008), citing the *Financial Times*, February 2002
7. *Annual Report 98-1199 For the Year 1984*, U.S. House of Representatives Select Committee on Narcotics Abuse and Control, p. 32.
8. Jonathan Beaty and S. C. Gwynne, *The Outlaw Bank: A Wild Ride into The Secret Heart of BCCI* (Washington, DC: Beard Books, 2004), p. 306.
9. Interview with the authors in Kabul, 2002.
10. Ibid.
11. Conversations with American journalists, Kabul, October 2002.
12. Interview with the authors in Kabul, 2002.
13. *Crosslines Global Report*, September 15, 2002.

14. Ibid.
15. Authors' interview with Chris Hondros of Getty Images, Kabul 2002.
16. Authors' interview with Steve Komarow, *USA Today*, Kabul 2002.
17. Ibid.
18. Ben Fenton, "General Warns of Unwinnable Guerrilla War," *Telegraph*, March 22, 2002.
19. Gates, p. 433.
20. Mahmood Karzai, Hamed Wardak and Jack Kemp, "Winning the Other War," *Washington Post*, April 7, 2003.
21. Ibid.
22. April Witt, "Afghan Political Violence on the Rise," *Washington Post*, August 3, 2003.
23. Robyn Dixon, "Afghans on Edge of Chaos," *Los Angeles Times*, August 4, 2003.
24. Jonathan Steele, "Red Kabul Revisited," *Guardian*, November 13, 2003.
25. Ibid.
26. Owais Tohid, "Pakistani Nuclear Scientist Confesses to Sharing Secrets," *Christian Science Monitor*, February 2, 2004.
27. Michael Janofsky, "Security Efforts Turning the Capital Into an Armed Camp," *New York Times*, February 22, 2004.
28. Michael Meacher, "The Pakistan Connection," *Guardian*, July 22, 2004.
29. Ibid.
30. Amy Davidson, "Bush's Afganistan Problem," *New Yorker Online,* April 12, 2004. Interview with Seymour Hersh.
31. Ibid.
32. Ibid.
33. Ibid.
34. Médecins sans Frontières (http://www.msf.org) had operated out of Afghanistan throughout the Soviet occupation and the brutal civil war.
35. Paul Kennedy, "For Whom the Bell Tolls," *Guardian*, August 6, 2004.
36. Carlotta Gall, "A Hoard of Gold That Was Quietly Saved; 2000-Year-Old Heritage Narrowly Escaped the Taliban," *New York Times*, June 24, 2004.
37. Ibid.
38. Nick Meo, "Afghanistan Wants Its 'Dead Sea Scrolls of Buddhism' Back from UK," *Independent*, November 12, 2004.
39. "Musharraf: Look to Terrorism Roots," CNN.com, December 6, 2004.
40. Ibid.
41. Eric Schmitt, 'The Reach of War: Drug Eradication; Afghans' Gains Face Big Threat In Drug Traffic," *New York Times*, December 11, 2004.
42. Ron Suskind, "Faith, Certainty and the Presidency of George W. Bush," *New York Times Magazine*, October 17, 2004.
43. "Outsider forged Cold War Strategy," *Washington Post*, March 18, 2005.
44. Ibid.
45. Robin Cook, "The Struggle against Terrorism Cannot Be Won by Military Means," *Guardian*, July 8, 2005.
46. Ibid.
47. Gaby Hinsliff, Mark Townsend and Martin Bentham, "Robin Cook Dies After Collapse on Mountain," *Guardian/Observer,* August 7, 2005.
48. Carlotta Gall, 'Mood of Anxiety Engulfs Afghans as Violence Rises," *New York Times*, June 30, 2005.
49. Eric Schmitt and Tom Shanker, "Washington Recasts War as 'Struggle,'" *International Herald Tribune*, July 27, 2005.
50. "God Told Me to Invade Iraq, Bush tells Palestinian Ministers," BBC, http://www.bbc.co.uk/pressoffice/pressreleases/stories/2005/10_october/06/bush.shtml (accessed July 10, 2008).

51. In Briefing to Security Council, Secretary-General's Representative Reports Continuing, Intensifying Violence in Southern Afghanistan, http://www.unis.unvienna.org/unis/pressrels/2006/sc8610.html, (accessed July 20, 2008).
52. Tom Coghlan, "Mass Grave Haunts the Afghan Election," *Telegraph*, October 8, 2005.
53. Sidney Blumenthal, "Democracy Was Only an Afterthought," *Guardian*, July 25, 2005.
54. Simon Tisdall and Ewen MacAskill, "America's Long War," *Guardian*, February 15, 2006.
55. Paul Krugman, "The Treason Card," *New York Times*, July 7, 2006.
56. Isambard Wilkinson, "Kabul Erupts into Violence over an Accident," *Telegraph*, May 30, 2006.
57. Sebastian Rotella, "War on the West Shifts Back to Afghanistan," *Los Angeles Times*, October 25, 2006.
58. Used during the Iran revolution to describe the United States, the term now applies in general throughout the Islamic world as a metaphor for American imperialism.
59. Sebastian Rotella, "War on the West Shifts Back to Afghanistan," *Los Angeles Times*, October 25, 2006.
60. Declan Walsh, "Pakistani Taliban Gaining Strength," *SFGate.com* Monday, April 3, 2006, http://www.sfgate.com/c/a/2006/04/03/MNGN8I2DKL1.DTL (accessed July 10, 2008).
61. Ibid.
62. News clipping from authors' files.
63. Laura K. Donohue, "Battlefield: U.S. Pentagon Spies Are Treating the Homeland Like a War Zone," *Los Angeles Times*, May 18, 2006.
64. Ibid.
65. Ann Jones, "Ann Jones on Bush's Poppy Wars in Afghanistan," *TomDispatch.co*m, October 29, 2006.
66. David Corn, "Who's Running Afghan Policy?" *Nation*, October 30, 2006.
67. Ibid.
68. "Wrong War, Wrong Time," *International Herald Tribune*, February 6, 2007.
69. Peter Bergen, "Waltzing with Warlords," *Nation*, January 1, 2007.
70. Ibid.
71. Ibid.
72. Isambard Wilkinson, "Islamist Militants Claim Vaccines are U.S. Plot," *Telegraph*, February 17, 2007.
73. Mark Mazzetti and David Rohde, 'Terror Officials See Al Qaeda Chiefs Regaining Power," *New York Times*, February 19, 2007.
74. Matthias Gebauer, 'Not a Good Omen for Afghanistan," *Der Spiegel*, February 27, 2007.
75. Syed Shoaib Hassan, "Profile: Islamabad's Red Mosque," BBC News, July 27, 2007.
76. "Obituary: Ex-king Zahir Shah," BBC News, July 23, 2007.
77. The last member of the two-hundred-year-old Pashtun dynasty to rule as king, Zahir Shah was deposed in 1973 by his cousin Mohammed Daoud and Communist Babrak Karmal.
78. David S. Cloud, "U.S. Set to Offer Huge Arms Deal to Saudi Arabia," *New York Times*, July 28, 2007.
79. Craig Murray, "Britain is Protecting the Biggest Heroin Crop of All Time," *Daily Mail*, July 21, 2007.
80. Selig Harrison, "Simmering Discord in the Tribal Badlands," *Boston Globe*, August 1, 2007.

CHAPTER 16—AFGHANISTAN AND THE REGION

1. The Constitution of Afghanistan, 1963, http://www.constitution.org/cons/afghan/const1963.htm (accessed July 10, 2008).
2. The Constitution of Afghanistan, 1976, http://www.constitution.org/cons/afghan/const1976.htm (accessed July 10, 2008).
3. "Tenet Failed to Prepare for al-Qaeda Threat," *Washington Post*, August 21, 2007.
4. Ibid.

5. Dreyfuss, p. 291
6. Camelia Fard and James Ridgeway, "The Accidental Operative," *Village Voice*, June 12, 2001.
7. Correspondence with the authors, 2006.
8. M. K. Bhadrakumar, "Deep Flaws in Afghan Peace Drive," *Asia Times*, September 14, 2007.
9. Ibid.
10. Ibid.
11. "Ann Jones on the Nightmare of Afghan Women," TomDispatch.com, February 5, 2007, http://www.tomdispatch.com/post/163092/ann_jones_on_the_nightmare_of_afghan_women (accessed July 10, 2008).
12. Sima Wali, "West Point Remarks," (unpublished), March 2, 2006.
13. Ahmed Rashid, "Bush Didn't Listen," *Washington Post*, August 17, 2007.
14. Ibid.
15. James Rupert, "Afghanistan Has Slipped Backward into a Political 'Danger Zone,'" *RAWA News*, September 9, 2007, http://www.rawa.org/temp/runews/2007/09/09/afghanistan-has-slipped-backward-into-a-political-danger-zone.html (accessed July 10, 2008).
16. Selig Harrison, "Simmering Discord in the Tribal Badlands," *Boston Globe*, August 1, 2007.
17. Ibid.
18. Conversation with the authors, September 2007.
19. Arthur Kent, "The Canadian Forces in Afghanistan Have Been Left Exposed," Student Operated Press, November 11, 2007, http://thesop.org/index.php?article=8256 (accessed July 10, 2008).
20. Ibid.
21. Eric Schmitt and Thom Shanker, "U.S. Adapts Cold-War Idea to Fight Terrorists," *New York Times*, March 18, 2008.
22. Ibid.
23. Correspondence with Afghan-Americans.
24. Kaplan, p. 10.
25. Ian Traynor, "Pre-emptive Nuclear Strike a Key Option, NATO Told," *Guardian*, January 22, 2008.
26. Gen. John Shalikashvili, former chairman of the U.S. joint chiefs of staff and NATO's former supreme commander; Gen. Klaus Naumann, Germany's former top soldier and ex-chairman of NATO's military committee; General Hank van den Breeman, former Dutch chief of staff; Admiral Jacques Lanxade, former French chief of staff; and Lord Inge, field marshal and former chief of the general staff in the UK.
27. Ian Traynor, "Pre-emptive Nuclear Strike a Key Option, NATO Told," *Guardian*, January 22, 2008.
28. Kathy Gannon, "Arab Militants Join Fight in Afghanistan," *Boston Globe*, June 24, 2007.
29. Interview with the authors, September 2007.
30. Ibid.
31. Ibid.
32. Selig Harrison, "Simmering Discord in the Tribal Badlands," *Boston Globe*, August 1, 2007.
33. Ibid.
34. Craig Murray, "Britain is Protecting the Biggest Heroin Crop of All Time," *Daily Mail*, July 21, 2007.
35. Ibid.
36. Ibid.
37. M. K. Bhadrakumar, "Deep Flaws in Afghan Peace Drive," *Asia Times*, September 14, 2007.
38. Vladimir Socor, "CIS Collective Security Treaty Organization Holds Summit," *Eurasia Daily Monitor* June 24, 2005, http://jamestown.org/edm/article.php?volume_id=407&issue_id=3380&article_id=2369935 (accessed July 10, 2008).
39. Ibid.
40. M. K. Bhadrakumar, "Deep Flaws in Afghan Peace Drive," *Asia Times*, September 14, 2007.

CHAPTER 17—GEOPOLITICAL REALITIES VS. OSAMA BIN LADEN, SUPERSTAR

1. "The Good War, Still to Be Won," editorial, *New York Times*, August 20, 2007.
2. Greg Miller, "Pakistan Backs Off Al Qaeda Pursuit," *Los Angeles Times* September 23, 2007
3. James Rupert, "Afghanistan Has Slipped Backward into a Political 'Danger Zone,'" *RAWA News*, September 9, 2007, http://www.rawa.org/temp/runews/2007/09/09/afghanistan-has-slipped-backward-into-a-political-danger-zone.html (accessed July 10, 2008).
4. Ibid.
5. Ahmed Rashid, "A Distraction from Washington's Grand Design," *Telegraph*, September 11, 2007.
6. Ismail Khan, "Missile Attack, Possibly by NATO, Kills 8 in Pakistan," *New York Times*, February 29, 2008 (this article cites a little known Al Qaeda associated group from Turkmenistan "working under the name Abu Hamza.") According to the U.S. Department of State Web site http://travel.state.gov/travel/cis_pa_tw/cis/cis_1047.html, the country-specific information for Turkmenistan warns, "Supporters of extremist groups such as the Islamic Movement of Uzbekistan, Al-Qaeda, and the Eastern Turkistan Islamic Movement . . . may attempt to target U.S. Government or private interests in the region, including Turkmenistan. The CIA's World Fact book designates Turkmenistan as a "transit country for Afghan narcotics bound for Russia and Western European markets, transit point for heroin precurser chemicals bound for Afghanistan." www.cis.gov/library/publications/the-world-factbook/geos/tx.html
7. Ahmed Rashid, "A Distraction from Washington's Grand Design," *Telegraph*, September 11, 2007.
8. Joseph R. Biden, "Senate Committee On Foreign Relations Holds A Hearing On Afghanistan," January 31, 2008. Political/Congressional Transcript Wire, Congressional Quarterly Inc., February 1, 2008.
9. Ibid.
10. Ibid.
11. Jonathan S. Landy, "Insurgencies Spread in Afghanistan and Pakistan," McClatchy Newspapers, February 3, 2008.
12. Declan Walsh, "Bhutto Loyalist is Named Pakistan Prime Minister," *Guardian,* March 24, 2008.
13. Graham Allison, "Reading the Tea leaves in Pakistan," *Boston Globe,* February 21, 2008.
14. Ibid.
15. Declan Walsh, "Pakistani Military 'Misspent up to 70% of American Aid," *Guardian,* February 28, 2008.
16. C. J. Chivers, "Supplier Under Scrutiny on Arms for Afghans," *New York Times*, March 27, 2008.
17. M. K. Bhadrakumar, "Intrigue Takes Afghanistan to the Brink," *Asia Times*, February 6, 2008.
18. Ibid.
19. Thom Shanker, "Gates Says Anger Over Iraq Hurts Afghan Effort," *New York Times*, February 9, 2008.
20. Editorial, "Gates, Truth and Afghanistan," *New York Times*, February 12, 2008.
21. Ashraf Khan, "Envoy to Pakistan: US Won't Meddle in Politics," Associated Press, March 28, 2008.
22. Robin Wright and Joby Warrick, "U.S. Steps Up Unilateral Strikes in Pakistan," *Washington Post*, March 27, 2008.
23. Carlotta Gall and Abdul Waheed Wafa, "Karzai Escapes Attack in Kabul by Gunmen," *New York Times*, April, 28, 2008. Gall and Wafa refer to the event as Mujahideen Day in paragraph seventeen of the article.
24. Ullrich Fichtner, "The Third World War: Why NATO Troops Can't Deliver Peace in Afghanistan," *Der Spiegel Online*, May 29, 2008, http://www.spiegel.de/international/world/0,1518,556304,00.html (accessed July 11, 2008).
25. Carlotta Gall and Abdul Waheed Wafa, "Afghan President Was Warned of Attack," *New York Times,* April 30, 2008
26. Ibid.

27. Ullrich Fichtner, "The Third World War: Why NATO Troops Can't Deliver Peace in Afghanistan," *Der Spiegel Online*, May 29, 2008, http://www.spiegel.de/international/world/0,1518,556304,00.html (accessed July 11, 2008).
28. Laura King, "U.S. Is Uneasy as Pakistan Bargains with Militants," *Los Angeles Times*, June 15, 2008.
29. *Progress in Afghanistan, Bucharest Summit, 2-4 April 2008*, NATO, http://www.nato.int/ISAF/docu/epub/pdf/progress_afghanistan.pdf (accessed July 11, 2008).
30. Ibid., p. 19.
31. Ibid., p. 18.
32. Ibid., p. 17.
33. Ullrich Fichtner, "The Third World War: Why NATO Troops Can't Deliver Peace in Afghanistan," *Der Spiegel Online*, May 29, 2008.
34. Paul Gallis, "NATO in Afghanistan: A Test of Transatlantic Alliance," Congressional Research Service Report for Congress, updated January 7, 2008, http://www.fas.org/sgp/crs/row/RL33627.pdf (April 4. 2008)
35. Ibid.
36. Matthias Gebaur, "'More than Promises' Needed in Afghanistan," *Der Spiegel*, March 31, 2008.
37. Robert Burns, "May's Afghan Deaths Surpass Iraq's," *Associated Press*, June 13, 2008.
38. See Gates, pp. 131-134, 143-149.
39. M. K. Bhadrakumar, "Russia Joins the War in Afghanistan," *Asia Times*, June 25, 2008.
40. Seth G. Jones, *Counterinsurgency in Afghanistan*, RAND Counterinsurgency Study Vol. 4, RAND Corporation, June 2008.
41. M. K. Bhadrakumar, "Russia Joins the War in Afghanistan," *Asia Times*, June 25, 2008.
42. James Phillips and Lisa Curtis, *The War in Afghanistan: More Help Needed*, Heritage Foundation Backgrounder No. 2124, Heritage Foundation, April 17, 2008.
43. Ibid.
44. Ullrich Fichtner, "The Third World War: Why NATO Troops Can't Deliver Peace in Afghanistan," *Der Spiegel Online*, May 29, 2008, http://www.spiegel.de/international/world/0,1518,556304,00.html (accessed July 11, 2008).
45. Paul Marshall, "Taliban-Lite," *National Review Online*, November 7, 2003 citing the U.S. Commission for International Religious Freedom.
46. "CIA Worked in Tandem with Pak to Create Taliban," *Times of India*, March 7, 2001.
47. Ibid.
48. Jason Straziuso, "US Report Says Pakistan Helped Afghan Insurgents," *Associated Press*, June 10, 2008.
49. See Dupree, p. 320 (map, "Empire of Ahmad Shah Durrani").
50. James Phillips and Lisa Curtis, *The War in Afghanistan: More Help Needed*, Heritage Foundation Backgrounder No. 2124, Heritage Foundation, April 17, 2008.
51. Azadi Afghan Radio interview with Ambassador Peter Tomsen June 7, 1999 (transcript from authors' files).
52. Seth G. Jones, *Counterinsurgency in Afghanistan*, RAND Counterinsurgency Study Vol. 4, RAND Corporation, June 2008.
53. Syed Saleem Shahzad, "US Terror Drive Stalled in Political Quagmire," *Asia Times*, May 31, 2008.
54. Isambard Wilkinson,, "Storming the Mosque Humiliated Pakistan," *Telegraph*, July 11, 2007.
55. Syed Saleem Shahzad, "US Terror Drive Stalled in Political Quagmire," *Asia Times*, May 31, 2008.
56. Jane Perlez, "Taliban Leader Flaunts Power Inside Pakistan," *New York Times*, June 2, 2008.
57. Ibid.
58. Joby Warrick, "U.S. Cites Big Gains Against Al-Qaeda," *Washington Post*, May 30, 2008.
59. Karen DeYoung, "Intelligence Official Sees Little Progress Before Bush Exit," *Washington Post*, May 31, 2008.
60. *Afghanistan Security*, GAO-08-661 June 2008.

61. Karen DeYoung, "GAO Criticizes U.S. Strategy on Afghan Forces," *Washington Post,* June 19, 2008.
62. *Combating Terrorism,* GAO-08-806, June 2008.
63. Robin Wright, "U.S. Funding to Pakistan Plagued with Problems", GAO Report Says, *Washington Post* June 25, 2008.
64. Zulfiqar Ali and Henry Chu, "Pakistan Military Blames U.S. for Deaths of 11 Soldiers," *Los Angeles Times* June 11, 2008.
65. Carlotta Gall and Eric Schmitt, "Pakistan Angry as Strike by U.S. Kills 11 Soldiers," *New York Times* June 12, 2008.
66. Thomas Harding and Lashkar Gah, "Afghan Insurgents 'On the Brink of Defeat,'" *Telegraph,* June 2, 2008.
67. Carlotta Gall, "Taliban Free 1,200 in Attack on Afghan Prison," *New York Times,* June 14, 2008.
68. Carlotta Gall, "Karzai Threatens to Send Soldiers Into Pakistan," *New York Times,* June 16, 2008.
69. Roger Gathman, "Ahmed Rashid's 'Descent into Chaos': Terrifying," *Austin American-Statesman,* June 1, 2008, http://www.statesman.com/life/content/life/stories/books/06/01/0601rashid.html (accessed July 11, 2008).
70. Carlotta Gall, "Karzai Threatens to Send Soldiers Into Pakistan," *New York Times,* June 16, 2008.
71. Mark Tran, "Afghanistan: Kandahar Braces for Taliban Attack as Thousands Flee," *Guardian,* June 17, 2008.
72. Ibid.
73. M. Karim Faiez, "Afghan Forces Drive Taliban from Villages," *Los Angeles Times,* June 20, 2008.
74. Ibid.
75. Ibid.
76. Rahim Faiez, "Afghan Aide Faults Pakistan in Attacks," Associated Press, June 26, 2008.
77. Rahim Faiez, "2 NATO Soldiers Die near Kabul," Associated Press, June 25, 2008.
78. Jane Perlez and Pir Zubair Shah, "Taliban Imperil Pakistani City, a Major Hub," *New York Times,* June 28, 2008.
79. Gideon Rachman, "Afghanistan Backlash," FT.com international affairs blog, June 18, 2008, http://blogs.ft.com/rachmanblog/2008/06/afghanistan-backlash (accessed July 11, 2008).
80. Ivan Watson, "Experts: Lessons of Soviets in Afghanistan Ignored," National Public Radio, *All Things Considered,* June 6, 2008.
81. Ibid.

CHAPTER 18—WHAT CAN THE NEXT U.S. PRESIDENT DO?

1. Ullrich Fichtner, "The Third World War: Why NATO Troops Can't Deliver Peace in Afghanistan," *Der Spiegel Online,* May 29, 2008, http://www.spiegel.de/international/world/0,1518,556304,00.html (accessed July 11, 2008).
2. Seth G. Jones, *RAND Counterinsurgency Study Vol. 4 Counterinsurgency in Afghanistan,* June 2008.
3. Mark Mazzetti and David Rohde, "Amid Policy Disputes, Qaeda Grows in Pakistan," *New York Times* June 30, 2008.
4. See *Report of the Independent Counsel on International Human Rights Concerning Violations of the Laws of War in Afghanistan,* UN Doc. A/42/667; Coll, p. 177 ("'The war in Afghanistan was in itself criminal, a criminal adventure,' he [Andrei Sakharov] told them.")
5. Emram Quereshi, "Misreading 'The Arab Mind,'" *Boston Globe,* May 30, 2004.
6. Michael Scheuer, "A Catalogue of Errors in Afghanistan," *Asia Times,* May 9, 2007.
7. Nyrop and Seekins.
8. Clare Lockhart, "The Failed State We're In," *Prospect,* June 2008.
9. Aunohita Mojumdar, "Afghanistan Adrift in Misplaced Aid," *Asia Times,* March 29, 2008.
10. Ibid.
11. Authors' correspondence with an American aid worker in Afghanistan.

12. Sarah Sewall, "A Heavy Hand in Afghanistan," *Boston Globe,* June 15, 2007.
13. Uwe Klussman interview with Dmitri Rogosin, "The Attempt to Push Georgia into NATO Is a Provocation," *Der Spiegel,* March 10, 2008.
14. Ibid.
15. "France and Germany thwart Bush's Plans," *Der Spiegel*, April 3, 2008.
16. "Poppy for Medicine," Senlis Council, http://www.senliscouncil.net/modules/P4M (accessed July 11, 2008).
17. Joseph Gerson, "The War in Afghanistan: Goals, Future, and Alternatives," CommonDreams.org, June 7–8, 2008, http://www.commondreams.org/archive/2008/06/09/9508 (accessed July 11, 2008).
18. Cooley, p. 145.
19. Jane Perlez, "Pakistan Taliban Blamed in Killing of Peace Committee Members," *New York Times News Service,* June 26, 2008.
20. William Pfaff, "The Illusion of Saving Nations from Themselves," Truthdig, June 30, 2008, http://www.truthdig.com/report/item/20080630_the_illusion_of_saving_nations_from_themselves (accessed July 11, 2008).
21. Ibid.
22. David Walker, "Learn From the Fall of Rome, US Warned," *Financial Times*, August 14, 2007.
23. "The War in Iraq, September 4-8, 2007," CBS/NYTimes Poll, released September 9, 2007 http://CBSnews.com/htdocs/pdf/sep07a-iraq.pdf (accessed July 11, 2008).
24. "Bush, Congress at Record Low Ratings," Reuters poll, September 19, 2007, http://www.reuters.com/article/politicsNews/idUSN1844140220070919?sp=true (accessed July 11, 2008).
25. "George W. Bush's Overall Job Approval Drops," American Research Group, June 20, 2008, http://www.Americanresearchgroup.com/economy (accessed July 11, 2008).
26. Samira Goetschel interview with Milt Bearden, *Our Own Private Bin Laden.*
27. "The Delusions of Hegemony: A Tomdispatch Interview with Andrew Bacevich," Tomdispatch.com May 25, 2006, http://www.tomdispatch.com/post/85723/tomdispatch_interview_bacevich_on_the_limits_of_imperial_power (accessed July 11, 2008).
28. Kaplan, p. 10.
29. Chet Raymo, "In the New Mexico Desert, The Test Was of Physics Itself," *Boston Globe*, November 2, 1992.
30. Greg Herkin, review of *John Von Neumann* by Norman Macrae, *Boston Globe*, November 1, 1992.
31. Kaplan, p. 223.
32. Ibid.
33. H. D. S. Greenway, "The Ghost of Neville Chamberlain," *Boston Globe*, May 27, 2008.
34. James Risen, "The Return of the Neocons," Truthout, June 19, 2008, http://www.truthout.org/article/the-return-neocons (accessed July 11, 2008).

EPILOGUE—THE TWENTY-FIRST CHAPTER

1. See Anthony Burgess, "Introduction: A Clockwork Orange Resucked," in *A Clockwork Orange* (New York: W. W. Norton, 1986), p. ix.
2. Ibid.
3. Ibid.
4. Ibid.
5. "Anthony Burgess," Wikipedia, http://en.wikipedia.org/wiki/Anthony_Burgess (accessed July 11, 2008).
6. Anthony Burgess, "Introduction: A Clockwork Orange Resucked," in *A Clockwork Orange* (New York: W. W. Norton, 1986), p. ix.
7. George M. Young Jr., "Fedorov's Transformations of the Occult," in *The Occult in Russian and Soviet Culture*, Bernice Glatzer Rosenthal, ed. (Ithaca, NY: Cornell University Press), p. 182.

Bibliography

Abbas, Hassan. *Pakistan's Drift into Extremism: Allah, the Army, and America's War on Terror.* M. E. Sharpe, 2005.

Adamec, Ludwig W. *Afghanistan 1900–1923: A Diplomatic History*. Berkeley: University of California Press, 1967.

Afghanistan: The Making of U.S. Policy 1973–1990, National Security Archive Microfiche Collections, http://www.gwu.edu/~nsarchiv/nsa/publications/afghanistan/afghanistan.html.

Andrew, Christopher and Oleg Gordievski, ed. *Comrade Kryuchkov's Instructions: Top Secret Files on KGB Foreign Operations, 1975–1985*. Stanford, CA: Stanford University Press 1993.

Bamford , James. *Body of Secrets: Anatomy of the Ultra-Secret Agency.* New York: Anchor Books, 2002.

———*A Pretext for War: 9/11, Iraq, and the Abuse of America's Intelligence.* New York: Anchor Books, 2005.

Beal, Samuel, trans. *Xuanzang's Record of the Western Regions*, Book One. Seattle: Silk Road, 2003 (http://depts.washington.edu/silkroad/texts/xuanzang.html).

Bearden, Milt, and James Risen. *The Main Enemy: The Inside Story of the CIA's Final Showdown with the KGB*. New York: Ballantine Books, 2003.

Beaty, Jonathan, and S. C. Gwynne. *The Outlaw Bank: A Wild Ride into the Secret Heart of BCCI.* Washington, DC: Beard Books, 2004.

Bennigsen, Alexandre, and Marie Broxup. *The Islamic Threat to the Soviet State.* New York: St. Martin's Press, 1983.

Berntsen, Gary, and Ralph Pezzullo. *Jawbreaker: The Attack on Bin Laden and Al Qaeda: A Personal Account by the CIA's Key Field Commander.* New York: Crown Publishers, 2005.

Blavatsky, H. P. *The Secret Doctrine: The Synthesis of Science Religion, and Philosophy*. London & Benares: Theosophical Publishing Society, 1897.

Bradsher, Henry S. *Afghan Communism and Soviet Intervention*. New York: Oxford University Press, 2000.

_____. *Afghanistan and the Soviet Union*. New and expanded edition. Durham, NC: Duke University Press, 1985.

Burgess, Anthony. *A Clockwork Orange.* New York: W.W. Norton & Company, 1986.

Burnham, James. *Suicide of the West: An Essay on the Meaning and Destiny of Liberalism*. New York: John Day, 1964.

Cahn, Anne Hessing. *Killing Détente: The Right Attacks the CIA*. University Park, PA: Pennsylvania State University Press, 1998.

Cherne, Leo M., ed. *Business and Defense Coordinator*. New York: Research Institute of America, 1941.

Chomsky, Noam. *Hegemony or Survival: America's Quest for Global Dominance*. New York: Metropolitan Books, 2003.

_____. *Year 501: The Conquest Continues*. Boston: South End Press, 1993.

Cohen, Jack, Maurice Cornforth, E.J. Hobsbawm, Nicholas Jacobs, Martin Milligan, and Ernst Wangerman, ed. *Karl Marx, Frederick Engels, Collected Works*, Volume 18. New York: International Publishers, 1982.

Coll, Steve. *Ghost Wars: The Secret History of the CIA, Afghanistan and Bin Laden, From the Soviet Invasion to September 10, 2001*, New York: Penguin Books, 2004.

Cooley, John K. *Unholy Wars*. London: Pluto Press, 1999.

Cooney, John. *The American Pope: The Life and Times of Francis Cardinal Spellman*. New York: Times Books, 1984.

Cordovez, Diego, and Selig S. Harrison. *Out of Afghanistan: The Inside Story of the Soviet Withdrawal*. New York: Oxford University Press, 1995.

Corson, William R, Susan B. Trento, and Joseph Trento. *Widows: The Explosive Truth Behind 25 Years of Western Intelligence Disasters*. New York: Crown Publishing, 1989.

Corwin, Philip. *Doomed in Afghanistan: A UN Officer's Memoir of the Fall of Kabul and Najibullah's Failed Escape, 1992*. New Brunswick NJ: Rutgers University Press, 2003.

Crile, George. *Charlie Wilson's War*. New York: Atlantic Monthly Press, 2003.

Cronin, Isaac, ed. *Confronting Fear: A History of Terrorism*. New York: Thunder's Mouth Press, 2002.

Crozier, Brian. *Free Agent: The Unseen* War, *1941–1991*. London: HarperCollins, 1993.

Daraul, Arkon. *A History of Secret Societies*. New York: Citadel Press, 1962.

Davies, C. Collin. *The Problem on the North-west Frontier, 1890–1908: With a Survey of Policy since 1849*. 2nd ed., revised and enlarged. London: Curzon Press, 1975.

Draft Defense Planning Guidance (DPG) excerpt. Nuclear Vault, http://www.gwu.edu/~nsarchiv/nuclearvault/ebb245/doc03_extract_nytedit.pdf (accessed July 10, 2008).

Dreyfuss, Robert. *Devil's Game: How the United States Helped Unleash Fundamentalist Islam*. New York: Metropolitan Books, 2005.

Dupree, Louis. *Afghanistan*. Karachi: Oxford University Press, by arrangement with Princeton University Press, 1997.

Encyclopaedia Britannica, 15th ed. Chicago: Encyclopaedia Britannica, 1993.

Epstein, Edward Jay. *Deception: The Invisible War Between the KGB and the CIA*. New York: Simon and Schuster, 1989.

Fischer, W. B., Ilya Gershevitch, and Ehsan Yarhster, ed. *The Cambridge History of Iran*. Cambridge: Cambridge University Press, 1969–1991.

Fisher, James T. *Dr. America: The Lives of Thomas A. Dooley 1927–1961*. Amherst: University of Massachusetts Press, 1997.

Fraser-Tytler, William Kerr, with Sir Gillet Michael Cavenagh. *Afghanistan: A Study of Political Developments in Central Asia*, 1907, 3rd ed., revised. London: Oxford University Press, 1967.

Gankovsky, Yu. V., et al. *A History of Afghanistan*. Translated from the Russian by Vitaly Baskakov. Moscow: Progress Publishers, 1985.

Garthoff, Raymond L. *Detente and Confrontation: American-Soviet Relations from Nixon to Reagan*. Washington: Brookings Institution Press, 1985.

_____. *Detente and Confrontation: American-Soviet Relations from Nixon to Reagan*. Revised ed. Washington: Brookings Institution Press, 1994.

Gates, Robert M. *From the Shadows: The Ultimate Insider's Story of Five Presidents and How They Won the Cold War*. New York: Touchstone, 1997.

Ghaus, Abdul Samad. *The Fall of Afghanistan: An Insider's Account*. Washington: Pergamon-Brassey's International Defense Publishers, 1988.

Gladstone, Cary. *Afghanistan Revisited*. Huntington, NY: Nova Publishers, 2001.

Goldman, Marshall I. *Soviet Foreign Aid*. New York: Praeger, 1967.

Goodrick-Clarke, Nicholas. *The Occult Roots of Nazism: Secret Aryan Cults and Their Influence on Nazi Ideology*. New York: New York University Press, 1992.

Gregorian, Vartan. *The Emergence of Modern Afghanistan: Politics of Reform and Modernization, 1880–1946*. Stanford, CA: Stanford University Press, 1969.

Heckethorn, Charles William. *The Secret Societies of All Ages and Countries: In Two Volumes*, Vol. I. New ed. London: George Redway, 1897.

Holt, Frank L. *Into the Land of Bones: Alexander the Great in Afghanistan*. Berkeley: University of California Press, 2006.

Hopkirk, Peter. *The Great Game: The Struggle for Empire in Central Asia*. New York: Kodansha America, 1994.

_____. *Like Hidden Fire: The Plot to Bring Down the British Empire*. New York: Kodansha America, 1994.

Hudson, Geoffrey Francis, Richard Lowenthal, and Roderick MacFarquhar. *The Sino-Soviet Dispute*. New York: Praeger, 1961.

Hussain, Arif. *Pakistan: Its Ideology and Foreign Policy*. Routledge, 1966.

Jan, Abid Ullah. *From BCCI to ISI: The Saga of Entrapment Continues*. Ottawa: Pragmatic Publishing, 2006.

Johnston, Alastair Iain, and Robert S. Ross, ed. *New Directions in the Study of China's Foreign Policy*. Stanford, CA: Stanford University Press, 2006.

Kabbani, Muhammed Hisham. *Classical Islam and the Naqshbandi Sufi Tradition.* Washington DC: Islamic Supreme Council of America, 2004.

Kakar, Mohammed Hassan. *Afghanistan: The Soviet Invasion and the Afghan Response, 1879–1982.* Berkeley: University of California Press, 1995.

Kaplan, Fred. *The Wizards of Armageddon.* New York: Simon and Schuster 1983.

Khan, Munawwar. *Anglo-Afghan Relations, 1798–1878: A Chapter in the Great Game in Central Asia.* Peshawar: University Book Agency [1964 or 5].

Khrushchev, Nikita Sergeevich. *Khrushchev Remembers.* Boston: Little, Brown, 1970.

Kipling, Rudyard. *Plain Tales from the Hills (With a Biographical Sketch by Charles Eliot Norton).* Garden City, NY: Doubleday, Page & Company, 1912.

Kleveman, Lutz. *The New Great Game: Blood and Oil in Central Asia.* New York: Atlantic Monthly Press, 2003.

Kwitny, Jonathan. *Man of the Century: The Life and Times of Pope John Paul II.* New York: Henry Holt and Company 1997.

Lohbeck, Kurt. *Holy War, Unholy Victory: Eyewitness to the CIA's Secret War in Afghanistan.* Washington: Regnery Gateway, 1993.

Male, Beverley. *Revolutionary Afghanistan: A Reappraisal.* New York: St. Martin's Press, 1982.

Marchetti, Victor, with John D. Marks. *The CIA and the Cult of Intelligence.* New York: Dell Publishing, 1980.

McCoy, Alfred W. *The Politics of Heroin: CIA Complicity in the Global Drug Trade.* New York: Lawrence Hill Books, 1991.

Mendelson, Sarah E. *Changing Course: Ideas, Politics and the Soviet Withdrawal from Afghanistan.* Princeton NJ: Princeton University Press, 1998.

Meyer, Karl E. *The Dust of Empire: The Race for Mastery in the Asian Heartland.* New York: Public Affairs, 2003.

Meyer, Karl E., and Shareen Blair Brysac. *Tournament of Shadows: The Great Game and the Race for Empire in Central Asia.* Washington: Counterpoint, 1999.

Meyerowitz, Joanne, ed. *History and September 11.* Philadelphia, PA: Temple University Press, 2003.

Mickiewics, Ellen Propper. *Changing Channels: Television and the Struggle For Power in Russia.* Revised and expanded ed. Durham, NC: Duke University Press, 1999.

Miller, Charles. *Khyber, British India's North West Frontier: The Story of an Imperial Migraine.* New York: Macmillan, 1977.

Mitrokhin, Vasily, Christian F. Osterman, and Odd Arne Westad, ed. *The KGB in Afghanistan.* Working Paper No. 40, Cold War International History Project. Washington D.C.: Woodrow Wilson International Center, 2001.

Munshi, Mir, and Sultan Mahomed Khan, ed., *The Life of Abdur Rahman Amir of Afghanistan G.C.B, G.C.S.I, in Two Volumes*, Vol. II. London: John Murray, 1900.

Musharraf, Pervez. *In the Line of Fire: A Memoir*. New York: Free Press, 2006.

Nayar, Kuldip. *Report on Afghanistan*. New Delhi: Allied Publishers, 1981.

Newell, Nancy, and Richard S. *The Struggle for Afghanistan*. Ithaca, NY: Cornell University Press 1981.

Nyrop, Richard F., and Donald M. Seekins, ed. *Afghanistan: A Country Study*. Washington, DC: Supt. of Docs., GPO, 1986.

Pauwels, Louis, Jacques Bergier, and Rollo Myers. *The Morning of the Magicians*. Chelsea, MI: Scarborough House, 1991.

Poullada, Leon B. *Reform and Rebellion in Afghanistan, 1919–1929*. Ithaca, NY: Cornell University Press, 1973.

Poullada, Leon B., and Leila D. J. Poullada. *The Kingdom of Afghanistan and the United States 1828–1973*. Lincoln, NE: Dageford Publishing, 1995.

Rapson, Edward James, with Wolseley Haig, Richard Burn, and Henry Dodwell. *Cambridge History of India* , vol. VI. India: University Press, 1962.

Rashid, Ahmed. *Taliban: Militant Islam, Oil and Fundamentalism in Central Asia*. New Haven: Yale University Press, 2000.

Reiss, Curt. *Total Espionage*. New York: G. P. Putnam's Sons, 1941.

Roosevelt, Archie. *For Lust of Knowing: Memoirs of An Intelligence Officer*. Boston: Little, Brown and Company, 1988.

Rosenthal, Bernice Glatzer, ed. *The Occult in Russian and Soviet Culture*. Ithaca: Cornell University Press, 1997.

Ross, Colin A. *Satanic Ritual Abuse: Principles of Treatment*. Toronto: University of Toronto Press, 1996.

Roy, Olivier. *Afghanistan: From Holy War to Civil War*. Princeton, NJ: Darwin Press, 1995.

Russell, Dick. *The Man Who Knew Too Much: Hired to Kill Oswald and Prevent the Assassination of JFK*. New York: Carroll & Graf, 1992.

Sachau, Edward C. *Alberuni's India: An Account of the Religion, Philosophy, Literature, Geography, Chronology, Etc.* Vol. II. London: Kegan Paul, Trench, Trubner & Co., 1910.

Sampson, Anthony. *The Arms Bazaar: From Lebanon to Lockheed*. New York: Viking Press, 1977.

Scheer, Robert. *With Enough Shovels: Reagan, Bush & Nuclear War*. New York: Random House, 1982.

Schweizer, Peter. *Victory: The Reagan Administration's Secret Strategy That Hastened the Collapse of the Soviet Union*. New York: Atlantic Monthly Press, 1994.

Snyder, Alvin A. *Warriors of Disinformation: American Propaganda, Soviet Lies and the Winning of the Cold War*. New York: Arcade Publishing, 1995.

Sontag, Raymond James, and James Stuart Beddie. *Nazi-Soviet Relations 1939–1941: Documents from the Archives of the German Foreign Office Etc.*, New York: Didier [1948].

Truell, Peter, with Larry Gurwin. *False Profits: The Inside Story of BCCI, the World's Most Corrupt Financial Empire*. Boston: Houghton Mifflin Company, 1992.

Waller, John H,. *Beyond the Khyber Pass: The Road to British Disaster in the First Afghan War.* New York: Random House, 1990.

Weiner, Tim. *Blank Check: The Pentagon's Black Budget.* New York: Warner Books, 1990.

Wirsing, Robert G. *Pakistan's Security Under Zia, 1977–1998: The Policy Imperatives of a Peripheral Asian State.* New York: St. Martin's Press, 1991.

Whitcomb, Roger S. *The Cold War in Retrospect: The Formative Years.* Westport, CT: Praeger, 1998.

Yates, Frances. *The Occult Philosophy in the Elizabethan Age.* London: Routledge Classics, 2003.

Index

"Passim" (literally "scattered") indicates intermittent discussion of a topic over a cluster of pages.

ABOUT THE AUTHORS

PAUL FITZGERALD and ELIZABETH GOULD, a husband-and-wife team, began working together in 1979, coproducing a documentary for Paul's television show, *Watchworks*, called *The Arms Race and the Economy, A Delicate Balance*. They found themselves in the midst of a swirling controversy that was to boil over a few months later with the Soviet invasion of Afghanistan. The first U.S. television crew granted visas to enter Afghanistan in the spring of 1981, they arrived in the middle of the most heated Cold War controversy since Vietnam. But the pictures and the people inside Soviet-occupied Afghanistan told a very different story from the one being broadcast on the evening news.

Following their exclusive news story for *CBS Evening News with Dan Rather*, they produced a documentary, *Afghanistan Between Three Worlds*, for PBS, and in 1983 they returned to Kabul for *ABC Nightline* with Harvard Negotiation project director Roger Fisher. Next the two wrote a film script about Afghanistan for director Oliver Stone. In 1998 Paul and Liz began collaborating with Afghan human rights expert Sima Wali. Along with Wali, they contributed to the book *Women for Afghan Women: Shattering Myths and Claiming the Future*. In 2002 they filmed Wali's first return to Kabul since her exile in 1978. The film they produced about Wali's journey home, *The Woman in Exile Returns*, gave audiences the chance to discover the message of one of Afghanistan's most articulate voices and Wali's hopes for her people.

SIMA WALI has received numerous citations and awards for her pioneering efforts in the field of civil society building. She is the recipient of the Gloria Steinem "Women of Vision Award" and in 1999 was awarded the Amnesty International USA's Ginetta Sagan Fund Award for Women's and Children's Rights. In 2002, due to her long-standing service to peace, democracy and women's rights, Sima Wali was invited to serve as a delegate—the only woman from the United States—to the peace talks on Afghanistan held in Bonn, Germany, which brought peace and the establishment of the Karzai government in Afghanistan. The creation of the Ministry of Women's Affairs was based on Wali's advocacy in Bonn. During the same time period she served as the chief organizer of the Afghan Women's Summit held in Brussels. In May 2002, Smith College awarded Ms. Wali a doctorate of humane letters for her "superb courage, tenacity and resourcefulness" in her work. During her years as a civil society organizer her life was often threatened for exposing the realities of the Afghan crisis she never backed down. Today she fights another battle, this time for her own health, as she faces a life-altering crisis due to the unrelenting stresses of the Afghan war.